BREAKING THE CYCLE OF MASS ATROCITIES

Breaking the Cycle of Mass Atrocities investigates the role of international criminal law at different stages of mass atrocities, shifting away from its narrow understanding solely as an instrument of punishment of those most responsible. The book is premised on the idea that there are distinct phases of collective violence, and international criminal law contributes in one way or another to each phase. The authors therefore explore various possibilities for international criminal law to be of assistance in breaking the vicious cycle at its different junctures.

Breaking the Cycle of Mass Atrocities

Criminological and Socio-Legal Approaches in International Criminal Law

Edited by

Marina Aksenova
Elies van Sliedregt
and
Stephan Parmentier

•HART•
OXFORD · LONDON · NEW YORK · NEW DELHI · SYDNEY

HART PUBLISHING

Bloomsbury Publishing Plc

Kemp House, Chawley Park, Cumnor Hill, Oxford, OX2 9PH, UK

HART PUBLISHING, the Hart/Stag logo, BLOOMSBURY and the Diana logo are
trademarks of Bloomsbury Publishing Plc

First published in Great Britain 2019

A catalogue record for this book is available from the British Library.

Library of Congress Cataloging-in-Publication data

Names: Aksenova, Marina, editor. | Sliedregt, E. van, editor. | Parmentier, Stephan, 1960- editor.

Title: Breaking the cycle of mass atrocities : criminological and socio-legal approaches in international
criminal law / edited by Marina Aksenova, Elies van Sliedregt, Stephan Parmentier.

Description: Oxford, UK ; Chicago, Illinois : Hart Publishing, 2019. |
Includes bibliographical references and index.

Identifiers: LCCN 2018054817 (print) | LCCN 2018055182 (ebook) |
ISBN 9781509919451 (EPub) | ISBN 9781509919444 (hardback)

Subjects: LCSH: International criminal law—Social aspects. | BISAC: LAW / International. |
LAW / Criminal Law / General. | SOCIAL SCIENCE / Criminology.

Classification: LCC KZ7050 (ebook) | LCC KZ7050 .B74 2019 (print) | DDC 345/.0251—dc23

LC record available at https://lccn.loc.gov/2018054817

ISBN: HB: 978-1-50991-944-4
        ePDF: 978-1-50991-946-8
        ePub: 978-1-50991-945-1

Typeset by Compuscript Ltd, Shannon
Printed and bound in Great Britain by TJ International Ltd, Padstow, Cornwall

To find out more about our authors and books visit www.hartpublishing.co.uk.
Here you will find extracts, author information, details of forthcoming events
and the option to sign up for our newsletters.

Dedicated to everyone trying to make this world a better place ...

ACKNOWLEDGEMENTS

This project was funded by the Danish National Research Foundation Grant Number DNRF105 and conducted under the auspices of iCourts, the Danish National Research Foundation's Centre of Excellence for International Courts.

CONTENTS

LIST OF CONTRIBUTORS

Marina Aksenova, Professor of International and Comparative Criminal Law, IE Law School, University of Madrid.

Anette Bringedal Houge, Head of Humanitarian Needs and Analysis, Norwegian Red Cross.

Kerstin Carlson, Assistant Professor, Department of Law, University of Southern Denmark.

Amani Chibashimba, Head of VOKI Project, Vivo International e.V. in the DRC.

Matilde Gawronski (Oxford University) DPhil candidate at the Centre for Socio-Legal Studies and Nuffield College.

Christopher Harding (Aberystwyth University), Emeritus Professor.

Stefan Harrendorf, Professor of Criminology, Criminal Law, Criminal Procedure and Comparative Criminal Law and Justice, University of Greifswald.

Barbora Holá, Senior Researcher Netherlands Institute for the Study of Crime and Law Enforcement, Associate Professor VU University Amsterdam.

Stephan Parmentier, Professor of Criminal Law and Criminology, KU Leuven.

Colleen Rohan (ICTY Association of Defence Counsel).

Milena Tripkovic, Lecturer in Law, University of Birmingham.

Elies van Sliedregt, Professor in Comparative and International Criminal Justice, University of Leeds.

Harmen van der Wilt, Professor of International Criminal Law, University of Amsterdam.

LIST OF CASES

UN Mechanism for International Criminal Tribunals

International Criminal Tribunal for Rwanda

Special Tribunal Lebanon

Special Court for Sierra Leone

International Criminal Court

Constitutional Court of Uganda

The International Crimes Division of the High Court of Uganda at Kampala

Supreme Court of Uganda

Supreme Court of the Republic of Rwanda

Rwanda Criminal Courts

High Court of Justice (UK)

Supreme Court in The Hague (Netherlands)

US Supreme Court

US District Court, ED North Carolina

US District Court for the Southern District of New York

PART I

Cycle of Mass Atrocities

1

Introduction: Breaking the Cycle of Mass Atrocities: Criminological and Socio-Legal Approaches to International Criminal Law

MARINA AKSENOVA

I. The Cycle of Mass Atrocities

International criminal law addresses dramatic situations in the collapse of societal structures leading to the inability of various actors to distinguish between 'good' and 'evil'. 'Collapse' does not necessarily entail physical destruction or dissolution of institutions responsible for the enforcement of values, although this is a very common scenario, but may also occur in the presence of authoritarian non-accountable institutions acting as a 'façade of justice', while in reality serving as an instrument of oppression.

Christian Gerlach's concept of 'extremely violent societies' is helpful in explaining the general loss of a moral compass in society.[1] Gerlach does not define violence as a structural or cultural characteristic and permanent condition of societies but rather locates events and maps campaigns triggering further escalation.[2] Such description accurately captures the state of confusion accompanying war crimes, crimes against humanity, and genocide, jointly known as 'atrocity crimes' or 'mass atrocities'.[3] These crimes are manifestations of collective violence perpetrated during periods of chaos. They are particularly heinous because they threaten the survival of entire communities. These are not singular instances of criminal

---

[1] C Gerlach, 'Extremely Violent Societies: An Alternative to the Concept of Genocide' (2006) 8 *Journal of Genocide Research* 455.

[2] ibid, 460.

[3] D Scheffer, 'The Merits of Unifying Terms: "Atrocity Crimes" and "Atrocity Law"' (2007) 2(1) *Genocide Studies and Prevention* 91, 92; W Schabas, 'Semantics or Substance? David Scheffer's Welcome Proposal to Strengthen Criminal Accountability for Atrocities' (2007) 2(1) *Genocide Studies and Prevention* 31, 34; S Karstedt, 'Contextualizing Mass Atrocity Crimes: Moving Toward a Relational Approach' (2013) 9 *Annual Review of Law and Social Science* 383, 388.

conduct but rather symptoms of a bigger crisis in the respective society. Rwandan genocide, for example, was preceded by decades of successive victimisation of Tutsi and Hutu communities – a situation leading to perpetual re-enactment of onslaught and culminating in one of the most brutal massacres of the twentieth century.[4]

The terminology of 'atrocity crimes' used in the title of this book follows the concept introduced by David Sheffer in 2002 to reflect the law of international criminal tribunals and subsequently adopted by criminologists and official UN bodies.[5] In the 2005 World Summit Outcome Document, United Nations Member States made a commitment to protect populations from genocide, war crimes, ethnic cleansing and crimes against humanity, a principle referred to as the 'Responsibility to Protect'.[6] The purpose of inventing the legal concept of 'atrocity crimes' was therefore to highlight the importance of timely intervention of the international community during the early phases of such crimes.[7] The emphasis is thus on the escalating nature of collective violence with less severe crimes, such as forcible transfer or looting, often preceding more serious crimes, such as genocide.[8] This approach stresses the fluid nature of collective criminality, making the terminology of 'atrocity crimes' most suitable for distinguishing between different stages of collective violence.[9]

The present volume investigates the role of international criminal law at different points in time in the course of collective violence. It shifts away from law's narrow construction solely as an instrument of punishment of those most responsible for mass atrocities[10] and rather views it as a broader force, which is both practical and universal.[11] International criminal law enables the dissemination

---

[4] Karstedt, ibid, 385.

[5] The term 'mass atrocities' or 'atrocity crimes' is used to refer to three legally defined international offences: genocide, crimes against humanity and war crimes and ethnic cleansing (the latter, while not defined as an independent crime under international law, includes acts that are serious violations of international human rights and humanitarian law).

[6] D Scheffer in 'The Future of Atrocity Law' (2002) 32 *Suffolk Transnational Law Review* 398; United Nations, *Framework of Analysis for Atrocity Crimes – A tool for prevention* (2014) available at: www.un.org/en/preventgenocide/adviser/pdf/framework%20of%20analysis%20for%20atrocity%20crimes_en.pdf.

[7] Sheffer, 'The Merits of Unifying Terms', above (n 3).

[8] D Scheffer, 'Genocide and Atrocity Crimes' (2006) 1(3) *Genocide Studies and Prevention* 229, 232.

[9] Susanne Karstedt argues, 'atrocity crimes disconnect an ultimate legal judgment from preventive and protective action, which necessarily has to precede it'. See Karstedt, above (n 3) 388.

[10] Article 1 of the ICTY/R Statutes defines competence of the *ad hoc* tribunals as 'have the power to prosecute persons responsible for serious violations of international humanitarian law' committed in the respective territory. Article 1 of the Rome Statute makes it clear that the Court has 'the power to exercise its jurisdiction over persons for the most serious crimes of international concern'. See UN Security Council, Statute of the International Criminal Tribunal for the former Yugoslavia (as amended on 17 May 2002)', 25 May 1993; UN Security Council, 'Statute of the International Criminal Tribunal for Rwanda (as last amended on 13 October 2006)', 8 November 1994; UN General Assembly, 'Rome Statute of the International Criminal Court (last amended 2010)', 17 July 1998.

[11] According to Derrida the language of law is imposed on people to satisfy their demand for infinite justice. In doing this, law must hold force or appeal to it. J Derrida, 'Force of Law: "The Mystical Foundation of Authority"' in G Anidjar (ed), *Acts of Religion* (London, Routledge, 2002).

of norms about the prohibited conduct and sets the standard for behaviour in conflict situations. A good example to illustrate the wider implications of international criminal law, which go far beyond mere adjudication, would be the effect of the ratification of the Rome Statute of the International Criminal Court (ICC) on deterrence. Studies show that ratification of the Statute and not necessarily the engagement of the ICC as such created certain deterrent effects in a number of African states.[12]

In this vein, one can view international criminal law as a point of refence for, or a measure of, international consensus about universally condemned conduct. Cultural criminology provides a suitable theoretical framework for this statement. Criminologist Wayne Morrison observes that life is anchored in fixed points of symbolic reference, or monuments, that incorporate and preserve a sense of collective identity (for example, the Statue of Liberty). On a non-physical plane, he continues, the *legal order* serves as a vitally important monument.[13] Globally, formal recognition of human rights is one of the pillars of the emerging universalist legal order and a symbol of consensus.[14] Mass atrocities are human rights violations on a big scale and they shake the consciousness of humanity as a whole by undermining this order. Their occurrence is thus a reminder of the need for accountability, but it is also a call for action to prevent future escalation. With such a strong symbolic appeal, international criminal law bears prospective qualities and must be viewed in broader temporal terms.[15]

The foundation of the discussion in the present volume is the contextual embedding of mass atrocity crimes. The work of Susanne Karstedt is helpful in understanding this context. Karstedt views atrocity crimes as linked to macro conflicts and micro dynamics at the local level. This vision follows from her understanding of mass atrocities as a phenomenon to be studied *both* in the light of the general structures of international power relations and technologies of war and by identifying localised events, patterns of victimisation, involvement, and resistance at the community level.[16] This book however suggests a somewhat different

---

[12] Beth Simmons and Allison Marston Danner found evidence that merely the ratification of the Rome Statute by a government tends to be correlated with a pause in civil war hostilities. See BA Simmons and A Danner, 'Credible Commitments and the International Criminal Court' (2010) 64 *International Organization* 225. See also G Dancy, B Marchesi, F Montal and K Sikking, 'The ICC's deterrent impact – what the evidence shows', *Open Democracy* (3 February 2015), available at www.opendemocracy.net/openglobalrights/geoff-dancy-bridget-marchesi-florencia-montal-kathryn-sikkink/icc%E2%80%99s-deterrent-impac.

[13] W Morrison, *Theoretical Criminology: From Modernity to Post-Modernism* (London, Cavendish, 1995) 77.

[14] T Dahl-Eriksen, 'R2P and the "Thin Cosmopolitan" Imagination' (2016) 40(2) *The Fletcher Forum of World Affairs* 127.

[15] For the discussion on temporality and restorative justice see Adam Crawford, who argues that questions of time and time-consciousness are essential components in the project of restoring trust. See A Crawford, 'Temporality in Restorative Justice: On Time, Timing and Time-consciousness' (2015) 19 *Theoretical Criminology* 470.

[16] Karstedt, above (n 3) 390–93.

approach. Instead of focusing on 'general-to-specific' dimension of mass atrocities, it rather examines its individual stages and possible causal linkages between them. Individual stages form a cycle, which serves as a starting point, or a framework, assisting in studying collective violence and the role international criminal plays in containing it. The cycle points to the fact that mass atrocities and tensions preceding them are not singular events but rather that they keep occurring over a prolonged period of time, manifesting as a symptom of a society exposed to violence and oppression.[17]

The cyclical nature of collective violence is reinforced by recurrent events unfolding during shorter temporal intervals and often serving as a build up for a major genocidal event.[18] For example, in Guatemala, the period of extreme violence starting in 1977 was preceded by more than a decade of lower intensity crimes such as arbitrary executions and torture.[19] A more recent example is the persecution of the Rohingya Muslims and other ethnic minorities in Myanmar. The UN Fact Finding mission found that the process of 'othering' the Rohingya had started long before the worst atrocities unfolded.[20] It follows that mass atrocities are not exceptional, or 'one-off', incidents but rather repetitive occurrences.[21] Having said that, it is fair to assume that the cycle of mass atrocities, in its various manifestations, has features that distinguish it from 'regular' criminality usually tackled by domestic criminal law.

Admittedly, representing criminality as a cycle risks painting the picture in black and white, obfuscating important nuances and using a general mould to fit a variety of scenarios. The point here is rather to use the cycle as an analytical tool for understanding the wider context of collective criminality and without a claim to its universal applicability.

This volume contrasts the cycle of mass atrocities with the cycle of 'regular' criminality and argues that these are different processes. What is it then that makes the cycle of collective violence unique? Schemes 1 and 2 presented below

---

[17] The cycle of mass atrocities has some resonance with the idea of the intergenerational cycle of violence, denoting psychological violence that is passed from parent to child, or sibling to sibling. The cycle of mass atrocities, however, focuses less on family ties and more on collective perpetuation of criminality and on institutional structures (or lack thereof) that allow this to happen. For recent empirical studies on traumatic experiences or symptoms of post-traumatic stress disorder that facilitate or enhance intergenerational transfer of violence see A Crombach, 'Children and the Cycle of Violence in Post-Conflict Settings: Mental Health, Aggression, and Interventions in Burundi' (PhD Dissertation, University of Konstanz, 2013); M Roth, F Neuner and T Elbert, 'Transgenerational Consequences of PTSD: Risk Factors for the Mental Health of Children Whose Mothers Have Been Exposed to the Rwandan Genocide' (2014) 8 *International Journal of Mental Health Systems* 12.

[18] Crombach, ibid, 392.

[19] TR Gulden, 'Spatial and Temporal Patterns in Civil Violence: Guatemala, 1977–1986' (2002) 21(1) *Politics and the Life Sciences* 26.

[20] UNHRC, 'Report of the Independent International Fact-Finding Mission on Myanmar', UN DOC A/HRC/39/64 (24 August 2018) para 20.

[21] Karstedt posits that while the history of the twentieth century supports the idea of genocide being an exceptional event (Nazi Germany, Rwanda in 1994), the same does not hold true for other mass atrocities, typically taking place beneath the level of the nation state and following the historical trajectory of a violent conflict in a given society. See Karstedt, above (n 3) 386; Gerlach, above (n 1).

demonstrate crucial distinctions. **Scheme 1** outlines the phases of 'regular' criminality in a society not affected by conflict, while **Scheme 2** visualises the cycle of mass atrocities divided into various stages. A brief comparison of these two diagrams demonstrates varying levels of contextual embedment of the two cycles of criminality, with collective violence posing additional challenges both in the area of prevention and enforcement. The 'regular cycle' comprises the following steps: offence, criminal justice's response to it, reintegration of former perpetrators into society, and prevention. The cycle of mass atrocities derives its distinctive features from the context in which it occurs and incorporates the following stages: the commission of a crime; criminalisation of the relevant conduct; punishment of those responsible; re-entry of victims and perpetrators into society; and prevention.

The key distinctions lie in the nature of the conduct in question: as a rule, the cycle of 'regular' criminality includes singular instances of offending, whereas mass atrocities are by definition a collective endeavour. The reaction to these crimes varies as well and depends on whether there exists effective enforcement. Societies experiencing extreme violence are unlikely to have the resources and political support for effective and fair investigations. Moreover, the cycle of regular criminality presupposes that the offences are criminalised well in advance, while 'criminalisation' becomes a separate step in the cycle of mass atrocities because the

Scheme 1 Cycle of 'Regular' Criminality

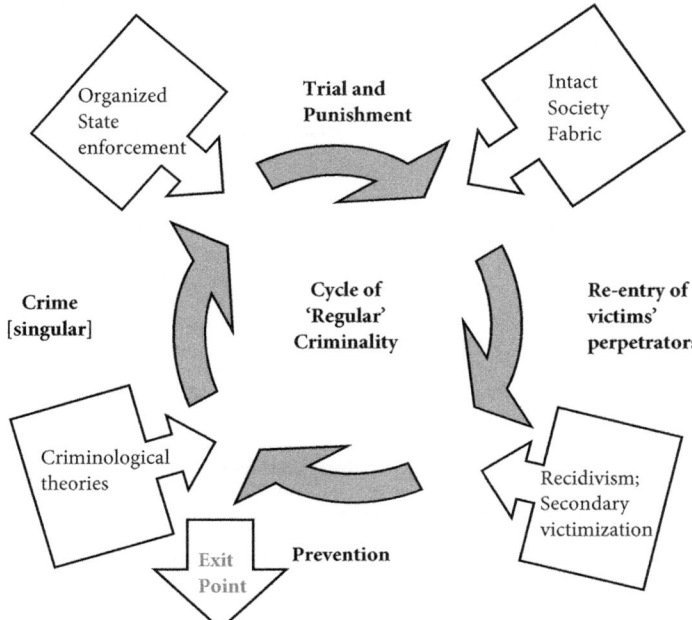

content and variety of offences under international criminal law are continuously expanding. The stage of 're-entry of victims and perpetrators' within the two processes intends to achieve different goals: while international criminal law and other transitional justice mechanisms aim to rebuild trust in society and mend its torn fabric, domestic instruments grapple with the issue of recidivism, which may or may not be as pronounced in the context of collective violence. The challenge for international criminal law therefore is to respond to the specific type of criminality.

Finally, the emphasis of most domestic criminological theories is on preventing deviant behaviour because the aim is to reduce incentives for offending. Crime and social control are therefore objects of study within the field of criminology. The purpose is to answer the primary question about how and why people come to act in violation of the law.[22] As a result, criminological theories do not only explain crime but also contribute to its prevention, thereby providing an 'exit point' from the cycle of offending. Paradoxically, while national policymakers have long benefited from criminological science when crafting responses to various types of offence, advocates of international criminal justice still rely on sporadic surveys and work in the absence of reliable empirically tested theories.[23] Possible explanations for this vacuum in the field of international criminal law lie in the difficulty of developing plausible theories accounting for mass criminality.

The patterns of collective offending are not so easily broken down into single analytical pieces. Such patterns often emerge from complex organisational hierarchies and shifts in the psychology of persons exposed to the severe stress of war and violence. Would traditional criminological theories explain the processes leading to mass atrocities? Let us take, for instance, 'neutralization theory', which is prominent in many domestic criminological explanations of criminal behaviour. This theory, developed by Sykes and Matza, argues that much delinquency is based on what is essentially an unrecognised extension of defences to crimes.[24] The delinquent justifies his or her deviance by reasons appearing as valid to him or her but not to the legal system or society at large.[25] Neutralization theory thus focuses on life narratives and the offender's self-representation. In line with this

---

[22] I Loader and R Sparks, 'Situating Criminology: On the Production and Consumption of Knowledge about Crime and Justice' in M Maguire et al (eds), *The Oxford Handbook of Criminology* (Oxford, Oxford University Press, 2012) 19. See also J Bennett, *Oral History and Delinquency: The Rhetoric of Criminology* (Chicago, IL, University of Chicago Press, 1981).

[23] Rothe and Mullins identified this gap and made the first attempt to come up with a general theory. Their framework combines different variables but lacks predictive value. See DL Rothe and CW Mullins, 'Toward a Criminology of International Criminal Law: An Integrated Theory of International Criminal Violations' (2009) 33 *International Journal of Comparative and Applied Criminal Justice* 97.

[24] G Sykes and D Matza, 'Techniques of Neutralization: A Theory of Delinquency' (1957) 22 *American Sociological Review* 664, 666.

[25] ibid.

subjective approach to understanding criminality, modern 'cultural criminology' aims at integrating creative and interpretative practices into the study of crime. Wayne Morrison insists that much criminality is a way of reclaiming self-control in situations where the locus of this control is lost outside the self, due to immutable societal structures.[26]

Both the neutralization theory and the postulates of the cultural criminology lead to the conclusion that changing faulty cognitions in individual offenders may be less of a psychological or clinical matter than a sociological one.[27] In a follow-up analysis to the Sykes and Matza study, Copes and Maruna identify research confirming the idea that all of us make predominantly external attributions for our failures and predominantly internal attributions for our successes.[28] If failures are attributed to external societal factors, then deterrence efforts are also to be focused on changing an offender's way of relating to them rather than just working with his internal psychological state of being. Copes and Maruna further 'normalised' human justificatory processes, stressing that neutralisation techniques are commonplace and do not necessarily attest to the existence of a 'criminal personality'.[29] The same possibly holds true for high-level perpetrators. Stanley Cohen notes that politicians, military commanders and industrial leaders might be said to owe their careers to their ability to neutralise.[30]

It is plausible to apply neutralization theory and its extensions to the context of mass atrocities.[31] However, there are some peculiarities and limitations. What is particularly striking is that the atmosphere of lawlessness accompanying the rupture of society creates a uniquely fertile ground for attributing one's conduct to externalities (orders by superiors, despair, confusion about the value of human life). One could call this phenomenon the 'alternative reality of war'. At the same time, the scale and gravity of misconduct also increases exponentially, requiring stronger shifts in cognition to come to terms with one's role in mass atrocities. Consequently, while it is easy to see how neutralisation techniques are an inalienable part of the human condition and do not necessarily attest to 'criminal personality', a distinct set of justificatory mechanisms, based on the 'alternative reality of war', must be in place in the situations of extreme violence.[32] One may

---

[26] Morrison, above (n 13) vi.

[27] S Maruna and H Copes, 'What Have we Learned from Five Decades of Neutralization Research?' (2005) 32 *Crime and Justice* 221, 283.

[28] ibid, 286 citing M Zuckerman, 'Attribution of Success and Failure Revisited, or: The Motivation Bias Is Alive and Well in Attribution Theory' (1979) 47 *Journal of Personality* 245.

[29] Maruna and Copes, ibid, 286.

[30] See S Cohen, *States of Denial* (Cambridge, Polity Press, 2001) 35.

[31] For more discussion of the applicability of 'neutralization theory' to mass criminality see Stefan Harrendorf's contribution to this volume, ch 10.

[32] Some researchers argue that neutralization theory can explain participation only in minor forms of crime and delinquency and is ineffective at explaining participation in more serious criminal behaviour. See J Mitchell and R Dodder, 'An Examination of Types of Delinquency through Path Analysis' (1980) 9 *Journal of Youth and Adolescence* 239.

justify bank robbery by social injustices and economic inequalities, but how does one justify persecuting civilians fleeing from the danger of war?[33]

In other words, if one adopts Morrison's starting point that much criminality is a way of reclaiming self-control in situations when the social structures are impermeable, one keeps wondering how the very same process of reclaiming control unfolds when fixed structures break down at war or during an institutional stalemate created by a repressive regime. Such drastic scenarios open the door to discourses that establish a different hierarchy of the dominant values in society, thereby allowing individuals to reclaim control relying on the new reality. The question is whether the changes in societal structure lead to personal engagement in mass atrocities, resistance to it or complacency.

Finally, the challenge of criminology of mass atrocities is a challenge of comparative criminology more generally. Criminology, strictly construed, presupposes the study of causes and consequences of crimes on the basis of a plethora of criminological theories.[34] The latter provide for the specific indicators against which scientists measure criminality. For example, sociology-oriented theories, such as the theory of social control or social disorganisation, point towards urbanisation, peer group pressure and family disruption as relevant factors indicative of the propensity to offend. In contrast, 'rational choice theory' and 'economic theory of crime' place more emphasis on poverty, unemployment and deterrence.[35] In practice, such theoretical distinctions are often difficult to maintain. For instance, a comparative study on criminality in EU Member States, conducted at the turn of the twenty-first century, revealed that poverty and employment are essential for understanding social disorganisation, while peer groups and neighbourhood effects belong to the discussion of economics.[36] Thus viewing criminology narrowly as a constellation of theories fails to respond to wider global challenges.[37] Moreover, in the context of a breakdown of state institutions, the indicators produced by the traditional criminological theories may be skewed. A more satisfying approach is to attach a criminological analysis to empirical data or the expertise in the other fields of knowledge rather than to a particular theory.[38]

---

[33] Stefan Harrendorf in his contribution to this volume argues that neutralization theory explains how perpetrators of mass atrocities overcome moral inhibitions but falls short of explaining why they come to commit crimes in the first place. See Harrendorf, ch 10, p 209.

[34] See, eg, GB Vold, TJ Bernard and JB Snipes, *Theoretical Criminology*, 4th edn (Oxford, Oxford University Press, 1998) 4.

[35] H Entorf and H Spengler, *Crime in Europe: Causes and Consequences* (Berlin, Springer, 2002) 173.

[36] ibid.

[37] K Soothhill, M Peelo and C Taylor, *Making Sense of Criminology* (Cambridge, Polity Press, 2002) 152. See also F Cullen and P Wilcox (eds), *Oxford Handbook of Criminological Theory* (Oxford, Oxford University Press, 2013) that is built around a number of themes rather than specific theories. For instance, it examines the context of offending, individual and biological factors.

[38] P Rock, 'Sociological Theories of Crime' in M Maguire et al (eds), *The Oxford Handbook of Criminology* (Oxford, Oxford University Press, 2007) 33.

Scheme 2 Cycle of Mass Atrocities

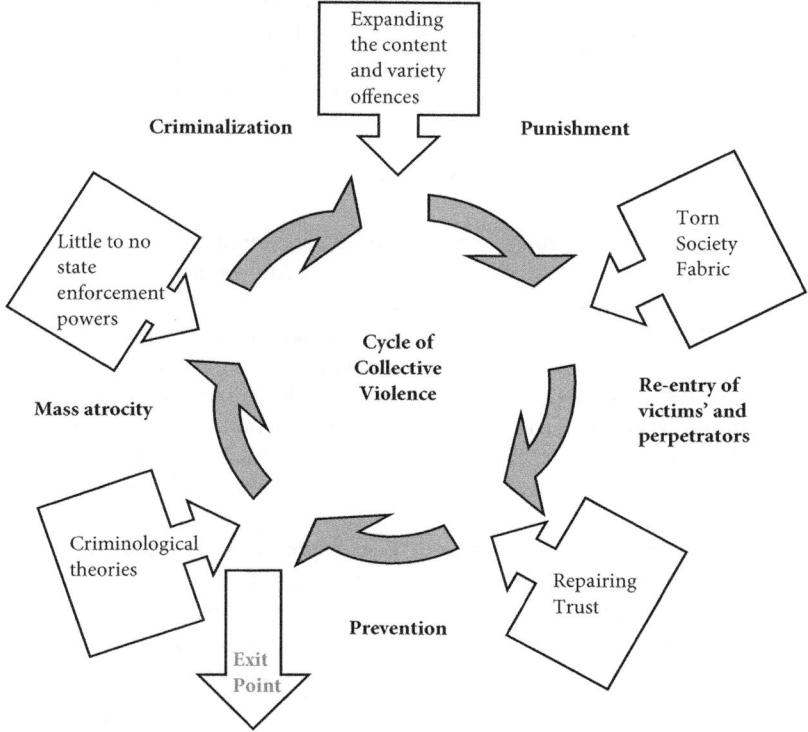

II. Structure of the Book

This collection of chapters[39] embraces the temporal dimension of international criminal law and is premised on the idea that there are distinct phases of mass atrocities. Legal tools available through international and domestic communities contribute in one way or another to understanding and dealing with each phase. The authors explore whether international criminal law, broadly conceived, can be of assistance in breaking the vicious cycle at its different junctures and what are the limitations to such exercise.

A comprehensive understanding of the process of collective criminality in its *entirety* is thus of utmost importance in devising the most appropriate mechanisms for breaking down the vicious cycle. The role of international criminal law must be reassessed in this wider context. Contributions to this volume follow the phases of mass atrocities shown in **Scheme 2** illuminating the role of international

---

[39] Descriptions of the chapters in this section are based on the abstracts provided by the authors.

criminal law at each stage. The aim is to introduce anchors for scholarly and practically oriented discussion of collective violence. Each section of the book provides an insight into one of the stages of mass atrocity with the aim of strengthening the effectiveness and legitimacy of international criminal law as well as exploring the possibilities of linking this field of law to other relevant disciplines.

A. The Nature of Mass Atrocities

There is much debate on what constitutes an international crime, but no real one convincing answer.[40] Dawn Rothe and Christopher Mullins made the first attempt to provide a comprehensive definition when they combined different features of international crimes and came up with the schematic model.[41] The authors categorised various factors influencing the chances of collective violence grouping them by levels: state-level (ideological character of the ruling elite, type of regime); organisational level (patterns of human rights violations, bureaucratic institutions); and interactional level (social power of decision-makers, motivations). The integrated theory provides a good framework for analysis but lacks predictive value.

This collection offers in the introductory chapter a unique take on the nature of mass atrocities by Christopher Harding, who links it to the notion of memory. Harding's chapter suggests a framework for the discussion of atrocity offending, emphasising the primacy of biological and psychological factors in explaining and understanding such offending. Harding argues that atrocity stems from natural human tendencies towards violence, aggression, hostility and suspicion towards others, and that such tendencies are moderated by ethical, social and political calculations. External circumstances, involving economic, environmental and cultural factors may act as the *triggers* of violence, hostility and aggression. Bearing in mind this frame of reference and discussion, the chapter examines the role of memory and its erasure in both the commission and the resolution of atrocity, as both a stimulus of extreme and systematic violence and as a subsequent route to resolution, thus testing the strategy of 'forgive and forget'. This part of the discussion takes as an example the fictional imagining of atrocity in post-Roman Britain presented in Kazuo Ishiguro's recent work, *The Buried Giant* (2015).

B. Criminalisation

Part II focuses on the process of criminalisation often preceding or occurring simultaneously with the trial and prosecution of mass atrocities at an international

---

[40] The debates about the scope of international crimes are ongoing. For example, on 20 October 2015, the European Court of Human Rights rendered a judgment examining in detail the definition of the crime of genocide. The Court's Grand Chamber remained highly divided as to what comprises this definition. See *Vasiliauskas v Lithuania* App no 35343/05 (ECHR, 20 October 2015).

[41] Rothe and Mullins, above (n 23).

level. The process of criminalisation is a mechanism whereby international courts and tribunals push forward collective agendas on the conduct not to be tolerated on a global scale. The choice of the term 'criminalisation' over 'interpretation' is deliberate. It is true that the process whereby judges engage with the sources of international law – treaty, custom and the general principles of law – is commonly referred to as 'interpretation'. The structure of international law is such however that it allows a lot of discretion as to the manner of interpretation and the choices of supporting sources. The question thus remains whether judges, as well as other stakeholders applying international criminal law, work with an already existing body of law when they define and elaborate on the elements of crimes and other related concepts, or whether they constantly partake in the development of the new norms. It is possible to view the two processes – interpretation and criminalisation – not as mutually exclusive, but rather as emphasising different aspects of international criminal law. 'Interpretation' refers to the way in which legal sources are processed. In contrast, the terminology of 'criminalisation' highlights the dynamic nature of international criminal law, which is in the constant state of flux when it comes to the content of offences.

A good example demonstrating inconsistency in the definition of certain crimes in the practice of international courts and tribunals would be the acquittal and the subsequent conviction of a Serbian nationalist politician Vojislav Šešelj. First, the Trial Chamber of the International Criminal Tribunal for the former Yugoslavia (ICTY) acquitted Šešelj, who is known to have made open calls for the expulsion of the non-Serbian population from Vukovar in Croatia and Vojvodina in Serbia. This outcome raised questions as to the definition of hate speech and incitement in international criminal law.[42] The acquittal was then reversed on appeal by the successor court – the Mechanism for International Criminal Tribunals – which held that the Trial Chamber erred in concluding that Šešelj's speeches did not call for ethnic cleansing, but merely contributed to the general war effort.[43]

The stage of criminalisation is largely missing in the cycle of 'regular' criminality because domestic penal law is traditionalist in nature and denotes the feelings collectively shared by society.[44] The authority of the penal rule is thus a societal custom *formed over time*.[45] Consequently, most offences remain firmly codified in the respective criminal codes or statutes and undergo little challenge over time. The response of the criminal justice system amounts to trial in a court of law and punishment, which is administered in a systematic fashion because all members of society are presumed to share the values and agree to submit the offender to censure.[46]

---

[42] *Prosecutor v Šešelj* (Summary Judgment) ICTY Case No IT-03-67-T (31 March 2016).
[43] *Prosecutor v Šešelj*, UN Mechanism for International Criminal Tribunals, Summary Judgment, Appeals Chamber, 11 April 2018, available at: www.irmct.org/sites/default/files/casedocuments/mict-16-99/appeals-chamber-judgements/en/180411-vojislav-seselj-judgement-summary-en.pdf.
[44] E Durkheim, *The Division of Labour in Society* (Basingstoke, Macmillan, 1984) 37.
[45] ibid, 35.
[46] ibid, 45.

This is not to suggest that national legal systems never problematise the issue of criminalisation. It simply happens in a sporadic rather than systematic fashion. Modern societies occasionally struggle with drawing the boundary between conduct that is morally wrong and that which is criminal. For example, policing protest presents a challenge to democracies and totalitarian states alike. It is difficult to strike the right balance in deciding whether to punish non-conforming individuals who question the legitimacy of the established rules with the of aim changing them for the perceived greater good. These very same protestors may be viewed as a group committing crimes against the established state order.[47] The exercise of state power over protesters becomes even trickier in cases of state criminality.[48]

The approach of the ICC to criminalisation is a prime example of how international criminal law solidifies certain prohibitions. The ICC's pilot case focused exclusively on offences against children.[49] The Trial Chamber devoted considerable attention to outlining the elements of the crime of conscripting or enlisting children under the age of 15 years, which was not defined in the Rome Statute or the Elements of Crimes.[50] A more recent example from the ICC includes efforts by the Prosecutor to give 'particular consideration' to cases resulting in the 'the destruction of the environment, the illegal exploitation of natural resources or the illegal dispossession of land'.[51] Prosecutorial strategy therefore becomes an instrument of promoting the agenda of international criminal law and expanding our understanding of the content of certain offences. One may be critical of reprimanding some conduct and not other, but this seems to be the only feasible solution given the limited resources available to the international community.

Both chapters in this Part explore the nature of criminalisation in international criminal law. The first chapter by Matilde Gawronski offers a practitioner's perspective on the quality of international crimes. She suggests that international criminalisation can be best understood as a knowledge-building institutional practice which transforms open-ended information about mass atrocities into triable cases. This process is captured by the coined term 'pragmatic criminalisation'. Gawronski adopts an empirical lens when she discusses constructing international criminality by contrasting the trials of Dominic Ongwen at the ICC and a factually similar trial of Thomas Kwoyelo in Uganda. She argues that while the conduct of these two individuals is similar, it was not criminalised in the same way because of the legal framework and instruments available to the courts. She thus dwells on

---

[47] Soothhill et al, above (n 37)152. See also Cullen and Wilcox, above (n 37) 140.

[48] E Stanley and J McCulloch, *State Crime and Resistance* (London, Routledge, 2012).

[49] Article 8(2)(7)(vii) of the Rome Statute of the ICC.

[50] *Prosecutor v Thomas Lubanga Dyilo*, ICC-01/04-01/06, Trial Chamber I, Judgment Pursuant to Article 74 of the Statute, 14 March 2012, para 600 *et seq*.

[51] ICC Office of the Prosecutor, 'Policy Paper on Case Selection and Prioritization', 15 September 2016, para 41, available at: www.icc-cpi.int/itemsDocuments/20160915_OTP-Policy_Case-Selection_Eng.pdf.

a de facto empirical challenge stemming from the actual practice of courts trying international crimes. Gawronski concludes that the judicial body's institutional and legalistic capacity is crucial to the outcome of the criminalisation process of conduct amounting to international crimes, and ultimately to case building.

In contrast, I adopt a more theoretical lens in exploring the category of crimes against humanity. I use the criminologically related work of Emile Durkheim to develop a societal foundation of this group of core international crimes. It is evident from the ongoing debates on whether state policy is an element of crimes against humanity that this category of offences still struggles with establishing its own identity. Originally conceived at Nuremberg as an extension of war crimes, it grew into an independent and ambitious legal category, which seeks to address gross human rights abuses committed on a massive scale in peace- and wartime alike. At the same time, its legal foundation is shaky due to over reliance on customary international law, which is not always clear. With all the fluidity engendered by the weakness of the sources, where does one find justification for international prosecution of crimes against humanity? The purpose of the chapter is to illuminate the process of criminalisation using the category of crimes against humanity as an example. The argument is that criminalisation in international criminal law is a *sui generis* process that requires an insight from other disciplines to promote better understanding of the nature of atrocity crimes. In the case of crimes against humanity, the Durkheimian idea of solidarity offers a possibility to solidify its moral and legal foundations.

C. Trial and Punishment

Part III – and the third element of the cycle of mass atrocities – is trial and punishment, facilitated by the institutions applying international criminal law. This part of the book includes contributions by Colleen Rohan, Kerstin Carlson, and Barbora Holá and Amani Chibashimba.

The 1990s witnessed the creation of the *ad hoc* tribunals dealing with geographically and temporarily limited conflicts. The 2000s marked the beginning of the operation of the permanent treaty-based ICC and the hybrid courts situated in the region and employing both international and local staff members with the aim of bringing international criminal justice 'closer to home'. The latter category of institutions included the Extraordinary Chambers in the Courts of Cambodia (ECCC), the Special Tribunal for Lebanon (STL), and the Special Court for Sierra Leone (SCSL). Internationally created courts are not the sole venue for holding high-ranking officials accountable. The principle of universal jurisdiction contained in many domestic criminal codes allows for prosecutions of those responsible for the commission of core international crimes irrespective of their nationality or place where the crimes occurred. This mechanism caused a surge of enthusiasm in legal activists and scholars in the 1990s and early 2000s. Later on, however, this eagerness was significantly tapered due to clear enforcement deficits, such as the failure to act upon high-profile arrest warrants.[52] The concept of universal jurisdiction is not buried, however, with new courts being created under this principle specifically for the purpose of prosecuting former dictators, such as, for example, the Extraordinary African Chambers set up in Senegal to try former Chadian president Hissène Habré.

Institutions applying international criminal law are thus diverse and strive to be prolific. This is a laudable development but there are pitfalls associated with the emerging practice. In their work these courts reinvent some principles borrowed from domestic law: their procedure combines, with occasional success, elements of civil and common law. Prosecutions follow certain patterns exposing the selectivity bias and raising concerns about fairness. The sentences these courts render vary significantly. Colleen Rohan relies on her experience as a defence lawyer in multiple international criminal law cases and argues that at present there exists no unified 'international criminal law system' as such. In her chapter she explores the practical implications of the 'mixed' system of civil and common law principles, both substantive and procedural, which are in use by the various international courts and tribunals. The chapter comes up with several case-based challenges to international and 'internationalised' systems of criminal justice with particular emphasis on the questions of transfer of knowledge and expertise from international to domestic level and the adaptation of national criminal law values to international trials. Rohan warns against assumptions and generalisations, for every system is only as good as its participants, and advocates for more attention to be paid to defining the purpose of international criminal law.

Kerstin Carlson continues the discussion on diversity within the field of international criminal law by focusing on novel methods of assigning culpability for violations of international humanitarian law to individual actors. Such methods differ by institution, leading to variability (some would say fragmentation) within the corpus of the discipline. This chapter offers a new normative contestation of the assessment of the culpability of participants. It does so by considering prison guards' liability in international criminal law. Carlson's analysis demonstrates that dominant methods of evaluating blameworthiness elide elements of the 'general part' of international criminal law – applicable to all content – with elements of what should be a distinct 'specific part', namely the definitions of offences. This doctrinal imprecision, the chapter argues, functions to subvert normative challenges to the application of collective liability onto individual actors, which is the project of international criminal law. The chapter concludes with a call for more rigorous analytical work towards a model code defining the general and specific parts of international criminal law.

---

[52] In 2002, the International Court of Justice (ICJ) contributed to this trend finding Belgium in violation of international law for issuing the arrest warrant under the principle of universal jurisdiction against the incumbent Minister for Foreign Affairs of the Congo. The ICJ held that Belgium failed to respect the immunity from criminal jurisdiction. See *Case Concerning the Arrest Warrant of 11 April 2000 (Democratic Republic of the Congo v Belgium)*, International Court of Justice (ICJ), 14 February 2002.

One of the aims of the book is to add empirical insights in the discussion of the role of international criminal law in breaking the cycle of mass atrocities. Barbora Holá and Amani Chibashimba do precisely this by focusing on the notion of sentences meted out by both international and domestic courts that have prosecuted perpetrators of international crimes committed during the genocide in Rwanda in 1994. Few of 'the most responsible' individuals have been tried at the international level by the International Criminal Tribunal for Rwanda (ICTR), while the vast majority of perpetrators have been dealt with by domestic criminal courts and the *Inkiko Gacaca* tribunals in Rwanda.[53] The simultaneous operation of these different legal systems – with different legal traditions and differing dogmatic underpinnings – has generated widely reported incidents of 'vertical inconsistency' of international sentencing. However, these claims are often based on flawed anecdotal comparisons, while no systematic empirical inquiry of sentencing of perpetrators of international crimes committed during the Rwanda genocide has ever been conducted. This chapter purports to fill this lacuna and presents preliminary findings of an original, explorative empirical study comparing sentencing of genocide, the crime of crimes, at the ICTR and ordinary courts in Rwanda and reflects upon the allegations of vertical inconsistency of international sentencing.

The section on trial and punishment therefore goes to the core of the day-to-day operation of international criminal law, examining its strengths and inconsistencies and pointing to the ways in which one may rethink some of its core features.

D. Reintegration of Victims and Perpetrators

Part IV of the book focuses on the fourth stage of the cycle of mass atrocities: the reintegration of victims and offenders into society. This step is shared by both cycles of criminality. If one looks at a 'regular' cycle, reintegration of the offender is the focus of rehabilitation often listed as one of the objectives of punishment in many national laws. For example, the Russian Penal Code ensures that punishment 'is applied with the purpose of restoring social justice, as well as rehabilitating the convicted person and preventing the commission of new crimes'.[54] The same goal is featured in human rights documents, such as the International Covenant on Civil and Political Rights.[55] Victim participation in domestic criminal justice processes and attention to victims' rights outside the criminal trial are also gaining

---

[53] *Gacaca*, or grassroots lay court system, emerged in Rwanda as an alternative to the prosecutions by the International Criminal Tribunal for Rwanda (ICTR) and domestic national courts is a self-contained regime operating in accordance with its own rules. Gacaca may also be described as a community justice mechanism dealing with low level perpetrators of genocide. See R Haveman, 'Doing Justice to Gacaca' in A Smeulers and R Haveman, *Supranational Criminology: Towards a Criminology of International Crimes* (Antwerp, Intersentia, 2008).

[54] Article 43 of the Russian Penal Code (1996).

[55] Article 10(3) of the International Covenant on Civil and Political Rights (ICCPR).

momentum. Various systems across the the globe are now gradually incorpo-
rating restorative principles contained in a number of UN Documents, such as
the Declaration of Basic Principles of Justice for Victims of Crime and Abuse of
Power (1985).[56]

The main challenge posed by the restorative justice objective in the context
of mass violence is the fact that communities meant to reintegrate victims and
offenders may not be capable of doing so because the societal fabric is torn.
Communal rupture, manifested by the state's failure to prevent and prosecute
collective violence, always accompanies the cycle of mass atrocities. This essential element of mass offending often perplexes domestic criminal lawyers entering
the field of international criminal law as they draw links between gang violence
and mass atrocities.[57] This comparison is of limited explanatory value. Whereas
the former is susceptible to pressure from state enforcement agencies and often
goes underground to avoid it, the latter always occurs with unable or unwilling
institutions in the background. A state's failure to act creates conditions of general
lawlessness, thus continuing the cycle of mass atrocities.

Milena Tripkovic utilises an international criminal justice lens in her contribution to this volume when exploring how this field conceives of the relevant
'communities' as the authors and owners of criminal justice that is administered
by international criminal courts. To do so, she contrasts the traits of relevant
communities at the national and international levels. Tripkovic argues that while
there is *only one* relevant community at the national level – the domestic community – that oversees punishment, there are in fact *two* relevant communities at the
international level – the 'domestic' community from which the perpetrators prosecuted before the international tribunals come, and the 'international' community
in whose name the perpetrators are punished before international tribunals. This
duality of communities at the supranational level creates tensions, because while
the international community can be considered as both the creator and recipient of
international justice, the domestic community is merely its addressee, but hardly
plays any other role. Thus, even if crimes over which international criminal courts
have jurisdiction are universally condoned, the way in which international justice
operates alienates and excludes the domestic community, while punishment at the
international level does little to strengthen the domestic moral order. The chapter
argues that it is this problem – more than issues of geographical distance or the
lack of outreach – which accounts for why international trials fail to achieve beneficial effects and offers some insights into whether this problem could be resolved.

The notion of 'community' is thus essential for understanding the relevance
of the restorative justice rationale in the aftermath of mass atrocities: this type

---

[56] UN DOC A/RES/40/34, 29 November 1985; C Hoyle, 'Victims, the Criminal Process, and Restorative Justice' in M Maguire et al (eds), *The Oxford Handbook of Criminology* (Oxford, Oxford University
Press, 2012). See also C Hoyle, 'Can International Justice be Restorative Justice? The Role of Reparations' in N Palmer et al (eds), *Critical Perspectives on Transitional Justice* (Antwerp, Intersentia, 2012).

[57] *cf* P Collier, *Economic Causes of Civil Conflict and their Implications for Policy* (Department of
Economics, Oxford University, 2006).

of criminality breeds group victimisation and stems from large-scale organisation and state participation with a long-term effect on victims and their whole communities.[58] As a result, victims emerge not only as individuals suffering from an attack on their person or property, but also as bearers of collective identity representing the disasters of the havoc of war. There is therefore an immense expressive value in the engagement of victims in the international criminal justice process. This line of thinking produced a powerful criticism of the *ad hoc* tribunals treating victims as objects of moral concern, rather than subjects with any rights.[59] Responding to these worries, the ICC and the ECCC made victim participation one of the pillars of their operation.[60] The purpose was to give voice to the affected communities and facilitate truth-telling, leading to subsequent healing.

Another related discussion international criminal law literature focuses on is the idea of a shifting victim/perpetrator divide. There is a strong pull away from 'vilifying' the offenders and towards a more comprehensive understanding of their motivations and driving forces. Many times, the portraits of perpetrators of mass criminality are far from what popular media may wish to paint. Take, for example, the case of the former child soldier Dominic Ongwen, abducted by the Ugandan Lord's Resistance Army at the age of nine and standing trial at the ICC for war crimes 25 years later.[61] His trial at the ICC evidences a lack of agreement about what culpability entails.[62] Dominic Ongwen was recruited as a very young person and subsequently rose up the ranks for lack of better alternatives. His trial stirs debate as to the distinction between victims and perpetrators and the importance of environmental factors in shaping future perpetrators of mass atrocities – do we place former child soldiers in the same category as those offenders who joined the army voluntarily as adults?[63]

The contribution by Anette Bringedal Houge offers a window into this field of enquiry. Houge explores the construction of life narratives by those convicted for participating in mass atrocities. She focuses specifically on perpetrators of sexual violence prosecuted by the international criminal tribunals following the wars in the former Yugoslavia and the genocide in Rwanda. Houge observes that tribunals

---

[58] eg, MS Groenhuijsen and A Pemberton, 'Genocide, Crimes Against Humanity and War Crimes: A Victimological Perspective on International Criminal Justice' in R Letschert et al (eds), *Victimological Approaches to International Crimes: Africa* (Antwerp, Intersentia, 2011); L Moffett, *Justice for Victims before the International Criminal Court* (London, Routledge, 2014) 10–12.

[59] C Jorda and J de Hemptinne, 'The Status and Role of the Victim' in A Cassese, P Gaeta and JRWD Jones (eds), *The Rome Statute of the International Criminal Court: A Commentary* (Oxford, Oxford University Press, 2002).

[60] Articles 43, 54, 64, 68, 75 and 79 of the Rome Statute; new Article 33 Law on the Establishment of the ECCC.

[61] For the discussion of this case please see contribution of Matilde Gawronski in this volume, ch 3.

[62] See 'The Dominic Ongwen Trial and the Prosecution of Child Soldiers', Justice in Conflict Symposium, available at: justiceinconflict.org/2016/04/11/the-dominic-ongwen-trial-and-the-prosecution-of-child-soldiers-a-jic-symposium/.

[63] B Sander, 'We Need to Talk About Ongwen: The Plight of Victim-Perpetrators at the ICC', Justice in Conflict Symposium, available at: justiceinconflict.org/2016/04/19/we-need-to-talk-about-ongwen-the-plight-of-victim-perpetrators-at-the-icc/.

allow stories about sexual war violence from the perspectives of survivors, perpetrators and other parties to the conflict but constrain them according to the needs and purposes of the legal framework. In the face of a perpetrator 'gap' in research on sexual war violence, court cases focusing on direct perpetrators of sexual war violence provide interesting material for increasing our knowledge about this phenomenon and the ways in which we conceptualise it.[64] This expertise is particularly relevant for exploring the 'agency versus structure' debate in relation to the collective violence for which defendants are tried. Criminal proceedings and the arguments of the parties epitomise this debate. The chapter thus shifts the focus from doctrinal debates over legal principles and case law development, to the insights of stories, or narratives, that these legal proceedings produce.

E. Prevention

The book's penultimate section (Part V) is dedicated to prevention, which is one of the least studied stages in the cycle of mass atrocities. A purely legalistic focus invites a distortion of the broader picture of offending for it offers a limited view on enforcement, thereby omitting important factors conducive to mass violence. Adding to the challenge is the fact that the criminology of mass atrocities is a relatively new field of enquiry that has benefited from some preliminary groundwork *within* the discipline (law or criminology, respectively). What is currently missing and what this book seeks to start developing is a study framed in a way that facilitates meaningful cross-disciplinary exchange, allowing for a better systematic understanding of the phenomenon of atrocity crimes. The two chapters in this section thus offer a combination of criminological and legal intake on the issue of prevention.

Stefan Harrendorf uses criminological discourse to investigate the claim that international crimes are an exceptional category, not only with respect to the scale of these crimes, but also with respect to their inherent qualities. The relationship between ordinary and international crimes is often described as a dichotomy between crimes of obedience or conformity on the one hand and crimes as acts of individual deviance from social and legal norms on the other. Harrendorf advocates a different view: he proposes viewing the spectrum of crimes more like a continuum with international crimes as an extreme form of criminal conduct, which, however, could be explained by the same, comprehensive theory as ordinary crimes. He rejects purely situationist or individualistic approaches

---

[64] Maruna and Copes highlight that the interest in life narratives among many contemporary social scientists is not so much in the substantive events these stories depict but the meanings the person attaches to such facts. How people choose to frame the events of their lives says as much about the psychology of the individual – his or her personality, identity, or self – as it does about the events and structural conditions experienced. See Maruna and Copes, above (n 27) 222. See also J Bruner, *Making Stories: Law, Literature, Life* (Cambridge, MA, Harvard University Press, 2002).

to explain international crimes, suggesting an interactionist theory as the only viable option. Based on 'social identity theory' and 'self-categorization theory', the chapter provides a first glance of a social identity approach to international crimes, integrating other situational forces such as ideology or obedience processes as far as possible into the overall social identity scheme.

Elies van Sliedregt in her contribution offers an international lawyer's perspective on the link between regional accountability efforts and prevention. She critically examines the Malabo Protocol, which is a constituent instrument for the African Court of Justice and Human Rights (ACJHR). Van Sliedregt oscillates between two competing conceptualisations of the ACJHR. The first one pictures it as a 'rebel court' since the Malabo Protocol distorts the definition of crimes solidified at an international level and offers immunity to the sitting heads of state, making both cooperation with the ICC and domestic enforcement more complicated. A competing view is that of a 'model court' due to the possibility of the prosecutions of corporate entities within the African regional criminal justice system. This is steps ahead of the ICC, which currently lacks such powers. Van Sliedregt praises these developments and concludes by stressing the paramount importance of the threat of criminal sanctions when it comes to the business activities of corporations in deterring future atrocities in Africa and elsewhere.

F. Epilogue

The book concludes with the Epilogue by Harmen van der Wilt which summarises the discussion in the volume. It points to the gaps in legal framing of the phenomenon of mass atrocities and recognises the need for multidisciplinary perspectives going beyond the 'comfort zone' in developing international criminal law. The view of the entire cycle of mass criminality is essential in order to understand how best to respond to the ruptures in the societies described as 'extremely violent' or 'oppressive'. This comprehensive approach also allows enhancing the role of international criminal law in combating collective offending.

III. Methodological Approach

From the time of the Nuremberg tribunal onwards, international criminal law has developed largely along doctrinal lines. This field of law was born out of political consensus reached in the aftermath of the Second World War and in the existing legal vacuum. Until recently, both scholars and practitioners overlooked criminological considerations when discussing and dealing with collective offending. Legal instruments and exponentially increasing case law served as a basis for accumulating knowledge related to perpetrators, causes of mass atrocities and the effectiveness of the international criminal justice system. Empirical research on the work of international criminal tribunals is miniscule compared with the massive body of literature on the law applied by these courts.[65] This gap is best explained by considering two factors: the general nature of legal scholarship, and additional challenges posed by international criminal law.

Legal scholarship tends to be static and focuses primarily on developing an argument rather than on processing empirical observations.[66] In contrast, empirical socio-legal research takes a dynamic form and must account for the ever-changing world full of contradictions and inconsistencies. As a result, many areas of law lack general theories capable of grasping patterns or structures of data or phenomena.[67] International criminal law is no exception – the systematic accumulation of scientific knowledge is frequently replaced by the concrete application of doctrine within the constraints of the specific argument. The situation is quickly changing with the growing interest in interdisciplinarity and empirical scholarship in international law. There is clear impetus to rearticulate the methods of legal research.[68]

When it comes to studying international criminal law more specifically, the most well-travelled path would be to engage with tightly crafted legal provisions and the case law emanating from the institutions applying these provisions. This approach, however, is no longer sufficient in the light of the mounting criticism of international criminal justice as well as its imminent (and desired) appropriation by regional and national policymakers. Empirical legal scholarship in the new realist tradition[69] is the best way to respond to the increased awareness of political and social reality. It pushes the scientific agenda forward by using research to shift familiar paradigms and reconstruct the habitual frames of reference.[70]

Points of tension created by the lack of relevant empirical and sociological studies include such issues as the length and appropriateness of sentences imposed on the perpetrators of mass atrocities or the nature of international crimes. What does a specific number of years in prison stand for and how does it compare across different courts? Is it feasible to expand the jurisdiction of the ICC to cover the responsibility of corporate entities? This volume tackles these questions by going beyond purely legal discourse into the fields of sociology,

---

[65] SMH Nouwen, '"As You Set out for Ithaka"': Practical, Epistemological, Ethical, and Existential Questions about Socio-Legal Empirical Research in Conflict' (2014) 27 *Leiden Journal of International Law* 227, 228. See also I Bantekas, 'Introduction: An Interdisciplinary Criminology of International Criminal Law' in I Bantekas and E Mylonaki (eds), *Criminological Approaches to International Criminal Law* (Cambridge, Cambridge University Press, 2014); S Karstedt and S Parmentier, 'Introduction to the Special Issue Atrocity Crimes and Transitional Justice' (2012) 9 *European Journal of Criminology* 465.

[66] A Peters, 'Realizing Utopia as a Scholarly Endeavour' (2013) 24 *European Journal of International Law* 536.

[67] ibid.

[68] I Venzke, 'International Law and its Methodology: Introducing a *New Leiden Journal of International Law* Series' (2015) 28 *Leiden Journal of International Law* 185.

[69] See below (n 79).

[70] A Lang, 'New Legal Realism, Empiricism, and Scientism: The Relative Objectivity of Law and Social Science' (2015) 28 *Leiden Journal of International Law* 231 240.

philosophy and criminology.[71] The book therefore adopts a wider approach to international criminal law and views it *in relation* to the divisions and ruptures in a given society or within the institution.

IV. Urgency in Developing Multidisciplinary Approaches to International Criminal Law

There are at least three compelling reasons why international criminal law as a discipline calls for further exploration from multiple angles, including sociological and criminological perspectives.

The first reason is the increasing importance of regional and national courts in prosecuting collective violence.[72] The Extraordinary African Chambers in the Senegal court system set up by the African Union to try the former dictator of Chad, Hissène Habré, and the EU-backed Special Tribunal for Kosovo are just two examples of the strong pull towards 'regionalisation' of international criminal law. The complementarity principle of the ICC also provides for 'domestication' of international criminal justice.[73] This principle facilitates strong ties between international and local judiciary in addressing atrocity crimes. For instance, the ICC's normative framework played a significant role in the determination of possible sentences to be meted out by the Colombian courts to different parties in the conflict. Adequate punishment meeting international standards proved to be crucial in the ongoing peace negotiations between the government and the guerrillas.[74] This trend towards 'regionalisation' fosters a growing demand for the transfer of knowledge and expertise from the purely international level to hybrid or domestic courts. Without a more profound understanding of atrocity crimes and their contextual elements, this transfer is incomplete.

Secondly, and related to the first point, there is an ongoing critical discussion in scholarly and professional circles about the legitimacy of international courts and international justice.[75] The ICC is often assessed from the standpoint of its

---

[71] Rock, above (n 38).

[72] Olusanya describes 'collective violence' as usually perpetrated in a systematic fashion by a large number of participants possessing a high degree of heterogeneity. See O Olusanya, 'Using the Macro–micro Integrated Theoretical Model to Understand the Dynamics of Collective Violence' in I Bantekas and E Mylonaki (eds), *Criminological Approaches to International Criminal Law* (Cambridge, Cambridge University Press, 2014) 226.

[73] Article 17 of the Rome Statute of the ICC.

[74] M Aksenova, 'Values on the Move: Colombian Sentencing Practice and the Complementarity Analysis of the International Criminal Court' (2015) iCourts Working Paper Series No 24; See also M Aksenova, 'Achieving Justice Through Restorative Means in Colombia: New Developments in Implementing the Peace Deal' *EJIL: Talk!* (3 May 2017), available at: www.ejiltalk.org/achieving-justice-through-restorative-means-in-colombia-new-developments-in-implementing-the-peace-deal/.

[75] See, eg, M Scheinin, H Krunke and M Aksenova (eds), *Judges as Guardians of Constitutionalism and Human Rights* (Cheltenham, Edward Elgar Publishing, 2016).

ability, or lack thereof, to achieve a number of conflicting objectives.[76] How to reconcile different competing rationales and conflicting views on what international criminal law must deliver. The ICC's lack of enforcement powers and the selectivity of its prosecutions targeting only a fraction of potentially responsible individuals may present insurmountable obstacles on the road to much sought-after legitimacy. This strand of thought leads to the discussion of the alternatives to international criminal justice or modifications to its current architecture that allow for broader acceptance of its ideals. Criminological research of atrocity crimes rooted in empirics, socio-legal studies and pragmatic considerations of restoring affected lives and communities may contribute towards this goal. For example, criminology may assist in determining the motivations of perpetrators of mass violence, thereby grounding the goal of preventing future atrocities. In this instance, academic scholarship goes beyond its role as a material source of law and serves to influence practice, thereby fostering the development of international law.[77]

Finally, promoting multidisciplinary research that connects doctrinal approaches in international criminal law to what is happening on the ground is consonant with reviving interest in legal realism.[78] Gregory Shaffer describes New Legal Realism as building 'from a jurisprudential tradition that asks how actors use and apply law in order to advance our understanding of three inter-related questions – how law obtains meaning, is practised (the law-in-action), and changes over time'.[79] The empirical study of law's operation in relation to social and political forces is backward looking, while the analysis of its capacity to address problems, however they may be conceived, is forward looking.[80]

International criminal law arguably reached the outer limits of legalism. It can no longer afford to ignore social and political reality because these are factors crucial for its further development. Judith Shklar pointed to the discrepancy between, on the one hand, legalistic values that were constitutive at Nuremberg and paved way to the future of international criminal law, and wilful disregard by the architects of Nuremberg of the political and social environment that gave

---

[76] See, eg, M Osiel, 'The Banality of Good: Aligning Incentives Against Mass Atrocities' (2005) 105 *Columbia Law Review* 1751; M Aksenova, 'Symbolism as a Constraint on International Criminal Law' (2017) 30 *Leiden Journal of International Law* 475. For a critical discussion see contribution of Colleen Rohan to this volume, ch 5.

[77] C Stahn and E de Brabandere, 'The Future of International Legal Scholarship: Some Thoughts on "Practice", "Growth", and "Dissemination"' (2014) 27 *Leiden Journal of International Law* 1, 4.

[78] Karstedt and Parmentier emphasise that problems tackled by international criminologists are far from theoretical and concern day-to-day realities and ongoing conflicts in different parts of the world. Karstedt and Parmentier, above (n 65) 466. See also Elies van Sliedregt on 'connecting law to life' in E van Sliedregt, 'International Criminal Law: Over-studied and Underachieving?' (2016) 29 *Leiden Journal of International Law* 1, 8–9.

[79] G Shaffer, 'International Legal Theory: International Law and its Methodology: The New Legal Realist Approach to International Law' (2015) 28 *Leiden Journal of International Law* 189.

[80] ibid, 194.

rise to the trial, on the other.[81] In the absence of positive law at the time of the creation of the International Military Tribunal, such 'blindness' was a 'legalistic way of coping with violence, vengeance, disorder, and even, the future of German politics'.[82] But the same approach cannot subsist today when the novelty of the new field of law has worn off and the capital of trust vested in it by different stakeholders ran out. Difficult contextual questions accompanying the commission of mass atrocities and their subsequent prosecutions require answers in order for international criminal law to continue benefiting from wide international support, which is the sole and precious impetus for its development.

[81] JH Shklar, *Legalism: An Essay on Law, Morals and Politics* (Cambridge, MA, Harvard University Press, 1964) 146–47. John Hagan and Scott Greer point however to the fact that one criminologist influenced by legal realism served as a member of the US delegation at the London conference resulting in the Nuremberg Charter: Sheldon Glueck insisted on treating Nazi perpetrators as criminally responsible as opposed to irrational 'in order to inform public opinion ... and to fix the record of history'. See J Hagan and S Greer, 'Making War Criminal' (2002) 40 *Criminology* 231, 236.

[82] Shklar, ibid, 147.

2

The Biology and Psychology of Atrocity and the Erasure of Memory

CHRISTOPHER HARDING

I. The Search for Criminological Understanding: The Criminology of Atrocity and Confronting the 'Monster Within'

The striking and distinguishing feature of atrocity[1] or 'mass' or 'system' criminality is its scale, extremity, discriminatory motivation, and its collective nature of perpetration. In this way it is differentiated from the individualised and specific nature and context of 'classic' or 'ordinary' criminality, and the number of victims, the extent of their suffering and the number of human offenders required to bring about that outcome has now led to a distinctive moral, legal and political reaction. Morally, this is a phenomenon which 'shocks the conscience of mankind';[2] legally, the conduct now qualifies as 'international crime' and a serious violation of human rights;[3] and politically, it has become the basis for exceptional intervention and the compromise of state sovereignty.[4] At the same time, the subject embodies its own

---

[1] The term 'atrocity' will be used in this discussion as a convenient shorthand term. It is a useful sociological/criminological/ethical epithet for what lawyers now often call 'crimes against humanity' as a form of 'international crime', and that generally conveys a sense of criminality which is large-scale, extreme in consequent human suffering, highly organised, and discriminatory in its motivation.

[2] Such descriptive language has been widely used during the twentieth century: 'abhorrent crimes ... which struck at the whole of mankind and shocked the conscience of nations' (District Court of Jerusalem in *Attorney-General for the Government of Israel v Eichmann* (1961) ILM 5; 'in order to liberate mankind from such an odious scourge' (preamble to the Convention on the Prevention and Punishment of the Crime of Genocide, 1948).

[3] There are thus two main routes of legal control: via criminal law, usually as a crime against humanity or genocide (accountability of individuals), or under human rights protection treaties (accountability of states and governments).

[4] Although humanitarian intervention and the more recent 'responsibility to protect' remain a contested area of international law (consider for example the case of Rwanda in 1994, as discussed below), in political terms such interventions have sometimes taken place, with significant outcomes, for instance in Kosovo in 1999. For an overview, see: S Zifcak, 'The Responsibility to Protect' in MD Evans (ed), *International Law*, 4th edn (Oxford, Oxford University Press, 2014).

enigma – while it has a manifestly exceptional and traumatic quality, expressed in strong and evocative vocabulary ('holocaust',[5] 'armageddon', 'inferno'), it also involves the participation of the ordinary and the routine – hence the use of the term 'banality of evil'.[6]

In this way the subject presents a particular challenge to criminology,[7] and indeed overturns and subverts the very idea of the 'criminal'. The special task for criminology, or at least the criminology of atrocity, is then to explain and understand the involvement of the otherwise good citizen in outrageous conduct, and most disturbingly, confront the existence of the 'monster' within everybody.

Another problem for criminal science and criminology in its traditional form is that it is largely an enquiry and scholarship rooted in methodological individualism, and an atomised view of humanity as operating through a number of specific and individual personal interactions, seeing the criminal as an individual bounded by his or her own personal circumstances, rather than as an item in a more complex whole.[8] In this way, the egocentricity of each individual human being (itself an important distinguishing feature of the human species) has been projected on to the traditional explanations offered by criminal science. The dilemma for theory in this field has then been that of squaring this circle of interaction of the individual and collective units.[9] In attempts (for instance by ethicists, political scientists and jurists) to penetrate the puzzle of the banality of evil, there has been a tendency to dehumanise the all too human individual and transform that actor into a cog in the machine. But this has left a disturbing ethical aftertaste in the resultant denial and removal of individual responsibility, for instance shifting accountability to the state or some criminal enterprise. This dilemma and these uneasy conclusions have led to a burgeoning of philosophical and legal literature,[10] accompanying the practical and political demands of

---

[5] 'Holocaust', now a widely applied description, originates in Greek, signifying a sacrificial burning. An equivalent term in Hebrew is 'shoah', broadly translated as 'catastrophe'. Another evocative term, but more specific in its application, is 'pogrom', from Russian, denoting a violent assault, and used first to describe large-scale anti-semitic attacks in Russia and parts of central Europe during the nineteenth and twentieth centuries.

[6] Reputedly the term first used by Hannah Arendt, in her book, *Eichmann in Jerusalem: A Report on the Banality of Evil* (New York, Viking Press, 1963).

[7] Other, perhaps it may be said more 'banal', challenges for criminologists have been identified as political and professional in character. For instance, see the view of Daniel Maier-Katkin et al that 'the safer course to academic respectability and official support for an aspiring discipline was to focus on the scientific study of agreed-upon national concerns such as violent crime, delinquency and drug abuse' (D Maier-Katkin, DP Mears and TJ Bernard, 'Towards a Criminology of Crimes Against Humanity' (2009) 13 *Theoretical Criminology* 227, 230).

[8] What may be conveniently summarised as the issue of 'agency', or the problem of identifying the relevant actor on a global stage increasingly populated by significant organisational entities (states, corporations, IGOs and NGOs, criminal and terrorist organisations, to mention just some).

[9] See generally, C Harding, *Criminal Enterprise: Individuals, Organisations and Criminal Responsibility* (Cullompton, Willan, 2007).

[10] For a summary, see Harding, ibid; T Schwinn, 'Individual and Collective Agency' in W Outhwaite and SP Turner (eds), *The SAGE Handbook of Social Science Methodology* (London, Sage Publications, 2007).

developing human rights and international criminal law. But it is now timely for criminology to be called in aid to help resolve these ethical, legal and political puzzles.

Among sociologists and criminologists there appears to be some self-awareness of a tardiness and even some nervousness in approaching this subject. For instance, Hagan and Rymond-Richmond have referred to a sense of new venturing and scholarly risk: having taken a long time to confront 'more deadly neglected topics, namely genocide, war crimes, and crimes against humanity' and so bring 'a rich array of theories and methods to this crucial task', criminologists will 'first have to engage more fully and embrace the topic of genocide', but will 'incur the inevitable scholarly risks of traveling to new intellectual locations'.[11] Maier-Katkin, Mears and Bernard have interrogated more fully what they describe as 'the silence of mainstream criminology about crimes of such magnitude' in a discussion which calls upon the discipline to 'overcome its historic inattention'.[12] Those authors also identify a main task for the mainstream of the subject in taking up such an enterprise: that of selecting and applying approaches from its existing menu of explanations and theories, which have to a large extent been worked out in the context of 'individualised' criminality as observed in national study of such crime.

But then there may be some risk in over-complicating the response to what is in essence a simple main question. As Olaoluwa Olusanya has observed: the central question in the subject is 'what motivates people to murder, rape or torture their neighbours, friends and family members?'[13] Expressed in such terms, it becomes easier to view this criminological endeavour as a criminology of the non-criminal actor, in some respects a more extreme version of what has been involved in the study of white-collar crime.[14] But phrasing the subject in this way should serve as a reminder that it is subject matter that has been defined for criminologists by those working in other disciplines who were, so to speak, the first on the scene – political theorists, historians, psychologists, moral philosophers and lawyers.[15] Indeed, the essential nature of the subject has been identified most sharply, evocatively and graphically by writers of a more wide-ranging and less academic provenance, such

---

[11] J Hagan and W Rymond-Richmond, 'Criminology Confronts Genocide: Whose Side Are You On?' (2009) 23 *Theoretical Criminology* 503, 503.

[12] Maier-Katkin et al, above (n 7) 228–29.

[13] O Olusanya, 'A Macro–Micro Integrated Theoretical Model of Mass Participation in Genocide' (2013) 53 *British Journal of Criminology* 843, 844.

[14] Maier-Katkin et al, above (n 7) point out the pioneering role of the study of white-collar crime in beginning to address the issue of crime within the organisation, leading to an interest in crime within government and sponsored by the state, and then to the present topic of large-scale atrocity offending. A common point, naturally enough, is the anonymity of the individual within an organisational context. The comparison also prompts thoughts about a catchy descriptor to match 'white collar', to capture pithily the idea of the latent enemy within the friend, colleague or neighbour.

[15] See Maier-Katkin et al, above (n 7) 230.

as Hannah Arendt,[16] Primo Levi[17] and Leonard Cohen.[18] The possible explanations for such apparently incomprehensible criminality therefore have been batted to the criminologists from a variety of disciplinary perspectives and there has been a late-in-the-day scrabble among the competing solutions to the puzzle – it is inherent in our biological make-up, it resides in the psychology of obedience and compliance, or in the force of propaganda and ideology, it originates in cultures of fear and distrust of the 'other', it depends upon a combination of authoritarian governance and economic or environmental breakdown or catastrophe. In that sense, the field is rich already in possible, and in many respects quite plausible and convincing explanations.[19] The problem for the criminologist is then how to use this fertile source of data and theoretical analysis, and how to locate this material in the long-running debate within criminology as a discipline, as between the significance on the one hand of individualised explanations (broadly speaking the 'micro-level' biology and psychology of human actors) and on the other hand, of social-structural explanations (broadly speaking, the 'macro-level' political, social, economic and environmental context of action).[20] The present main task for criminology is then outlined by Maier-Katkin et al in the following terms:

> [A] criminologist might well be struck by the extent to which closely related disciplines have advanced a discourse on genocide and crimes against humanity,

but that the existing literature

> does not put forward a theory to explain how these factors come together to generate the behavior of groups of normal citizens who become perpetrators of evil,

so that

> there is much more to be done and that criminology as an intellectual enterprise has much to offer and much to gain by turning an eye towards crimes against humanity.[21]

Taking up that mission, the present discussion will next suggest a *clarifying theoretical framework* for this debate on the way forward (a 'theory to explain how the factors come together'),[22] but without going so far as to recommend, as do, for instance Maier-Katkin et al and Olusanya,[23] a unifying or key component of such a theory.

---

[16] As a journalist: Arendt, above (n 6).

[17] As a victim and survivor, Primo Levi: P Levi, *The Drowned and the Saved* (trans Raymond Rosenthal) (New York, Vintage International, 1988).

[18] As a poet, Leonard Cohen: L Cohen, 'All There is to Know About Adolf Eichmann' from *Flowers for Hitler* (Toronto, McClelland and Stewart, 1964).

[19] As a teacher of the subject, the present author would feel duty bound to list and examine all those possible explanations and understandings of the subject; in other words, they all have something to offer.

[20] See generally, KS Williams, *Textbook on Criminology*, 7th edn (Oxford, Oxford University Press, 2012) 8–9.

[21] Maier-Katkin et al, above (n 7) 232–33.

[22] While acknowledging that what criminology has to offer in this enterprise is some more widely applicable understanding of criminal motivation.

[23] For Maier-Katkin et al, it is 'normal people and group structures and dynamics – including socialization and conformity to the dominant norms of the moment – through which individuals are brought

II. A Framework for Discussion: It Begins in Biology But Includes Much Else

An essential clarifying task is to provide some order for discussion, proceeding on the assumption that there is something of value in most of the explanations and 'theories' of atrocity offending offered so far, and that any search for a single, overarching explanation is likely to be a chimera. The following is offered then as a 'simple plan' or more exactly an orientation within the subject as an aid for ideas, argument and the deployment of data.

The underlying element in explaining and understanding atrocity is – unpalatable as it may be – human nature in itself: the fact that, as a species, humans have a capacity for violence, and are prone to behaviour that is aggressive, suspicious and in various ways hostile towards others of the same species. This is a clutch of biological and psychological traits common to all humans. Furthermore, for humans in a more advanced state of social organisation, there is also a strong tendency towards obedience to authority and the need to fit into a hierarchy (resulting in what is often then referred to as an attitude of compliance) and this characteristic may be seen as a psychological need for security. Finally, another significant and arguably distinctive feature of the human make-up is also psychological – a capacity for critical reflection, for rationality and reasoning and for self-judgement, leading then to a capacity for normative ordering of action and an associated reflexive mental process, or 'conscience'.[24]

These are all 'individual' or 'micro' features of human behaviour in criminological parlance. But the important point of clarification is that the 'negative' biological and psychological elements – violence, aggression, suspicion, and to some extent obedience, may be and are moderated through rationality and critical judgement of the self and others. A central point of enquiry is how and when that process of moderation occurs, and that is a question in particular for moral philosophers, psychologists, lawyers and criminologists.

But also the external dimension (social and structural explanations) is important, indeed crucial, in any analysis of atrocity. Any resort to violent, aggressive or hostile action towards others (which is then in need of rational restraint or modification) will be triggered by external circumstances which generate a condition of fear, leading to violence or other aggression. Such external factors may be various and historically contingent but may be broadly classified as sources of economic and environmental stress, combining with certain political and cultural conditions (typically, for instance, authoritarian governance).

---

to participate in crimes against humanity, and perhaps many other forms of crime as well': see above (n 7) 247). For Olusanya, the central element in his integrated conceptual framework is the notion of cognitive dissonance (Olusanya, above (n 13) 845 *et seq*).

[24] For some recent debate on the validity and relevance of 'biosocial criminology', especially as judged in the writings of 'critical criminology', see the papers and discussion in (2015) 7 *Journal of Theoretical and Philosophical Criminology*.

This broad scheme of analysis could then be reordered as a kind of timeline into the following general equation:

(capacity for violent, aggressive and hostile behaviour) × (obedience to authority within a culture of authoritarian governance) × (conditions of economic or environmental stress) × (insufficient or ineffective critical self-restraint) = atrocity conduct.

'Atrocity conduct', it will be recalled, is broadly understood here as action which is large-scale, extreme in its injurious effect, systematic and organised, and discriminatory in its motivation (thus legally, for example, a grave and manifest violation of human rights, a crime against humanity). The equation or formula given above will help to explain why and how, for example, atrocity occurred in the former Yugoslavia in the early 1990s but not in Scandinavia; or in Rwanda in 1994 but not in Botswana; in continental Europe in the early 1940s but not in North America.[25]

Some of this may be elaborated on a little more. While the external or structural factors are well noted in discussion of predictive and preventive strategies (in so far as the latter are politically feasible),[26] it is well to remember and emphasise the underlying biology and psychology as the human seedbed of atrocity offending. This is a key to understanding the puzzle of the ordinary citizen turned into *génocidaire*. In the words of Leonard Cohen, what should we expect? 'Medium, and distinguishing features, none',[27] so very much most of us ourselves, bearing a capacity for violence, aggression, suspicion of the 'other', and a tendency to respect authority, but tempered by a certain degree of self-awareness and self-restraint.

Jared Diamond provides a concise summary of the self-destructive irony embodied in human nature:

But among our unique qualities are two that now jeopardize our existence: our propensities to kill each other and to destroy our environment. Of course, both propensities occur in other species: lions and many other animals kill their own kind, while elephants and others damage their environment. However, these propensities are much more threatening in us than in other animals because of our technological power and exploding numbers.[28]

[25] Examples of well-attested atrocity, often described legally as genocide, as subsequently addressed by the International Criminal Tribunal for the former Yugoslavia (ICTY), the International Tribunal for Rwanda (ICTR), and the International Military Tribunal (Nuremberg Tribunal).

[26] A notorious example of accurate prediction coupled with political refusal to act pre-emptively is the warning given by UN peacekeeping force commander Roméo Dallaire on the eve of the Rwandan genocide in 1994. See Dallaire's own account in *Shake Hands with the Devil: The Failure of Humanity in Rwanda* (Toronto, Random House, 2003); and also former UN Secretary-General Kofi Annan's later expressions of regret that the international community had failed to intervene in Rwanda in 1994. Also, on the trigger for genocidal conflict in Rwanda, note the argument of Jared Diamond: 'I conclude that population pressure was *one* of the important factors behind the Rwandan genocide, that Malthus's worst-case scenario may sometimes be realized and that Rwanda may be a distressing model of that scenario in operation. Severe problems of overpopulation, environmental impact, and climate change cannot persist indefinitely; sooner or later they are likely to resolve themselves, whether in the manner of Rwanda or in some other manner not of our devising' (J Diamond, *Collapse: How Societies Choose to Fail or Survive* (London, Allen Lane, 2005) 327–28.

[27] Cohen, above (n 18).

[28] J Diamond, *The Rise and Fall of the Third Chimpanzee* (London, Vintage Books, 1992) 2–3.

The violent and aggressive urge may then be tied to fear of the unknown, in particular of the stranger or 'other'.[29] A useful basis for exploring the concept of the 'other' in modern societies is provided by the work and theorising of the Polish sociologist Zygmunt Bauman. In the first place, Bauman has distinguished the *anthropophagic* tendency of primitive societies to incorporate and assimilate strangers, from the *anthropoemic* tendency of modern societies to exclude or keep separate such strangers – thus, contrasting inclusive and exclusive social strategies.[30] For Bauman, a characteristic feature of modernity is the need to remove unknowns and uncertainties, and the latter is represented in particular by the 'danger-carrying stranger'.[31] Related to this analysis is Bauman's other explanatory metaphor of the 'gardening state'. This is a way of understanding modern societies as 'gardens' in which the natural and individual roots of antisocial phenomena are tended into some kind of social order (rational self-restraint, but also obedience to authority). In such modern societies, there is an 'indispensability of the supra-individual power of the state in securing and perpetuating an orderly relationship among men'.[32] But while obedience to authority may be harnessed to the positive project of collective self-restraint (law as an ethical 'good') it may also be employed in the service of organised and systemic attacks on the 'other' (authority and law as an ethical 'wrong'). Experimental research such as that carried out some time ago by Milgram and Zimbardo also suggests the impact of authority as a means of unlocking the capacity for violent behaviour and loosening the restraint of ethical inhibition.[33]

This ordering of the subject would then suggest that an important focus for criminological research should be that point of exercising self-restraint in the context of action being contemplated or taken in relation to the perceived threat of the 'other'. As Maier-Katkin et al argue,

> it is not personal pathology or an anomic state of affairs but rather normal people and group structures and dynamics – including socialization and conformity to the

---

[29] Note, for instance, the tragic fate of James Cook in Hawaii, but also the extermination of the aboriginal population of Tasmania. For a useful overview of the latter, see: Diamond, *Rise and Fall*, above (n 28) 252–55. Cook's death appears to have occurred as part of a classic 'clash of culture', although the circumstances were complicated; see: *Journal of William Ellis: A Narrative of a Tour through Hawaii in 1823* (introduction by Lorrin A Thurston, Hawaiian Gazette Co, 1917).

[30] Z Baumann, *Life in Fragments* (Oxford, Blackwell, 1995) 179–92.

[31] Z Baumann, *Modernity and Ambivalence* (Ithaca, NY, Cornell University Press, 1991).

[32] Z Baumann, *Legislators and Interpreters* (Oxford, Polity Press, 1987) 55.

[33] S Milgram, 'Behavioural Study of Obedience' (1963) 67 *Journal of Abnormal & Social Psychology* 371; for a fuller account, see S Milgram, *Obedience to Authority: An Experimental View* (New York, Harper & Row, 1974). Milgram's research, conducted at Yale University in the early 1960s, while ethically controversial, has been replicated subsequently with some similar results by other researchers (for instance, the 'Stanford Prison Experiment', carried out by Philip Zimbardo in 1971: C Haney, WC Banks and PG Zimbardo, 'A Study of Prisoners and Guards in a Simulated Prison' (1973) 30 *Naval Research Review* 4). This research took place in a particular historical and political context, at the time of the trial of Adolph Eichmann in Jerusalem, charged with crimes against humanity for his role as a Nazi bureaucrat, and the debate engendered by Hannah Arendt's analysis of the 'banality of evil'.

dominant norms of the moment – through which individuals are brought to participate in crime against humanity.[34]

But personal pathology and anomic state should not be so easily discarded. These latter are the raw material of the subject, the biological and psychological seedbed for destructive socialisation, and for that reason should be kept in the forefront of the mind in any analysis of atrocity conduct.

III. Memory and the Erasure of Memory

The second part of this chapter will build upon the scheme of discussion laid out above by addressing more specifically a particular aspect of the psychology of atrocity and its manipulation: memory of past atrocity and the erasure of that memory, both as a component of the atrocity and as a strategy for its resolution. Much of this discussion will build upon Diamond's argument that:

> Genocide, often considered a human hallmark confined to rare perverts, actually has many animal precedents and used to be considered socially acceptable or admirable. Whether we will succeed in curbing our modern power to commit it depends on our coming to recognize its frequency in human history, the potential for it in all of us, and the way in which ordinary people try to rationalize becoming killers.[35]

Memory is important in relation to a number of aspects of atrocity offending. In more practical terms it is a significant element of evidence and the proof of atrocity for legal and other purposes. After the event and in any attempt to recall and establish the facts of atrocity, the memory of victim-survivors, witnesses and perpetrators is often crucial in any reconstruction and understanding of the relevant events, yet it is clearly recognised that such memory may be problematical. It is well understood that memory is *selective* (for a number of reasons, some of which are self-evident), may be of *doubtful accuracy*, may be based upon a *partial experience*, and is subject to *interpretation and re-evaluation* by the memorising person. The psychology of memory and recollection is a well-established field of study,[36] and much may be drawn upon in that area of expertise for purposes of application to both legal and political processes which may be used to address atrocity situations. In the context of legal process, for example, policies and rules have been developed to deal with the sufficiency and admissibility of eye-witness testimony which is necessarily based on memory of past events. As Patricia Wald, for some time a judge in the International Criminal Tribunal for the former Yugoslavia (ICTY), has observed in relation to the work of that particular

---

[34] Maier-Katkin et al, above (n 7) 247.

[35] Diamond, *Rise and Fall*, above (n 28) 250.

[36] For a convenient overview and entry into the topic, see; JK Foster, *Memory – A Very Short Introduction* (Oxford, Oxford University Press, 2008).

court: 'the Balkan offenders – again unlike their Nuremberg predecessors – did not engage in "meticulous record keeping". They left few paper trails behind, and thus witnesses had to be relied upon for most of the evidence at trial'.[37] In the context of international criminal law, therefore, the vagaries and psychology of memory have engaged a fair amount of attention.

But memory is also very important in both the generation of atrocity, in understanding how it may come about, and in relation to subsequent feeling about and response to the occurrence of atrocity, and in that sense may be seen as a substantive component of atrocity. It is evident for instance that during the Balkans conflict of the 1990s longer-term memory among both Serbs and Croats of inter-ethnic atrocity committed during the 1940s served to ignite violence and aggression, and may help to understand and explain the phenomenon and paradox of 'friend and neighbour turned into enemy'. Similarly, and more generally, some of the 'healing' strategies of atrocity-avoidance, ranging from amnesty to truth and reconciliation procedures, depend upon both memory and erasure of memory as part of a longer-term and continuing process of managing inter-ethnic relations. Memory in this context may be encapsulated in the metaphor of the 'buried giant', as used to notable literary effect by Kazuo Ishiguro in his recent novel, *The Buried Giant*.[38]

A. The Buried Giant: An Imagining of Atrocity and its Erasure

In his recent novel Ishiguro engages in a fascinating reimagining of a partly 'forgotten' period of British history, that of the British westward 'retreat' before the advancing Germanic (or Anglo-Saxon) settlement (or 'invasion') of the British islands during the fifth and sixth centuries (AD). This has sometimes been regarded as a 'lost' period of history, largely on account of the scarcity of written and documentary evidence (part of the 'dark age'), made all the more tantalising for historians since it was at the same time a period of significant ethnic migration and demographic change, resulting in the emergence of an Anglo-Saxon England and Celtic western belt within the British islands. Even now, there remains some argument among historians regarding the extent to which these changes (which were long term, extending over some two hundred or more years) were either violent and confrontational or peaceful and consensual. To pose the question in more dramatic terms, was it a matter of violent push and ethnic cleansing, or

---

[37] PM Wald, 'Dealing with Witnesses in War Crimes Trials: Lessons from the Yugoslav Tribunal' (2002) 5 *Yale Human Rights & Development Law Journal* 217, 220. The discussion there is a good example of critical analysis of some of the procedural and evidential issues in that particular jurisdiction.

[38] K Ishiguro, *The Buried Giant* (London, Faber & Faber, 2015). Ishiguro was awarded the Nobel Prize for Literature in 2017.

gradual integration? More heroic historical conjecture ('legend') has favoured the former view, while more rigorous and painstaking examination of archaeological and other evidence seems to be moving towards the latter view.[39]

For his literary purposes and fictional device, Ishiguro takes up the 'legendary' account, and employs as a focal point of his narrative the partly historical, partly legendary military victory of the British (and Christian) war leader Aurelius Ambrosius (legendary 'King Arthur') at Mount Badon in the last decade of the fifth century.[40] Ishiguro's fictional conceit, central to the narrative of the novel, is a kind of mistiness which has covered much of the British territory during the earlier part of the sixth century, inducing among its inhabitants a kind of collective amnesia. This is eventually explained as the act of the 'sage' Master Merlin, acting for the war leader Arthur after his notable victory over the Saxons. Merlin used the breath of a female dragon to bring about the condition of forgetfulness, as a political strategy for ensuring longer-term peace in the strife ridden and ethnically divided country – a means of consolidating the British military victory and preventing a return to the earlier culture of ethnic tension. It is finally revealed that a particular objective of Arthur and Merlin's plan was to erase memory of a large-scale massacre, or attempted genocide of innocent Saxons in the wake of the Saxon military reversal at Bladon. Arthur the legendary hero is thereby transformed into Arthur the war criminal and génocidaire, attempting to rewrite the historical record and erase human memory – although in the cause of a peaceful future. In the words of the fictional Gawain (agent and nephew of Arthur) to the fictional Axl (a proponent of peaceful reconciliation in the wake of the battle):

> Master Axl, what was done in these Saxon towns today my uncle would have commanded only with a heavy heart, knowing of no other way for peace to prevail. Think, sir. Those small Saxon boys you lament would soon have become warriors burning to avenge their fathers fallen today. The small girls soon bearing more in their wombs, and this circle of slaughter would never be broken. Look how deep runs the lust for vengeance ... Yet with today's great victory a rare chance comes. We may once and for all sever this evil

[39] See, for instance, JE Pattison, 'Is it necessary to assume an apartheid-like social structure in early Anglo-Saxon England?' (2008) 275 *Proceedings of the Royal Society: Biological Sciences* 2423. Pattison comments: 'It is now commonly accepted by archaeologists and historians that most, if not all, of the invasion groups arriving in Britain, from the Romans to the Normans, were relatively small migrations of vigorous people who used force and fear to control the considerably larger indigenous population. Although major battles and massacres took place, there was no mass extermination of the indigenous Britons as was once thought: the new settlers assimilated with their indigenous neighbours' (2423). Also, for an argument that there was a longer-term assimilation and integration, and indeed continuity of 'supplanted' culture, see S Laycock, *Britannia: The Failed State: Tribal Conflicts and the End of Roman Britain* (Stroud, The History Press, 2008).

[40] While the more exact location and date of the Battle or Siege of Mount Badon remain open to argument (the most favoured identification is close to Bath, during the 490s), there is little doubt regarding the nature and consequence of the historical event – a final military action as part of a successful British counter-offensive which pushed back and slowed down the Anglo-Saxon advance over 'English' territory, resulting in stable and peaceful British governance over the western part of England during the first half of the sixth century. See: J Morris, *The Age of Arthur: A History of the British Isles from 350 to 650* (London, Weidenfeld & Nicolson, 1973) 112 *et seq*.

circle, and a great king must act boldly on it. May this be a famous day, Master Axl, from which our land can be in peace for years to come.[41]

Thus, Arthur and Merlin conceived a kind of 'final solution'.[42] But the solution proves to be temporary. Some memory survives, the ageing dragon's breath will not endure, and Gawain, the dragon's appointed protector, has become old and weakened, and cannot prevail against Wistan, the Saxon warrior intent on rekindling memory and the craving for retribution. In the final exchange between Axl and Wistan, the former recalls his long-forgotten policy of peaceful reconciliation:

[W]ho knows what old hatreds will loosen across the land now? We must hope God yet finds a way to preserve the bonds between our peoples, yet custom and suspicion have always divided us. Who knows what will come when quick-tongued men make ancient grievances rhyme with fresh desire for land and conquest?[43]

But Wistan's response is uncompromising:

How right to fear it, sir … The giant, once well buried, now stirs. When soon he rises, as surely he will, the friendly bonds between us will prove as knots young girls make with the stems of small flowers. Men will burn their neighbours' houses by night. Hang children from trees at dawn. The rivers will stink with corpses bloated from their days of voyaging. And even as they move on, our armies will grow larger, swollen by anger and thirst for vengeance … And country by country, this will become a new land, a Saxon land, with no more trace of your people's time here.[44]

And then Wistan is transformed from warrior-hero into génocidaire, suggesting analogy with the speeches of Hitler and the Hutu radio broadcasts against Tutsi 'cockroaches'; and the book's final message is that history teaches us that the 'evil circle' of suspicion, fear, aggression and violence, encased in memory – the buried giant – is likely to endure.

B. Managing the Buried Giant and the Circle of Violence

Ishiguro's imagined history rehearses three main strategies of managing inter-ethnic conflict. First, there is Axl's lately recalled policy of rational and peaceful

---

[41] Ishiguro, above (n 38) 232–33. Axl had earlier negotiated a peace treaty, but it had not held: 'And yet, sir, the wars didn't finish. Where once we fought for land and God, we now fought to avenge fallen comrades, themselves slaughtered in vengeance. Where could it end? Babes growing to men knowing only days of war. And your great law already suffering violation' (298).

[42] There are a number of analogies with 'well-intentioned' solutions within the historical record: for instance in 1945, the bombing of Hiroshima and Nagasaki, or the Potsdam Agreement redrawing the map of Europe and authorising large-scale ethnic cleansing and population relocation in much of post-war Europe (similarly in the Indian sub-continent later in the 1940s).

[43] Ishiguro, above (n 38) 323. It is as though Axl has read Baumann, and knows his theory of fear of the 'other'! His speech is an eloquent evocation of the power of the demagogue and propaganda and the stirring of self-interested aggression.

[44] ibid, 324.

reconciliation and compromise, the diplomatic solution. Secondly there is Arthur, Merlin and Gawain's final solution, violent then peaceful, comprising an erasure of memory and a rewriting of history. Finally, there is Wistan's different final solution, drawing upon the revival of memory and its manipulation, and violent in its intended finality. And as a moral tale, Ishiguro's narrative is nicely instructive. For the historical evidence would tend to support the view that Axl's policy, intuitively the most commendable, often struggles to succeed in the face of 'custom and suspicion' and the argument of 'quick-tongued men'. The other two policies provide in themselves significant models of atrocity but exploit collective memory in opposite ways. What is then especially enlightening in Ishiguro's telling of the story is the way in which management of memory, as a key strategy, involves the manipulation of a number of the elements, explanations and theories of atrocity listed earlier in the discussion – elements of suspicion and fear of and aggression towards the 'other', and the manufacture of obedience and compliance through the exploitation of adverse circumstances (in Ishiguro's setting, the economic and political collapse of post-Roman Britain). On some reflection, the tale of *The Buried Giant* supplies some convincing analysis for many historical examples of genocide and atrocity, as already indicated above. Most significant examples of inter-ethnic tension will have longer histories of custom and suspicion and, one way or another, the collective memory of those longer histories will have an important role in any later or future atrocity, as borne out in the final dialogue between Axl and Wistan. Realisation of that fact, and an understanding of the latent power in the activation of memory, is then an important perception and tool for political leaders (Arthur), strategists and propagandists (Merlin), diplomats and negotiators (Axl), and military commanders (Wistan). In that analysis, what is or would be valuable for the present discussion and theory of the subject is what may be described as the missing criminology of memory.

In this context memory is not just an important resource – a storehouse or repository of information and feeling and as such something which is an essential element of psychological phenomena such as national and ethnic identity and culture more generally (indeed none of these could exist without a collective history and memory of that). But it is also a psychological force, a process of recollection which is both cognitive and emotive, and in that aspect is less predictable and controllable. To employ a legal analogy, memory comprises both evidence and the way in which that evidence is at a later time selected and used. Seen in those terms, memory is then a powerful force in determining action and that perception in turn is important in the analysis of any attempt to colour or even erase memory of action which may qualify as atrocity. In *The Buried Giant* both Arthur and Wistan recognise the powerful effect of erasing memory, both in genocidal action and then in amnesia of the event afterwards.[45] But another aspect of the power of

---

[45] Although the routes to amnesia appear different, and indeed this does point to some choice of strategy. Arthur opts for a chemically induced amnesia which would affect the whole population and take away a memory of the whole past, with cataclysmic consequences for the whole society. In a sense,

memory is that it can serve as a weapon on both sides. As Arthur perceived, if it is not erased completely, then it will not only haunt but also act as a motor of retaliation, hence, in Axl's words, the 'evil circle'.

The expert génocidaire will therefore have an understanding of memory and its uses. It should follow that the expert anti-génocidaire (assumed to include the author, the audience and the readership of this chapter!) will also need an understanding of memory and its uses. That observation then provokes an agenda-setting exercise, a kind of mapping of key tasks for criminology in relation to this subject. Four main fields of enquiry and further study come to mind at this point.

i. Memory as a Strategy

A first subject for criminological investigation would be in relation to an awareness of the power of collective memory and its deployment by those contemplating the commission of atrocity, both regarding their own motivation and how they may perceive the impact of such collective memory on others. Typically, in this context such collective memory will comprise both a history of events and an established culture and world view. Also, in the light of what has been said above, a strategic appreciation of such memory may lead either to a policy of exploitation or one of suppression and erasure, or both, emphasising certain facts and suppressing others in order to present a particular, if biased account of the past. The criminological interest resides in the exploitation of memory and the choice of strategy, since what is being examined here is the delinquent motivation, the aim to draw upon memory (or not) in the perpetration of atrocity. One way to view this kind of enquiry is to understand it as the study of propaganda and propagandists, but analysing such activity as a presentation of history and particular events through the medium of collective memory and the manipulation of the latter – the work, for example of a leading propagandist such as Goebbels, combining a reading of recent Germany history and a culture of anti-Semitism into a collective memory of a wronged nation.[46] Many other examples from the historical record could be cited of how memory of past events may be presented in different ways as different readings of history. Just briefly for present purposes, for instance, a number of examples of influential public statements about native-settler encounters in North America may be examined and compared.[47] On the one hand, there is the quotation of President Theodore Roosevelt: 'the settler and pioneer have at bottom, had justice on their side; this great continent could not have been kept as nothing but

---

Wistan's proposed strategy is cleaner – through a complete physical eradication of a people and its culture, the traces would be removed and eventually result in a forgetting. Whatever the strategy, it is likely to be a tall order, given the number of people involved and the resilience of some kinds of evidence (a lesson of the Holocaust).

[46] See J Herf, 'The "Jewish War": Goebbels and the Antisemitic Campaigns of the Nazi Propaganda Ministry' (2005) 19 *Holocaust Genocide Studies* 51.

[47] Diamond, *Rise and Fall*, above (n 28) presents a thought-provoking anthology of 'Indian policies of some famous Americans' 277–78.

a game preserve for squalid savages'.[48] While on the other hand, there is the example of the significant American tradition and celebration of Thanksgiving Day, drawing upon the memory of a benign and bonding encounter between Native Americans and 'Pilgrim Fathers'.[49] It is all too easy to speculate on the political and ideological motivation informing such resort to the memory of the European settlement of North America.

ii. The Subjective Psychology of Memory

The psychological aspect of such enquiry relates first to the fact of memory, its existence and its meaning for the memorising agent. Memory, whether personal or collective, is an important guide to decision-making and action, but people remember differently, according to their capacity, experience and circumstances. What is of special interest here is the deeper memory and the development of longer-term and collective memory, all of which may have consequences for any emotional response. It is axiomatic that feelings of like and dislike, resentment, grudge, or victimisation may be nurtured and sharpened by particular memory and its interpretation. The mundane observation that all humans are formed by their own past is more exactly a statement that human character and action may be significantly a result of each person's own memory. In seeking to understand the psychology of fear, hostility and suspicion, an understanding of the role of memory in such psychological states is important. An obvious example in the present context would be the deeper memory of Hutu–Tutsi inter-ethnic relations in central Africa. It is readily accepted that an important element in the infamous Rwandan genocide in 1994 was the memory of earlier treatment of the Hutu community, in particular the massacre of Hutu by Tutsi in Burundi in 1972–73, and earlier still the successive German and Belgian policy of promoting the Tutsi above Hutu in the colonial administration of the territory[50] – 'pre-existing ethnic hatreds fanned by cynical politicians for their own ends'.[51]

iii. Memory Survival and Memory Loss

Thirdly, there is the question of memory and the absence of memory. *The Buried Giant* is essentially a study of the personal, social and political consequences of the

[48] ibid, 278.

[49] 'Memory' asserts that the first Thanksgiving celebration was in 1621, at the Plymouth Plantation in Massachusetts, to celebrate the Pilgrims' first successful harvest, following Native American support – supply of food and advice on how to grow corn there.

[50] See generally on the background to the Rwandan Genocide: C Newbury, *The Cohesion of Oppression: Clientship and Ethnicity in Rwanda, 1860–1960* (New York, Columbia University Press, 1988); Human Rights Watch, *Leave None to Tell the Story: Genocide in Rwanda* (Human Rights Watch, 1999); P Gourevitch, *We Wish to Inform You That Tomorrow We Will Be Killed With Our Families* (New York, Farrar, Straus and Giroux, 1998).

[51] Diamond, *Collapse*, above (n 26) 317. Again, the fictional Axl in *The Buried Giant*, was right to fear, in his recovered memory of the earlier treatment of Saxons by Britons, the fictional Wistan's intention to fan the flames of this recovered memory among the Saxons.

survival and the loss of memory. Ishiguro poses questions regarding the possibility of both, and such possibilities are a matter of sociological and psychological enquiry. Certainly, that author posited challenging questions regarding the feasibility of either Arthur and Merlin's or Wistan's project to erase memory. There is a rich body of historical evidence of atrocity committed at different times and in different places and circumstances and this may be drawn upon to test both the resilience and the vulnerability of memory. It is intriguing to speculate for instance whether there are examples of genocide that have proven so successful that they and their subjects have effectively been erased from the collective memory of humankind – some form of never-knowable 'dark figure'. Or, on the other hand, it is worthwhile to study survival in the wake of attempted genocide, and assess the role of collective memory in such endurance and in the face of huge material destruction. The Nazi Holocaust would be a natural candidate for such study, both regarding the material challenge of bringing about a complete obliteration of millions of people and a historically significant and embedded culture, and also the subsequent considered policy of preservation of the memory of those events. Preserved Holocaust sites such as Auschwitz represent a particular strategy of reminder – 'lest we forget', to use the common British memorial heading.[52] A particular question worth investigation is the feasibility of strategies of erasure, and then the impact of the subsequent memory of attempts to take away memory – for instance, the criminalisation of Holocaust denial or revisionism in some European countries. Such a field of enquiry will demonstrate both the destructive potential of memory in the perpetration of atrocity, and also the conserving and restorative role of memory in the survival and endurance of particular groups and peoples.

A related question concerns the way in which first-hand individual or collective memory may be preserved or transmitted, leading to the construction of a longer but more indirect form of memory. In some more recent scholarship, researchers in the field of Holocaust studies have employed the concept of 'postmemory' (that of a second generation) to address this aspect of the subject. As Eva Hoffman has explained:

> The guardianship of the Holocaust is being passed on to us. The second generation is the hinge generation in which received, transferred knowledge of events is being transmuted into history, or into myth. It is also the generation in which we can think about certain questions arising from the Shoah with a sense of living connection.[53]

In more general terms, Marianne Hirsch has identified this as the issue of 'the "guardianship" of a traumatic personal and generational past with which some of us have a "living connection" and that past's passing into history',[54] and indicates

---

[52] There are countless other examples, ranging from Remembrance Sunday in the UK to old armoured vehicles displayed at tourist sites in Dubrovnik as reminders of 'Serb–Montenegrin aggression'.

[53] E Hoffman, *After Such Knowledge* (New York, PublicAffairs, 2004) xv.

[54] M Hirsch, 'The Generation of Postmemory' (2008) 29 *Poetics Today* 103, 104.

other contexts for the study of such intergenerational transmission – American slavery, the Vietnam War, the Dirty War in Argentina, South African apartheid, Soviet and East European communist terror, and the Armenian and Cambodian genocides. This is a related field of enquiry, already under way, which may have much to offer in insight and argument.

iv. *The Lessons for Policies of Prevention and Resolution*

Fourthly, the criminological and psychological study of memory in this context may serve policies and strategies of both prevention and *ex post facto* resolution.

In a pre-emptive context, this may be a means of alerting observers of a situation to the warning signs of imminent atrocity while also suggesting the benefits of educational and informative strategies which enable a more fully informed and balanced popular reading of history. Atrocity alert, the potential awareness of imminent atrocity, is now well developed, and the problem would seem to be the feasibility and will for political action rather than awareness, as the sad example of Rwanda in 1994 has shown.[55] On the other hand, there may be a huge potential benefit in educating populations of potential génocidiaires regarding the way in which histories and collective memory have been and may be manipulated in the ways discussed above.

In the context of resolution after the event, the choice of a number of strategies may be informed by a consideration of the effects of drawing upon memory in different ways. It is necessary to ask, for example, whether the resolution of a bad memory is better addressed by the closure effected through a trial or other formal process leading to criminal responsibility, punishment or compensation, or the compromise of memory involved in a process of amnesty or some aspects of reconciliation and social or political restoration. Compromise of memory, as embodied in the maxim 'forgive and forget', is a strategy which inevitably is set within the frame of an ethical debate which seeks to mediate between retributive and restorative argument. For present purposes, amnesty may be taken as a convenient example which illustrates such argument in a stark form. As Ben Chigara points out[56] *amnesty* and *amnesia* have the same etymological root in the Greek word *amnestia* which may be translated as 'forgetfulness'. Amnesty in the present context is a total and strategic forgetting of certain events to serve a utilitarian benefit – typically, the grant of legal immunity in relation to serious alleged or proven offences in order to ensure a peaceful transition to stable democratic governance.[57] Chigara has rehearsed the ethical and jurisprudential arguments

---

[55] See above, and in particular the account by Dallaire, above (n 26).

[56] B Chigara, *Amnesty in International Law: The Legality under International Law of National Amnesty Laws* (Harlow, Longman, 2002) 8.

[57] There are many recent examples. The history of legal process in Argentina is instructive: in particular, the use of legislation and presidential amnesty in relation to former members of the ruling Junta in the 1980s, and subsequent judicial declaration (for instance by the Argentinian Supreme Court

and argues forcefully against the extent of the compromise of victim rights and interests and retributive justice involved in amnesty relating to crimes against humanity:

> If they were accepted as part of statecraft in modern international law, national amnesty laws which purport to expunge criminal and civil liability of agents of a prior regime potentially would threaten to convert jurisprudence from a study of positive laws to a study of sacrificial philosophy ... The suggestion that rehabilitation of a State from totalitarian rule to democratic practice is mutually exclusive to justice is an apology for setting to zero the inalienable rights of victims of crimes against humanity. It protects and perpetuates violence and fraud in the State system.[58]

The strategy of amnesty is an extreme, at one end of the spectrum. But other restorative processes, such as truth and reconciliation, may involve some degree of moderation of formal retributive justice, for instance the procedure famously used in post-apartheid South Africa. There is now a vigorous debate regarding many measures of such 'transitional justice'[59] and this debate may be usefully informed by some of the reflection on the use of collective memory which has been urged in this discussion.

IV. Sign-Off

By its nature, much of the present discussion, in addressing a missing criminology of atrocity and the memory of atrocity, is speculative and tentative, and at the present stage agenda-setting rather than conclusive. But the purpose has been twofold: first to recommend a framework for discussion and analysis of these questions, and then to recommend a focus in this discussion on the role of memory, both individual and collective, in relation to the perpetration of atrocity and the reaction to such events. Much of this discussion has taken as a starting point a perceived primacy of biological and psychological elements as components of atrocity offending, in order then to appreciate the significance of human memory of atrocity and the management and manipulation of such memory.

---

in 2005) that such amnesty was illegal and unconstitutional. The legal saga relating to former Junta member Jorge Videla is especially illuminating (also an example of an individual invoking a particular memory of history to justify his own actions).

[58] Chigara, above (n 56) 22.

[59] See generally, eg, D Sullivan and L Tifft (eds), *Handbook of Restorative Justice: A Global Perspective* (London, Routledge, 2006) especially section 5.

PART II

Criminalisation

PART II

Criminalisation

3

International Criminalisation as a Pragmatic Institutional Process: The Cases of Dominic Ongwen at the International Criminal Court and Thomas Kwoyelo at the International Crimes Division in the Situation in Uganda

MATILDE GAWRONSKI*

I. Introduction

International crimes are a *sui generis* phenomenon, which in order to be effectively addressed, call for responses able to capture as much as possible their absolute, abhorrent, brutal nature and impact. The criminalisation of a certain conduct as an international crime through international or domestic legal instruments, on the basis of which international criminal prosecutions are built, is one of the responses devised by the international community to this end. Others include transitional justice mechanisms such as truth-telling, amnesties, or traditional justice. These, although they also contribute to defining a certain conduct as 'wrong' and to rectifying it, do not do so though criminalisation processes, but rather through restorative mechanisms. What then differentiates international criminalisation-based mechanisms from these restorative ones? What is, in other words, international criminalisation? How does it work in practice? And to what extent are institutional criminal justice mechanisms able to capture the absolute

* The author would like to thank Rod Rastan, Hans Bevers, Nora Stappert and other reviewers for their helpful advice, as well as the editors of this volume for their encouragement in exploring the concept of criminalisation through a *sui generis* lens.

abhorrent reality of international crimes through the tools offered by international criminalisation?

I suggest that criminalisation in the context of international criminal justice, or what I call 'international criminalisation', could be seen as more than just a formalistic legislative process which focuses on proscribing certain conduct through law in an abstract sense, or what I call 'black letter criminalisation'. If international criminalisation in fact originates this way – and as many would argue also ends this way – its proscriptive objectives are realised in pragmatic form, when abstract proscriptions are connected to facts. Its purpose, in other words, is realised when a certain conduct occurred in reality is codified as an international crime by a body with the power to do so for the purpose of enabling its prosecution. Why then, not consider this leap from an abstract to a concrete form as part and parcel of what international criminalisation is or, at the very least, can do?

On the basis of this proposition, in this chapter I explore the possibility of viewing international criminalisation as a pragmatic knowledge-building practice that takes place within judicial bodies with an international criminal justice mandate, and that transforms open-ended information about mass atrocities into evidence and evidence into individual triable cases.[1] I suggest that this pragmatic process, which normally culminates in 'case-building', will result from the interplay between two aspects: a legalistic one, which pertains to its 'black letter' legislative origin, and which relates to how international criminal justice bodies can frame a certain conduct on the basis of their overall legal framework, mandate, rules and regulations, among others; and an institutional one, which pertains to the capabilities, know-how, policy, inner workings, decision-making processes, and contextual opportunities that these judicial bodies have. Altogether, I call this process 'pragmatic international criminalisation' (or 'pragmatic criminalisation'), to differentiate it from the traditional notion of criminalisation, as the process which culminates in the abstract legislative prohibition of a certain conduct, and to identify instead the concrete process by virtue of which certain individual conduct occurred in a real situation of mass violence, is codified by a judicial body as 'crime' and transformed into a triable case.

The process of pragmatic criminalisation that I so define is the focus of this chapter's empirical analysis. Specifically, in this chapter I explore this notion by reference to the processes of pragmatic criminalisation that took place during the pre-trial phases of the Dominic Ongwen case at the International Criminal Court (ICC) in The Hague and of Thomas Kwoyelo at the International Crimes Division (ICD) in Uganda. Both cases derive from the situation in Uganda and

---

[1] On the applicability of the concept of 'practice' in the field of empirical studies of international criminal justice institutions see, in general, J Meierhenrich, 'Foreword: The Practices of the International Criminal Court' (2013) 76 (3–4) *Law & Contemporary Problems* i, i–ii; J Meierhenrich, 'The Practice of International Law: A Theoretical Analysis' (2013) 76 (3–4) *Law & Contemporary Problems* 1.

of the crimes committed by the Lord's Resistance Army (LRA) between 1986 and 2008. By exploring how Ongwen and Kwoyelo went from being LRA commanders at large to defendants in criminal cases against them, I demonstrate how the outcome of their respective pragmatic criminalisation processes depended on legalistic and institutional factors that pertained to the ICC and the ICD at the time when they were building the two cases. The Ugandan case studies thus allow me to show that within the same historical reality of mass violence and vis-à-vis comparable cases, processes of pragmatic criminalisation can take different routes and achieve different outcomes. As a result, they help me to demonstrate the overall contingent and institution-dependent nature of the international pragmatic criminalisation process vis-à-vis its ambition to capture, as one of my informants once put it, 'the total package of suffering' of a situation.

The chapter will first provide a brief discussion of the black letter origin of international criminalisation. It will then explore the processual and dual nature of the process of pragmatic criminalisation. Finally, it will produce an analysis of the two case studies and draw, on their basis, some general conclusions.

II. Beyond the 'Black Letter' Origin of International Criminalisation

Criminalisation *stricto sensu* pertains to the practice of criminalising through law a certain conduct. The core focus of the process of black letter criminalisation is to define through law and core principles the 'frontiers of criminal liability'.[2] This occurs both at the domestic and at the international level. However, while at the domestic level black letter criminalisation may constitute the central node of the practice and the debate, in this chapter I argue that, owing to the specific nature of international crimes and of the judicial institutions tasked with their pursuit, international criminalisation can be seen as expanding beyond the process of codifying on paper in legal form a certain conduct or act.

Black letter criminalisation, even in the context of international criminal justice, may be the trigger of its pragmatic criminalisation processes, for there could not be international criminal trials in the present age without a certain conduct having first been proscribed through law, as clearly captured by the *nullum crimen sine lege* principle. International criminalisation starts, in other words, just like domestic criminalisation, from the proscription of certain conduct in an abstract legal form. At present, the Rome Statute of the ICC is the most comprehensive contemporary example of this process of black letter criminalisation at the international level. When it was drafted, it was designed to be the state-of-the-art international criminalisation code, not only for the ICC but also as a symbol of a newly established

---

[2] A Ashworth and J Horder, *Principles of Criminal Law*, 7th edn (Oxford, Oxford University Press, 2013) 23.

paradigm of international justice. The domestication by national jurisdictions of the Rome Statute is testimony to this orientation and constitutes a particularly relevant shift for states where no other legislation covering international crimes is otherwise present.

This formal codification is the sine qua non precondition of the process of international criminalisation. In the context of judicial bodies with an international criminal justice mandate, however, the same legal codes do not just define the conduct liable to be prosecuted by them in abstract terms. Legal instruments criminalising a certain conduct as international crimes are often also the foundational pillars upon which international criminal judicial bodies are established and on which basis they are moulded. They therefore also define the boundaries of the possible and of the impossible for the practice of such judicial bodies as a whole. They function, therefore, not just as a legal code, but as a practical blueprint for action. The clearest example of this is the symbiotic relationship between the Rome Statute and the ICC: while the Rome Statute defines the crimes that the ICC can investigate and prosecute, it also defines how these processes can take place.

Black letter criminalisation therefore is at the origin of international criminalisation theoretically speaking, in at least two ways: as the process which establishes through law the boundaries of conduct liable to be prosecuted as an international crime; and as a framework which shapes the bodies where international criminalisation as the institutional practice analysed in this chapter takes place. The process of pragmatic criminalisation analysed in this chapter, therefore, can be said to take its cue in multiple ways from the existence of codes that criminalise certain conduct as international crimes. However, once 'activated', that is, once a judicial body is established, and once this body begins to undertake processes of assessment of criminality in a certain situation and vis-à-vis specific individuals, the criminalisation process defined on paper as a matter of legal prohibition begins to take a processual, institution-specific form. In this way, international criminalisation moves beyond its black letter origin and becomes the process that I have defined as pragmatic criminalisation.

III. Pragmatic Criminalisation as a Dual-Nature Institutional Process

Having established in which way international criminalisation could be viewed as an institutional process, in this section I explore its two enabling aspects, in order to understand how pragmatic criminalisation might work in practice. I suggest that if pragmatic criminalisation is a knowledge-building process which results in the transformation of a situation of mass criminality into triable cases, then the success of this process must depend on the interplay between two factors that are at the basis of the practice of judicial bodies in general: a legalistic one, which pertains to the legal framework available to said body; and an institutional one, which pertains to the body's material institutional capabilities and the contextual opportunities around it.

A. The Legalistic Aspect of the Pragmatic Criminalisation Process

In a legalistic sense, pragmatic criminalisation depends on the judicial body's overall legal framework, as captured, normally, by its statute or other foundational document. This comprises a number of legalistic aspects, as for example the judicial body's mission, mandate, jurisdiction, triggering and relational mechanisms, rules and regulations among others. All, I argue, contribute to shaping in a legalistic sense the breadth and limitations of the scope of action of a judicial body, beyond the definition of conduct that a body can prosecute, thus affecting in different ways the pragmatic criminalisation process.

The mandate and jurisdiction of a judicial body, by definition, define its scope of action and competence. While a mandate does so in more aspirational terms, as a matter of tasked mission, jurisdiction does so in terms of defining the broadest legal boundaries within which the action of a judicial body can take place. For instance, the International Criminal Tribunal for the former Yugoslavia (ICTY) and International Criminal Tribunal for Rwanda (ICTR) had competence over international crimes committed within two specific situations – the conflict in the former Yugoslavia since 1991[3] and the 1994 Rwandan genocide[4] respectively. This rendered them *ad hoc* international tribunals. Their jurisdictions were limited in space and time to the crimes allegedly committed within specific situations of mass violence. The ICC, instead, as an international criminal court with universal aspirations, has an open mandate to investigate and prosecute 'the most serious crimes of international concern',[5] and thus retains a much broader scope of action. It is able to cover *at a minimum* any conduct amounting to international crimes under the Rome Statute, committed within the territory of a State party to it – of which so far there are 123 – within a time frame starting no earlier than its year of activation, 2002. Domestic bodies with international justice mandates, similarly, will also have established jurisdictional parameters, as demonstrated by the example of the ICD in Uganda, explored below.

Triggering and relational mechanisms will also matter for the legalistic ability of a judicial body to undertake a pragmatic criminalisation process. There are, for example, at least four mechanisms that can trigger and expand the ICC's jurisdiction over a situation. States themselves have the power to refer situations to the ICC,[6] and the Office of the Prosecutor (OTP) can start investigations *proprio motu*

---

[3] Updated Statute of the International Criminal Tribunal for the former Yugoslavia 2009, Article 1.
[4] Statute of the International Criminal Tribunal for Rwanda 1994, Article 1.
[5] Rome Statute of the International Criminal Court 1998, Article 1.
[6] ibid, Article 14.

if the conduct was committed within the territory of a State Party or by one of its citizens.[7] The ICC also has the possibility of obtaining jurisdiction over situations occurred within the territory of states not parties to the Statute through mechanisms such as a Security Council referral[8] or a state declaration under Article 12(3).[9] The use of these relational mechanisms, crucially, is the reason why, regardless of the fact that mass atrocities are currently being committed in a number of situations, they cannot all fall under the jurisdiction of the Court.[10] Similarly, relational mechanisms of cooperation, as those established for the ICC and states in Part IX of the Rome Statute, play a crucial role in the processes of pragmatic criminalisation of concern to this chapter. Triggering and relational mechanisms exist for all judicial bodies, including those with an international criminal justice scope.

Statutory requirements, rules and regulations are also legalistic aspects that will contribute to defining a process of pragmatic criminalisation, shaping one important layer of the invisible framework of action of a judicial body guided by them. They define, for example, aspects such as the legal criteria that need to be met for a situation or a specific case to be investigated, as for example does Article 53(1) of the Rome Statute for the ICC's process of preliminary examinations, the form that filings will have to take, the sequence of interactive moments, for example between prosecution, chambers and defence, in terms of bringing a case, for instance, from investigation to trial.

These are just some of the legalistic aspects that will play a role in a judicial body's pragmatic criminalisation processes. It follows that international tribunals and domestic courts with an international criminal justice mandate, therefore, will have different 'legalistic' shapes, based on these factors. However, in addition to the legalistic mould with which a judicial body is endowed and that I have just described, processes of pragmatic criminalisation will also depend on a judicial body's extra-legal institutional factors, ie, on a body's material institutional capacity.

B. The Institutional Aspect of the Pragmatic Criminalisation Process

Beyond the legalistic capacity of a judicial body, which I have described above, pragmatic criminalisation will also concomitantly depend on the same body's concrete institutional capacity to bring this process to fruition. That is, an

---

[7] ibid, Article 15(1).
[8] ibid, Article 13(b).
[9] ibid, Article 12(3).
[10] See, eg, United Nations, 'Referral of Syria to International Criminal Court Fails as Negative Votes Prevent Security Council from Adopting Draft Resolution' (22 May 2014), available at: www.un.org/press/en/2014/sc11407.doc.htm.

institution's ability to transform a broad situation of mass criminality into discrete prosecutable cases will depend, beyond its legalistic mould, on myriad interlinked institutional aspects and conditions of a material or contextual nature.

Investigative abilities, for example, will contribute to determining which type of evidence can be collected and processed. This was clear, for example, in the Ongwen case, as describe below, where access to intercept material proved crucial to building a case around him and the LRA leadership. Internal work processes will determine which type of analysis must be conducted and how. An example in point is the process of preliminary examinations which the OTP of the ICC follows in order to determine whether the opening of an investigation is warranted on the basis of criteria set by the Rome Statute and further explained by the relevant policy paper.[11] Internal case selection policies will define which cases will make the cut for investigation and prosecution, as well as which types of conduct will be prioritised or focused on. The recent policy paper on case selection and prioritisation[12] or the two policy papers issued by the OTP on sexual and gender-based violence[13] and children,[14] are cases in point. The degree of discretion attributed to a prosecutorial body will also influence the institutional execution of pragmatic criminalisation processes.

Another factor that is likely to influence the process of pragmatic criminalisation of concern to this analysis will be the availability of resources – staff and financial. Both might contribute to determining the overall institutional investment into a certain situation, including possibly its withdrawal from it or its prioritisation. Resources will also likely influence the evolution of a judicial body's staff's know-how and their ability to be knowledgeable in specific analytical, investigative or prosecutorial techniques. It is common knowledge, for example, in the case of the ICC, that access to financial resources is an issue debated year on year at the Assembly of States Parties to the Rome Statute.

The need for external cooperation and support, with regard for example to an institution's ability to arrest a suspect or having them arrested or summoned for trial (provided their presence is required for trial), is another factor that will impact on a judicial body's ability to bring a 'pragmatic' criminalisation process to completion. At the ICC the opposite scenarios of Ahmed Al-Faki Al-Mahdi, who was arrested in the Mali situation and handed over to the Court for trial in September 2015, Bosco Ntaganda who turned himself in to the Court in March 2013 for crimes he allegedly committed in the situation in the Democratic

---

[11] ICC OTP, 'Policy Paper on Preliminary Examinations' (2013), available at: www.icc-cpi.int/iccdocs/otp/OTP-Policy_Paper_Preliminary_Examinations_2013-ENG.pdf.
[12] ICC OTP, 'Policy Paper on Case Selection and Prioritisation' (2016), available at: www.icc-cpi.int/itemsDocuments/20160915_OTP-Policy_Case-Selection_Eng.pdf.
[13] ICC OTP, 'Policy Paper on Sexual and Gender-Based Crimes' (2014), available at: www.icc-cpi.int/iccdocs/otp/OTP-Policy-Paper-on-Sexual-and-Gender-Based-Crimes--June-2014.pdf.
[14] ICC OTP, 'Policy on Children' (2016), available at: www.icc-cpi.int/iccdocs/otp/20161115_OTP_ICC_Policy-on-Children_Eng.PDF.

Republic of Congo (DRC), or the Omar Bashir case in the situation in Darfur, who despite the arrest warrant against him and much international travel, is so far still at large, all show this point. The level of self-sufficiency or dependence of a judicial body from external stakeholders will be crucial to its ability to bring a pragmatic criminalisation process to fruition.

The momentum surrounding a situation or a case, and the ability of a judicial body to exploit it, will also play a role in enhancing the chances of success of specific investigation or case-building processes. An example in point, again referring to the ICC, is the shift in support that the Court saw in its Sudan and Libya cases. To date the Security Council, despite its initial referral of the two situations to the ICC and many calls for support by the OTP, has seemingly done little to further support the Court towards the arrests of the suspects wanted in the two situations.[15]

Together these institutional factors, among other possible ones, will play a role in the process of pragmatic criminalisation analysed in the chapter in a way often less immediately visible than, but equally meaningful to, the legalistic factors described above.

C. Pragmatic Criminalisation as the Interplay Between Legalistic and Institutional Factors

Overall, I suggest that the power of international criminalisation can be better understood if this is thought of not just as a *de jure* proscriptive process, but also a *de facto* knowledge-building institutional practice. I have further argued that this process will be the result of the pragmatic interplay between legalistic and institutional elements, between the formal and the material, between broad principles of law and the ability of a judicial body to take these principles, apply them to facts, and turn them into criminal cases. This conceptualisation makes international criminalisation much more than a purely legislative proscriptive process. It turns it, rather, into a concrete process that has to do with institutional structures, know-how and contextual opportunities as much as the law. As a whole, therefore, pragmatic international criminalisation is a dual nature process, whose outcome will be contingent on the institutional and legal context from which it emerges, as I explore in the two Ugandan case studies below.

---

[15] See, on this issue, the most recent calls for support issued by the ICC OTP: ICC, 'Statement to the United Nations Security Council on the Situation in Libya, pursuant to UNSCR 1970 (2011)' (9 May 2018), available at: www.icc-cpi.int/Pages/item.aspx?name=180509-otp-stat-UNSC-lib; ICC, 'Statement to the United Nations Security Council on the Situation in Darfur, pursuant to UNSCR 1593 (2005)' (12 December 2017), available at: www.icc-cpi.int/Pages/item.aspx?name=171212-otp-stat-UNSC.

IV. International Criminalisation as a Pragmatic Institution-Dependent Process in the Situation in Uganda

Based on the framework provided above, it follows that in order to understand how the process of pragmatic international criminalisation works and what its implications may be for addressing atrocity crimes through prosecutorial means, it can be studied empirically. The interplay between its legalistic and institutional aspects, in fact, can only be observed through the lens of specific cases, which in turn unfold within a specific institutional setting. To this end, in this section I analyse two examples of pragmatic criminalisation that emerge from the situation in Uganda. This choice is not accidental. The situation in Uganda is quite unique in so far as it allows to observe two parallel and rather different processes of pragmatic criminalisation taking place out of the same context of conflict, criminality, and with reference to two similar cases. I explore how the conduct of Dominic Ongwen, a former LRA commander, came to be criminalised pragmatically by the ICC and how the conduct of Thomas Kwoyelo, also a former LRA commander, came to be criminalised pragmatically by the ICD, the ICC's domestic counterpart in Uganda. By following the two processes I show the extent to which pragmatic criminalisation and its effectiveness, in terms of triggering a trial process, depended on what the ICC and the ICD were capable of doing based on the legal framework available to them and on their institutional capacity and standing in the Ugandan context of operation.

A. The Pragmatic Criminalisation Process in the Case of Dominic Ongwen at the Office of the Prosecutor of the International Criminal Court in the Hague

The process of pragmatic criminalisation in the case of Dominic Ongwen developed in two phases. The first took place between 2003 and 2005, with the ICC's OTP's first investigation and the issuing of his and four other arrest warrants. The second phase took place between 2015 and 2016, with his capture, transfer to The Hague and the update of his indictment by the OTP for presentation at his confirmation of charges hearing in January 2016. Both phases show the interplay between the legalistic and the institutional aspects described above.

i. Ongwen's 2002–05 Pragmatic Criminalisation Phase

The pragmatic criminalisation process by the ICC's OTP of the conduct of alleged perpetrators of crimes in the context of the 1986–2008 northern Uganda conflict began with the 2003 referral of the Ugandan situation by the government of

Uganda to the Court.[16] This referral gave the Court the power to investigate and prosecute international crimes committed in the course of the conflict from 2002 onwards. Uganda was the first situation falling under the jurisdiction of the ICC, which had only entered into force in 2002, after being established in 1998 upon the adoption of the Rome Statute.

In light of this jurisdictional capacity and subsequent investigations, the manner in which Ongwen's conduct – and that of four others – had been 'criminalised in practice' by the ICC became visible when, in 2005, the Court issued five arrest warrants against as many LRA leaders for crimes allegedly committed in the context of the non-international armed conflict that was taking place in northern Uganda, between 2002 and 2004.[17]

The arrest warrant against Dominic Ongwen charged him with seven counts of war crimes and crimes against humanity for the attack against the Ugandan village of Lukodi, carried out in 2004.[18] Notably Ongwen had already been in the LRA since his abduction, which as he claimed, took place in 1988, and had been climbing its ranks ever since, becoming one of its top commanders.[19] However, due to the ICC's jurisdictional framework and the timing of Uganda's referral to the ICC, Onwgen's criminality was at that point attached solely to one attack, committed against one location in northern Uganda in 2004 and for 'only' seven counts, compared with the larger number of counts brought against four other LRA commanders, including LRA leader Joseph Kony.

This framing of Ongwen's conduct was the result of both the legalistic framework that defined the ICC's formal relationship with Uganda and its mandate, but also the ICC's own internal capabilities, investigative opportunities, policies and the overall momentum that existed in the early 2000s around the LRA problem. At the time of the Ugandan referral, the situation in northern Uganda had been defined by Jan Egeland, UN Undersecretary General for Humanitarian Affairs and Emergency Relief Coordinator, as 'the biggest forgotten, neglected humanitarian emergency in the world today'.[20] The momentum around the situation therefore was strong and contributed to pushing it towards the ICC.

When the Ugandan situation was referred to the ICC – upon invitation by the Court – it signalled the beginning of a new formative moment for the Court in

[16] Republic of Uganda, 'Referral of the situation concerning the Lord's Resistance Army' (16 December 2003) (on file with author).

[17] ICC OTP, 'Warrant of Arrest unsealed against five LRA Commanders' (Press release, 14 October 2005), available at: www.icc-cpi.int/pages/item.aspx?name=warrant+of+arrest+unsealed+against+five+lra+commanders.

[18] ICC Pre-Trial Chamber II, 'Warrant of Arrest for Dominic Ongwen, ICC-02/04' (8 July 2005), available at: www.icc-cpi.int/CourtRecords/CR2006_01112.PDF.

[19] 'Lord's Resistance Army Commander Appears Before Hague Court' *The Guardian* (26 January 2015), available at: www.theguardian.com/world/2015/jan/26/lords-resistance-army-commander-hague-court-kony.

[20] 'Northern Uganda "world's biggest neglected crisis"' *The Guardian* (22 October 2004), available at: www.theguardian.com/world/2004/oct/22/2.

general, and the OTP in particular.[21] The referral meant that the newly established OTP could for the first time test its own capacity to carry out investigations on the ground and transform the evidence collected into trial-ready cases.[22] According to an OTP 2003 report, in just over nine months, the OTP's investigators conducted over 50 missions to the field, over 20 missions to meet with local leaders, and meetings in The Hague with national authorities and local community leaders.[23] During this phase, the OTP collected 'statements from former LRA commanders, victim or witness accounts, radio broadcast recordings and short-wave radio LRA communications as intercepted by Ugandan investigative authorities'.[24] This evidence-collection phase proved highly successful from the OTP's own point of view and it enabled the OTP's subsequent case-building phase.

Notably, these investigations took place in an environment that presented a number of external operational challenges that the OTP openly recognised and navigated. First, at the time of the first investigation, northern Uganda was still a theatre of conflict, which rendered the security situation volatile. Secondly, a climate of hostility to the ICC's intervention began to spread in Uganda, in light of factors such as a preference among some affected communities and prominent local actors towards giving amnesties to the LRA, as opposed to prosecuting them.[25] Thirdly, the OTP, during its investigations, had received cooperation from the Ugandan authorities. This factor meant that, as the OTP recognised, the efficiency of its investigations was enhanced.[26] At the same time this also meant that some grassroots actors, for example communities who during the conflict had also felt victimised by the actions of the Uganda Peoples' Defence Forces (UPDF), read this as a sign of a possible lack of impartiality.[27] The challenging nature of the Ugandan investigative theatre was exacerbated further when after two years of peace negotiations at Juba, in South Sudan, the LRA failed to sign the final

---

[21] ICC OTP, *Report on the activities performed during the first three years (June 2003–June 2006)* (12 September 2006) 7, available at: www.icc-cpi.int/NR/rdonlyres/D76A5D89-FB64-47A9-9821-725747378AB2/143680/OTP_3yearreport20060914_English.pdf.

[22] ICC Assembly of States Parties, *Report on the Activities of the Court* (ICC-ASP/3/10) (22 July 2004) para 36, available at: asp.icc-cpi.int/iccdocs/asp_docs/library/asp/ICC-ASP-3-10_report_from_the_court_english.pdf.

[23] ICC OTP, 'The Investigation in Northern Uganda' (Press Conference, 14 October 2005) 2, available at: www.icc-cpi.int/NR/rdonlyres/E996F31C-5AB0-43C7-B518-69A13844FBAD/143734/Uganda_PPpresentation.pdf; see also: ICC OTP, *Report on the activities performed during the first three years*, above (n 21) paras 26, 34.

[24] ICC Pre-Trial Chamber II, *Warrant of Arrest for Joseph Kony Issued on 8th July 2005 as Amended on 27th September 2005* (ICC-02/04-01/05-53), para 11, available at: www.icc-cpi.int/pages/record.aspx?uri=97185.

[25] On this issue, see eg, Acholi Religious Leaders Peace Initiative, 'ARLPI's Position on the International Criminal Court (ICC)' (9 July 2009), available at: www.arlpi.org/international-criminal-court-s-icc-uganda.

[26] As a 2006 OTP report stated, 'The efficiency of the Northern Uganda investigation was a consequence of the cooperation received from the people and the authorities of Uganda'. ICC OTP, *Report on the activities performed during the first three years*, above (n 21) para 31.

[27] Many of my Ugandan informants, whom I interviewed in 2014 and 2016, held this perception.

agreement, reportedly also in light of the pending ICC arrest warrants against its leadership. As one Ugandan CSO representative, who had taken part in the Juba Peace Process and who had met Kony several times, explained to me in 2014: 'Kony was worried about the ICC arrest warrants … He also saw himself as a powerful warlord, and could not imagine himself being brought in chains in Uganda, locked up in some prison or arraigned in court'.[28] Notably, at the same time a number of stakeholders, including the Ugandan government, also recognised that the arrest warrants had likely contributed to bringing the LRA to the negotiating table.[29] In sum, the fact that this climate existed did not mean that the ICC's early investigation had no support in northern Uganda. It did mean, however, that the investigations out of which Ongwen's case emerged, were carried out within the bounds and opportunities created by this environment.[30]

Beyond these contextual factors, the singling out of Dominic Ongwen as one of five leaders of the LRA worthy of indictment out of a plausibly much larger group, derived from the interplay between the available evidence and the OTP's own policy to target those most responsible for the most egregious crimes, as the Rome Statute prescribed. A public presentation made by the OTP in 2005 showed how the OTP had come to select Ongwen and the others as the top leaders of the LRA. A number of organigrammes demonstrated – as well as crystallised – the evolving hierarchy of the LRA during the period from 2002 to 2004, showing how Ongwen had come close to its top, thus making him a likely person of interest for the OTP.[31] This evolution of Ongwen's position within the command structure of the LRA, linked to the available evidence and filtered through the OTP's case selection policy, determined that the OTP built for itself a convincing picture around Ongwen's criminal role in one of the most notorious attacks of the LRA, the Lukodi massacre of 2004.

The OTP's selection of cases in the Ugandan situation, as it emerged in 2005, resulted from the interplay of all these factors. Effectively, it was the OTP's policy focus on the most responsible together with the temporal and geographical

---

[28] Extract from transcript of an interview conducted by the author with a local CSO representative at Kampala, Uganda, in 2014. This was also widely reported in the media: 'Ugandan Rebel Leader Fails to Sign Peace Deal' *The Guardian* (11 April 2008), available at: www.theguardian.com/world/2008/apr/11/uganda; 'Ugandan rebel leader wants ICC warrant lifted before peace deal' *Voice of America* (22 August 2008), available at: reliefweb.int/report/uganda/ugandan-rebel-leader-wants-icc-warrant-lifted-peace-deal.

[29] ICC Pre-Trial Chamber II, *Submission of Information on the Status of the Execution of the Warrants of Arrest in the Situation in Uganda* (ICC-02/04-01/05) (6 October 2006) para 25, fn 48, available at: www.icc-cpi.int/CourtRecords/CR2007_02807.PDF; United Nations Security Council, 'Under-Secretary-General Calls For Greater Security Council Commitment To Ending Conflicts In Democratic Republic of the Congo, Northern Uganda' (Press release, 15 September 2016), available at: www.un.org/press/en/2006/sc8831.doc.htm.

[30] This was explicitly recognised by the OTP in a 2006 report: 'The on-going conflict resolution efforts and the volatile security situation were all part of the context in Northern Uganda at the outset of the investigation'. ICC OTP, *Report on the activities performed during the first three years*, above (n 21) para.33.

[31] ICC OTP, Press Conference 14 October 2005, above (n 23).

focus, within which the OTP operated by virtue of its jurisdiction, that guided the OTP towards the selection of Ongwen and his four co-indictees. Ongwen's selection, therefore, was the result of a convergence of institutional and contextual factors that reflected the ICC's capability and position at the time and not just the absolute abhorrent nature of his conduct. The contingent nature of Ongwen's pragmatic criminalisation process by the ICC, became even more visible once Ongwen was captured in 2015 and his case, after a hiatus of 10 years, was revived in a new form.

ii. Ongwen's 2015–16 Pragmatic Criminalisation Phase

Dominic Ongwen was captured by the Seleka rebels in the Central African Republic in mid-January 2015[32] and transferred to The Hague on 20 January 2015[33] with the acquiescence of the Ugandan government.[34] His capture, 10 years after his arrest warrant was first issued, was a liminal moment not only in the Ugandan situation in front of the ICC, but also in the development of Ongwen's own case. In light of the lack of arrests, the LRA case at the ICC had become dormant. The OTP had by now expanded its portfolio of cases to other situations and its attention had altogether shifted elsewhere. In addition, all of Ongwen's co-indictees, save for Joseph Kony who was still at large, had by now died.[35] This made Ongwen's arrest all the more meaningful for the ICC as an institution which by now believed that its Ugandan situation had reached a dead end.

With Ongwen in custody the OTP was presented with the opportunity to give the Ugandan situation and the Ongwen case a new lease of life. To this end a new investigation phase was carried out, this time solely focusing on his figure, between January 2015 and June 2016.[36] The intention of the OTP, as declared by OTP senior trial lawyer Benjamin Gumpert on the occasion of Onwgen's status conference on 19 May 2015, was to now bring charges against him beyond the single Lukodi attack imputed to him originally.[37] The result was an expansion of Ongwen's

---

[32] 'LRA Chief Ongwen Surrenders,' *The Daily Monitor* (7 January 2015), available at: www.monitor.co.ug/News/National/LRA-chief-Ongwen-surrenders/688334-2580798-6y7cre/index.html.

[33] ICC Registry, *Report of the Registry on the voluntary surrender of Dominic Ongwen and his transfer to the Court* (ICC-02/04-01/05, submitted to Pre-Trial Chamber II on 22 January 2015), available at: www.icc-cpi.int/CourtRecords/CR2015_00477.PDF.

[34] Republic of Uganda Media Centre, 'Statement by the Government on the Dominic Ongwen Case' (2 February 2015), available at: www.mediacentre.go.ug/press-release/statement-government-dominic-ongwen-case.

[35] Notably, as a result of their deaths, which the ICC verified, the ICC terminated its proceedings against Raska Lukwiya and Okot Odhiambo, respectively in 2007 and 2015. However, despite unofficial reports that Vincent Otti was also killed, the ICC never officially managed to verify his death. As a consequence, the arrest warrant against him still stands.

[36] On the timeline of this investigation see: ICC OTP, *Prosecution Submissions in Accordance with the Scheduling Order of 4 May 2016* (ICC-02/04-01/15, submitted to Trial Chamber IX on 18 May 2016), available at: www.icc-cpi.int/CourtRecords/CR2016_03503.PDF, para 5, and para 25.

[37] ICC YouTube Channel, 'Ongwen Case: Status Conference, Pre-Trial Chamber II' (19 May 2015), available at: www.youtube.com/watch?v=xovczlB8k4E, 2:27–2:49.

charges, as became most visible in the list provided by the OTP during his 'Confirmation of Charges' hearing on 21 January 2016. His 'refreshed case' now attributed to Ongwen the responsibility for a number of incidents not previously connected with him. It also reflected systemic conduct, namely his involvement in sexual and gender-based crimes and the recruitment and use of child soldiers, neither of which were present in the original charges.

This development meant that a more detailed picture of Ongwen's roles became clear, as well as the degree of his involvement in the identified LRA crimes during the entire period under scrutiny. According to the OTP's view as presented in 2015, Ongwen had risen up the hierarchy of the LRA, from the rank of major, which he held in July 2002,[38] to that of brigadier general, which he acquired in December 2004.[39] While climbing the ranks of the LRA he had covered key command roles. For example, Ongwen had been the commander of Oka battalion in August 2002, the second in command of the Sinia brigade in September 2003, the brigade's commander in March 2004,[40] and a member of Control Altar, the central command of the LRA, since September 2003.[41] In 2005, he had become 'the most senior LRA commander in Uganda', in charge of fighters from brigades other than his own.[42]

In these roles, the OTP alleged, Ongwen could be held responsible for 70 charges of war crimes and crimes against humanity.[43] These included crimes such as carrying out attacks against the civilian population, murder, attempted murder, torture, other inhumane acts, cruel treatment, enslavement, pillaging, persecution, and destruction of property, within the context of attacks against four settlements, namely Pajule, Odek, Lukodi and Abok.[44] 'These locations', according to the OTP's statement during the opening of the Ongwen trial in December 2016, 'ha[d] been selected because they are attacks about which the Prosecution has been able to find a significant and coherent body of evidence which demonstrates what happened in detail and which links them to Mr Dominic Ongwen.'[45]

---

[38] ICC OTP, Prosecution's Pre-Trial Brief, para 105.

[39] ibid, para 119.

[40] ICC Pre-Trial Chamber II, *Decision on the confirmation of charges against Dominic Ongwen* (ICC-02/04-01/15, 23 March 2016), available at: www.icc-cpi.int/CourtRecords/CR2016_02331.PDF, para 58.

[41] ICC OTP, *Prosecution's Pre-Trial Brief* (Situation in Uganda in the Case of The Prosecutor v Dominic Ongwen, ICC-02/04-01/15, submitted to Trial Chamber IX on 6 September 2016), available at: www.icc-cpi.int/CourtRecords/CR2016_06511.PDF, para 111.

[42] ibid, para 119.

[43] ICC OTP, *Document Containing the Charges* (Situation in Uganda in The Case of The Prosecutor v Dominic Ongwen, ICC-02/04-01/15, submitted to Pre-Trial Chamber II on 22 December 2015), available at: www.icc-cpi.int/RelatedRecords/CR2015_25222.PDF.

[44] ibid, sections VI–IX.

[45] ICC OTP, 'Statement of the Prosecutor of the International Criminal Court, Fatou Bensouda, at the opening of Trial in the case against Dominic Ongwen' (6 December 2016), available at: www.icc-cpi.int/Pages/item.aspx?name=2016-12-06-otp-stat-ongwen.

In addition, the OTP charged Ongwen with multiple counts for the crime of persecution of the northern Uganda civilian population,[46] sexual and gender-based crimes,[47] and the conscription and use of child soldiers.[48] In the OTP's view Ongwen had 'faithfully carried out the LRA's brutal policy toward girls and women',[49] including by personally forcibly marrying, raping and sexually enslaving a number of women. He had also ensured that the same policy would be followed by his subordinates in the Sinia brigade.[50] In addition the OTP alleged, 'From at least 1 July 2002 until 31 December 2005, Dominic Ongwen, Joseph Kony and the Sinia brigade leadership implemented a common plan to abduct children, including those under 15, in northern Uganda and use them as active participants in hostilities'.[51]

Ongwen's criminal responsibility for these charges was codified by the OTP according to multiple modes of liability.[52] As a result he was charged concomitantly as a direct perpetrator, an indirect perpetrator and a co-perpetrator in the implementation of the LRA's 20-year long campaign of violence. In addition, he was held responsible for ordering crimes, and for his failure to prevent and/or punish those under his command, who had committed them.[53]

Ultimately, in light of this new investigative and case (re-)building process, Ongwen was charged with 10 times as many counts as those originally charged in 2005. This shift, which most clearly symbolised the evolution that the Ongwen case had undergone during this period, speaks clearly of the institution-dependent nature of the process of pragmatic criminalisation followed by the OTP in Ongwen's case. Though this shift occurred within the fixed legalistic boundaries of the Rome Statute, which designated the conduct attributed to Ongwen as criminal, it was a series of pragmatic factors and opportunities that effectively enabled it. Ongwen's arrest had created the sine qua non condition for the process to take new life. It had also created a new momentum around the ICC's Uganda situation, placing it anew in the limelight. The OTP responded to this unique opportunity with great energy, reviewing and taking stock of the evidence, and taking into account also newly developed policy foci: crimes committed against children and sexual and gender-based crimes, both of which largely applied to Ongwen's expanded case.

iii. The Evolution of Ongwen's Pragmatic Criminalisation Process

Altogether the evolution of Ongwen's case shows how, within the stable legalistic framework of the Rome Statute, the same case developed in different ways

---

[46] ICC OTP, Prosecution's Pre-Trial Brief, section V.
[47] ibid, section X.
[48] ibid, section XI.
[49] ibid, para 502.
[50] ibid.
[51] ibid, para 704.
[52] ibid, para 89.
[53] ibid, paras 138–55.

based on contingent factors, such as operational opportunities and institutional momentum. In 2005, the symbolic value of Dominic Ongwen's case was shared with that of his co-indictees – Joseph Kony, Vincent Otti, Raska Lukwiya and Okot Odhiambo. In 2015, instead, in light of the fact that his case was severed from that of his co-indictees, the narrative and context of the case became focused on Ongwen alone, rather than Ongwen with other top commanders. This did not mean that his role was atomised from that of the LRA as such. It meant instead that owing to the contextual developments triggered by Ongwen's arrest, the OTP now had to focus its prosecutorial efforts on one single individual. In turn, as I described above, this resulted in a 'narrative' shift towards his particular case. With this finding in mind I now turn to presenting the pragmatic criminalisation process that took place at the ICD in Uganda in the Thomas Kwoyelo case.

B. The Pragmatic Criminalisation Process in the Case of Thomas Kwoyelo at the International Crimes Division in Uganda

The pragmatic criminalisation process in the Thomas Kwoyelo case went hand-in-hand with the establishment of Uganda's first bespoke body dedicated to the domestic pursuit of international crimes. The idea of a domestic body that could deal with the LRA crimes in a manner complementary to the ICC and to other domestic mechanisms first emerged during the Juba Peace Process, which between 2006 and 2008 had brought the LRA and the Ugandan government to the negotiating table in Sudan. Although a final peace agreement was never signed, the parties signed an 'Agreement on accountability and reconciliation' on 29 June 2007,[54] whose 'Annexure' stipulated among others the creation of 'a special division of the High Court of Uganda … to try individuals who are alleged to have committed serious crimes during the conflict'.[55] This ultimately resulted in the establishment of the ICD in 2011, as a body mandated to prosecute cases of international and transnational crimes, in accordance with the Ugandan Constitution and the rules of procedures and evidence applicable to criminal trials in Uganda.[56]

The process of pragmatic criminalisation in the Kwoyelo case took place as the ICD was still taking shape, notably within a context which was widely supportive of this initiative. Compared with Ongwen's case, the ICD pragmatic criminalisation process in Kwoyelo's case followed a different path and achieved qualitatively different outcomes, but it also could be said to have taken shape in two phases.

---

[54] 'Agreement on Accountability and Reconciliation Between the Government of the Republic of Uganda and the Lord's Resistance Army/Movement Juba, Sudan' (29 June 2007) (on file with author).

[55] 'Annexure to the Agreement on Accountability and Reconciliation' (19 February 2008) para 7 (on file with author).

[56] 'The High Court (International Crimes Division) Practice Directions, 201, Legal Notice No 10 of 2011' (*The Ugandan Gazette* Vol CIV No 38, 31 May 2011) (on file with author).

The first began with Kwoyelo's arrest in 2009, upon which his first and second indictments were issued by the ICD and his trial was initiated. During this phase Kwoyelo's case went through a five-year-long admissibility challenge, which took it first from the ICD to the Constitutional Court and then from the Constitutional Court to the Supreme Court of Uganda. At the end of this phase Kwoyelo was once again remanded to trial. The second phase ran from 2015 onwards and continues to this day. During this phase, after the Supreme Court established that contrary to the Constitutional Court's decision, Kwoyelo could be tried, the ICD's prosecution team reframed his conduct under a new light, through a third (amended) indictment.

The two phases, as I describe them below, show a different interplay between the legalistic and the institutional aspects of the process of pragmatic criminalisation compared with what was observed in the Dominic Ongwen case at the ICC.

i. Kwoyelo's 2009–11 Pragmatic Criminalisation Phase

Thomas Kwoyelo, a former high-ranking LRA commander, was reportedly captured by the UPDF in March 2009 in the DRC and soon after transferred to Uganda.[57] In April 2009, the Ugandan police department attached to the ICD received instruction to commence investigations into his case.[58] In June 2009, after preliminary investigations had shown 'that Kwoyelo was suspected to have committed criminal offences', the Ugandan police requested the Ugandan army to hand him over for prosecution.[59] His capture and profile offered the ICD an opportunity to activate its newly established mandate, the chance of building a case around him constituting a unique and favourable opportunity for the new judicial body. For the ICD, therefore, the pragmatic criminalisation process in Kwoyelo's case began from his physical presence, rather than from the theoretical construction of a case around him with a suspect still at large, as had been initially in Ongwen's case at the ICC.

From the investigative point of view, according to ICD stakeholders I interviewed, investigations into Kwoyelo's conduct had been overall successful. The ICD prosecution team relied on a wide network of local intermediaries to help. It had some access to evidence granted by government and army stakeholders and later also obtained some evidence from the ICC's OTP.[60] However, despite the seeming success of these investigations, the process of pragmatic criminalisation in the Kwoyelo case took a less than straightforward path, primarily as a result

---

[57] Jack Kimball, 'Uganda says captures LRA rebel commander' *Reuters* (4 March 2009), available at: uk.reuters.com/article/uk-uganda-rebels/uganda-says-captures-lra-rebel-commander-idUKTRE5235VJ20090304>.

[58] 'The Republic of Uganda in the Constitutional Court at Kampala, 1st Respondent's Affidavit (Lawrence Ogen Mungu) (Constitutional Reference No 36 of 2011 sworn at Kampala on 16 August 2011)' para 2 (on file with author).

[59] ibid, para.6.

[60] ICC OTP, *Weekly Briefing 23–29 November 2010* (Issue 65) 1 (on file with author).

of the legalistic mismatch between the ICD's mandate and the legal instruments available to it, but also as a result of the ICD's limited institutional capabilities.

Kwoyelo was charged in a prima facie manner in June 2009.[61] A first indictment against him was then issued on 31 August 2010 at Gulu Magistrates' Court. This included 12 charges for crimes he allegedly committed as a member of the LRA, under Uganda's domestic Penal Code.[62] A second amended indictment, built on the back of the 2010 indictment, was then issued for Kwoyelo on 5 July 2011.[63] From a factual perspective this indictment attributed to Kwoyelo the responsibility for eight attacks, which primarily occurred in Pabo sub-county, a hotspot of Kwoyelo's activity and operations when in the LRA and his area of origin. In the course of these attacks, according to this indictment, Kwoyelo allegedly killed, abducted, injured, and treated inhumanely civilians not involved in the hostilities and looted and destroyed their villages.[64] From a temporal perspective the charges covered 12 years of Kwoyelo's membership in the LRA, a much larger time span than that covered by the ICC in its own LRA arrest warrants. In terms of criminal liability, the indictments alleged that the attacks had been committed under Kwoyelo's leadership, and that Kwoyelo had been 'at all material times ... a senior commander/officer in the LRA rebel group under the overall command of Joseph Kony'.[65]

In total, Kwoyelo's 2011 indictment included 12 substantive counts, charged under the Geneva Conventions Act of 1964, and 53 alternative counts, charged under the Uganda Penal Code. Framing Kwoyelo's conduct through these legal instruments was, rather than a matter of choice, one of necessity. Not unproblematically, the domestic Penal Code and the Geneva Conventions Act were the only legal instruments that the ICD had available at the time to frame Kwoyelo's conduct. Notably however the 1964 Geneva Conventions Act only criminalised grave breaches at the domestic level, thus being applicable only to conflicts of an international character, but not Common Article 3, applicable instead to conflicts not of an international character. In addition, although in 2010 Uganda had domesticated the Rome Statute through the ICC Act, this was not applicable to the time frame in which Kwoyelo's criminal conduct had allegedly taken place.

This limited available legal framework highlighted the nature and extent of the legalistic challenge faced by the ICD. Practically speaking, charging Kwoyelo under the Geneva Conventions Act could only 'work' if the northern Uganda conflict,

---

[61] '1st Respondent's Affidavit (Lawrence Ogen Mungu)' para 7.

[62] Directorate of Public Prosecutions Uganda Police, *Charge Uganda v Kwoyelo Thomas alias Latoni M/A 39 Years* (Police Form 53, Gulu Police Station, Gulu CRB 337/2004 31 August 2010) (on file with author).

[63] Directorate of Public Prosecutions, Ammended (sic) Indictment Uganda (Prosecutor) v Kwoyelo Thomas Alias Latoni (Accused) (Case No A-09 of 2010, issued on 5 July 2011), available at: www.judiciary.go.ug/files/downloads/Final%20Amended%20Kwoyelo%20Thomas%20indictment%20.pdf (also known as Second Amended Indictment).

[64] ibid.

[65] Second Amended Indictment, para 2.

within which the alleged offences had taken place, was framed as an international armed conflict. Notably, this conflict had always been considered, including by the ICC, as not of an international nature. Despite this, the approach adopted in Kwoyelo's second indictment reflected this non-conventional interpretation. Its preamble described that Kwoyelo's

> offences contained and charged ... were committed in the context of an international armed conflict that existed in Northern Uganda, Southern Sudan and North Eastern Democratic Republic of Congo between the [LRA] ... with the support of and under the control of the government of Sudan, fighting against the government of the Republic of Uganda as by law established, between 1987 and 2008.[66]

The choice of this framing was a matter of strategy, as an ICD investigator explained to me:

> We charged Kwoyelo under the Geneva Conventions Act, which covers the international armed conflict aspect. Then we also used alternative counts under domestic law, the Penal Code, which covers non-international armed conflict. In case we were challenged in Court that this was not an international armed conflict, then we had a fall-back position.[67]

This quote shows that while the ICD's prosecution team was aware of the apparent controversial nature of this approach, it had also decided to take it nonetheless. The reasons for this choice were seemingly multiple, but overall framing Kwoyelo's conduct as international crimes was a matter of institutional necessity as much as a search for institutional coherence, which the ICD derived from its international criminal ambition and mandate. By contrast, following a (more correct) legal route that criminalised Kwoyelo's conduct only through the domestic Penal Code would have been seen by the ICD prosecution team as a failure of this body to live up to its own mandate.

This situation would become even more challenging when, following Kwoyelo's trial commencement on the basis of its 2011 indictment, the ability of the ICD to try him was challenged *tout court* at Uganda's Constitutional Court by Kwoyelo's defence team. Kwoyelo's lawyer argued in this context that, in light of the Amnesty Law which had been in place since 2000 and had already been applied to thousands of LRA returnees, including high-ranking LRA commanders, Kwoyelo should not have been considered for trial in the first place. Kwoyelo's lawyers argued that Kwoyelo's case should never have been allowed to take shape, since Kwoyelo had applied for amnesty while in custody at Luzira prison and renounced rebellion in January 2010. Kwoyelo, in addition, in their view, had been abducted as a child and thus was to be seen a victim of the LRA and not a perpetrator.

This challenge led to a five-year-long 'admissibility challenge' about the right of the ICD's prosecution team to bring Kwoyelo to trial vis-à-vis Kwoyelo's right

---

[66] ibid, para 1.
[67] Extract from transcript of an interview conducted by the author with an ICD investigator at Kampala, Uganda, in 2014.

to be granted amnesty. The Constitutional Court, in September 2011, agreed with Kwoyelo's defence team that Kwoyelo's trial should be halted and he be granted amnesty. However, the ICD prosecution team appealed the Constitutional Court's decision at Uganda's Supreme Court. In a new turn of events, in April 2015, the Supreme Court argued against the lower court that Kwoyelo's right to receive an amnesty had not been infringed upon by his indictment and that his trial should instead resume.[68]

The analysis of this phase shows that differently from the ICC, for the ICD, the challenge in the pragmatic criminalisation process in the Kwoyelo case had less to do with institutional factors – though the institutional weakness of the ICD had also mattered in this respect – and more with legalistic factors. Contrary to the ICC's OTP, which could frame Ongwen's conduct in both in 2005 and 2015 through the straightforward and internally consistent legal framework of the Rome Statute, the ICD faced the challenge of wanting to achieve similar results, in terms of framing Kwoyelo's conduct as international crimes, without having the appropriate instruments to do so.

The ICD, despite its mandate and institutional ambition, operated from within a national legal and contextual framework not streamlined for the purpose for which it had been set up. The obstacles faced by the ICD included the concomitant existence of an amnesty law, which was effectively at odds with Uganda's commitment to prosecute those most responsible for the commission of the gravest of the LRA crimes, and the lack of applicable international or domestic legal instruments that could successfully enable the prosecution of international crimes as such. This legalistic conundrum rendered Kwoyelo's case unfit for trial, at least up to 2015, when the Supreme Court ordered its resumption.

ii. Kwoyelo's 2015–17 Pragmatic Criminalisation Phase

The year 2015 provided the ICD's prosecution team with a new opportunity not just for resuming Kwoyelo's trial but also for reframing his criminality in a new light. Having faced the challenge brought against Kwoyelo's case through the highest Ugandan courts and having observed the ICC's own reframing of Onwgen's charges from afar, the ICD reframed Kwoyelo's charges through a third amended indictment.

Kwoyelo's third indictment remained true to the ICD's mandate and aspiration to prosecute him for international crimes but gave Kwoyelo's charges a new form. Aware of the weakness of the previous framing, the ICD's prosecution team took this time a different – but again legally creative – approach.[69] First, they now viewed

---

[68] *Uganda v Kwoyelo* (Constitutional Appeal No 01 of 2012) [2015] UGSC 5 (8 April 2015), available at: ulii.org/ug/judgment/supreme-court/2015/5.

[69] See Directorate of Public Prosecutions, *Re: Notice of Amendment of Indictment in Case of Uganda vs Thomas Kwoyelo* (Ref: WCD-CO-001-2015) (24 January 2017) (on file with author); Directorate of Public Prosecutions, *Final Pre-Trial Submission in the case Uganda (Prosecutor) vs Kwoyelo Thomas*

the northern Uganda conflict as a conflict not of an international character.[70] They did so explicitly noting that this had also been the ICC's approach in Ongwen's case.[71] Secondly, and as a result, they framed Kwoyelo's conduct as war crimes committed under Common Article 3 of the Geneva Conventions, applicable to conflicts not of an international character, pursuant to customary international law, no longer making reference to the Geneva Conventions Act of 1964.[72]

Specifically, the Prosecution's submission argued that war crimes had been criminalised since the time of the International Military Tribunal (IMT) at Nuremberg and Control Council Law 10 and later developed through the case law, in particular, of the ICTY and ICTR. These, in their view, had established that Common Article 3 crimes were prohibited as a matter of international customary law. All its elements – the existence of and the nexus of the conduct with an armed conflict, and that the crimes must be committed against civilians – were satisfied by Kwoyelo's conduct, which was thus liable to be prosecuted under the grave breaches regime of the Geneva Conventions.[73] On the same legal basis they also charged Kwoyelo for crimes against humanity.[74] The Prosecution argued that this was a 'category of recognized international crimes that was developed decades prior to the conduct of the accused KWOYELO (*sic*)'.[75] It thus could be 'applied by the Ugandan courts without violating the principle of legality'.[76] Referring back to the jurisprudence of and the definition of crimes against humanity produced by the IMT, Control Council Law 10, the ECCC, the ICTY, ICTR, and a number of UN resolutions, the submission concluded that crimes against humanity had been sufficiently criminalised, effectively as of 1945, as a matter of customary international law. It followed that by the time Kwoyelo committed the imputed conduct, they had been clearly defined. An obligation to prosecute them domestically had also been established in the same way.[77]

Overall, the Prosecution's view was that 'the charged offenses were all crimes under [customary international law] and the ICD ha[d] the ability and duty to prosecute them as such', 'even in the absence of specific domestic legislation'.[78] In their eyes there was no doubt about the correctness of the chosen approach and on this basis asked the bench to uphold the newly framed charges, despite the Defence's challenge against them. However, to keep in line with the 'safe' approach

---

Alias Latoni (Accused) (Case No HCT-00-ICD-CR-SC-N0 02 of 2010, submitted on the 24 April 2017) (on file with author).

[70] Directorate of Public Prosecutions, *Amended Indictment Uganda (Prosecutor) vs Kwoyelo Thomas Alias Latoni (Accused)* (Case No 02 of 2010, filed in the International Crimes Division of the High Court of Uganda at Kampala on 30 January 2017) para 2 (on file with author) (also known as Third Amended Indictment).

[71] DPP, Final Pre-Trial Submission, 47.

[72] Third Amended Indictment, para 1.

[73] DPP, Final Pre-Trial Submission, 11–19.

[74] Third Amended Indictment, para 1.

[75] DPP, Final Pre-Trial Submission, 19.

[76] ibid.

[77] ibid, 19–22.

[78] ibid, 5.

already taken during the previous phase, the indictment also continued to include charges in the alternative, under the Uganda Penal Code, for domestic offences.[79]

In terms of Kwoyelo's responsibility, the amended indictment confirmed that Kwoyelo had been a long-term member of the LRA, and that he had held multiple roles between 1992 and 2005 directly under the authority of Joseph Kony, including commander of operation, director of military intelligence and 'charged of all sick bays', a title which within the LRA defined an individual in charge of the areas designated for the treatment of the sick and the wounded.[80] In these roles, the Prosecution alleged throughout the indictment, Kwoyelo was to be considered individually criminally responsible for the crimes committed directly by him and by those under his command.[81]

The result of this reframing was that Kwoyelo was now charged with 93 counts of war crimes, crimes against humanity and domestic offences. The new charges included a number of counts of sexual and gender-based crimes, something which the earlier indictments had not included.[82] Given the timing, this very much appeared to echo the ICC OTP's own focus on Ongwen's responsibility for sexual and gender-based crimes, suggesting that the reframing of Ongwen's charges also had a contextual impact on the ICD's own process.

This narrative shift had not been due to a new investigative effort, as had been the case for the ICC and Ongwen's case. The 'Notice of amended indictment' issued by the ICD prosecution in January 2017, explicitly stated that no new evidence had been incorporated in the newly framed charges.[83] Rather this reframing had been the result of creative legal crafting driven by the institutional objective of framing Kwoyelo's criminality through the international crimes lens. Of course, despite proclaiming a belief in its approach, the ICD prosecution team was aware of its possible limitations.[84] Therefore, in an unprecedented leap of legal faith, they also proclaimed the 'strength' of their reasoning, by arguing that ultimately they had been driven by the primary duty of 'prohibiting and punishing any conduct that is socially harmful or causes danger to society, whether or not the conduct has already been legally criminalized at the moment it is taken', in the name of the 'legal order'.[85] This was true, all the more so because, in their view, Kwoyelo's conduct had breached multiple legal regimes, namely Ugandan law, international humanitarian law and the prohibition on crimes against humanity.[86]

---

[79] Third Amended Indictment para 1.

[80] ibid, para 8.

[81] See, generally, Third Amended Indictment.

[82] Third Amended Indictment, Counts 81–93.

[83] DPP, Notice of Amendment of Indictment, 2.

[84] The problematic nature of this approach has also been noted by some commentators: P Bradfield, 'Reshaping Amnesty in Uganda: The Case of Thomas Kwoyelo' (September 2017) 15 *Journal of International Criminal Justice* 827, 848. Others have instead written in favour of the approach taken in Kwoyelo's third amended indictment: KT Seelinger, 'Uganda's Case of Thomas Kwoyelo: Customary International Law on Trial' (April 2017) 8 *California Law Review* 19, 21, available at: scholarship.law.berkeley.edu/cgi/viewcontent.cgi?article=1101&context=clrcircuit.

[85] DPP, Final Pre-Trial Submission, 39.

[86] ibid, 41.

According to this reasoning little mattered that Kwoyelo's alleged conduct could only be framed in a legally convincing manner under the domestic Penal Code or that he had applied for amnesty as around 25,000 others had already successfully done by then. Satisfying the 'mandate' of the ICD, the 'expressive value of addressing atrocities as more than individual, regular crimes',[87] as well as the 'paramount interest of substantive justice',[88] appeared to be factors that could override the weakness of the available legal framework in the name of a higher mission. Such 'legal gymnastics', as one of my informants called it, was therefore justified as a matter of strategy, given the legalistic limitations imposed on the ICD by the Ugandan legal framework and the strong institutional desire to bring to trial a case worthy of its international aspirations.

Notably, the path to confirming the newly reframed charges against Kwoyelo proved tortuous and dotted with false starts, greatly due to Kwoyelo's Defence's continuous objections to the modality of his charging as well as technicalities. After many 'failed' pre-trial confirmation hearings,[89] Kwoyelo's charges were finally confirmed on 30 August 2018, over three years after the Supreme Court had ordered the resumption of his trial.[90] Kwoyelo's trial was set to commence in earnest on 24 September 2018. During the hearing, in a final stroke of wishful thinking, Justice Gawaga recalled: 'The case made a journey to the Supreme Court [of Uganda] and we lost seven years until the Supreme Court pronounced itself on the matter. We pray that we do not encounter such challenges again'.[91] However, on 26 September 2018, in light of translation issues, the trial was adjourned to November 2018.[92] The flaws that had emerged in the Kwoyelo case during the pragmatic criminalisation process described above, therefore, continue to reverberate to this day.

iii. *The Evolution of Kwoyelo's Criminalisation at the ICD*

The evolution of Kwoyelo's pragmatic criminalisation process showed how highly dependent this process was on the ICD's ability to bring it to fruition from a legalistic perspective. If the ICC's challenge in Ongwen had been primarily one of

---

[87] ibid, 48.

[88] ibid, 39.

[89] Lino Owor Ogora, 'Confirmation of Charges Hearing against Thomas Kwoyelo Postponed Again' *International Justice Monitor* (14 June 2018), available at: www.ijmonitor.org/2018/06/confirmation-of-charges-hearing-against-thomas-kwoyelo-postponed-again/.

[90] Lino Owor Ogora, 'Ten Years Later, Ugandan Court Finally Confirms 93 Charges Against Thomas Kwoyelo' *International Justice Monitor* (24 September 2018), available at: www.ijmonitor.org/2018/09/ten-years-later-ugandan-court-finally-confirms-93-charges-against-thomas-kwoyelo/.

[91] Lino Owor Ogora, 'Thomas Kwoyelo's Trial Commences in Uganda' *International Justice Monitor* (25 September 2018), available at: www.ijmonitor.org/2018/09/thomas-kwoyelos-trial-commences-in-uganda/.

[92] Julius Ocunugi, 'Kwoyelo trial adjourned over poorly translated charges' *Daily Monitor* (26 September 2019), available at: www.monitor.co.ug/News/National/Kwoyelo-trial-adjourned-over-poorly-translated-charges/688334-4777882-hav408z/index.html.

operational opportunities and momentum, the ICD's challenge in Kwoyelo manifested itself predominantly at the point of producing a solid legalistic framing of
his conduct (even though material challenges were also not lacking in the process).
As a result, Kwoyelo's case evolved differently from Ongwen's case. Ongwen's
case evolved both in form and substance. Upon his capture, new investigations
were carried out and as a result the number of charges against him grew tenfold.
Kwoyelo's case instead evolved primarily in form, as demonstrated by the three
amended indictments that were issued against him and by the lengthy admissibility
challenge that his case underwent. The conundrum faced by the ICD in Kwoyelo's
case was thus different from the one faced by the ICC. While institutional factors
also mattered, including in terms of funding and external support, the outcome of
the pragmatic criminalisation process in the Kwoyelo case depended primarily on
the lack of a streamlined legal framework that the ICD could apply to transform
his conduct into a product that could be successfully taken to trial.

V. Conclusions

To this day little has been written from a socio-legal perspective about the concept
of criminalisation in the field of international criminal justice. This chapter paves
the way in this direction suggesting that international criminalisation could be
explored – and better understood – if considered as an institutional practice, liable
to being analysed through empirical methods by reference to case studies unfolding within distinct institutional settings. I put forward this proposition, aware that
viewing international criminalisation as a pragmatic process may be at odds with
how criminalisation is traditionally viewed. I hope nonetheless that by exploring
international criminalisation as a *de facto* institutional process stemming from a
de jure one, I could shed some light on what international criminalisation implies
in practice.

On the basis of this proposition I coined the term 'pragmatic criminalisation'. This term captures the idea that international criminalisation can be seen
as extending beyond its black letter origin, becoming the pragmatic process that
judicial bodies seeking to prosecute international crimes follow in order to link
abstract prohibitions to real facts and transform them into discrete criminal cases.
I suggested that this process could be seen as the result of the interplay between a
legalistic aspect – the judicial body's legal framework, mandate, rules and overall
legal shape – and institutional aspects – the judicial body's institutional capabilities
and the momentum around it. In this sense, I argued, pragmatic criminalisation
is an institutional-dependent process whose outcome has more to do with what
a judicial body *can do*, than with the objective, historical, abhorrent reality of the
alleged criminal conduct under scrutiny.

In order to illustrate the validity of this theoretical proposition, I analysed the
processes of pragmatic criminalisation that took place in the Dominic Ongwen

case at the ICC in The Hague and the Thomas Kwoyelo case at the ICD in Uganda. I used these case studies as a lens through which I could observe the interplay between the legalistic and the institutional taking place in these two judicial settings, and to test its outcome. This analysis showed that within the same situation of mass criminality, processes of pragmatic criminalisation can take very different routes and shapes depending on which judicial body is undertaking them, when and how. This was evident from the different evolutions of the two Ugandan case studies, which both changed from one phase to the other, but also from the comparison between them.

The Ugandan case studies thus give credence to my argument that in the field of international criminal justice, possibly much more than in the field of domestic criminality, the outcome of pragmatic criminalisation processes, or how a case – as well as which case – is created for prosecution, emerges from the compromise between an institution's capacity and internal functioning, the legal framework available to it and its context of operation. It is therefore a contingent process. It follows that if solid prosecutions are wanted, both the legalistic and the institutional strengthening of the judicial bodies undertaking them should be sought. At the same time it also follows that by definition, pragmatic criminalisation processes, will always fall short of capturing the total and absolute nature of atrocity crimes, and will always instead, if at all, contribute to rectifying the wrong caused by them, qualitatively and quantitatively, in a limited and contingent manner.

4

Solidarity as a Moral and Legal Basis for Crimes Against Humanity: A Durkheimian Perspective

MARINA AKSENOVA

I. Introduction

Crimes against humanity, along with war crimes, crime of aggression and genocide, form the core of international criminal prosecutions.[1] They denote universal consensus about prohibited conduct in the times of war and peace. But what makes these offences 'worthy' of such status? What are the prerequisites for launching them to an international plane? Taking a more criminological approach to international criminal law (ICL), this chapter is concerned with the process of 'criminalisation' of international offences with the specific focus on crimes against humanity.

The term 'crimes against humanity' first entered positive criminal law through Article 6(c) of the Nuremberg Charter.[2] The notion was originally introduced as an extension of war crimes and served the practical purpose of addressing atrocities committed by the Nazi regime against its own Jewish citizens. The records of the UN War Crimes Commission indicate that crimes against humanity were included in the Charter primarily due to the fact that war crimes were traditionally directed only against foreign citizens. The Commission held that 'offences committed by the enemy could not technically be regarded as war crimes *stricto sensu* on account of one or several elements, which are of different nature.'[3]

---

[1] Article 5 of the Rome Statute of the ICC confers upon it jurisdiction over these four offences. They are jointly referred to as 'core international crimes'.

[2] MC Bassiouni, *Crimes Against Humanity: Historical Evolution and Contemporary Application* (Cambridge, Cambridge University Press, 2014) 96.

[3] *History of the United Nations War Crimes Commission and the Development of the Laws of War compiled by the United Nations Commission* (London, His Majesty's Stationery Office, 1948) (UN War Crimes Commission) 174, available at: www.cisd.soas.ac.uk/Files/docs/97813052-history-of-the-unwcc-chapter-8.pdf.

The reference was made to the nationality of victims. Bassiouni highlights the evolutionary nature of crimes against humanity as a legal phenomenon that grew out of necessity imposed by the circumstances into a distinct category.[4]

Following its inclusion in the Nuremberg Charter, the novel crime rapidly entered the vocabulary of international lawyers. Despite its rising importance, the category of crimes against humanity struggles with establishing its own identity independent from other core international crimes. This is partially due to the lack of solid legal foundation in international law – there is still no treaty specifically addressing crimes against humanity. The second major complexity relates to the lack of clarity as to the state's role in the commission of these offences.

This chapter seeks to engage the criminologically related work of Emile Durkheim to develop a societal foundation of the category of crimes against humanity in international criminal law. The purpose is to show the process of its criminalisation in international criminal law by invoking one of the most influential sociological theories, developed over a century ago. The theory is relevant as it can form the background for building up legitimacy of this group of international offences. The main argument flowing from the application of Durkheim's ideas to the modern notion of crimes against humanity is that it derives its moral legitimacy from the feelings collectively shared by individuals across state borders. Repulsion towards certain acts is ingrained in the collective consciousness of people worldwide. And that solidarity is key for gluing societies together in the Durkheimian perspective.

The above statement does not attempt to oversimplify the complexity and controversy of Durkheim's ideas. As will be explained in the following section, his philosophy serves only as a starting point in my analysis of the foundation of crimes against humanity as a set of norms of societal importance. It is impossible to ignore the context of late nineteenth-century industrialisation in which these pieces were written. Yet, the relevance of *The Division of Labour in the Society* and subsequent works, such as *The Elementary Forms of Religious Life*, for exploring the foundations of international criminal law is nevertheless striking, as I will argue. Section two of this chapter focuses on the reasons for turning to Durkheim in the present study. The 'why' question in section two is followed by the 'what' question in section three that turns attention to the complexities inherent in the category of crimes against humanity. The same section relies on the theories of Emile Durkheim, in particular the idea of solidarity and collective consciousness, to resolve ambiguities of this category of offences. Section four, in line with Durkheim's general approach to law, focuses on the process rather than the content of crimes against humanity. It argues that international criminal trials are a form of ritual expressing of beliefs collectively held across state borders.

---

[4] MC Bassiouni, 'Revisiting the Architecture of Crimes Against Humanity: Almost a Century in the Making, with Gaps and Ambiguities Remaining – The Need for a Specialized Convention' in LN Sadat (ed), *Forging a Convention for Crimes Against Humanity* (Cambridge, Cambridge University Press, 2011) 44.

The final concluding section establishes the links between the past, the present and the future of the category of crimes against humanity.

II. Reasons for Looking at Durkheim in 'Grounding' International Criminal Law

Legal and political sciences have long been the first ports of call for scholars of international law and international courts. This leaves theories with great explanatory potential available in the domain of sociology out of the picture.[5] This chapter attempts to remedy this gap by engaging with the work of Durkheim, who was one of the founders of the discipline. His external observer's perspective and concern with the role of law in the process of social integration gives much needed perspective to the study of international criminal law.[6] There are at least three reasons for looking deeper into Durkheim's analysis.

The first 'contextual' reason for exploring Durkheim's work is the fluidity and adaptability of his ideas in explaining the 'moral glue' that holds communities together. Durkheim focused on the function of law in the society at different stages of its development. The context of late nineteenth-century industrialisation and political struggles between labour and capital in the workplace strongly affected the author's way of thinking.[7] He was also influenced by the First World War, in which he lost his son, seeing the nascent modern society's darker sides flourish before his eyes.

What is the value of Durkheim's theory for international criminal law – a discipline that came into existence only a few decades after his death? Durkheim's search for the appropriate internal ties binding society in any given moment in time is comforting for a field of law that derives its legitimacy from the progressive push that occurred in the aftermath of the Second World War. The emergence of the new field of law can be explained not only by the content thereof but also by the combination of factors that fostered its creation – grave human suffering, the sequence of the two successive world wars and realisation by states and activists comprising the international community that those responsible for mass atrocities must be held responsible regardless of their high-level position within the state.[8] These external dimensions of international criminal justice are often overlooked.

---

[5] See MR Madsen, 'Sociological Approaches to International Courts' in K Alter, C Romano and Y Shany (eds), *The Oxford Handbook of International Adjudication* (Oxford, Oxford University Press, 2013) 388 *et sq*.

[6] R Cotterrell, *Emile Durkheim: Law in a Moral Domain* (Stanford, CA, Stanford University Press, 1999) 32.

[7] ibid, 182.

[8] For the dynamic perspective on international criminal law see K Sikking, *The Justice Cascade: How Human Rights Prosecutions Are Changing World Politics* (New York, WW Norton & Company Inc, 2011) 5.

Durkheim did not attempt to hide inconsistencies and modified his views throughout his career. One can trace the evolution of his approach to law and society comparing the earlier work *The Division of Labour in Society* and the one written towards the end of his life – *The Elementary Forms of Religious Life*. The former focuses on collective consciousness as a basis for ensuring social solidarity in less advanced societies (mechanical solidarity) and the division of labour and ensuing interdependence in more advanced and differentiated societies (organic solidarity). Durkheim argues that the scope of collective consciousness as a platform for shared beliefs becomes smaller as society progresses and differentiates.[9] This position was reversed later, with Durkheim's acknowledgement of the importance of shared beliefs in advanced societies. He later held that morality transcends time and social organisation and remains the dominant societal cement.[10] The emphasis shifted to religion as a facilitator of the process of social cohesion.[11] Law, however, might well be another cross-sectorial glue of specialised societies, notably higher order law such as constitutions and human rights.[12]

Following *The Division of Labour in Society*, Durkheim abandoned the analytical distinction between mechanical and organic solidarity in favour of the notion of collective representation, which is a less static way of explaining the attachment of individuals to society and the way in which the group conceives of itself in relation to objects that affect it.[13] Another important alteration in Durkheim's thinking was the place he assigned to human dignity. In *The Division of Labour*, Durkheim rejects the idea that the value of human dignity can provide the moral foundation of modern law – he claims it is not a unifying force but rather binds us to ourselves. Subsequently, he came to see individualism as the only system of beliefs, which can ensure the moral unity of the country.[14]

Related to that is the second 'emotive' reason for exploring Durkheim's work – it provides a much sought after moral foundation for international criminal law. Durkheim found a way to externalise humanism and the value of individual dignity. He used it as a function in the society rather than as an independent variable. This approach served as a precursor for the subsequent development of the human rights movement later in the twentieth century. Durkheim admitted that the content of collective consciousness transforms, and morality becomes universalised, in a 'collective ideal' of 'humanity as a whole'.[15]

In *The Division of Labour*, he explores the nature of treaties prohibiting wars and argues that that growing interdependence of European societies, which he

---

[9] S Lukes, *Emile Durkheim: His Life and Work: A Historical and Critical Study* (London, Allen Lane, 1973) 5.

[10] Cotterrell, above (n 6) 62.

[11] ibid, 54.

[12] MR Madsen and G Verschraegen (eds), *Making Human Rights Intelligible: Towards a Sociology of Human Rights* (Oxford, Hart Publishing, 2013).

[13] Lukes, above (n 9) 5–6.

[14] E Durkheim, 'Individualism and Intellectuals' (trans S Lukes and J Lukes), reprinted in W Pickering (ed), *Durkheim on Religion* (London, Routledge & Kegan Paul, 1975) 66 cited by Cotterrell, above (n 6) 112.

[15] Lukes, above (n 9) 157.

calls 'negative solidarity', is not enough to deter wars. It is rather a growing recognition that they are all part of the same society, or 'positive solidarity', that leads to the formation of the global consciousness. This way, he sets the framework for the discussion of universal values shared across the societies. At the same time, Durkheim lays down limitations to universalisation. In an ideal of human brotherhood wars would no longer govern international relations, but for this to happen all men must be part of one and the same society and subject to the same laws. Inter-society conflicts can be contained only by the society that embraces all other societies and this is a challenging task due to many divergences across the world.[16] Durkheim underlines that we do not know whether it is possible to forge one single human society, but he mentions continuous transformations.

The final 'operational' motivation for exploring Durkheim in the context of international criminal law is his functionalism and stride towards explaining the way society operates.[17] The distinction between mechanical and organic solidarity, the theory of representation as a method of holding societies together, and the study of the functions of law, religion and morality is highly pertinent to the relatively young discipline of international criminal law. A functionalist approach allows for deeper exploration of the categories and institutions of the new field of law. Durkheim achieves a high level of generalisation in his discourse, thus providing an opportunity for scholars to go up and down the 'abstraction elevator' and apply his theories to present day circumstances.[18] Of course, the latter is also what has been criticised by some scholars of international law. One sociologist of international law, Mikael Rask Madsen, has for instance pointed to the circularity of the argument of the functional approach to international law and its tendency to aloof abstraction which fails to treat empirical material in a rigorous way.[19] I accept that critique of functionalism but for the purpose of the present study, I will maintain that although it is a general abstracted theory it provides a suitable theoretical tool for analysing the key question of the grounding and justification of crimes against humanity.

III. Problems with the Category of Crimes Against Humanity

Crimes against humanity as a legal category still struggles with establishing its distinctive identity in international law. Recent years has seen the proliferation of

---

[16] E Durkheim, *The Division of Labour in Society* (originally published 1893; Basingstoke, Macmillan 1984) 336–37.

[17] Madsen, above (n 5) 394–95.

[18] *cf* Dupuy who criticises Durkheim for taking away individual suffering from Christianity and reducing it to abstraction. See JP Dupuy, *The Mark of Sacred* (Stanford, CA, Stanford University Press, 2013) 123.

[19] Madsen, above (n 5).

scholarship on the legal and normative content of crimes against humanity.[20] This trend only underlines the growing need for international instruments that address gross violations of human rights committed in peacetime.[21] It is appealing to think of the International Criminal Court (ICC) as being able to intervene prior to the escalation of hostilities and even prevent the worst atrocities committed in an armed conflict.[22] This classic prevention function, well known from penal theories and criminology, is an addition to its main function, namely post-factum prosecutions. The Court alone, however, cannot provide such a deterrent effect – it must be supported by the network of treaties alerting states about the parameters of the prohibited conduct and creating a reputational and penal risk in cases of breaches. The following subsections purport to resolve two major concerns hampering the development of crimes against humanity – their weak legal foundation and the uncertain role of the state – by invoking considerations stemming from the work of Emile Durkheim as laid out above.

A. Problem One: Weak Legal Foundation

The first problem is the weak legal foundation of the crimes in international criminal law. Notwithstanding the mounting efforts to solidify the status of crimes against humanity by codifying them in the Convention,[23] this group of offences still largely relies on customary international law.

'Crimes against humanity' were among the first categories of international offences to serve as a pre-text for the future field of international criminal law. As early as 1915, the governments of France, Great Britain and Russia issued a joint declaration condemning the Turkish government's massacre of the Armenian population as constituting 'crimes against civilization and humanity', for which all members of the Turkish government would be held responsible.[24] This was the first time the term 'humanity' was used in the legal context. Four years later, the Treaty of Versailles allowed prosecutions of German military personnel for war crimes.[25] It failed, however, to include crimes against humanity, primarily due to the objection raised by the United States that the content of 'the laws on humanity' could not be defined because it was based on natural law, which did not form

---

[20] eg, L May, *Crimes Against Humanity: A Normative Account* (Oxford, Oxford University Press, 2005); D Luban, 'A Theory of Crimes Against Humanity' (2004) 29 *Yale Journal of International Law* 85; LN Sadat, 'Crimes Against Humanity in the Modern Age' (2013) 107 *American Journal of International Law* 334; G Robertson, *Crimes Against Humanity: The Struggle for Global Justice* (London, Penguin Books, 2007); Bassiouni, 'Revisiting the Architecture of Crimes Against Humanity', above (n 4).

[21] Schabas points to the analogy between crimes against humanity and serious violations of human rights. W Schabas, 'Crimes Against Humanity' in DL Shelton (ed), *Encyclopaedia of Genocide and Crimes Against Humanity* (Detroit, MI, 2005) 209.

[22] Sadat, 'Crimes Against Humanity in the Modern Age', above (n 20) 334.

[23] Sadat, *Forging a Convention for Crimes Against Humanity*, above (n 4).

[24] Bassiouni, 'Revisiting the Architecture of Crimes Against Humanity', above (n 4) 88–89.

[25] Article 228 of the Treaty of Versailles.

part of international law at that time. Two decades later, the United States changed its view: Justice Robert H Jackson, in his capacity as Chief Counsel for the United States in the Nuremberg prosecution wrote to the President of the United States that crimes against humanity 'have been assimilated as a part of International Law at least since 1907'.[26]

Accordingly, the Nuremberg Charter extended the jurisdiction of the International Military Tribunal (IMT) over crimes against humanity 'namely, murder, extermination, enslavement, deportation, and other inhumane acts committed against any civilian population, before or during the war, or persecutions on political, racial or religious grounds' *provided* they were committed 'in execution of or in connection with any crime within the jurisdiction of the Tribunal'. The pragmatic reason for the inclusion of crimes against humanity in the Nuremberg Charter was the existence of the legal lacuna because war crimes were traditionally conceived as offences committed solely against enemy citizens.

Despite the absence of positive law on crimes against humanity at the time of the drafting of the Nuremberg Charter, the judges at the IMT did not address their ex post facto nature.[27] The Tribunal discussed war crimes and crimes against humanity together under the same subheading.[28] The judges pointed out that war crimes had been recognised under international law prior to the adoption of the Charter.[29] With regard to crimes against humanity, the judgment made it clear that only offences committed in connection with other crimes within the jurisdiction of the court, ie, after the initiation of war in 1939, qualify as crimes against humanity.[30] Thus, in the light of the possible *nullum crimen* objection, the IMT preferred to deal with war crimes and crimes against humanity together. The Tribunal found most accused guilty of both classes of offences, thus avoiding the need to draw a distinction between the two.[31]

The uncertainty about the distinctive nature of this group of core international crimes was reinforced by the persistent practice of cumulative charging and cumulative convictions for war crimes and crimes against humanity at the *ad hoc* tribunals. The inevitable side effect of such practice is blurring the important boundaries between two distinctive categories. The practice of the ICC is mixed when it comes to disentangling these two groups. Crimes against humanity are charged in all nine situations under the Court's investigation. In six instances they go hand-in-hand with war crimes, while three other situations address exclusively

---

[26] Bassiouni, 'Revisiting the Architecture of Crimes Against Humanity', above (n 4) 93.

[27] Nuremberg Judgment, 217–18.

[28] ibid, 224–25, 248 *et sq.*

[29] ibid, 248.

[30] The *Tadić* Appeal Chamber subsequently held that nexus requirement to other crimes as formulated in the Nuremberg Charter was unique to that tribunal and customary international law no longer required a connection of crimes against humanity to an armed conflict. See *Tadić* (Jurisdiction Decision) para 141; *Prosecutor v Kupreškić et al* (Trial Judgment) IT-95-16-T (14 January 2000) (*Kupreškić* Trial Judgment) paras 577–78.

[31] A Cassese, *International Criminal Law*, 2nd edn (Oxford, Oxford University Press, 2008) 106.

offences committed in peacetime – post-electoral violence in Kenya and Cote d'Ivoire, and civil unrest prior to the collapse of the Gaddafi regime in Libya.[32]

As a result, there exists currently uncertainty about the definition of the general contextual elements of crimes against humanity, as well as the underlying acts. The customary nature of crimes against humanity frequently creates confusion notwithstanding the extensive body of jurisprudence produced in the past two decades. Critical voices draw attention to the fact that some findings of the *ad hoc* tribunals relying on customary international law are not supported by the actual cases.[33]

Modern definitions of the general elements of crimes against humanity require that they be perpetrated as part of a widespread or systematic attack against the civilian population.[34] An attack is a course of conduct involving the commission of violence, which may be part of an armed conflict, but not necessarily.[35] The target of the attack, which may also happen also during military operations pursuing legitimate objectives, must predominantly be the civilian population. What is essential is that a party to the conflict has specifically or indiscriminately targeted civilians.[36] 'Population' is understood as a collective entity residing in a certain geographical area rather than a loosely connected group of individuals.[37] The attack must be 'widespread' or 'systematic'. These adjectives are used disjunctively. 'Widespread' refers to the large-scale nature of violence and the number of victims, whereas 'systematic' describes the organised nature of the attack and the improbability that individual acts occurred randomly. These two components often overlap and require normative assessment on a case-by-case basis. Criteria for such assessment include, inter alia, possible participation of officials or authorities and identifiable patterns of crime.[38]

The Rome Statute embraced general uncertainty as to the scope of crimes against humanity by supplementing the list of the specific underlying acts contained in Article 7 with a catch-all provision covering 'other inhumane acts of a similar character intentionally causing great suffering, or serious injury to body or to mental or physical health'.[39]

---

[32] These two situations were the most contested on admissibility grounds.

[33] L van den Herik, 'Using Custom to Reconceptualise Crimes Against Humanity' in S Darcy and J Powderly (eds), *Judicial Creativity at the International Criminal Tribunals* (Oxford, Oxford University Press, 2010); A Zahar and G Sluiter, *International Criminal Law: A Critical Introduction* (Oxford, Oxford University Press, 2008) 199 *et sq*.

[34] Article 3 of the ICTR Statute; Article 2 of the SCSL Statute; Article 7 of the Rome Statute; *Tadić* (Trial Judgment) paras 644–49.

[35] eg, *Prosecutor v Kunarac* (Trial Judgment) ICTY Case No IT-96-23-T & IT-96-23/1-T (22 February 2001) (*Kunarac* Trial Judgment) para 415; *Kunarac* (Appeal Judgment) para 86; *Prosecutor v Tadić* (Appeals Chamber Judgment) ICTY Case No IT-94-1 (15 July 1999) para 251 (*Tadić* Appeal Judgment); G Mettraux, *International Criminal and Ad Hoc Tribunals* (Oxford, Oxford University Press, 2005) 156.

[36] *Kupreškić* Trial Judgment, para 524.

[37] *Kunarac* Appeal Judgment, para 90.

[38] ibid, para 95; *Mettraux*, above (n 35) 190.

[39] Article 7(1)(k) of the Rome Statute of the ICC.

There is a growing demand for an international convention that will codify crimes against humanity, enhance interstate cooperation and dispel ambiguities engendered by the customary law status of these crimes.[40] This work resulted in the recent decision of the International Law Commission to add the drafting of a treaty to its active agenda.

B.   Problem Two: The Uncertain Role of the State

The second major question to be resolved is: can non-state actors commit crimes against humanity?

The element of the definition that caused a lot of controversy at the ICC is the requirement of a policy to commit crimes. The *ad hoc* tribunals took a clear jurisprudential stance on the matter claiming that policy was not an element of crimes against humanity under customary international law.[41] Nonetheless, it is widely accepted that the evidence of the existence of a policy or plan to commit crimes serves to support the widespread or systematic nature of the attack.[42] In contrast, the Rome Statute of the ICC expressly requires that the acts be perpetrated in furtherance of a state or organisational policy.[43]

This additional element in the definition of crimes against humanity in the Rome Statute divided the Pre-Trial Chamber in the Kenya case, which concerned post-electoral violence allegedly perpetrated by the Kenya police jointly with a number of non-state actors. Accordingly, the judges had to determine whether these non-state actors might nonetheless be regarded as an organisation for the purposes of Article 7 of the Rome Statute. The majority answered this question in the positive.[44] The judges noted previous jurisprudence of the *ad hoc* tribunals and interpreted 'organisation' broadly as a group with 'the capability to perform acts which infringe on basic human values'.[45] The Chamber held that the formal nature of the group and its level of organisation should not be the defining criterion.[46]

In contrast, the dissenting Judge Kaul pointed towards the express requirement of 'state or organisational' policy as a distinguishing feature of the Rome Statute.[47]

---

[40] To that effect, there is an initiative launched by Professor Sadat at Washington University School of Law to develop a Convention on Crimes Against Humanity. Crimes Against Humanity Initiative: A Rule of Law Project of the Whitney R Harris World Law Institute, available at: crimesagainsthumanity. wustl.edu/.

[41] *Kunarac* Appeal Judgment, para 98.

[42] Mettraux, above (n 35) 172.

[43] Article 7(2)(a) of the Rome Statute of the ICC.

[44] Decision Pursuant to Article 15 of the Rome Statute on the Authorization of an Investigation into the Situation in the Republic of Kenya, ICC-01/09, International Criminal Court (ICC), 31 March 2010, para 90.

[45] ibid, para 92.

[46] ibid.

[47] Dissenting Opinion of Judge Hans-Peter Kaul to the 'Decision Pursuant to Article 15 of the Rome Statute on the Authorization of an Investigation into the Situation in the Republic of Kenya', ICC-01/09-19-Corr (Dissenting Opinion of Judge Kaul) para 32.

He interpreted 'organisation' strictly as an 'entity which may act like a State or has quasi-State abilities'.[48] The features of 'organisation' include hierarchy, collectivity, common purpose and authority to implement policy.[49] Only state-like entities may engage in this crime.[50] Underlying Kaul's restrictive interpretation is the premise central to this chapter: there must be a clear demarcation line between international crimes of concern to the international community as a whole and common crimes, albeit of a serious nature, prosecuted domestically.[51] Judge Kaul concluded that with respect to crimes against humanity, it is the presence of state policy that elevates them to the international level.[52] Consequently, non-state actors do not reach the level of organisation required by Article 7.[53]

C. Durkheim's Approaches Elucidating Problem One: The Idea of Solidarity[54]

What makes crimes against humanity 'worthy' of international prosecution? It is challenging to provide moral and legal justifications for the category of crimes against humanity, known for its amorphous body not (yet) solidified in a comprehensive treaty. Open-ended lists of underlying acts and contested legal definitions create uncertainty that frequently results in legal techniques further blurring the boundaries of these crimes.

Arguably, what makes this group of offences 'special' is that it protects citizens of a state, which is depriving them of the natural protection of a sovereign. Durkheim's theory of collective consciousness assists in understanding the process whereby the international community reaches out to individual victims trapped inside state borders. It also explains how solidarity justifies international interventions.

Durkheim's view of solidarity is premised on the idea of modern societies moving towards greater specialisation of tasks that are divided among its members.[55] He argues that this process is visible not only in the area of industrial relations, where the division of labour boosts productivity, but also in other walks

---

[48] ibid, para 51.
[49] ibid.
[50] ibid, para 66.
[51] ibid, para 8.
[52] ibid, para 60.
[53] ibid, para 52.
[54] In his early works, Durkheim distinguished between organic and mechanical solidarity. The former, characteristic of more advanced societies, had been premised on interdependence and law effectuating it, while the latter had been supported by penal law that represented shared beliefs in the society. He later abandoned this distinction and admitted that shared beliefs are also important for modern societies. This article accordingly does not place much emphasis on the distinction between organic and mechanical solidarity.
[55] Durkheim, *The Division of Labour in Society*, above (n 16) 4.

of life such as art and science.[56] As the activity of various actors becomes more concentrated and focused, social cohesion gains its importance for sustaining political equilibrium. Members of the society need to interact effectively with each other in order to exchange the results of their activity. Thus, the division of labour becomes a source of social solidarity.[57]

Law serves to organise relationships either with one another or with a group collectively. Law is the glue that holds social life together in an organised and precise way. It cements the relationships that exist in society; new relationships cannot subsist without being consolidated in law. Solidarity within any particular group may arise from a diverse core, and can be national, professional or domestic. What is important is a shared understanding in the society that law is the instrument of maintaining and regulating links between different actors.

Legal rules are divided into two big groups: purely restitutory, or civil, rules and repressive, or penal, sanctions. The latter group is administered on behalf of society and seeks to cause harm to the offender. Durkheim hinted at a great diversity of acts prohibited by penal sanctions across different societies and, yet, a certain degree of universality of values that underlie the notion of a crime.[58] This point is not instrumental for Durkheim's claim, but it is for this chapter. He proceeded to argue that the essence of crime is not in the intrinsic properties of acts prohibited by penal sanctions because they display great diversity, but in the relationship they entertain with some condition outside themselves.[59]

What defines a crime, according to Durkheim, is the antagonism between the act and the wider interests of the society. A crime disturbs feelings that in any one type of society are to be found in every healthy consciousness. The sentiment is not only strongly held, but also precise.[60] It is for this reason ignorance of the law is not a criminal law defence: any potential offender is expected to know and share the values collectively held in the community.[61] The purpose of the governmental authority is to defend beliefs commonly held. In other words, the authority to create crimes and impose penalties grows out of the need to preserve the collective consciousness and defend it from the enemy, internal or external.[62]

The society 'outsources' the tasks of defining crimes and the administration of punishment to an organised entity acting on its behalf (for example, legislators, juries and judges).[63] This structure ensures that any crime is an attack not only on the collective interests, but also on the authority itself. Punishment is an act of solidarity of the society to an act offending its collective consciousness; it is an emotional reaction, graduated in its intensity depending on the interests

---

[56] ibid, 14.
[57] ibid, 23.
[58] See also Cotterrell, above (n 6).
[59] Durkheim, *The Division of Labour in Society*, above (n 16) 25–32.
[60] ibid, 38.
[61] ibid, 34.
[62] ibid, 43.
[63] ibid, 37.

harmed. Punishment is imposed in a systematic fashion because all members of the community are presumed to share the values and agree to submit the offender to censure.[64] Durkheim later refined his thesis and acknowledged the role of the state as a moderator between the offender and shared beliefs by regulating the severity of punishment.[65]

Durkheim's work concerns primarily singular societies. Is it possible to conceive of solidarity as beliefs shared universally? Durkheim made a passing reference to this question when he noted that resemblance exists not only among crimes provided in the legislation of a single nation, but also among all crimes recognised and punished in different societies for they 'universally strike the moral consciousness of nations in the same way'.[66] He then added that the acts that are universally regarded as criminal constitute only a tiny minority.

On the face of it, there is some contradiction in this thesis since it seems to suggest simultaneously a strong resemblance among crimes recognised by different states and, at the same time, the scarcity of such crimes. One way to reconcile these two statements (in present-day reality) is to think of them as a reflection of the dichotomy of purely domestic criminal offences versus crimes subject to universal jurisdiction. The first statement can be said to refer to wrongful acts found in the majority of criminal codes around the world for they offend moral consciousness of different nations in the same way. The second claim may be interpreted as singling out a small fraction of offences that by virtue of injuring values essential to the entire world community drop their nexus to a particular state. Crimes against humanity attack the authority higher than the state authority, they attack the *jus cogens* core of international law. Solidarity across nations is achieved only with respect to this second category of acts that are of international concern.

Durkheim presents national penal law as traditionalist in nature – its authority is a societal custom formed over time. Domestic criminal law has an indispensable regulatory function because by guarding dominant values shared by its citizens it may be said to preserve the identity of a state.[67] Due its high value to the society, criminal law is backed by the sanctions enforced on behalf of the community. In contrast, international criminal law – a relatively young discipline dating back just a few decades – does not limit itself to the values traditionally shared by the citizens of a particular state, but claims universality and adherence to the project of protection of the fundamental legal values of humanity as a whole.[68] Its legitimacy derives not so much from the regulatory function, but rather, its moral standing.[69]

---

[64] ibid, 43–52.
[65] Cotterrell, above (n 6) 73.
[66] Durkheim, *The Division of Labour in Society*, above (n 16) 31.
[67] ibid, 45.
[68] K Ambos, *Treatise on International Criminal Law, Volume 1: Foundations and General Part* (Oxford, Oxford University Press, 2013) 65.
[69] See CA Thomas, 'The Uses and Abuses of Legitimacy in International Law' (2014) 34 *Oxford Journal of Legal Studies* 729, 741 on the moral legitimacy of international law.

Durkheim described two distinct consciousnesses that exist within each individual: one is personal and characterises each one of us separately; whereas the other is collective in that it comprises states common to the whole of society. The two consciousnesses coexist in every person and give rise to a solidarity, which binds the individual to society.[70] Arguably, since the time when this claim was made, a new additional type of consciousness emerged, ie, the global one, which exists in every individual, along with personal and collective consciousness, and embraces a set of characteristics not unique to a particular society, but common to all in the interconnected world order. Solidarity, in its modern understanding, stems from the interplay among these three types of consciousness.

International prosecutions of crimes against humanity derive their justification from the beliefs held at the level of global consciousness: these offences attack basic human rights considered universal and belonging to every person regardless of their national affiliation. The horrors of the Second World War led to the proliferation of the thematic treaties with the universal focus. The exact point in time when the human rights movement reached its critical mass opens it for reproach of being eurocentric, rather than truly universal. It took atrocities in Western Europe, and not the enslavement of Africans or the brutal colonisation of Asians, to create a collective sense of responsibility for the worst human rights violations.[71] While it is true that core international crimes conceived following the Second World War are not free from ideological baggage, the deep social trauma caused by the aggressive military ambition of Nazism constructed a suitable narrative whereby evil could be easily distinguished from good by the majority of countries and their citizens, thereby creating a strong ethical pull of values superior to that of individual state interests.[72] Thus, the accused of crimes against humanity are tried on behalf of redeeming humanity.[73]

Thus, the legitimacy capital of international criminal law thrives on solidarity felt across state borders. There must be a shared understanding that certain acts hurt the interests of the global community in a way that justifies international intervention. Universal cohesion carries practical significance for international criminal law because it lacks the enforcement apparatus akin to the one that allows individual states to exercise their executive powers.[74] Support from national

---

[70] Durkheim, *The Division of Labour in Society*, above (n 16) 61.

[71] M Mutua, 'Savages, Victims, and Saviors: The Metaphor of Human Rights' (2001) 42 *Harvard International Law Journal* 201, 201–11.

[72] JC Alexander, *Trauma: A Social Theory* (Cambridge, Polity Press, 2012) 39.

[73] E Bikundo, 'Humanity's Exemplary Justice: from "hostis" to "hostia humani generis"' in B van Beers, L Corrias and WG Werner (eds), *Humanity Across International Law and Biolaw* (Cambridge, Cambridge University Press 2013) 44.

[74] eg, Article 27 of the ICTY Statute and Article 26 of the ICTR Statute (enforcement of sentence). To that effect Bodansky argues that an institution's lack of coercive power means that it must rely more on perceived legitimacy as a basis of influence. See D Bodansky, 'Legitimacy in International Law and International Relations' in JL Dunoff and MA Pollack (eds), *Interdisciplinary Perspectives on International Law and International Relations: The State of the Art* (New York, Cambridge University Press, 2012) 325.

governments as well as local populations is thus essential for keeping the discipline operational because failure to secure cooperation may lead to the denial of justice as, for instance, happened with South Africa's failure to arrest the president of Sudan, Omar Al Bashir, for whom the ICC issued the arrest warrant. Such enforcement-deficit makes international criminal law particularly susceptible to questions of moral legitimacy.

D. Durkheim's Approaches in Support of Problem Two: The Importance of Human Dignity

The second issue pertaining to crimes against humanity, namely the role of the state element in the definition of this group of offences, continues to provoke intense scholarly discussions,[75] and, in the light of its paramount importance to defining the nature of crimes against humanity, is likely to receive more attention in the future jurisprudence of the ICC.

Judge Kaul largely relies on historical explanation in supporting this claim.[76] While in agreement with the general assessment that the state element is crucial for the crime to fall under the radar of international community, this article argues that historical and legal narratives alone fail to eliminate doubts about the distinctive nature of crimes against humanity. Historically speaking, they were conceived as an extension of war crimes and, along with other core international crimes, travelled from Nuremberg to The Hague. The scrutiny of their legal foundations exposes significant gaps that undermine the principle of legal certainty essential for the perceived legitimacy of international trials. Historical narrative does not always elucidate the specific elements required to construct legal definitions. One needs to push the analysis further to account for an extra variable, namely the function of this category of offences.

What is then the function of crimes against humanity? Answering this question may assist in answering the queries pertaining to the role of the state in the definition of these offences. Arguably, the special character of crimes against humanity as a legal category stems from their role as guardian against the most egregious human rights abuses either committed or overlooked by the state. The legal criteria that they are perpetrated as a part of the widespread or systematic attack against a civilian population establishes a certain level of severity required for triggering the feeling of collective repulsion across borders. Philosophers of international criminal law, in particular Larry May and David Luban, developed normative criteria for assessing the margin of appreciation afforded to states in dealing with gross violations committed within their borders, ie, the threshold of gravity that brings

---

[75] For the extended discussion and references to relevant scholarship see Sadat, 'Crimes Against Humanity in the Modern Age', above (n 20) fn 6.

[76] Dissenting Opinion of Judge Kaul, para 65.

these crimes under the radar of the global community. May adopts what he calls a 'moral minimalist' understanding of crimes against humanity. In his view, only the violation of basic human rights to security and subsistence warrants the violation of state sovereignty and justifies international prosecutions.[77]

Luban attributes less importance to sovereignty.[78] He notes that crimes against humanity are of international concern because of the vulnerability of the population under state control: people are defenceless against political violence inflicted on them collectively. Luban distinguishes between two meanings of the word 'humanity', which are not equivalent. Humanity can denote humanness as a quality or a value reflecting the nature of being human. The attack on diversity is the attack on humanness.[79] The same term may refer to humankind as an entity or a collection of individuals.[80] The argument is that crimes against humanity are simultaneously both things – they are offences against humankind and injuries to humanness. These crimes are so universally odious because they make the offender the enemy of the whole of humankind and injure something fundamental to being human that national legal systems fail to address.[81]

Although Durkheim focuses primarily on the processes of administration of law, his work also assists in reconciling these two positions by bringing into light the value of human dignity – something Durkheim held dear, especially later in his career. For Durkheim, human dignity transcends state boundaries and replaces religion as the social glue holding societies together. He identifies the cult of the individual as a basis of popular morality – man is both believer and god.[82]

Individualism – which Durkheim duly separates from egoism and selfishness – is a new religion and system of beliefs that ensures moral unity.[83] Individualism, if it is not purely utilitarian self-interest, sacralises the human person in a ritual sense of the world. This makes an attempt on human life a violation. The cult of the individual sanctifies the idea of individual rights and liberties and the state guarantees them.[84]

What happens if the state fails in its duty to protect individuals subject to its jurisdiction? The gravest example of this would be the state's failure to prevent crimes committed against civilians on a widespread or systematic basis. In such circumstances, social cohesion within the state based on respect for human dignity is ruptured and the international community is forced to intervene and

---

[77] May, above (n 20) 12.

[78] D Luban, 'Beyond Moral Minimalism: Response to Crimes Against Humanity' (2006) 20 *Ethics & International Affairs* 353, 356.

[79] Luban, 'A Theory of Crimes Against Humanity', above (n 20) 87.

[80] ibid, 90. See also C Macleod, 'Towards a Philosophical Account of Crimes Against Humanity' (2010) 21 *European Journal of International Law* 281, 283.

[81] Macleod, above (n 80).

[82] Durkheim, *The Division of Labour in Society*, above (n 16) 122; Durkheim, Individualism and Intellectuals', above (n 14) 81.

[83] Lukes, above (n 9) 166–67

[84] Cotterrell, above (n 6) 115–16.

pick up where the state stopped fulfilling its duties as a protector. Global collective consciousness comes into action because the sentiment that no one must be subjected to crimes violating human dignity and bodily integrity – such as torture or extermination – is strongly held and precise across different communities.

Durkheim located the individual within the state and highlighted the importance of social links holding groups together. Morality created the source of obligation in the community. Law ultimately expressed the moral code.[85] In the light of the dwindling role of states in a modern highly globalised world, it is essential to develop similar links between individuals and the wider international community.

Morality could hold the same unifying power at an international level. Crimes against humanity are offending global morality and thus require adequate legal response. One can argue that standards of morality differ from place to place. This is only partially true. When it comes to the gravest violations of human dignity, a common denominator comes into play, ie, empathy. The feeling of human pity and compassion is universal.

Crimes against humanity appeal to human empathy like no other core international crime. Emotions such as compassion or abomination are widely recognised across the communities. It is peculiar that already at Nuremberg, ie, at the time of their creation, crimes against humanity were described in very strong emotive language. The Tribunal used adjectives such as 'horrifying' and 'revolting' when describing the policy of terror that existed in Germany prior to the commencement of the Second World War.[86] Finally, crimes against humanity are dynamic in nature.[87] In the absence of a fixed legal definition, these crimes gradually transformed themselves to accommodate for the shifts in global architecture. Originally introduced as a legal solution for the specific issue, the new category of offences had the effect of redefining states' powers with respect to individuals under its authority. The level of permissiveness afforded to states by the international community significantly decreased.

IV. The 'How' Question: International Criminal Trials as Religious Rituals

In *The Division of Labour in Society*, Durkheim argued that modern societies subsist on interdependence stemming from the allocation of functions to different actors. He later modified his view to account for a more complex picture rooted in value systems that are expressed by religious or quasi-religious practices.[88]

---

[85] ibid, 54.

[86] Nuremberg Judgment, 249.

[87] It is peculiar that during the course of his life Durkheim moves away from static to dynamic interpretation of social organisation. See Cotterrell, above (n 6).

[88] Cotterrell, above (n 6) 49–51.

The deep unsettling query of Durkheim's analysis is his search for the moral foundations of the new legal order. He came to realise early on that the division of labour and the distribution of tasks is insufficient to facilitate the processes of integration, thus he turned to religion. The special emphasis is on the process of expressing beliefs – religious ritual is a method for society to renew itself and tie together its members.

Religion consists of acts, which have the object of perpetually making and remaking the soul of the collectivity and of individuals, thus its function is to strengthen the bonds attaching the individual to the society.[89] For Durkheim, religion has social function both as a system of communication of ideas and sentiments and as means of specifying and regulating social relationships.[90] Religion represents society and social relationships in a cognitive sense as means of understanding social reality and in a sense of expressing or symbolising human relationships.[91] What is essential in religious representation is a search for truth – whether justified or not.[92]

In *The Elementary Forms of Religious Life* written towards the end of Durkheim's life, he pointed to the lack of a moral basis in modern societies. What happened to religious rituals in the industrialist societies? Do they still hold the same power? In Durkheim's view, religious enthusiasm (of Christianity) that filled our forefathers no longer exists for 'the old gods are growing old or already dead, and others are not yet born'.[93] In these circumstances, law comes to replace religion as a forum for effectuating common beliefs. Durkheim saw it along with religion as fulfilling social functions, acting as a source of duty and obligation. For Durkheim protecting human dignity is not only the end result of the administration of law, but also part of its process. The result of this trend is curtailing barbaric punishments in modern life.[94]

Placing Durkheim's ideas in a contemporary context, it is possible to conceptualise international criminal trials as religious rituals. Procedure plays an essential role in bringing those responsible to justice.[95] Victims of mass atrocities are the 'new gods', dominating international criminal proceedings. The exponential growth of mass media (and in particular television) in the 1970s and social media in the 2000s made it possible to draw public attention to gross human rights violations worldwide. Various media outlets widely disseminated information on the basic human rights standards. Media also contributed to the development of victims' movement by allowing the general public to embrace victims' suffering and experience, viewing it as 'common and collective, rather than individual

---

[89] E Durkheim, *The Elementary Forms of Religious Life* (originally published in 1912; New York, The Free Press, 1995) 471.

[90] Lukes, above (n 9) 471.

[91] ibid, 465.

[92] ibid, 491.

[93] Durkheim, *The Elementary Forms of Religious Life*, above (n 89) 427.

[94] Cotterrell, above (n 6) 79.

[95] ibid, 111.

and atypical.[96] Such self-identification with the victim strengthened collectively held feelings of aversion towards the perpetrator of atrocities.

Victims become a focal point in the discussion of the state's failure to protect its own citizens when crimes against humanity occured. This discourse symbolises the universality of human values.[97] Victims are sacralised for they fulfil an important function, that of containing vengeance. Identification of victims streamlines moral outrage flowing from the fact that mass atrocities have been committed by placing a barrier between the aggrieved and the rest of the world. The state is no longer at the centre of the debate and its failure and abuse does not stigmatise the whole population, but rather attaches to the selected few high-level perpetrators. Shifting the emphasis from the state to the individual is the new modus operandi of transnational politics.

International criminal courts and tribunals fulfil an important social function in international affairs – they identify a victim and an offender, while simultaneously placing a barrier between the two. Thus, in the aftermath of mass atrocities, the international community comes together to craft an institution that religiously follows legal procedure in creating a space between the perpetrator and the victims. The state is left out of the process, while international actors feel united around common ideals. Sikking coined the term 'justice cascade' – a situation whereby the proliferation of criminal trials of high-level politicians and army officials led to the legitimation of the idea of international criminal prosecutions.[98] Durkheim allows for explaining why this shift occurred – a quickly evolving international community was in dire need of the new ritual, a new process to preserve itself, while allowing individual states to subsist.

V. Conclusion: The Rising Significance of the Category of Crimes Against Humanity

International criminal law is still in search of its identity.[99] It is particularly true when it comes to the process of criminalisation of core international crimes. It seems that lawyers and activists have been able to come up with definitions that are subject to general agreement, but the moral basis of these categories is lagging behind. This leads to uncertainties when it comes to the elements of various international crimes. It could be that by virtue of creating international courts and tribunals, the international community is working towards common definitions

---

[96] D Garland, *The Culture of Control: Crime and Social Order in a Contemporary Society* (Oxford, Oxford University Press, 2001) 144.

[97] Dupuy, above (n 18) 187.

[98] Sikking, above (n 8) 5.

[99] D Robinson, 'Identity Crisis of International Criminal Law' (2008) 21 *Leiden Journal of International Law* 925.

and joint understandings. The creation of the ICC and growing recognition of international crimes may be the moment that Durkheim described as a day 'when our societies will know again those hours of creative effervescence, in the course of which new ideas arise and new formulae are found which serve for a while as a guide to humanity'.[100] It appears that the international community comes to accept that certain crimes committed within state borders cannot be overlooked even if the state fails to address them. Would this trend qualify as the moment of 'effervescence' discussed by Durkheim?

This seems to be the case with the rising significance of crimes against humanity as a category of core international offences. It is true that they lack clear legal foundation in an international treaty, yet prohibition of torture or extermination of civilians effectuated as a part of a widespread or systematic attack produces moral outrage globally. Atrocities perpetrated by ISIS against the Yazidis in Iraq or the massacre of students in Kenya by Al-Shabaab stir little disagreement in the international community as to the heinous and unacceptable nature of these acts.

One last paradox in Durkheim's philosophy of crime and punishment must be addressed in this closing section. Durkheim considered crime and shared sentiments of the collective consciousness as symbiotic; thus one cannot exist without the other.[101] This position undermines the claim that crimes against humanity must be prosecuted internationally – if they exist to hold the international community together, why, then, create international courts to address them?

The picture is more nuanced however. Indeed, Durkheim upholds the value of crime per se in *The Division of Labour in Society*. He claims that it would be impossible to have a society without crime because the intense sentiments that crime offends would fade unless they were strengthened through the punishment of offenders.[102] This is a much criticised point because Durkheim fails to link punishment to policies, rather than just shared beliefs, and also to reiterate its value in modern organic societies, as opposed to mechanical societies that rely on penal law.[103] Later in his career, however, Durkheim saw punishment as an integral part of every healthy society, not just less developed ones.

Thus, it is the punishment following the crime that holds societies together. It is not feasible to accept at face value that a bare offence serves as 'social glue' prompting solidarity. For Durkheim, the attack on individual rights outrages not only because the victim suffers, but also because this attack threatens the whole humanity and thus must be punished.[104] In this sense, Durkheim comes very close to Kantian philosophy that embraces the principle of punishment as a categorical imperative.[105] Those who commit crimes violate the public order by treating

---

[100] Durkheim, *The Elementary Forms of Religious Life*, above (n 89) 427–28.

[101] Cotterrell, above (n 6) 75.

[102] Durkheim, *The Division of Labour in Society*, above (n 16) 63; Lukes, above (n 9) 161.

[103] Lukes, above (n 9) 159–60; Cotterrell, above (n 6) 71.

[104] Dupuy, above (n 18) 123.

[105] I Kant, *The Metaphysics of Morals* (1797) Cambridge Texts in the History of Philosophy (edn 1991) 141.

themselves as exceptions to the law.[106] They become unworthy citizens and need to be punished for the sake of re-establishing the equilibrium that they broke. Punishment becomes the instrument of justice, and justice is essential for the functioning of society; 'for if justice goes, there is no longer any value in men's living on the earth'.[107]

The conclusion of the above discussion is that international prosecutions of the category of crimes against humanity enhance solidarity across national borders. International crimes in general, and crimes against humanity in particular, assault the global conscience. These acts must be punished in the course of criminal trials that are rituals that serve to effectuate solidarity and enhance cohesion. Compared with domestic law, international criminal law is less concerned with the punishment of all those responsible for mass crimes because of the natural limitations of this field of law. At the same time, enhanced focus on victims makes the whole process of international trial appear as a ritual. The symbolic recognition of the suffering and the outrage caused by the collective criminality legitimises international responses to crimes against humanity.

[106] ibid, 140.
[107] ibid, 141.

PART III

Trial and Punishment

5

The Hybrid System of International Criminal Law: A Work in Progress or Just a Noble Experiment?

COLLEEN ROHAN

'The shepherd knows more about sheep than the most
dedicated of scholars'.[1]

I. Introduction

I have had the privilege, since I began to practise law as defence counsel at the International Criminal Tribunal for the former Yugoslavia (ICTY) in 2005, to give lectures, talks, speeches and seminars to students, lawyers, academics, journalists and others from around the world about the realities of practising law within the international criminal courts. One striking impression I have gained from discussions with members of these audiences is their assumption – understandable as it is on the part of observers outside the courts – that a 'system' of international criminal law (ICL) exists which is consistently applied in the various international courts. That is not the case.

It is also assumed that ICL courts, as claimed on their various websites, are solutions to international conflict, an effective way to end or deter impunity, vehicles for establishing peace and/or reconciliation in post-conflict societies,[2]

---

[1] Comment by mystery writer Phillip Kerr.

[2] ICTY: www.icty.org/en/about: 'Simply by removing some of the most senior and notorious criminals and holding them accountable the Tribunal has been able to lift the taint of violence, contribute to ending impunity and help pave the way for reconciliation'. ICTR: unictr.irmct.org/: 'As the Tribunal approaches the end of its mandate, its legacy lays the foundation for a new era in international criminal justice'. (Author's note: Individuals acquitted after trial at the ICTR are still being held in custody; a notorious situation which has been repeatedly raised with the UN Secretary General to no avail); STL: www.stl-tsl.org/en/about-the-stl/5881-victims: 'The STL is one of only a few international tribunals that give victims a platform to be recognised and heard'. (Author's note: This is a highly misleading claim. When the testimony of victims is part of the prosecution or defence case all ICL courts give them

and, in particular, places where the innocent victims of war will be afforded justice and appropriate reparations.[3] Laudable though all these aspirations are, that is also not the case.

The ICL courts are *criminal courts* in which criminal cases are brought against select individuals regarding their responsibility for specified serious international criminal offences. That task, alone, is formidable given the legal and factual complexity of the cases, the difficulty in obtaining access to reliable evidence in conflict and post-conflict situations, limits on resources, and numerous other obstacles confronted by all parties to the cases which are unknown in most domestic criminal law courts. It is important that the public understands this basic fact so that the real value of the courts will be recognised. It does no good to raise expectations which cannot realistically be met by the courts. Indeed, affirmative damage to the courts' reputations and loss of confidence or belief in their actual purpose results when unrealistic expectations are presented.

Convictions and acquittals obtained as a result of the criminal trial process, against the handful of people tried in the various ICL courts, may or may not achieve some valuable societal result above and beyond the conviction or acquittal itself. History, however, has thus far shown that ICL convictions have not contributed to peace, reconciliation, the end of impunity or fair reparations for victims. Whether and in what way such goals are achieved by individual societies and citizens is a multifaceted challenge that requires much more than the outcome of a criminal trial.

What the ICL courts have done (and can continue to do) is more limited. They can convict and punish individuals responsible for war crimes, crimes against

---

a platform to be recognised and heard – they testify at trial or submit written statements. If the only role of a victim is to seek reparations then, as described below, only some of the ICL courts permit that form of victim participation.); ICC: www.icc-cpi.int/about: 'International justice can contribute to long-term peace, stability and equitable development in post-conflict societies. These elements are foundational for building a future free of violence'.

[3] The ICC trust fund for victims asserts: 'The Fund's mission is to support and implement programmes that address harms resulting from genocide, crimes of humanity, war crimes and aggression. To achieve this mission, the TFV has a two-fold mandate: (i) to implement Court-Ordered reparations and (ii) to provide physical, psychological, and material support to victims and their families. By assisting victims to return to a dignified and contributory life within their communities, the TFV contributes to realizing sustainable and long-lasting peace by promoting restorative justice and reconciliation': www.icc-cpi.int/tfv. The Trust Fund for victims, according to its official website, states that from 2004 to 2014 it received more than 20.4 million euros: www.trustfundforvictims.org/en/financial-information. That is approximately two million euros a year. The paucity of resources speaks for itself regarding the likelihood that the hundreds of thousands of victims of war will ever obtain reasonable reparations for their actual losses. In addition, even when crimes against recognised victims are proved beyond a reasonable doubt at trial, ICC law provides that no reparations will be awarded unless the specific accused in the dock is convicted. (See Rome Statute, Article 75(2)) and see discussion of this issue by the Institute for Security Studies in 2015, 'The Great Gamble for Reparations', available at: reliefweb.int/report/world/great-gamble-reparations.) Hence, following the acquittal of Jean-Pierre Bemba at the ICC the trust fund announced its need to seek donations to launch various assistance programmes for victims in the Central African Republic: www.icc.cpi.int/Pages/item.aspx?name=180613-TFVPR.

humanity and/or genocide arising from armed conflicts and acquit individuals wrongfully accused of such crimes. That contribution is of considerable value.

Of course, the effectiveness and validity of the system rendering these verdicts can only be achieved when the proceedings and verdicts obtained in the ICL courts are fair and are perceived as such. The structural integrity, procedural and substantive, of any system of law requires no less.

This chapter will address the hybrid 'system' of law utilised in the ICL courts, with a focus on the International Criminal Court (ICC), the only permanent ICL court. This hybrid system, comprised of a mix of Western civil and common law procedures and traditions seems to have been consistently applied at various *ad hoc*, regional tribunals, such as the ICTY and the International Criminal Tribunal for Rwanda (ICTR). Questions have arisen regarding the consistency and use of this hybrid 'system' at the ICC, in particular regarding the application of the legal burden of proof and the admission and assessment of trial evidence, both of which are briefly examined here.

It is important to recognise, in raising these issues, that the current ICL courts have only been in existence for about 25 years which for a system of law is a very short time. These courts are still developing their procedures and substantive jurisprudence and to date only a relative handful of people have actually stood trial in the various ICL courts. Nonetheless, it is important for any new institution to learn from its successes and to recognise and ameliorate mistakes or failures as it develops. This necessarily will strengthen the institution and help to ensure its effectiveness and future influence.

II. A Short Overview of the Existing ICL Courts

The ICTY opened its doors in 1995 with the mandate to bring to justice those responsible for serious violations of international humanitarian law committed during the conflict in the former Yugoslavia and thus to contribute to the restoration and maintenance of peace in the region.[4] The ICTY was the first international criminal court established since the Nuremberg tribunals of 1945. Upon its inception an administrative and legal structure was created within which to carry out the various functions of the Tribunal. Rules of Procedure and Evidence, intended to govern the conduct of proceedings at the Tribunal were drafted by tribunal judges and published in February 1994.[5] Its investigations into alleged war crimes, identification of suspects, and the preparation of indictments began when the war in the former Yugoslavia was still ongoing. Prosecutions of the war crimes cases

---

[4] United Nations Security Council Resolution 827 (25 May 1993); and see: www.icty.org/en/about/tribunal/mandate-and-crimes-under-icty-jurisdiction.

[5] The ICTY Rules of Procedure (RPE) have been amended 50 times over the history of the ICTY to reflect changing circumstances and lessons learned from the ongoing litigation before the Tribunal.

within the Tribunal's jurisdiction were rapidly begun after that.[6] It is, on several bases, the most successful ICL court of all those established to date in the number, importance and success of its prosecutions, the development of a body of reasonably consistent and accessible jurisprudence and the competence and integrity of its proceedings.[7] One reason for this success was succinctly put by a member of the ICTY bench:

> There is also a core duty incumbent on all us judges to continue to think 'internationally'. We come from diverse domestic jurisdictions with many different methods of running criminal trials and somehow we have managed to blend these methods together to successfully adjudicate crimes on a scale never attempted or even fathomed in domestic jurisdictions. This is a testament to our vision, our cooperativeness and our empathy. The continued evolution and expansion of international criminal justice demands that we always maintain these three virtues.[8]

A number of international and internationalised regional courts were created thereafter to prosecute war crimes, crimes against humanity, and genocide arising from various regional conflicts, including the International Criminal Tribunal for Rwanda (ICTR), the Special Tribunal for Lebanon (STL), the Special Court for Sierra Leone (SCSL), and the Extraordinary Criminal Chambers in Cambodia (ECCC).[9] In August 2015 the latest iteration of an 'internationalised court' the Kosovo Specialist Chambers (KSC) was established with jurisdiction over crimes against humanity, war crimes and other crimes under Kosovo law in relation to allegations raised in the Council of Europe Parliamentary Assembly Report of 7 January 2011. The KSC is not an international court. It is a Kosovar court located in The Hague for the purpose of trying a limited number of individuals for offences alleged to have been committed during a discrete time frame during the armed conflict in Kosovo.[10] The Court has yet to bring any indictments; cause for critical

---

[6] The first trial at the ICTY began in May 1996 (*Prosecutor v Dusko Tadić*, ICTY Case No IT-94-1). As of that date 14 indictments had also already been prepared in other cases involving 57 accused; pretrial proceedings were under way in three cases involving six accused, and in July 1996 the first guilty plea was accepted (*Prosecutor v Drazen Erdemovic*, ICTY Case No IT-96-22).

[7] During its 20-year existence the ICTY indicted and processed 161 war crimes cases; the ICTR 93 cases during approximately the same period. The two tribunals have similar, albeit not identical, establishing Statutes. Trial proceedings at each tribunal are separate but they share the same Appeals Chambers.

[8] Judge O Kwan, 'The Challenge of an International Criminal Trial as Seen from the Bench' 2007 5 *Journal of International Criminal Justice* 360, and see: ldoi.org/10.1093/jicj/mql094.

[9] The ECCC is not an international court. It is a domestic court which functions with significant international financial and professional assistance.

[10] See official website of the Kosovo Specialist Chambers and Specialist Prosecutor's Office: www.scp-ks.org/en; and www.scp-ks.org/en/background. Two prosecutions of Kosovar Albanians were brought at the ICTY during its mandate; *Prosecutor v Limaj et al*, ICTY Case No IT-03-66-T and *Prosecutor v Haradinaj et al*, ICTY Case No IT-04-84-T and IT-04-84*bis*-T. Although the KSC is a domestic court of Kosovo its Rules of Procedure and Evidence and jurisprudence will be controlled by international as well as domestic law. The KSC was created in 2014 but has yet to bring any indictments.

comments from individuals familiar with its creation.[11] As explained by one: 'the court has yet to receive any indictments to adjudicate, despite a multi-year birthing process and a massive budget of 41 million euros'.[12]

The ICC – meant to be a permanent court of last resort able to adjudicate crimes arising from conflicts anywhere in the world – came into being upon passage and ratification of the Rome Statute in 2002.[13]

III. The ICL Legal 'System'

These criminal courts (except for the ECCC) utilise a 'hybrid system' of law; that is a *sui generis* system of law and procedure comprised of a mix of Western civil and common law traditions and procedures. This system was not imported from any particular Western domestic jurisdiction.[14]

Although this hybrid system of law and procedure has been in existence for over two decades and is relied upon daily in the ICL courts it does not yet enjoy universal acceptance by practitioners within the ICL courts. The debate is ongoing in the ICL community as to whether the civil law system is more time and cost efficient than the common law and vice versa or whether the common law system is more workable given the nature of international criminal proceedings. Partisans from both camps advocate on behalf of the superiority of their own domestic legal systems. Some find it difficult to adapt to the various peculiarities of the 'hybrid' ICL systems. This includes judges, prosecutors, legal officers and defence counsel. Some of these practitioners function within the 'mixed' system the same as they might in their own domestic courts, activities which can lead to discord and disagreement in the conduct of trials and the resolution of cases.[15]

The mixed, hybrid system of ICL law is not consistently adopted or utilised at the various ICL courts. The STL is conducting trials *in absentia*; none of the accused are in physical custody or before the court. That process has not been

---

[11] See, eg, Judge D Pineles, 'Ghost Court Delays Justice for Kosovo War Victims,' 21 March 2018, available at: www.balkaninsight.com/en/article/ghost-court-delays-justice-for-kosovo-war-victims-03-19-2018.

[12] ibid.

[13] ICC Statute of the International Criminal Court, 2187 UNTS 90 (17 July 1998, entered into force 1 July 2002). The ICC is not, of course, a regional court. It is intended to address relevant crimes arising from anywhere in the world.

[14] *Prosecutor v Blaškić* (Decision on the Standing Objection of the Defence to the Admission of Hearsay with No Inquiry as to its Reliability) ICTY Case No IT-95-14-T (21 January 1998) para 5; see further C Schuon, *International Criminal Procedure: A Clash of Legal Cultures* (The Hague, TMC Asser Press, 2010), containing an in-depth comparison of the many variations in procedural rules between civil and common law jurisdictions, the RPE at the ICTY and the RPE at the ICC.

[15] Some examples of this are discussed below regarding the application of the proper burden of proof and the admission of trial evidence. See also D Jacobs, 'A Tale of Four Illusions: The Rights of the Defense before International Criminal Tribunals' in C Rohan and G Zyberi, *Defense Perspectives on International Criminal Justice* (Cambridge, Cambridge University Press, 2017) (which discusses the existence of such disputes in various contexts within the courts).

employed at any other ICL court. The ICC specifically does not permit it. The ECCC utilises a civil law system based upon the French legal system, which varies dramatically from all the ICL courts. The ICC, ECCC, STL and KSC permit victims to participate in trial proceedings with representation of counsel as a means to seek reparations. The SCSL, the ICTY, ICTR (and now the MICT)[16] do not, although they do maintain extensive victim/witness support offices which cover a range of issues such as witness protection and relocation, physical and psychological support and family issues.[17] Each court has its own unique rules of procedure and evidence, its own internal rules governing the conduct of judges, prosecutors and staff, differing codes of ethical conduct for defence counsel and prosecutors, and internal structures which vary from institution to institution. The substantive criminal law relied on by the ICL courts is essentially the same, but the founding statutes of the courts differ in many respects as to elements of certain crimes, modes of liability and the availability and effect of certain defences. The jurisprudence created as a result of proceedings at one international criminal court is not binding on any other international criminal court.[18]

As noted by one commentator: 'Variability, unpredictability, and unreliability are not the hallmarks of a mature judicial institution – not if the institution wishes the public at large to recognize it as fair and unbiased, and to accept its decisions and results'.[19]

Any 'system' of international criminal law must have clear standards and consistent procedures. As already noted, to achieve this the courts must also have the ability and willingness to learn from their successes and failures, as well as a means to adapt accordingly.

Additionally, if the purpose of ICL trials, as often claimed, is to establish a historical record, end impunity and bring justice to victims, the proceedings in the courts must be transparent: accessible to the press, academics and the public at large.

The pre-trial and trial proceedings conducted in the ICL courts – despite procedural differences between the courts – share some general similarities based on their statutes, rules and procedures. Those similarities are outlined very briefly here to provide a backdrop and context to some of the specific issues raised regarding the way in which trial proceedings may actually unfold. It is also important

---

[16] The MICT is the International Residual Mechanism for Criminal Tribunals and is mandated to perform the various functions carried out by the ICTY and ICTR now that those two tribunals are officially closed, such as some remaining appeal procedures, issues arising from the custody of convicted individuals, receipt of newly discovered evidence and, in the case of the ICTR, trials of remaining fugitives should those fugitives ever been found. See: www.irmct.org/en/about.

[17] As mentioned, all the ICL courts permit the participation of victims when their testimony is part of the proof of the prosecution cases.

[18] The exception is that the ICTY and ICTR share the same Appeals Chambers. Jurisprudence from that Chamber is binding on the trial chambers at both tribunals.

[19] M Karnavas, 'Academy Collogium International Criminal Justice and the Enforcement Deficit: In Search of *Sui Generis* Theories and Procedures', available at: michaelgkarnavas.net/blog/2017/10/31/academy-colloquium/.

to keep in mind, as observed by Judge Kwan of the ICTY regarding the mix of Western civil and common law principles, that this 'hybrid system cannot be explained solely from the perspective of one of the two systems but must be seen in the light of both.[20]

These courts are guided by human rights standards as delineated in the International Covenant on Civil and Political Rights (ICCPR) and the European Convention on Human Rights (ECHR). The Rules of Procedure and Evidence enacted at the courts, though they come from diverse legal traditions, reflect the intention to enforce these international standards in the daily functioning of the courts during pre-trial, trial, appeal and post-conviction proceedings. For example, all the ICL courts have adopted the standard of proof beyond a reasonable doubt and the presumption of innocence.[21]

Pre-trial investigation of cases is done entirely by the parties – the prosecution and defence – unlike most civil law systems. There is no independent investigating magistrate or investigating prosecutor.[22] Each party puts together its own information and evidence, including witness statements, expert reports, intelligence data, photographic evidence, military reports and all other evidence relevant to its case. Thereafter each court has its own rules governing the details as to when and how this information must be made available or disclosed to the opposing party as the case progresses through trial and appeal.

There are no juries in the ICL courts, unlike common law systems which require them in criminal cases unless the right to a jury trial is waived. ICL criminal cases are decided by majority vote of a bench comprised of three judges. These judges determine the facts and the law of the case, unlike jury trials during which a single trial judge is generally only empowered to make legal findings. A common law trial judge is meant to function primarily as the gatekeeper or referee between the parties in the trial process. He or she is not intended to take an active part in the litigation by, for example, extensively questioning witnesses. The questioning of witnesses by the trial bench occurs routinely in ICL courts. In practice, however, judges in the ICL courts vary quite a bit on the extent to which they engage in this kind of intervention. In the *Prlic et al* case at the ICTY, for example, one member of the bench was famous for conducting lengthy examinations of witnesses despite objections from prosecutors and defence counsel throughout trial.[23]

In all the ICL courts all relevant evidence is admissible at trial as is the usual practice in civil law systems. The heavy reliance on evidentiary rules of admission and exclusion that prevail in common law courts does not exist in the ICL courts. The ICL courts initially expressed a preference for witness testimony to be presented orally, in court, subject to cross-examination by the opposing party.

---

[20] Kwan, above (n 8).

[21] See, eg, ICCPR, Article 14; ECHR, Article 6.

[22] See discussion of the importance of this fact regarding subsequent trial proceedings and the receipt of evidence in F Guariglia, '"Admission" v "Submission" of Evidence at the International Criminal Court: Lost in Translation?' (2018) 16 *Journal of International Criminal Justice* 315.

[23] See, eg, *Prosecutor v Prlic et al*, ICTY Case No IT-04-74.

That preference was consistent not only with common law practice but also with provisions in the ICCPR and ECHR requiring that an accused has the right to confront and cross-examine the witnesses against him or her at trial.[24] That preference has eroded over the years. The ICTY amended its rules to provide for a number of circumstances permitting receipt of uncross-examined written witness statements.[25] The ICC, which originally did not allow those procedures, has now adopted them. Its rules of evidence now include provisions for admission of written statements which essentially mirror those enacted at the ICTY.[26]

This chapter does not list every instance in which the Rules of Procedure and Evidence and practice at the ICL courts utilise civil law principles and procedures as opposed to common law principles and procedures, particularly given the numerous nuanced differences between the various courts.[27] Suffice it to say that substantive and procedural aspects of both systems have been incorporated into the practices and procedures which are now being relied upon, interpreted and enforced at all the ICL courts and have been for some time.

IV. The Standard of Proof at Trial: Actualising the Difference Between Proof Beyond a Reasonable Doubt and *Intime Conviction*

The judges in the ICL courts come from all over the world. They are products of their legal cultures and bring those ingrained sensibilities with them to the bench in the ICL courts. Although all practitioners in the ICL courts are required to know and follow the applicable rules and law, not everyone is adaptable. One major concern is the conflict in application and understanding of the legal burden of proof and, in that context, the proper means for the evaluation of evidence.

International criminal law requires that a conviction cannot be entered unless the prosecution proves the case against the accused beyond a reasonable doubt.

---

[24] ICCPR, Article 14; ECHR, Article 6.

[25] See ICTY Rules of Procedure and Evidence, Rule 92 *et seq.*

[26] ICC Rules of Procedure and Evidence, Rule 68.

[27] The differences between the common and civil law systems have been the subject of many articles over the years including analysis of the interplay of the two systems in the international criminal courts. See, eg, M Rheinstein, 'Common Law and Civil Law: An Elementary Comparison' (1952) 22 *Revista Jurídica de la Universidad de Puerto Rico* 90; CB Picker, 'International Law's Mixed Heritage: A Common/Civil Law Jurisdiction' (2008) 41 *Vanderbilt Journal of Transnational Law* 1083; revised 23 January 2014; M Caianiello, 'Law of Evidence at the International Criminal Court: Blending Accusatorial and Inquisitorial Models' (2011) 36 *North Carolina Journal of International Law and Commercial Regulation* 287; K Ambos, 'International Criminal Procedure: Adversarial, Inquisitorial or Mixed?' (2003) 3 *International Criminal Law Review* 1; R Christensen, 'Getting to Peace by Reconciling Notions of Justice: The Importance of Considering Discrepancies between Civil and Common Legal Systems in the Formation of the International Criminal Court' (2001) 6 *UCLA Journal of International Law & Foreign Affairs* 391.

The accused's right to the presumption of innocence requires that this burden of proof always rests with the prosecution.[28] The accused has no burden to prove his or her innocence and no burden to present affirmative evidence at trial to disprove the prosecution case.[29] Thus far, all ICL courts claim to generally follow these principles.

The standard is fundamentally an objective one and has been defined as follows:

> It need not reach a certainty but it must carry a high degree of probability. Proof beyond a reasonable doubt does not mean proof beyond the shadow of a doubt. The law would fail to protect the community if it admitted fanciful possibilities to deflect the course of justice. If the evidence is so strong against a man as to leave only a remote possibility in his favour, which can be dismissed with the sentence, 'of course it is possible, but not in the least probable', the case is proved beyond a reasonable doubt, but nothing short of that will suffice.[30]

This burden of proof never shifts to the accused.[31] A finding of guilt can be made only if, after evaluating the strength of the prosecution evidence, the majority of a trial chamber finds the prosecution's burden has been met. The standard is also not limited solely to the ultimate question of guilt. It applies to each of the underlying facts which are essential to reaching a finding of guilt such as each element of each of the charged crimes, each element of each of the charged modes of liability, and any fact which is indispensable to or aimed at obtaining a conviction, such as identification of the accused.[32]

In the civil law system, the standard of proof – *intime conviction* – is a far more subjective one. As a general matter,[33] the trial in a civil law system is preceded by an investigation made by an investigating magistrate or prosecutor who, after investigating both inculpatory and exculpatory evidence, prepares a dossier containing

---

[28] See, eg, Article 76(1)(i) ICC Statute which provides that the accused is entitled 'not to have imposed on him or her any reversal of the burden of proof or any onus of rebuttal'.

[29] These rights are also articulated in all major human rights convictions. See, Article 14(2), ICCPR; Article 6(2), ECHR; Article 8(2), Inter-American Convention on Human Rights; Article 7(b), African Convention on Human Rights.

[30] *Prosecutor v Delalić et al* (Trial Judgment) IT-96-21-T (16 November 1998) para 600; citing *Miller v Minister of Pensions* (1947) 1 All ER 373, 373–74. And see *Prosecutor v Halilovic* (Appeal Judgment) IT-01-48-A (16 October 2007); *Prosecutor v Milutinovic et al* (Trial Judgment) IT-05-87-T (26 February 2009) paras 4, 62, 63. And see comprehensive discussion of the definition and application of the beyond a reasonable doubt standard in G Guy-Smith, "Burden of Proof and Presumption of Innocence' in *Manual on International Criminal Defence: ADC-ICTY Developed Practices* (UNICRI, ADC-ICTY, OSCE-ODIHR, 2011) 10.

[31] ICTY RPE, Rule 87(A); ICTR RPE, Rule 87(A), ICC Statute, Article 66(3).

[32] See, eg, *Prosecutor v Ntagrura et al* (Appeal Judgment) ICTR-99-46-A (7 July 2006) paras 169–70, 174–75; *Prosecutor v Limaj et al* (Trial Judgment) IT-03-66-T (30 November 2005) (*Limaj* Trial Judgment).

[33] It must be pointed out that not all civil law systems function in the same way; there are many variations between them. As one commentator has noted lawyers from common law countries can practise in foreign common law countries with little trouble as a general issue. Lawyers from civil law countries cannot due to the large number of differences between civil law systems despite the similar basis for the systems. Rheinstein, above (n 27).

the results of that investigation. That dossier is provided to the trial judges and comprises most, if not all, of the trial evidence. To convict an accused the court must be convinced that the facts brought against the accused are true. Hence, the civil law standard is based on an entirely different procedure in the gathering and presentation of trial evidence and conceptualises the burden of proof differently from the common law. Proof is understood as a subjective conclusion in the judge's mind, based on all the available evidence. The trial is meant to be a search for the truth.[34]

Although the ICL standard of proof beyond a reasonable doubt is well defined, some examples of the practical application of this standard in ICL cases suggest that the judges do not consistently apply it or consistently appreciate the role this standard plays in the assessment of the trial evidence. There is a profound logical and psychological difference between a trial process which objectively requires the prosecutor to meet a standard of proof regardless of the evidence produced by the accused, and a trial process which subjectively seeks to find the 'truth' however that truth might be revealed. Indeed, in the latter case there is usually an expectation on the part of the judges that the accused will present affirmative evidence to refute the prosecution case to assist the bench in its truth-seeking function.[35]

The *Limaj et al* case at the ICTY represents an example of the objective nature of the 'beyond a reasonable doubt' standard: the requirement that the prosecution *always* bears the burden of proof. In that case one of the accused, Haradin Bala, put on an affirmative defence – an alibi – which was ultimately rejected by the Trial Chamber. The rejection of the alibi did not result in a finding of guilt, however. In keeping with the requirement that the accused has no burden to establish innocence or disprove the prosecution case, the Chamber held that: 'so long as there is a factual foundation in the evidence the accused bears no onus to establish that alibi; it is for the Prosecution to eliminate any reasonable possibility that the alibi is true.'[36] As the *Limaj* Chamber explained: '[A[finding that an alibi is false does not itself establish the opposite to what it asserts. The prosecution must not only rebut the validity of the alibi but also establish beyond reasonable doubt the guilt of the Accused as alleged in the Indictment.'[37]

However, a comparable appreciation of the legally applicable burden of proof as a factor influencing procedures at trial was never recognised by the Court in one

---

[34] For a more in-depth discussion of the conceptual differences between the civil and common law standards of proof, and the psychological differences for triers of fact in both systems, see C Engel, 'Preponderance of the Evidence versus *Intime Conviction*: A Behavioral Perspective on a Conflict Between American and Continental European Law' (2009) 33 *Vermont Law Review* 435.

[35] Conceptually, this expectation challenges rights embodied in international documents such as: the presumption of innocence, proof beyond a reasonable doubt and the right to not be a witness against oneself amongst others.

[36] *Limaj* Trial Judgment, para 11.

[37] ibid; and see *Prosecutor v Vasiljevic* (Trial Judgment) IT-98-32-T (29 November 2002) para 15, fn 7.

notable case at the ICC. In the *Ntaganda* case at the close of the prosecution trial evidence, Mr Ntaganda requested leave to file a motion of 'no case to answer'.[38] The Trial Chamber refused to allow it, requiring, in effect, that Mr Ntaganda must proceed with a defence case. On appeal from that refusal Mr Ntaganda argued, among other matters, that he should not be required to elect to present evidence as part of an affirmative defence case without a prior determination that the prosecution had established at least a prima facie case against him during its case-in-chief at trial. Mr Ntaganda submitted that refusing to conduct such a review placed 'an undue burden on the exercise of the right to remain silent and its corollary, the privilege against self-incrimination'.[39]

The Appeals Chamber held that the Trial Chamber had the inherent discretion to permit a no-case-to-answer motion on a 'case-by-case' basis.[40] It recognised, as established in the jurisprudence of the ICTY and other international courts, that a 'no-case-to-answer' procedure protects 'the right of an accused not to be called on to answer a charge unless there is credible evidence of his implication in the offence with which he is charged'.[41] Although not mentioned in *Ntaganda*, that standard is also consistent with the internationally recognised requirements mentioned above that the prosecution has the burden of proof at trial; a burden which *never* shifts to the accused.[42]

The Appeals Chamber agreed that Ntaganda's motion was appropriate given the structure of the trial proceedings; a trial format consisting of a prosecution case followed by a defence case which is procedurally suited to a 'no-case-to-answer' procedure, including that 'the conclusion of the presentation of inculpatory evidence by the prosecution is a particularly appropriate juncture for such a procedure to be conducted'.[43]

It went on to explain, however, that the ICC legal framework includes procedures taken from civil law practice which are not found in the common law including the obligation of the prosecution to investigate both exculpatory as well as inculpatory evidence[44] and the need for a pre-trial chamber to determine

---

[38] *Situation in the Democratic Republic of Congo, in the case of the Prosecutor v Bosco Ntaganda*, No ICC-01/04-02/06 OA6, Judgment on the Appeal of Mr Bosco Ntaganda against 'The Decision on Defence Request for leave to file a "no case to answer" motion' (5 September 2017) (*Ntaganda* Appeal Judgment).

[39] *Ntaganda* Appeal Judgment, para 16.

[40] ibid, paras 42–45.

[41] ibid, para 46, citing *Prosecutor v Strugar*, ICTY Case No IT-01-42, 'Decision on Defence Motion Requesting Judgment of Acquittal Pursuant to Rule 98 *bis*' (21 June 2004) para. 13. And see Rule 98 *bis* ICTY Rules of Procedure and Evidence; Rule 98 *bis* ICTR Rules of Procedure and Evidence; Rule 98 SCSL Rules of Procedure and Evidence; Rule 167 Special Tribunal for Lebanon Rules of Procedure and Evidence; Rule 127 Kosovo Specialist Chambers & Specialist Prosecutor's Office Rules of Procedure and Evidence.

[42] The no-case-to-answer proceeding also protects the rights of the accused by essentially assuring the prosecution will put on the substance of its case during its case-in-chief, rather than holding back on some evidence for rebuttal after an affirmative defence case.

[43] *Ntaganda* Appeal Judgment, para 50.

[44] ICC Statute, Article 54(1)(a).

whether there are sufficient grounds to find the accused committed the crimes charged prior to holding the person for trial.[45] On that abstract basis it held that Mr Ntaganda's fair trial rights were adequately protected even though he was not allowed to test the prosecution evidence which was actually presented at trial by means of the no-case-to-answer motion.[46]

One is left to conclude that the *Ntaganda* judges – consistent with the notion of *intime conviction* – and contrary to the ICL requirement that the burden of proof never shifts to the accused – did not wish to make any factual findings unless and until they heard a defence case.

This decision exemplifies the dissonance and unfairness which can arise when select portions of the civil or common law systems, which have been adopted in the ICL hybrid mix, are taken out of their international context and relied upon as they would be in a domestic proceeding.

The *Ntaganda* Appeals Chamber had no basis upon which to find, for example, that the prosecution had, in fact, investigated exculpatory evidence on Mr Ntaganda's behalf. Nor was there any basis to believe that any such evidence was provided to Mr Ntaganda or his counsel. In fact, ICC case law is replete with complaints that the prosecution fails to comply with this obligation.[47] Unlike the domestic civil law dossier system, there was no neutral entity in Mr Ntaganda's case monitoring prosecution pre-trial investigations to ensure impartiality or thoroughness. The independent, unsupervised party-driven investigations conducted by the prosecution at the ICC are not the functional equivalent of a civil law dossier system.

In effect, the Appeals Chamber relied on abstract civil law procedures which do not exist at the ICC to deny Mr Ntaganda a significant procedural protection; an illustration of combining the 'worst aspects of the two models'.[48]

As a final cause for concern, the accused in the *Ruto et al* case at the ICC *were* permitted to bring a no-case-to-answer motion in their case; a fact raised in *Ntaganda* as cause to recognise the availability and appropriateness of the procedure. The Prosecution in *Ntaganda* argued that the fact Mr Ruto was afforded this

---

[45] *Ntaganda* Appeal Judgment, para 52, citing ICC Statute, Article 61(7). This finding is incorrect. Numerous common law jurisdictions conduct grand jury proceedings and/or preliminary hearings pre-trial to determine if there is sufficient evidence to hold an individual accused for trial. The existence of those pre-trial events does not prevent presentation of a no-case-to-answer motion based on the evidence which is subsequently actually produced at trial.

[46] *Ntaganda* Appeal Judgment, para 52. Since the no-case-to-answer procedure was never permitted there was no ruling on the substantive merits of such a motion.

[47] See, eg, S Kay, 'The Prosecution of Uhuru Kenyatta at the International Criminal Court', available at: www.internationallawbureau.com/wp-content/uploads/2015/01/report.pdf, and see *Prosecutor v Thomas Lubanga Dyilo*, ICC Case No 01/04-01/06 (trial case initially dismissed for failure of prosecution to disclose exculpatory evidence in its possession).

[48] See Caianiello, above (n 27). (In the context of discussing the hearsay rules in ICL courts, Caianiello notes: 'Perhaps the worst hypothesis for the fairness of the system occurs when, despite the accusatorial structure, hearsay evidence is broadly admitted. In such cases the process combines the worst aspects of the two models') 298.

procedural protection in his case did not mean Mr Ntaganda was entitled to the same protection in his.[49] The Appeals Chamber agreed.[50]

That finding bodes ill for the development of ICL into a mature system of well-reasoned, consistent jurisprudence. It supports – indeed promotes – the view that individual chambers within the ICC are not required to provide all accused with the same procedural rights.[51]

Another case which has raised problems of application of the ICL hybrid mix is the *Katanga* case in which the Trial Chamber, by majority vote and over the strong dissent of Judge Christine Van den Wyngaert, recharacterised the charges against Mr Katanga under Rule 55 of the ICC Rules and then convicted him based on that recharacterisation.[52] In essence the Majority, after hearing all the trial evidence including testimony from Mr Katanga, recharacterised the mode of liability, which had been charged at the initial confirmation of charges hearing from 'commission' under Article 25(3)(a) of the Rome Statute, to 'common purpose liability' under Article 25(3)(d).

The recharacterisation, while permitted by statute under specified conditions, violated a series of Mr Katanga's rights under the circumstances of his case given its timing, including his right to notice of the charges against him, the time and facilities to prepare a defence to such charges, and his right to make an informed decision as to whether to remain silent at trial.

As pointed out by the dissent:

> While the Appeals Chamber has upheld the validity of the regulation generally, it has stressed the need to ensure the rights of the accused to a fair and impartial trial are 'fully' protected, and has suggested that safeguards in addition to those outlined in regulation 55(2) and (3) may be required depending on the circumstances of the case. The Appeals Chamber has indeed emphasised that recharacterisation must not render the trial unfair. As such, when making a regulation 55(2) assessment, the Chamber must remain mindful of the rights of the accused. The Chamber must ensure that the accused: (i) receives prompt notice of the specific facts within the 'facts and circumstances described in the charges' which may be relied upon; (ii) is given adequate time and facilities for the effective preparation of his or her defence; (iii) is afforded the right to examine and have witnesses examined; and (iv) that the accused's right not to be compelled to testify is not infringed.
>
> Through the invocation of regulation 55 at this late stage, the Majority has 'mould[ed] the case against the accused' in order to reach a conviction on the basis of a form of criminal responsibility that was never charged by the Prosecution. In doing so, and contrary to article 74 and regulation 55(1), the Majority has substantially exceeded the

---

[49] *Ntaganda* Appeal Judgment, para 27.

[50] ibid, para 54.

[51] It is emphasised here that Mr Ntaganda's case did not involve the substantive merits of his proposed no-case-to-answer motion, *but his right to even bring such a motion as part of the trial procedure.*

[52] *Situation in the Democratic Republic of Congo in the Case of the Prosecutor v Germain Katanga and Mathieu Ngudjolo Chui*, ICC-01/04-01/07-3319, Decision on the implementation of regulation 55 of the Regulations of the Court and severing the charges against the accused persons, 21 November 2012 (*Katanga* Decision).

scope of the facts and circumstances as confirmed by the Pre-Trial Chamber. For this reason alone, I consider the judgment to be invalid as a matter of law (see *infra*, II.A) (footnotes omitted).[53]

In addition, it appears that the *Katanga* Majority, unlike the *Ntaganda* Chambers, was *not* willing to rely on the assumed neutrality or the assumed thoroughness of pre-trial procedures, such as the confirmation of charges hearing, and the evidence produced at that time as a basis for in-trial legal rulings. That inconsistency appears to rest on the legally impermissible basis of the application, between ICC chambers, of random, subjective legal standards rather than the objective standards required by the rule of law.

V. Ruling on the Admission of Trial Evidence Only at the End of Trial

The *ad hoc* tribunals and the ICC follow essentially adversarial procedures regarding the presentation of the parties' cases at trial by means of the presentation of evidence. In general, the prosecution presents its case-in-chief first, the accused then presents the defence evidence, if any, and the prosecution is entitled to a rebuttal if necessary.[54] Each party is entitled to confront and cross-examine witnesses presented in court by the opposing party. Clarity and consistency in the enforcement of these procedures is mandatory for the parties to make informed decisions as to what witnesses and other evidence to present at trial, to meet the burden of proof (for the prosecution) or to raise a reasonable doubt as to the strength of the evidence (for the accused).

In the *Haradinaj et al* case at the ICTY, for example, the three accused elected, at the close of the prosecution case-in-chief, not to put on any affirmative defence case. Instead all three accused rested their cases on the prosecution evidence, arguing that the prosecution evidence failed to prove the charges beyond a reasonable doubt.[55] The Trial Chamber agreed. Two accused were acquitted of all 37 counts charged in the indictment; one was convicted of two counts of the indictment.[56]

Prior to the start of the *Haradinaj et al* trial the Prosecution filed with the Trial Chamber a list of the witnesses to potentially be called at trial as well as a list of potential documentary and other evidence. The prosecution, as with any other

---

[53] *Katanga* Decision, paras 11–12. The dissent is 170 pages long and is an excellent illustration and examination of a clash of legal understanding of what should be reasonably clear ICC law on the part of the majority, as well as identifying the fundamental failure of the majority in that case to protect the rights of the accused as enumerated under the hybrid mix embraced in international criminal law.

[54] See, in general, ICC Rule 140.

[55] *Prosecutor v Haradinaj et al* (Trial Judgment) IT-04-84-T (3 April 2008) para 6. The parties did not bring a 'no-case-to-answer' motion under ICTY RPE Rule 98 *bis*. Their decision to present no defence case ended the evidentiary portion of the trial.

[56] ibid, paras 502–04.

party to a criminal trial, assessed the need to present individual items of evidence as the case proceeded and developed. The accused did likewise, introducing items of documentary evidence during cross-examination of prosecution witnesses as called for given the content of such testimony and the issues it raised.

The case represents a straightforward application of the appropriate standard and burden of proof under international criminal law and the appropriate procedures which apply in the trial process adopted at the *ad hoc* tribunals as well as the ICC.

Subsequent decisions in the *Bemba* and *Gbagbo* cases at the ICC, however, regarding the timing for admission of evidence at trial suggests there is significant inconsistency regarding the appropriate application and implementation of the legal burden of proof at ICL trials. The cases also raise concerns about judicial understanding of those burdens and how they play out during the trial process.[57]

In *Bemba* the majority of the Trial Chamber initially ruled that all the evidence listed by the Prosecution in its list of evidence filed pre-trial, including all written witness statements, would be admitted in evidence '*prima facie*' at the beginning of trial.[58] It was the Majority's view that admitting all the evidence prima facie would save 'significant' trial time. It agreed the parties could affirmatively object to items of evidence during trial.[59]

This decision was based primarily on the incorrect assumptions that the Pre-Trial Chamber prepares the case for trial – not the parties – that the ICC legal framework permitted admission of all written witness statements prepared pre-trial, and that the wholesale prima facie admission of evidence, not yet offered by any party at trial, did not violate the rights of the accused.[60]

The decision was subsequently overturned on appeal.[61] The Appeals Chamber held that evidence is not 'submitted' at trial until it is actually presented by the parties, on their own initiative or at the request of the Trial Chamber, for the purpose of proving or disproving facts in dispute, the prima facie admission of evidence without an item-by-item evaluation was outside the legal framework of the ICC, and the admission into evidence of written witness statements without a 'cautious' item-by-item analysis and without satisfying the applicable rules of procedure and evidence was incompatible with the principle of orality.[62] These are fundamental principles of law designed to protect the rights of the parties and

---

[57] As mentioned earlier, the jurisprudence and procedures developed at one ICL court are not binding on any other ICL court. There is no 'system' of international criminal law as such.

[58] *Situation in the Central African Republic in the Case of Prosecutor v Jean-Pierre Bemba Gombo*, ICC-01/05-01/08, Decision on the Admission into Evidence of Materials Contained in the Prosecution's List of Evidence (19 November 2010) (*Bemba* Admission Decision).

[59] *Bemba* Admission Decision, paras 23, 24.

[60] ibid, para 25.

[61] *Situation in the Central African Republic in the Case of Prosecutor v Jena-Pierre Bemba Gombo*, ICC-01/05-01/08 OA 5 OA 6, Judgment on the Appeals of Jean-Pierre Bemba Gombo and the prosecutor against the Decision of Trial Chamber III entitled 'Decision on the admission into evidence of materials contained in the prosecution's list of evidence' (3 May 2011) (*Bemba* Appeal).

[62] *Bemba* Appeal, paras 1–3

the integrity of the trial process itself. It is disturbing, to put it mildly, that a court charged with responsibility for adjudicating complex international criminal cases needed these principles explained.

Nonetheless, directly ignoring the teachings of *Bemba*, in *Gbagbo*, and contrary to the positions of all the parties,[63] the Trial Chamber ordered that rulings on the *admissibility* of evidence would not occur at the time the evidence was offered at trial but only after the close of all the evidence.[64] It agreed that evidence is 'submitted' at trial, within the meaning of Article 74(2), when it is presented by the parties on their own initiative or pursuant to a request from the Chamber for the purpose of proving or disproving facts in issue.[65]

It expressed the view that the Trial Chamber can rule on admissibility at the time the evidence is offered or could defer any determination of its probative value until the end of trial or could wait until the end of trial to make these rulings as 'part of the assessment of the evidence when it is evaluating the guilt or innocence of the accused'.[66] It chose the latter course.[67] The parties would not have rulings, until after the close of all the evidence, as to what evidence was actually going to be admitted and what was not.[68]

The *Gbagbo* court opined that it is only after all the evidence has been submitted that the Chamber is in a position to meaningfully assess each item of evidence.[69] It also concluded that deferring all evidentiary rulings until after the close of evidence would prevent multiple rulings on the same evidence.[70]

The Chamber dismissed the concern that rejecting an item of evidence only after the trial was over would detrimentally affect a party's chance to replace it with some other more acceptable evidence. It stated that:

> In the view of the Majority, the need to ensure the impartiality of the proceedings does not allow the Chamber to assist the parties with their preparations for the case or, even less, to permit them to 'remedy' any flaws which might affect their case, including their possible failure to satisfy their respective burden of proof.[71]

These rulings are incompatible with international legal principles which require a fair, transparent trial proceeding which recognises and upholds the rights of the accused. If an accused does not know which items of evidence offered by the

---

[63] para 11 (the parties and participants asked that the Court rule on the admissibility of evidence at the time the evidence is offered, on a 'rolling' basis).

[64] *Situation in the Republic of Cote d'Ivoire in the Case of Laurent Gbagbo and Charles Ble Goude*, ICC-02/11-01/15, Decision on the Submission and Admission of Evidence (29 January 2016) para 12 (*Gbagbo*).

[65] *Gbagbo*, paras 5–6.

[66] ibid, paras 7, 9.

[67] ibid, para 12.

[68] See a full discussion of the implications of these decisions in Guariglia, above (n 22) 315.

[69] *Gbagbo*, para 13.

[70] ibid, para 14.

[71] ibid, para 18 (this observation is surprising given the Chamber's equal concern that it fulfils its obligation to search for the truth. If a fact is relevant and subject to proof, it undermines the search for truth to make it impossible for a party to present acceptable evidence just because an initial attempt was found wanting).

prosecution will actually be admitted at trial and given weight, until after all the trial evidence is heard, he or she is denied the ability to make informed decisions as to what evidence to challenge, what evidence to cross-examine, what evidence to present as part of a defence case, if any.[72]

The same is true for the prosecution. If the prosecution relies on particular evidence as a means to prove its case beyond a reasonable doubt but does not know whether that evidence will actually be admitted until it is no longer possible to present additional evidence, how can the prosecution assure that it is meeting its burden of proof.

A trial chamber which renders timely, comprehensive, transparent rulings on the admissibility of evidence as the trial proceeds is not violating its impartiality. It is assisting the parties and properly so. It assists them by providing an intelligent, focused basis upon which to proceed with a trial which addresses the legal and factual issues which are in dispute. Such procedures do not improperly remedy 'flaws'. They are consistent with fair trial rights.

VI. Other Challenges Affecting the Development of a Mature, Reasonably Consistent, Fair Trial Process in the ICL Courts

This chapter has only touched upon certain of the fundamental issues which are raising concerns regarding the future effective and transparent functioning of the hybrid legal 'system' as practised in the ICL courts. The topic is huge and subject to constant debate. Many questions remain in addition to the few addressed here.

There is, as mentioned at the outset of this chapter, significant misunderstanding among the public about the ICL courts, what they are meant to accomplish, what they can accomplish and how they function.

Additionally, these courts are, for example, increasingly relying on closed and private sessions during trials, a process which precludes public viewing of proceedings. At times, protected witnesses are testifying and their identities cannot be made public. At times, sensitive governmental information is being presented which cannot be publicly revealed. These kinds of proceedings – 'closed and private' sessions excluding the public – should be exceptional, and permitted only when clear reasons, based on fair, strict and objective legal standards, have been articulated mandating their use. Court proceedings exist to address public and community concerns. They have not been created for a select few to render decisions that can affect a nation or even world affairs from behind closed doors by unelected officials.

---

[72] As at the time of writing, it is anticipated that an evidentiary decision, such as that returned in *Gbagbo* will also be entered in the *Ongwen* case – now set for trial in September 2018. (See *Prosecutor v Dominic Ongwen*, ICC-02/04-01/15.)

Indeed, how can the international community benefit from ICL proceedings in any of the ways touted on the various ICL court websites when proceedings take place in secret session, when written submissions are filed confidentially or when proceedings or submissions are conducted ex parte? A history book that had large sections blacked out would not be published and most assuredly would not be relied upon as a full and accurate record. Yet that is precisely the 'historical record' that is being produced by documents and transcripts of the ICL proceedings.

The ICL courts, as a group, have also traditionally excluded the Defence Function from their internal structures and overlooked the critical role the defence plays in assisting in the fair conduct of trials and the creation and development of a balanced system of international criminal law.

Prosecutors, members of chambers or individuals working within the court registries, all of whom are part of the court structure, work in offices located at the seat of the courts and have resources and institutional support. Similar resources have not been made available to the defence.

The failure to include the defence in the planning, education and structural development of the ICL institutions is a mistake. As one commentator pointed out, regarding the challenges faced by defence counsel when called upon to defend an accused in an international criminal court:

> Furthermore, lessons from earlier tribunals suggest that the mixture of legal traditions in the ICC will prove awkward for defense counsel, with all that implies for the accused, unless the defense counsel is accustomed to practicing in such a mixed jurisdiction. Thus, the merger of the two traditions in the ICC may have an impact on the justice afforded the accused, and, consequently, that afforded victims and humanity in general.[73]

Although a successful defence organisation was created at the ICTY it functions with extremely limited resources.[74] Two years ago, the ICC Bar Association was created as an association for defence counsel and victims' counsel at the ICC. That association operates with no resources other than voluntary dues from those counsel of the ICC official list of counsel who wish to contribute. It has not yet been officially recognised by the ICC.

There is need for training for other actors in the ICL community as well. One highly placed legal officer at the ICC believes the defence should allow the prosecution to investigate its defence cases since the prosecution is required under ICC rules to investigate exculpatory as well as inculpatory evidence. The suggestion

---

[73] Picker, above (n 27) 1088, citing S Rosenne, 'Poor Drafting and Imperfect Organization: Flaws to Overcome in the Rome Statute' (2000) 41 *Virginia Journal of International Law* 164, 184 (suggesting only two areas of the world where counsel is adequately familiar with both (civil and common law legal) systems ... Quebec and Cameroon'). And see 'Report of the Expert Group to Conduct a Review of the Effective Operation and Functioning of the International Tribunal for the former Yugoslavia' para 204, UN Doc A/54/634 (1999).

[74] Since the closure of the ICTY the ADC is now recognised as the association of defence counsel for the MICT and is known as the Association of Defense Counsel Practicing Before the International Criminal Tribunals.

reflects profound misunderstanding of the reality of the practice of international criminal law and the defence function. Among many other issues, defence counsel are ethically precluded from revealing their client communications, work product or case strategies to the prosecution. There is no reason for this kind of fundamental misunderstanding to continue to prevail at this point in the current ICL courts.

The concern about competence and integrity also extends to chambers, a concern articulated years ago by one of the most respected minds in the development of modern ICL courts, specifically regarding the ICC. Professor Cherif Bassiouni stated:

> There is no justification in the world for electing judges who are non-lawyers, who have no experience, who are diplomats or for adopting UN bureaucratic rules that make tribunals non-functioning and extremely costly. These are things we can fix. We must keep our legal institutions, strengthen them, don't cover up mistakes.[75]

Indeed, a secondary but equally important concern is the massive bureaucratic structure of the ICC and the use of its limited resources. Millions of euros are being spent yearly on an institution that has processed only a handful of cases since its first trial (*Lubanga*) began in 2009.[76] Given the worldwide jurisdiction of the ICC one may easily question whether its stated mandate – prosecution of war criminals, justice and reparations for victims, facilitation of peace and reconciliation in conflict and post-conflict regions – are realistic or can ever be met particularly under the current structures of that court.

VII. Conclusion

In any developing system the ability to recognise the mistakes and successes of its actors and policies is of significant importance. The development of a new system of law requires courageous, thoughtful input by individuals who are willing to challenge themselves so as to forage new approaches to old problems using the wisdom of the past and the creativity of the future. Our current system of international criminal law is most certainly a work in progress. It is also a noble experiment. It will succeed if we never forget the need to provide justice, seek to ensure an orderly society, and assure fairness and consistency in our efforts to define and enforce the rule of law.

---

[75] MC Bassiouni, 'Efficiency and the ICC' lecture, available at: iccforum.com/forum/efficiency-lecture.

[76] According to the ICC website three cases are currently in trial (*Ntaganda*, *Ongwen* and *Gbagbo*); three cases have resulted in acquittals (*Chui*, *Mbarushumana* and *Bemba* (acquitted on appeal)); two cases collapsed and were dismissed during or before trial for lack of evidence (*Kenyatta et al* and *Ruto and Sang*); and there have been two convictions (*Lubanga* and *Katanga*). One individual conceded his guilt (*Al Mahdi*) and one individual is awaiting trial (*Al Hassan*). Charges are pending against another 14 people none of whom have been arrested: www.icc-cpi.int/cases.

6

Agents and Agency in International Criminal Law: Intent and the 'Special Part' of International Criminal Law

KERSTIN BREE CARLSON[1]

I. Introduction

In July 2015, Danish newspapers buzzed with the news that the well-known 'Nazi hunter' Ephraim Zuroff had requested that Danish authorities charge Helmuth Leif Rasmussen, aged 90, for his participation in a Nazi concentration camp.[2] A 2014 book[3] had asserted that Rasmussen, together with other members of a Danish volunteer brigade, worked as guards in the Bobruisk camp in Belarus in 1942, where over 1,400 Jews were murdered. Rasmussen maintains he was a 17-year-old trainee separated from, and not involved in, ill-treatment of Jewish prisoners.[4] Following the war, Rasmussen reported what he had seen and experienced to the Danish authorities and was sentenced to six years in prison for crimes which included treason.[5]

---

[1] This research was supported by the Danish National Research Foundation and iCourts.

[2] JA Bjørnager and M Alsen, 'Nazijæger vil anmelde 90-årig dansker for krigsforbrydelser' ('Nazi hunter will arrest a 90-year-old Dane for war crimes') *Berlinske* (17 July 2015).

[3] T Stræde and D Larsen, *En skole i vold* (*A School in Violence*) (Copenhagen, Gyldendal, 2014). The 2014 book identified Rasmussen based on an interview Rasmussen made with Danish police in June 1945. The authors also interviewed Rasmussen in 2009 and 2010.

[4] JA Bjørnager and M Alsen, '90-årig afviser del i grusomheder' ('90-year-old denies taking part in atrocities') *Berlinske* (17 July 2015), available at: www.b.dk/nationalt/90-aarig-afviser-del-i-grusomheder. See also, Malcolm Brabant, 'Nazi hunter targets 90-year-old former labor camp guard in Denmark' *PBS Newshour* (22 July 2015), transcript available at: www.pbs.org/newshour/bb/nazi-hunter-targets-90-year-old-former-labor-camp-guard-denmark/: 'The Germans treated the Jews very badly, which we could not help but see, but we had no influence over it. When you were 17 years old, what can you do? I can tell you that it was unpleasant to watch. They beat them up with bats. But I had never seen the Germans kill Jews. I did see some of the Jews lying dead'.

[5] 'Denmark to take Nazi case 'very seriously'' *The Local* (21 July, 2015), available at: www.thelocal.dk/20150721/denmark-to-take-nazi-case-very-seriously; Flemming Emil Hansen, 'Pictured: Danish

The case in Denmark against Helmuth Leif Rasmussen was halted due to a lack of evidence;[6] other recent cases in Germany have brought convictions.[7] These cases are demonstrative of a series of issues that accompany questions of culpability for actors caught up in state crimes,[8] a category this chapter calls 'prison guard cases', though in truth the group is larger and more diverse. Prison guard cases, which can be set in opposition to 'big fish cases' that try masterminds or leaders of violence, present a number of juridical, criminological and philosophical difficulties. These low-level offenders have proven foundation to the burgeoning jurisprudence of international criminal law (a field that holds individuals criminally liable for violations of international humanitarian law, crimes against humanity and genocide). International criminal law has determined that the liability of prison guards is not necessarily constructed on personal animus or malice; guards' knowledge of criminal conduct and their furtherance of criminal activities is sufficient participation to incur liability. This standard, as the Rasmussen case demonstrates, can be much less rigorous than domestic criminal law standards.[9] And as Germany's 2011 conviction of John Demjanjuk suggests, the international criminal law standard may be entering some domestic jurisdictions as well, for application to state-sponsored atrocity crimes.[10]

The collective nature of grave violations of international humanitarian law raises important questions regarding individuals' 'agency', ie, their capacity to meaningfully choose their own conduct and its character. The fact that these individuals may not consciously choose to violate the norms of international criminal

---

Nazi volunteer facing mass murder trial for horrors at death camp where 1,400 Jews were forced to dig their own graves and strip naked before being shot in the head' *The Daily Mail* (27 July 2015), available at: www.dailymail.co.uk/news/artinternational criminal lawe-3173507/Pictured-Danish-Nazi-volunteer-facing-mass-murder-trial-horrors-death-camp-1-400-Jews-forced-dig-graves-strip-naked-shot-head.html#ixzz3wSL4UiU9.

[6] E Toft, DR, 'Manglende beviser redder 91-årig dansker fra retssag om krigsforbrydelser' ('An absence of evidence saves 91-year-old Danish man from criminal investigation regarding war crimes') 4 November 2016, available at: www.dr.dk/nyheder/indland/manglende-beviser-redder-91-aarig-dansker-fra-retssag-om-krigsforbrydelser.

[7] O Groening, the 'book keeper of Auschwitz' was sentenced to four years in prison in 2016. This followed the 2011 conviction of John Demjanjuk and a revision of German criminal law. See D Lawrence, *The Right Wrong Man: John Demjanjuk and the Last Great Nazi War Crimes Trial* (Princeton, NJ, Princeton University Press, 2016).

[8] There are of course some prison guard cases where guards have committed violence outside their professional obligations; these are not the cases considered here.

[9] Explaining his office's decision not to indict Rasmussen, the prosecutor told the Associated Press: 'To be prosecuted for participation in mass killings requires a closer connection to the crime itself. You do not prosecute a known burglar for lots of burglaries in a neighborhood simply because he was in the area at the time of break-ins. You need evidence' (4 November 2016), reported at: www.dailymail.co.uk/wires/ap/artinternational criminal lawe-3904602/Denmark-ends-probe-Dane-WWII-murder-Jews.html.

[10] Germany has been prosecuting guard cases since reunification; its border guard prosecutions were also considered by the European Court of Human Rights. See discussion in R Geiger, 'The German Border Guard Cases and International Human Rights' (1998) 9 *European Journal of International Law* 540.

law challenges the justice ideals borrowed from domestic criminal law, specifically normative justifications for punishment which underwrite the discipline. At the same time, defendants before international criminal tribunals become, in effect, agents of international criminal law because the law is built on them. As the comparison between the Rasmussen and Demjanjuk cases demonstrates, individual adjudications, framed by lawyers for the prosecution and defence, have the capacity to move the ideals and principles underwriting international humanitarian law into criminalised action.

The chapter focuses on the problem of prison guards in order to illustrate the 'agency paradox' inherent in international criminal law, where defendants are both central agents of international criminal law (through their commission of acts deemed criminal, and through their legal construction of these acts) as well as stripped of agency (where justification, excuse and context are generally rejected by the special part of international criminal law defining crimes, and are considered instead as sentencing factors applicable to any crime, ie, part of the general part of international criminal law). This trend becomes particularly evident when one examines the doctrines of liability (usually belonging to the general part) applied disparately from case to case. The chapter argues that the agency paradox of prison guard cases highlights a muddling of the special and general parts of international criminal law, a doctrinal confusion and inconsistency that threatens the coherence and legitimacy of international criminal law, thereby challenging the human rights recognitions that accompany that project.

II. Prison Guard Cases

The power of international criminal law's normative reach is based on the observation that violations of core human rights, while often dreamed up in the heads of dictators and oligarchs and effectuated through complex organisations, are always, necessarily, carried out by individuals. International criminal law takes individual actors, and their specific culpability, as the subject of its mandate, because were regular people, ordinary foot soldiers, to reject the demands of dictators and oligarchs, many human rights violations could not be carried out.

This approach to international criminality, which borrows heavily from domestic systems' methods of social control[11] raises a number of moral and legal quandaries at the international level. This first section briefly outlines these arguments, and then turns to the discussions raised by a historical address of prison guard cases to consider the normative issues raised by prosecutions of individuals carrying out the dictates of human-rights-violating states.

---

[11] A Cassese, 'On the Current Trends Towards Criminal Prosecution and Punishment of Breaches of International Humanitarian Law' (1998) 9 *European Journal of International Law* 2.

A. Moral and Legal Quandaries Presented

Prison guard cases exhibit the conflicts inherent in the application of international criminal law. On the one hand, state crimes require individual participation, and therefore, the refusal by individuals to participate could slow or eliminate state commissions of atrocity. Human rights violations do not commit themselves but rather require discrete, individual action to accomplish them. On the other hand, requiring individuals to engage in a human rights calculus (or face liability under international criminal law) demands that they be, in Koskenniemi's analysis, 'heroes'[12] because it requires that they, acting outside prevailing social or state norms[13] determine which acts violate international criminal law and cease participation that in any way assists, furthers, or enables the violation of the prohibitions of international criminal law. To demand that people perform as 'heroes' in order to escape criminal liability violates key tenets of fairness enshrined in criminal justice and its normative justifications, however.[14] The burgeoning field of international criminal law, with its evolving norms, also therefore incorporates a certain amount of prospective crimes, which potentially violates *nullem crimen sine lege* norms.[15]

Related to the unresolvable hero/everyman dichotomy evident in international criminal law is an accompanying context/act dichotomy. Prison guard cases have the capacity to showcase how an act is either legal or illegal depending upon the wider context in which it is performed. This wider context is frequently, if not always, outside the control of the individual actor. Thus, in the Rasmussen case opening this chapter, Rasmussen's own account of his activities consists of serving as a trainee in a concentration camp, where one of his trainee rotations – guarding the camp perimeter – enabled him to see the mistreatment of Jewish prisoners in another area of the camp. According to Rasmussen's account, his professional duties brought him no closer to this mistreatment than witnessing its effects (dead bodies; starving inmates). In the context of international criminal law, however, Rasmussen's awareness, coupled with his service (which assisted the entity responsible for violations of prisoners' rights: had Rasmussen not patrolled the perimeter, someone else would have had to do it, depleting the state of resources put in service of human rights violations; or had Rasmussen not patrolled, perhaps escape or rescue for the camp's victims would have become more likely) establishes his

---

[12] M Koskenniemi, 'Between Impunity and Show Trials' (2002) 6 *Max Planck Yearbook of United Nations Law* 1.

[13] MA Drumbl, *Atrocity, Punishment, and International Law* (Cambridge, Cambridge University Press, 2007).

[14] S Mohammed, 'Deviance, Aspiration, and the Stories We Tell: Reconciling Mass Atrocity and the Criminal Law' (2015) 124 *Yale Law Journal* 1628.

[15] K Ambos, 'Remarks on the General Part of International Criminal Law' (2006) 4 *Journal of International Criminal Justice* 660.

culpability in committing a crime,[16] or alternatively aiding and abetting a criminal system.[17] Thus, the international criminal law standard for prison guards often amounts to a strict liability standard, where to participate in a criminal system is to assume legal responsibility for wider criminal acts perpetrated by that system.[18]

It is here important to distinguish prison guard cases, where guards are charged with working/serving an illegal entity, from those cases where guards are charged with committing violence outside their official or professional duties. Many prison guard cases involve situations where the violence of social dissolution has given free rein to sadists and miscreants who are acting as camp guards. These are not the cases this chapter is concerned with. Certain forms of violence and criminality are permissible when performed by legitimate states (imprisonment, interrogations, even arguably ethnic cleansing, when described as 'population transfer'), whereas certain forms of violence (beatings, murder, rape)[19] are likely never legally permissible under international criminal law. Yet within the sphere of permissible, legitimate state violence, prison guards at international criminal law will face the possibility of prosecution depending on what 'ultimate goal' the violence of the system they serve is pursuing. This observation challenges some normative justifications underwriting the normative legitimacy of punishment through the criminal law.[20]

A central problem of assigning culpability to prison guards is the *individual* guilt ascribed for what is essentially a *collective* crime. Again, when considering cases outside those where war allows deviant violence to flourish, prison guard cases often concern individuals who have no desire or intent to commit crime, and who are suddenly made the tools of state, group, or collective processes engaged in criminal behaviour. The incommensurate application of individual liability for collective acts has been a staple of critiques of both international criminal law[21] as well as other forms of criminal law.[22]

---

[16] See *Prosecutor v Miroslav Kvočka, Mlađo Radić, Zoran Žigić, and Dragoljub Prcać*, ICTY Case No IT-98–30/1-T (2 November 2001) (*Kvočka* Trial Chamber). *Prosecutor v Miroslav Kvočka, Mlađo Radić, Zoran Žigić, and Dragoljub Prcać*, ICTY Case No IT-98–30/1-A (28 February 2005). See also Article 25 (c)(3) Rome Statute.

[17] See *Prosecutor v Momčilo Perišić* (Judgment) IT-04–81 (6 September 2011).

[18] This participation, which is 'commission' at law, must be distinguished from 'membership' in organisations, which was found not to be criminalisable at the IMT at Nuremberg, and remains non-criminalised at international criminal law. Ambos, above (n 15) argues that certain international criminal law doctrines collapse this necessary distinction.

[19] But see Heidi Matthews, 'Redeeming Rape: Berlin 1945 and the Making of Modern International criminal law' (presented at iCourts 4 December 2015) (on file with author) imagining the possibility of 'legitimate rape' in service to a 'just war'.

[20] HLA Hart, *Punishment and Responsibility* (Oxford, Clarendon Press, 1968); A Ashworth, *Principles of Criminal Law*, 6th edn (Oxford, Oxford University Press 2009).

[21] P Allott, *Eunomia: New Order for a New World* (Oxford, Oxford University Press, 1990); Drumbl, above (n 13).

[22] GP Fletcher, *Rethinking Criminal Law* (Boston, MA, Little Brown & Co, 1977).

Finally, international criminal law arguably runs afoul of individual rights through its use of individuals to establish public policy via selective prosecutions. As currently practiced, the prosecution of certain, somewhat opportunistically chosen individuals before international criminal tribunals is justified both as legal and moral, under the rubric that such individuals violated international criminal law, and their violations are not lessened by the fact that not all similarly situated individuals will be prosecuted by international criminal tribunals. Yet criminal law domestically draws its legitimacy from rule of law norms that demand equal treatment for like offenders, and criminal law as social control thrives where state prosecution is the expected response to a criminal violation. At international criminal law, however, prosecution by a governing authority remains the infinitesimally unlikely exception, and not the rule.

Modern international criminal law, as applied by international criminal tribunals, functions within a utilitarian, policy-oriented landscape, situating part of its moral legitimacy in the example-making value of international prosecutions to put 'would-be' offenders on notice that their actions will not meet with impunity.[23] This utilitarian rationale challenges normative justifications of punishment that are located in the requirement that the individual punished, as part of a community, understands and acknowledges her wrong.[24]

B. Prison Guard Jurisprudence in International Criminal Law

International criminal tribunals (ICTs) face particular obstacles in trying criminal acts. Battlegrounds are not conducive to criminal investigation, and prosecution often occurs only years after the events. Unlike domestic criminal courts, ICTs usually cannot compel state organs to produce relevant documentary or physical evidence, even where such evidence exists. Thus, ICTs often face steep challenges in creating the necessary links in a causal chain of responsibility that would tie a victim of a particular violent event to an individual defendant.

So far, ICTs have developed distinct methods to address this problem. At the International Criminal Tribunal for the former Yugoslavia (ICTY), the method is a theory of criminal liability called 'joint criminal enterprise' (JCE). Stemming from an early appellate decision,[25] JCE has gone on to become the ICTY's workhorse, featuring in nearly all ICTY convictions. JCE applies legal reasoning developed in

---

[23] K Carlson, 'International Criminal Law and its Paradoxes: Implications for Institutions and Practice' (2017) 5 *Journal of Law and Courts* 33.

[24] DR Antony 'Can We Punish the Perpetrators of Atrocities?' in T Budholm and T Cushman (ed) *The Religious in Response to Mass Atrocity: Interdisciplinary Perspectives* (Cambridge, Cambridge University Press 2009); A Norrie, *Punishment, Responsibility and Justice: A Relational Critique* (Oxford, Oxford University Press, 2000).

[25] *Prosecutor v Duško Tadić* (Appeals Chamber Judgment) IT-94-1-A (15 July 1999) (*Tadić* Appeals Chamber Judgment).

the Second World War era case law to interpret Article 7.1. of the ICTY Statute concerning individual criminal responsibility.[26] At the ICTY, JCE is sometimes privately referred to as 'just convict everybody'.[27]

JCE mitigates the evidentiary challenges arising at international criminal law by making it possible to prosecute anyone found to share 'the same criminal intent'[28] with whoever perpetrated a crime, even where such perpetrator is unknown. This addresses difficulties in chain of command structures otherwise necessary in proving command responsibility,[29] as well as offering the possibility of tying various individuals to any given crime. Although the International Criminal Court (ICC), a permanent body hearing international criminal law cases, has formally declined to recognise JCE jurisprudence, it employs a similar theory of liability that makes it possible to capture 'participants' removed from immediate violence.[30]

As developed by the ICTY, there are three arms of JCE. JCE I concerns co-perpetration, cases where all actors, in pursuit of a common plan, possess the same criminal intention.[31] JCE II, termed a variant of JCE I, applies this common plan to concentration camp cases. In the most far-reaching and controversial arm of the doctrine, JCE III, guilt rides on the *foreseeability* that crime will result from conduct. Under the JCE III doctrine, the Appeals Chamber found the defendant guilty of a murder in a location it could not show he had physically been.[32] JCE has been heavily criticised by a wide range of commentators, and nearly universally critiqued outside the doctrinal halls of international criminal law practice. Within those doctrinal halls, however, JCE remains a fast standard, even while its evolution suggests an imprecision and unpredictability which would challenge its legality, as discussed further in section III.

C. Domestic 'Transitional Justice' Prosecutions of Prison Guards

Prison guards have also been the target of domestic prosecutions as elements of 'transitional justice' processes. Transitional justice is the process societies undergo

---

[26] Like the US jurisprudence regarding conspiracy, JCE must be defined as a means of 'doing' crime, because the ICTY statute specifically precludes 'being criminal' vis-à-vis guilt by association or culpability based on membership in a criminal group. *Report of the Secretary General pursuant to paragraph 2 of Security Council Resolution 808* (1993), 3 May 1993 (S/25704) §§ 50, 51. This was reaffirmed in *Prosecutor v Milomir Stakić*, ICTY Case No IT-97-24 (Appeals Chamber, 22 March 2006).

[27] Author interviews, The Hague, May 2005. See also J Ohlin, 'Joint Criminal Confusion' (2009) 12 *New Criminal Law Review* 406; ME Badar, '"Just Convict Everyone!" – Joint Perpetration: From *Tadić* to Stakić and Back Again' (2006) 6 *International Criminal Law Review* 293.

[28] *Tadić* Appeals Chamber Judgment, para 220.

[29] AM Danner and JS Martinez 'Guilty Associations: Joint Criminal Enterprise, Command Responsibility, and the Development of International Criminal Law' (2005) 93 *California Law Review* 75.

[30] Ohlin, above (n 27).

[31] *Tadić* Appeals Chamber Judgment, para 196.

[32] ibid.

in addressing past injustice as they move from war to peace or from a repressive regime to a democracy.[33] These domestic processes often borrow rationales or argumentation from international prosecutions, even as they face particular domestic legal obstacles: legal experts in Denmark queried on the Rasmussen case, for example, opined that Danish legal criteria foreclose prosecution,[34] which is precisely what the prosecutor ultimately determined. This has not been the case in Germany, however, where a recent wave of prosecutions of one-time prison guards now in their nineties has resulted in several prosecutions. This builds on the prosecutions of East German border guards following reunificiation,[35] upheld by the European Court of Human Rights.[36]

The question of the criminality of the East German border guards who shot defectors while following East Germany's policies showcases difficult moral and legal questions. While these guards were 'just following orders' it was also possible to shoot at defectors and miss – should those who shot not to miss be deemed criminals, given that others shot and missed? Yet even this question – the idea of shooting to miss – ignores the context in which these guards carried out their duties. East German border guards who successfully shot would-be defectors were awarded medals, state congratulations, and bonuses.[37] Moreover, these guards were under orders to 'ensure the security of the GDR's State border ... to [not] permit border crossings [Grenzdurchbrüche], to arrest "border violators" or to "annihilate" them [vernichten] and to protect the State border at all costs [unter allen Bedingungen]'.[38] In the case of a successful border crossing, guards were subject to military prosecution.[39] Here we see how the guards, agents of an illiberal state, were the tools of state criminality. Beyond resisting the objectives of their office and the commission of their duties, in order to deliberately shoot to miss, East German border guards would have needed to conceptualise defectors outside the frames in which they were working and in which they were socialised, the kind of heroism that criminal law does not require. Finally, questions of East German border guard culpability elide with the methods with which Germany, rather infamously, swept its Nazis under the rug in the post-war years as part of the national policy of *Vergangenheitsbewältigung*. Under this policy, the Holocaust is remembered in very particular ways, and not generally through the prosecution of Nazi war criminals.[40]

---

[33] J Quinn, *Reconciliation(s): Transitional Justice in Postconflict Societies* (Montreal, McGill-Queen's Press, 2009).

[34] See: www.pbs.org/newshour/bb/nazi-hunter-targets-90-year-old-former-labor-camp-guard-denmark/.

[35] Geiger, above (n 10).

[36] *Streletz, Kessler and Krenz v Germany* (App nos 34044/96, 35532/97 and 44801/98) European Court of Human Rights (22 March 2001).

[37] ibid, 15.

[38] ibid, 8.

[39] ibid, 69.

[40] N Frei, *Adenauer's Germany and the Nazi Past: The Politics of Amnesty and Integration* (New York, Columbia University Press, 2002).

The problematic themes emerging from these prosecutions perhaps help explain why defendants in prison guard cases generally profess that they do not 'feel guilty'. The 90-year-old Dane, Lief Rasmussen, for example, told interviewers that he was a '17 year old kid with no choices, I went where I was told'.[41] A former guard at Auschwitz, on trial in Germany in 2013, asserted he did not 'feel like a criminal'.[42] Oskar Groening, a bookkeeper at Auschwitz put on trial two years ago, told the Luneburg court that he felt a 'moral guilt' but rejected a legal culpability.

The responses of the accused are reminiscent of Karl Jasper's observations regarding guilt.[43] In his post-war lectures, Jaspers identified four categories of guilt: criminal; political; moral; and metaphysical. For many criminal law categories, particularly violent crimes, domestic criminal law imagines a harmonisation between acts recognised as criminal and other forms of guilt.[44] In interviews conducted with defendants before the ICTY, researchers Mina Raushenbach, Damien Scalia and Christian Staerklé[45] found that defendants charged with personally committing violent crimes generally recognised the criminality of their actions. Those charged with crimes resulting from the politics of their participation, however, generally averred they did not feel guilty.

The second issue raised by recent prosecutions is the question of the punishment extracted for sharing information. Transitional justice processes value information and the revelation of facts as themselves capable of promoting social and personal healing.[46] Yet transitional justice policy mechanisms have historically faced the question of 'truth versus justice'. Truth commissions often offer amnesties from criminal punishment in exchange for full disclosure. The 'truth versus justice' argument weighs the problem of the social benefits of truth commissions versus punitive measures like tribunals. Grave crimes admitted and unpunished challenge justice and fairness norms. Tribunals are imperfect fact-finders, however, and punishment can hamper knowledge and the free flow of information.

---

[41] Rasmussen further speculates that had he not lived with his Nazi uncle, he would never have joined the Danish Hitler youth brigade as a minor and been sent to Belarus.

[42] F Bohr, C Meyer and K Wiegrefe, 'Interview with an Auschwitz Guard: "I Do Not Feel Like a Criminal"' *Der Spiegel* 35/2014 (25 August 2014); see also Felix Bohr 'Auschwitz Trial: Late Case Raises Questions about Justice System' *Der Spiegel* 40/2013 (30 September 2013), available at: www.spiegel.de/international/germany/former-auschwitz-worker-hans-lipschis-faces-trial-a-925247.html.

[43] K Jaspers, 'The Question of German Guilt' in G Mettraux (ed), *Perspectives on the Nuremberg Trial* (Oxford, Oxford University Press 2008 [1948]).

[44] N Walker, *Why Punish?* (Oxford, Oxford University Press, 1991).

[45] M Rauschenbach, D Scalia and C Staerklé, 'Paroles d'accusés sur la légitimitée la justice pénale international' (2012) *Chronique de criminology* 727; M Rauschenbach, D Scalia and C Staerklé, 'Accused for Involvement in Collective Violence: The Discursive Reconstruction of Agency and Identity by Perpetrators of International Crimes' (2015) 37 *Political Psychology* 219.

[46] A Krog, *Country of My Skull: Guilt, Sorrow, and the Limits of Forgiveness in the New South Africa* (New York, Times Books, 1999); J Rowen, *Searching for Truth in the Transitional Justice Movement* (Cambridge, Cambridge University Press, 2017).

In recent domestic cases, these issues arise in a novel manner because prosecutions have been born of shared information. As Rasmussen noted:

> I should never have told about the ugly things I saw. I never thought [speaking about it] could harm me ... You don't imagine that if you tell what you saw other people doing, that you can suddenly be seen as a part of it.[47]

Examples such as Rasmussen's suggest that zealous prosecution can harm the search for information.

Finally, there is the issue of who gets prosecuted at international criminal law: leaders or followers. Opinion is divided over whether international criminal law is, and should be, primarily an instrument to punish designers and leaders of human rights violations, or whether international criminal law should be equally applicable to the rank and file. The Nuremberg and Tokyo tribunals focused on senior leaders; trials following, however, targeted both higher- and lower-level perpetrators. Kai Ambos, for example, argues that international criminal law's construction makes it 'clear that such a model of attribution targets primarily the leadership level of the given organization since only the leaders are able to control and dominate the collective action with full responsibility'.[48] The ICC, however, has issued contradictory opinions regarding who it will try, leaders versus lower-level perpetrators. The ICTY focused on low-level perpetrators at the beginning of its practice because they were the only defendants the Tribunal could lay its hands on, and because arguably low-level perpetrators would help set the scene for higher-level prosecutions. The goal of 'moving up the power pyramid' iterated by ICTY prosecutors, however, has largely not come to pass, as recent prosecutions of senior leaders have resulted in a series of contentious acquittals.[49]

III. The 'Special Part': Criminalising Action at International Criminal Law

Recent scholarship on the normative justifications for punishment is bringing focus to the question of 'criminalisation' – the question of definitions of crimes – in

---

[47] 'Nazijæger er på jagt efter 90-årige Helmuth Rasmussen: "Hvad er det, jeg har gjort forkert?"' ('What did I do wrong?') *Berlinske* (18 July 2015), available at: www.bt.dk/danmark/nazijaeger-er-paa-jagt-efter-90-aarige-helmuth-rasmussen-hvad-er-det-jeg-har-gjort. 'Jeg skulle aldrig have fortalt, at jeg så de grimme ting. Jeg tænkte ikke, at det kunne skade mig. Hvis du ser noget, tror du ikke, det skader dig. Man forestiller sig ikke, at fordi man fortæller, hvad man har set andre gøre og lave, at man så pludselig selv bliver en part i det' (translation by author).

[48] Ambos, 'Remarks on the General Part of International Criminal Law', above (n 15) 664.

[49] See, eg, *Prosecutor v Ante Gotovina, Ivan Čermak and Mladen Markač*, ICTY Case No IT-06-90-PT (16 November 2012); *Prosecutor v Milan Milutinović et al*, ICTY Case No IT-04-84 (26 February 2009) (Milutinović acquitted); *Prosecutor v Haradinaj et al*, ICTY Case No IT-04-84 (29 November 2012); *Prosecutor v Naser Orić*, ICTY Case No IT-03-68 (3 July 2008); *Prosecutor v Vojislav Šešelj*, ICTY Case No IT-03–67 (31 March 2016). Šešelj, was later sentenced to 10 years, or time served, by the Appeals Chamber. *Prosecutor v Vojislav Šešelj*, MICT-16-99 (UN Mechanism for International Criminal Tribunals (11 April 11 2018).

criminal law theory.[50] This part of the criminal law, which contains definitions of offences, is known as the 'special part'. The special part is distinguished from the 'general part,' which develops doctrines and rationales applicable across many particular crimes. While numerous surveys, following the seminal work of HLA Hart,[51] have considered the 'general part' of criminal law, ie, the doctrines, rules and definitions at issue in the criminal law, theoretical considerations of the special part are a relatively recent development.[52] Such considerations often focus on how distinctions between general rules and specific doctrines should be made.[53]

As international criminal law develops, theorists and practitioners have also debated the content of, and even the necessary distinctions between, a general and special part of international criminal law. The following section presents these debates and distinctions, in order to inform a discussion in the chapter's final section, regarding how elisions in these categories demonstrate normative gaps in the construction and application of international criminal law.

A. The General and Special Parts of Criminal Law

Criminal law is theoretically divided between its 'general' and 'special' parts. The special part consists of specific criminal offences, and categorises them by families.[54] The general part is comprised of doctrines (insanity, necessity, provocation etc) applicable to some or all of the special part.[55] Theoretical scholarship on criminal law, following the work of HLA Hart in the mid-twentieth century, typically focused on the general part of criminal law. Recent theoretical criminal law scholarship, however, has advocated greater attention for criminal law's special part. Anthony Duff and Stuart Green's 2005 edited volume queried movement between the categories describing the special part.[56] Nicola Lacey has critiqued organisation and theorisation more generally.[57]

---

[50] N Lacey, 'Legal Constructions of Crime' in M Maguire, R Morgan and R Reiner (eds), *The Oxford Handbook of Criminology* (Oxford, Oxford University Press, 2002); RA Duff and SP Green, 'Introduction: Defining Crimes' in RA Duff and SP Green (eds), *Defining Crimes: Essays on the Special Part in Criminal Law* (Oxford, Oxford University Press, 2005).

[51] Hart, above (n 20).

[52] N Lacey, 'Historicising Criminalisation: Conceptual and Empirical Issues' (2009) 72 *Modern Law Review* 936.

[53] Duff and Green, above (n 50).

[54] J Gardner, 'On the General Part of the Criminal Law' in RA Duff (ed), *Philosophy and the Criminal Law: Principle and Critique* (Cambridge, Cambridge University Press, 1998).

[55] J Horder, 'The Classification of Crimes and the Special Part of the Criminal Law' in RA Duff and SP Green (eds), *Defining Crimes: Essays on the Special Part in Criminal Law* (Oxford, Oxford University Press, 2005) 25.

[56] Duff and Green, above (n 50).

[57] N Lacey, 'Contingency, Coherence and Conceptualism: Reflections on the Encounter between "Critique" and "the Philosophy of the Criminal Law"' in RA Duff (ed), *Philosophy and the Criminal Law* (Cambridge, Cambridge University Press, 1998); Lacey, 'Historicising Criminalisation, above (n 52).

At the same time as domestic criminal law theorists have been calling for new attention regarding the organisation and normative legitimation of criminal law, the law and practice of international criminal law has been developing as a field.[58] Numerous volumes considering the theory and practice of ICTs have been produced in the past two decades, following the resurgence and explosive growth of international criminal law.[59]

Although the practice of the *ad hoc* tribunals for the former Yugoslavia and Rwanda, and the growing jurisprudence of the permanent ICC, have created rich and extensive materials regarding the doctrine and application of international criminal law, theoretical work regarding the doctrinal coherence of international criminal law is arguably still in its infancy. Although debates regarding the form and content of international criminal law accompanied the ICTs at Nuremberg and Tokyo and followed the historical considerations of these tribunals, it is only with the resurgence of international criminal law as a mechanism of transitional justice, ie, international criminal law as a global policy directive, that theoretical work regarding the socially constitutive potential of international criminal law has developed.

Nicola Lacey defines 'criminalisation' as a conceptual framework for gathering subjects of criminal law and criminology/criminal justice which is capable of

> [e]scaping the notion of crimes as 'given' ... captur[ing] the dynamic nature of the field
> as a set of interlocking practices in which the moments of 'defining' and 'responding to'
> crime can rarely be completely distinguished and in which legal and social (extra-legal)
> constructions of crime constantly interact.[60]

---

[58] MJ Christiansen, 'Preaching, Practicing and Publishing International Criminal Justice: The Role of Academic Expertise in the Development of an International Field of Law' (2017) 17 *International Criminal Law Review* 239.

[59] See, eg, R Cryer et al, *An Introduction to International Criminal Law and Procedure*, 3rd edn (Cambridge, Cambridge University Press, 2014); V Tochilovsky, *Jurisprudence of the International Criminal Courts and the European Court of Human Rights: Procedure and Evidence* (Leiden, Martinus Nijhoff Publishers, 2008); V Tochilovsky, 'The Nature and Evolution of the Rules of Procedure and Evidence' in KA Khan, C Buisman and C Gosnell (eds), *Principles of Evidence in International Criminal Justice* (Oxford, Oxford University Press, 2010); M Shahabuddeen, *International Criminal Justice at the Yugoslav Tribunal: A Judge's Recollection* (Oxford, Oxford University Press, 2012) 129–86; A Whiting, 'The ICTY as a Laboratory for International Criminal Procedure' in B Swart, A Zahar and G Sluiter (eds), *The Legacy of the International Criminal Tribunal for the Former Yugoslavia* (Oxford, Oxford University Press, 2011); R May and M Wierda, *International Criminal Evidence* (The Netherlands, Brill, 2002); JD Jackson and SJ Summers, *The Internationalization of Criminal Evidence: Beyond the Common Law and Civil Law Traditions* (New York, Cambridge University Press, 2012); MC Bassiouni, *Introduction to International Criminal Law* (The Netherlands, Martinus Nijhoff Publishers, 2012); J Doria, HP Gasser and MC Bassiouni (eds), *The Legal Regime of the International Criminal Court Essays in Honour of Professor Igor Blishchenko* (The Netherlands, Brill, 2008). But see discussion in R Vogler, 'Making International Criminal Procedure Work: From Theory to Practice' in R Henham and M Findlay (eds), *Exploring the Boundaries of International Criminal Justice: Strategies for Achieving Justice in Post-Conflict Societies* (Farnham Ashgate Publishing Group, 2011) (noting that international criminal procedure importantly neglects African and Islamic law traditions).

[60] Lacey, 'Legal Constructions of Crime', above (n 50) 282.

Lacey's analysis makes it possible to consider the impact that a variety of social actors has on criminal justice practices. Lacey's research, conducted within a domestic setting (the UK), is demonstrative of a growing perspective also encompassing international criminal law. The scholars of international criminal justice have begun debating the necessity of establishing 'general' and 'special' parts of international criminal law. Proponents of developing an established distinction between the general and special part of international criminal law include Elies van Sliedregt,[61] as well as Kai Ambos,[62] who has published a three-volume treatise establishing the distinction. Opponents include Alexander Greenawalt, who in 2011 argued against defining a 'general part' for international criminal law because it would too obviously conflict with domestic systems.[63]

The first volume of Ambos's three-volume set appeared in 2013. In it, Ambos situates international criminal law historically in order to define, over the course of several targeted chapters, concepts, sources and functions of international criminal law. Ambos has been a vocal critic of JCE, particularly the third variant hinging on foreseeability, as contrary to rule of law norms and as challenging international criminal law's legitimacy,[64] a critique which is revisited in the *Treatise*.

B. Criminal Justice Constructions of Intent at International Criminal Law: The General Versus the Special Part

In principle, international criminal law follows domestic criminal law in placing intent (which for common law lawyers is 'mens rea' [the guilty mind] and for civil law lawyers is 'dolus' [the subjective mental element])[65] at the centre of its jurisprudence. In domestic systems, not all criminalised behaviour requires that this 'mental element' be present: at common law, for example, some crimes adhere to a strict liability standard, where to commit the act is to commit the crime, regardless of what was intended (statutory rape is one oft-cited example). Likewise, crimes of negligence do not require that intent be present, though typically, negligence offences are lesser crimes. Thus, one can generalise that at domestic criminal law, the mental element of a guilty mind is usually central to defining criminality, particularly for most grave crimes.

---

[61] E van Sliedregt, 'Pluralism in International Criminal Law' Editorial (2012) 25 *Leiden Journal of International Law* 847.

[62] K Ambos, *Treatise on International Criminal Law, Volume 1: Foundations and General Part* (Oxford, Oxford University Press, 2013); K Ambos, Treatise on International Criminal Law: The Crimes and Sentencing, Volume II (Oxford, Oxford University Press, 2014); K Ambos, *Treatise on International Criminal Law: International Criminal Procedure, Volume III* (Oxford, Oxford University Press, 2016).

[63] A Greenawalt, 'The Pluralism of International Criminal Law' (2011) 86 *Indiana Law Journal* 1063.

[64] Ambos, 'Remarks on the General Part of International Criminal Law', above (n 15).

[65] ibid

International criminal law follows domestic criminal law examples in making 'intent' central to criminality.[66] The statute of the ICC specifically requires that the 'mental element' (Article 30) be present in order to commit a crime. While the ICTY statute does not address the question of intent, William Schabas concludes that 'the judges of the ICTY have treated mens rea as an element of all of the offenses within the Tribunal's subject matter jurisdiction'.[67] Yet Schabas shows that ICTY practice has developed some exceptions to the mens rea standard which have served to 'dilute' it:[68] he lists command responsibility and joint criminal enterprise (JCE) as two such examples. Command responsibility is included in the ICTY statute, although its application remains ambiguous.[69] JCE, on the other hand, is a theory of liability first articulated by judges at the ICTY. Since its first iteration by the *Tadić* Appeals Chamber in 1999,[70] JCE has become a juridical catch-all, and features in a majority of indictments and convictions.[71] Thus unlike the situation arguably existing in 2003 when Schabas contrasted word and practice, with ICTY jurisprudence concluding, jurisprudence challenging domestic notions of intent such as JCE can no longer be identified as 'the exception' but is instead much closer to a rule.

JCE is problematic from an intent perspective because it decreases, in its most exaggerated applications, the intent of the perpetrator to commit grave violations of international criminal law to mere 'foreseeability'. At domestic law, this would be a negligence standard, which is not generally applicable to grave crimes. Thus, in the *Tadić* case, Tadić was found liable for murders in a location the Tribunal could not demonstrate he had been. The *Tadić* Chamber reasoned that because Tadić had been engaged (in other places) in the types of crimes against humanity (persecutions, ethnic cleansing) that can foreseeably lead to death, he was liable for murders committed in conjunction with the types of activities in which he was engaged. Guilt by association is not criminalised at international criminal law, and is specifically prohibited at the ICTY.[72] Yet JCE arguably comes close to obviating the distinction between *doing* crime (commission, under which JCE was articu-lated) and *being criminal* (guilt by association).

JCE, and the Rome Statute's Article 25(3) dealing with modes of liability appli-cable before the ICC, are designed to address issues that arise when attempting

---

[66] WA Schabas, 'Mens Rea and the International Criminal Tribunal for the Former Yugoslavia' (2003) 37 *New England Law Review* 1015.

[67] ibid, 1025.

[68] ibid, 1033.

[69] Danner and Martinez, above (n 29); EV Sliedregt, 'Command Responsibility at the ICTY – Three Generations of Case-law and still Ambiguity' in B Swart, A Zahar and G Sluiter (eds), *The Legacy of the International Criminal Tribunal for the Former Yugoslavia* (Oxford, Oxford University Press, 2011).

[70] *Tadić* Appeals Chamber Judgment.

[71] Danner and Martinez, above (n 29).

[72] *Report of the Secretary General pursuant to paragraph 2 of Security Council Resolution 808*, above (n 26) §§ 50, 51. This was reaffirmed in *Prosecutor v Milomir Stakić*, ICTY Case No IT-97-24 (Appeals Chamber, 22 March 2006).

to prosecute, inter alia, grave breaches of international humanitarian law. Some of these issues are evidentiary: during violent conflict, collecting evidence related to events, victims, and hierarchies of responsibility are often particularly difficult. Yet some of these are 'justice' related, as well. Violent social dissolution turns the Durkheimian logic of deviance and social control on its head, where *not* participating or condoning social violence can become the socially deviant act, requiring the individual to push back against overwhelming social pressures and norm constructions (being the 'heroic' border guard who conceptualises the possibility of shooting to miss). Because international crimes are often committed by individuals acting in service to states, individuals violating international criminal law often do so while helping to define a majoritarian 'we' and not a minority 'them'. In fact, it is precisely this justice problem that transitional justice is designed to address, by creating a break between an unlawful, rights-abasing regime and a just, rights-respecting regime.

To bypass the contestation that violators of international criminal law serve political systems that define their behaviour as legal, moral, or 'normal' (non-deviant), theories of human rights are constructed on a natural law foundation, where certain rights are inviolable (non-derogable). This allows international criminal law to assess the mental element of perpetrators under an 'objective', should-have-known standard. Violators of international criminal law cannot escape liability by an absence of animus; *knowledge* that a perpetrator's actions will bring about an illegal result (or *foreseeably* bring such result about, in the most extreme applications of international criminal law doctrine) can be sufficient to demonstrate (shared) *intent* for many international criminal law violations. Without such an approach, international criminal law would be seriously handicapped in redressing, and therein deterring, atrocity; were perpetrators able to avoid liability by claiming they were 'ordered' to do something or were they able to avoid liability by claiming they didn't 'mean' for the crime to occur, international criminal law's promise would be hollow. Yet what this approach has bred is a complex jurisprudence of *aggravation* and *mitigation*, as judges at ICTs peer into perpetrators' 'guilty minds' and seek to judicially rationalise these findings.

Kai Ambos's project considering a general part of international criminal law, together with the work of other international criminal law scholars, is seeking to harmonise disparate jurisprudence and guide future endeavours. The following section follows examples of judicial constructions of 'intent' at international criminal law to demonstrate the uphill battle for such harmonisation, due largely to the central agency paradox present in international criminal law.

IV. Jurisprudential Constructions

This section examines the application of the ideas discussed above in select international criminal law cases. At international criminal law, we see in prison guard cases a muddling of the special and general parts. Recall that the special part consists of the crime – at international criminal law, this charge might include crimes against humanity or war crimes including murder, and so on. The general part interprets context and content, applying theories such as JCE, which defines 'commission'. Modern international criminal tribunals elide these two, however. The following section traces the development and application of the significance of 'intent' across ICTY jurisprudence to demonstrate how the doctrinal, theoretical role played by 'intent' is distinctive across crimes (ie, mirrors a 'special part') although typically, 'intent' would belong in the general part of international criminal law, as a doctrinal formulation.

A. Applying Second World War Era Rationales in the Modern Era: *Kvocka et al*

The seeds of the muddled, imprecise doctrinal standards extant at international criminal law today were sown, importantly, in the Second World War era jurisprudence following the International Military Tribunals. Following the Second World War, the Allied powers occupying Germany conducted thousands of trials; this jurisprudence has provided source material ('precedent') for modern tribunals applying international criminal law.[73] The jurisprudence of the Second World War era was largely the province of academics and historians prior to the construction of the two *ad hoc* tribunals for the former Yugoslavia and Rwanda in 1993 and 1994, respectively. The concise statutes of those two tribunals necessitated looking outside them to interpret and pronounce international criminal law, and lawyers and judges turned to Second World War era materials to supplement their arguments and interpretations.

In this vein, a 1946 *Velpke* case[74] was relied on in a 2001 decision by the ICTY, *Prosecutor v Miroslav Kvočka, Mlađo Radić, Zoran Žigić, Dragoljub Prcać.*[75] Kvočka and the other named defendants were all 'guards' at the Omarska prison camp, a hastily assembled detention centre for Bosnian Muslims built on the grounds of a former mining complex. Unlike his co-defendants, Miroslav Kvočka, a Bosnian Serb policeman deeply embedded in the Muslim community of his region, was not accused of committing or ordering any violence himself; rather, his culpability was based on what he knew, his position of authority as a policeman among amateurs, and what he failed to do to combat the manifest criminality of the camp.

---

[73] N Jain, *Perpetrators and Accessories in International Criminal Law: Individual Modes of Responsibility for Collective Crimes* (Oxford, Hart Publishing, 2014).

[74] *Velpke Children's Home*: Case No 42, Trial of Heinrich Gerike and Seven Others, British Military Court, Brunswick, *VII Law Reports of Trials of War Criminals* 76 (1948). Discussed in greater detail in K Carlson, *Model(ing) Justice: Perfecting the Promise of International Criminal Law* (Cambridge, Cambridge University Press, 2018, forthcoming).

[75] *Kvočka et al* (Judgment) IT-98-30/1-T (2 November 2001).

In *Kvočka et al* the Trial Chamber applied a two-pronged test to determine Miroslav Kvočka's criminal responsibility. First, it examined the evidence before it to determine whether the time Kvočka spent at Omarska (17 days) was sufficient to find that he *participated* in the 'joint criminal enterprise' of the camp. Second, the Trial Chamber reviewed the evidence to determine whether Kvočka's level of participation made him a *co-perpetrator* ('sharing the intent of the camp's evil goals') or an *aider or abettor*, characterised by the Chamber as performing only his discrete job, alleviating detainee suffering when he could, and committing no violations of his own.[76] While the Chamber acknowledged that such a line was finely drawn, it determined that, based on the standard emerging from Second World War case law, Kvočka was best characterised as a co-perpetrator.[77]

Finding that Kvočka was aware of the horrible conditions for detainees in the camp, of beatings, deaths, lack of food and miserable conditions, the Trial Chamber determined that such *awareness* (knowledge) of the terrible conditions in the camp was the legal equivalent of intent.[78] While the Trial Chamber found that Kvočka himself did not physically perpetrate any of the crimes committed at Omarska, it found that he

> could have done far more to mitigate the terrible conditions in the camp ... [by] tak[ing] steps within his designated authority to more actively prevent unauthorized outsiders from entering the camp and abusing detainees ... ensur[ing] more detainees received medical treatment ... prevent[ing] guards and other subordinates from beating or otherwise abusing detainees on arrival, in the dining room, or en route to the toilets.[79]

The Trial Chamber rejected Kvočka's contention that he lacked the authority to prevent abuses in the camp, in part relying on Kvočka's own testimony of intervention in 'grave' circumstances (releasing his brothers-in-law, though he later complied with an order to bring them back; intervening in a case of mistaken identity) to show that he did in fact have such authority. The Trial Chamber held that witness testimony that Kvočka's presence improved conditions was additionally indicative of his authority, and that Kvočka's police department had sufficiently increased in size that it could be viewed on a par with a station, putting Kvočka in a '*de facto* position of authority and influence in the Omarska police station ... parallel[ing] the function of a deputy commander or assistant commander'.[80]

Finally, the Trial Chamber concluded that Kvočka's participation in Omarska was not only 'knowing' but was also 'willing'.[81] The Trial Chamber accepted

---

[76] ibid, para 323.
[77] ibid, para 328.
[78] ibid, para 278.
[79] ibid, para 395.
[80] ibid, para 344.
[81] ibid, para 404.

Kvočka's citation of the individual detainees he saved or helped as proof that Kvočka harboured no personal animus towards Muslims. This did not impact Kvočka's liability for participation in a JCE, however, because the critical intent question the Trial Chamber addressed was not whether Kvočka *intended* to hurt Muslims, but rather whether he *knowingly* facilitated the JCE, which was the operation of the Omarska camp. The Trial Chamber found that Kvočka's knowing and continued participation both enabled the camp to continue its abusive practices and sent a message of approval to others in the camp.[82]

The Appeals Chamber largely upheld the Trial Chamber's findings and argumentation.[83] Kvočka argued that he was a policeman performing his duty, which due to circumstances far outside his control became a job of providing internal security at a holding centre (albeit a particularly odious and dangerous one). The Appeals Chamber dismissed this argument pithily:

> Incidentally, it does not appear that maintaining a camp which seeks to subjugate and persecute detainees based on their ethnicity, nationality or political persuasion and in which living conditions are intolerable and the most serious beatings are regularly meted out can possibly be considered as performing 'duties in accordance with the police requirements'.[84]

The Appeals Chamber rejected Kvočka's contention that his lawful job had become unlawful through no action of his own under the rationale that Kvočka should have been able to recognise the criminal nature of the Omarska enterprise; it was clear to the Appeals Chamber, and thus it must have been (or it should have been, which is the legal equivalent) clear to Kvočka. Recognising Omarska's criminality, Kvočka should have ceased participating; any other form of conduct, the case holds, is criminal. As noted, this is not a novel standard, but is in fact borrowed directly from Second World War era cases such as *Velpke Children's Hospital*, which is cited by the *Kvočka et al* Chamber.

---

[82] ibid.

[83] *Prosecutor v Miroslav Kvočka, Mlađo Radić, Zoran Žigić, Dragoljub Prcać*, ICTY Case No IT-98-30/1-A (28 February 2005). Agreeing with the Trial Chamber's determination that Kvočka was only responsible for those crimes that occurred during the period he was working at Omarska, the Appeals Chamber overturned two murder findings against Kvočka, citing an inability to place those murders during Kvočka's term. To follow its own legal logic, the Trial Chamber should have found Kvočka liable for *all* crimes against humanity committed while he held his position in the Prijedor police force. It found Kvočka not liable for crimes committed outside his working period at the camp, however, and applied this to questions of liability for atrocities committed during the two sick leaves Kvočka took. The Appeals Chamber did not revisit this legal logic, because it held that this was a *factual* finding on the part of the Trial Chamber (para 114). The standard for overturning a finding of fact by a lower court is more onerous than overturning an articulation of law by a lower court. On appeal, defendants raised the problematic lack of care taken by the Trial Chamber, where defendants in the case were never entirely sure of whom they were accused of/found guilty of persecuting, beating, or killing, and on what day. The Appeals Chamber found that the Trial Chamber erred in this area, thereby violating a principle of fair trial, but nonetheless found that this error did not invalidate the judgment (para 74).

[84] ibid, para 242.

B. Halting 'Ideological Creep': *Perišić*

A decade after the final *Kvočka et al* judgment, the ICTY Appeals Chamber acquitted the Serbian General Perišić of 'aiding and abetting' the Bosnian Serb army. The *Perišić* case is not a JCE case, but rather a (novel) formulation of the ICTY's aiding and abetting jurisprudence.[85] Regardless, it is interesting for our purposes because like *Kvočka et al*, *Perišić* addresses the question of individual culpability within the confines of institutional legitimacy. In *Perišić*, however, the ICTY reached a very different conclusion regarding individual culpability when framed within possibly criminal state behaviour.

The *Perišić* case addressed Perišić's culpability for aid provided by the Serbian army to the Bosnian Serbs. Violence in Bosnia owed a great deal to Serbian aid: ethnic Serbs were overrepresented in the Yugoslav army, particularly in the leadership, and as the country dissolved, these factions helped funnel Yugoslav resources into ethnic Serb hands in Bosnia and Croatia.[86] In Bosnia, Serbian paramilitary groups aided Bosnian Serb military campaigns, and Yugoslav army supplies and personnel also crossed the border. The Serbian General Perišić was at the top of the supply train, providing materials to the Bosnian army as it ethnically cleansed and murdered Bosnian Muslims and Croats in an attempt to expand the territory under Bosnian Serb control. The *Perišić* Trial Chamber found that Perišić could approve or deny requests (paragraph 948), and concluded that without assistance from the Serbian army, the Bosnian Serb army 'would have been hampered in conducting its operations in Sarajevo and Srebrenica' (paragraph 1622). Recall that such 'operations' consisted in the brutal siege of a civilian city for more than three years (and included two large marketplace bombings and a policy of snipers targeting civilians) and the genocidal murder of 8,000 men and boys, respectively. The *Perišić* Trial Chamber sentenced Perišić to 27 years in prison.

In acquitting Perišić in 2013, the Appeals Chamber, in a 3:2 decision, engaged in the precise intellectual distinction that the *Kvočka et al* Chambers had rejected. Although the Appeals Chamber accepted the Trial Chamber's findings of fact regarding the aid supplied, through Perišić as gate-keeper, from the Serbian army to the Bosnian Serb army, the Appeals Chamber distinguished the Bosnian Serb army from certain illegitimate elements of its practice, and then required showing that Perišić's aid had specifically assisted the criminal, illegitimate aims of the Bosnian Serb army. Concerning intent in the form of awareness – the doctrinal articulation that affirmed Kvočka's culpability for violations of international humanitarian law – three of the five judges in the Perišić Appeals Chamber determined that knowledge of crimes is insufficient to meet the doctrinal requirements of aiding and abetting as those three judges construed them in the case.

---

[85] M Aksenova, 'The Specific Direction Requirement in Aiding and Abetting: A Call for Revisiting Comparative Criminal Law' (2015) 4 *Cambridge Journal of International and Comparative Law* 88.
[86] L Silber and A Little, *The Death of Yugoslavia* (London, Penguin Books, 1997).

C. The Messy Present: *Stanišić and Simatović*

The *Perišić* and *Kvočka* cases are doctrinally apples and oranges: Kvočka was charged with co-perpetration and Perišić with aiding and abetting, and these disparate charges have amassed their own jurisprudence, which confounds a straight doctrinal comparison. Around the same time Perišić was acquitted, however, the ICTY acquitted two other senior Serb leaders indicted under JCE charges in the case of *Prosecutor v Jovica Stanišić and Franko Simatović*.[87] The Trial Chamber considered the actions of those two Serb generals, who it found directed, supplied, and organised troops who were active in violence in Croatia and throughout Bosnia, through an 'inference of intent ... to share common criminal purpose' paradigm. The Trial Chamber, in a 2:1 decision, found evidence insufficient to support this mens rea standard, which is much more lenient than the 'knowledge' standard applied in *Kvočka et al*.

On 15 December 2015, the ICTY Appeals Chamber issued its judgment, ordering a retrial in the case. Regarding the joint criminal enterprise portion of the 2013 judgment, the Appeals Chamber determined that 'the absence of a thorough analysis and prior findings on the existence and scope of a common criminal purpose shared by a plurality of persons as well as on Stanišić's and Simatović's contribution to it', meant that 'the Trial Chamber could not have properly adjudicated Stanišić's and Simatović's *mens rea*'. The *Stanišić and Simatović* trial lasted several years and involved nearly 5,000 exhibits and more than 100 witnesses. The Appeals Chamber judgment sending the case to retrial means, effectively, that we are again years away from seeing how an international tribunal applies juridical constructions of 'intent' to facts it establishes.

Finally, there is the case against Vojislav Šešelj. On 31 March 2016, the ICTY's 10-year prosecution of the Serbian paramilitary warlord ended in acquittal.[88] Relevant portions of the more than two thousand pages that constitute the judgment, concurrence, and dissent (from the three-judge panel hearing the case, each judge in effect writing her own opinion) iterate factual and legal findings, particularly regarding the structure and application of JCE, which are violently at odds with most previous ICTY jurisprudence (finding, for example, that there were no crimes against humanity in Bosnia because the element of widespread or systematic attack on a civilian population was not met). The *Šešelj* judgment thus joined several other failed cases against those alleged to be most responsible for the war.[89]

---

[87] *Prosecutor v Jovica Stanišić and Franko Simatović*, ICTY Case No IT-03-69 (30 May 2013).

[88] *Prosecutor v Vojislav Šešelj*, ICTY Case No IT-03-67 (31 March 2016).

[89] See, eg, *Prosecutor v Ante Gotovina, Ivan Čermak and Mladen Markač*, ICTY Case No IT-06-90-PT (16 November 2012); *Prosecutor v Ante Gotovina, Ivan Čermak and Mladen Markač*, ICTY Case No IT-06-90-PT (15 April 15 2011); *Prosecutor v Perišić*, ICTY Case No IT-03-69 (28 February 2013); *Prosecutor v Jovica Stanišić and Franko Simatović*, ICTY Case No IT-03-69 (30 May 30 2013); *Prosecutor v Vojislav Šešelj*, ICTY Case No IT-03-67 (31 March 2016); and *Prosecutor v Slobodan Milošević*, ICTY Case No IT-02-54 (case uncompleted due to *Milošević's* death).

In March 2018, the Appeals Chamber overturned part of the Trial Chamber judgment, finding Šešelj guilty for statements he made in 1992 calling for the expulsion of the non-Serb population there, and sentencing him to 10 years in prison. The judgment did not overrule the Trial Chamber's determinations regarding JCE, however. And for Šešelj, the sentence, which amounts to time served, may only impact him in so far as it may result in his no longer being permitted to hold his Serbian parliamentary seat.

In conclusion, the JCE and related 'intent' jurisprudence of the ICTY discussed above demonstrates doctrinal deficits that show a blurring of the general part of criminal law (theories of liability) with the specific part of criminal law (particularised elements applicable to every crime). This is demonstrated by the varying applications of 'intent' across judicial categories (between, for example, aiding and abetting jurisprudence and joint criminal enterprise jurisprudence), as well as the shifting standards and applications of 'intent' in categories that would appear to be uniform.

V. Conclusion

This chapter applies the developing theory constructing and distinguishing the 'special part' of the criminal law to cases against prison guards at international criminal law as a means of considering the problem of agents and agency at international criminal law. Prison guard cases showcase the doctrinal shortcuts, and the intellectual hurdles, that still lie before international criminal law.

Prison guard cases at international criminal law showcase individuals involved in reprehensible situations without a counterbalancing recognition of the larger circumstances in which those individuals found themselves. In *Kvočka et al*, defendants were faced with the real-life challenges of navigating states whose horrifying articulations of justice they did not share. Moreover, in many cases defendants were arguably resisting and seeking to rewrite these flawed articulations of justice through their actions. Yet instead of 'punish(ing) those who are truly responsible for a state's misbehavior',[90] ICTs trying these cases scapegoated state responsibility onto unfortunate, low-ranking, and often powerless individuals. This is made abundantly clear, in the *Perišić* and *Stanišić and Simatović* and *Šešelj* Trial Chamber judgments, as more lenient standards of intent have been applied exactly to those higher up whose positions of authority would have allowed them to change the tenor of the violence, or to curb it completely.

---

[90] LB Sohn, 'The New International Law: Protection of the Rights of Individuals Rather than States' (1982) 32 *American University Law Review* 1.

7

Punishment in Transition: Empirical Comparison of Post-Genocide Sentencing Practices in Rwandan Domestic Courts and at the ICTR

BARBORA HOLÁ AND AMANI CHIBASHIMBA*

I. Introduction

In about three-and-a-half months following 6 April 1994, a small faction of hardliners within Rwanda's ruling party and military took over power, organised and directed the most rapid mass killing campaign of the twentieth century.[1] One of the distinctive characteristics of the violence was a broad popular participation of the Hutu majority population. It was a deliberate, systematic, genocidal campaign executed by thousands of perpetrators, which led to the deaths of an estimated 500,000 to 1,000,000 Tutsi civilians.[2] Other Rwandans, including members of the former Habyarimana regime (1973–94), members of the political

* The authors would like to thank Thijs Bouwknegt, Alette Smeulers, Joris van Wijk, and Martin Witteveen for their invaluable comments on the earlier draft of this chapter; Jean Pierre Tuyishima, Kayumba Godfrey, Pascaline Umutesi and Mazimpaka Eddy for data collection and coding of judgments in Rwanda; and Jessica Kelder and Claire Boost for their research assistance. The research has been funded by the Dutch Organization for Scientific Research (NWO) as part of its VENI granting scheme.

[1] See, eg, S Strauss, *Making and Unmaking Nations, War Leadership, and Genocide in Modern Africa* (Ithaca, NY, Cornell University Press, 2015) 273–321.

[2] A historian and human rights activist Alison Des Forges in her seminal work on Rwandan genocide, which was relied on heavily by the ICTR (Des Forges testified as an expert witness in 10 ICTR trials), put the total number of victims at around 500 000 (A Des Forges, *Leave None to Tell the Story: Genocide in Rwanda*, 2nd edn (Human Rights Watch, 1998) 18). The 1999 UN Report estimates 800,000 victims of violence. (UN, *Report of the Independent Inquiry into the Actions of the United Nations during the 1994 Genocide in Rwanda*, 15 December 1999). The government of Rwanda on its website and in genocide memorials around Rwanda refers to over 1,000,000 Tutsi and moderate Hutu victims of genocidal violence (Brief History of Rwanda, available at: www.gov.rw/home/history/). The exact number of victims and their ethnic affiliation may never be determined, however, and remains a matter of ongoing debate.

opposition and Hutu opposed to the mass killings, also fell victim to the killing spree.[3] After the genocide ended in July 1994, both domestic and international courts have prosecuted the alleged perpetrators of violence, *génocidaires*.[4] The United Nations International Criminal Tribunal for Rwanda (ICTR) has tried a few dozen of 'the most responsible' in Arusha, Tanzania. The vast majority of individuals have been dealt with by domestic courts and the reinvented, neo-traditional *Inkiko Gacaca* tribunals (Gacaca) in Rwanda.[5] These courts, situated in different settings (international versus domestic) and governed by different sets of laws, had been, independently of each other, handing out sentences for perpetrators of international crimes committed within the same episode of violence.[6] Legal scholars and the public assume – based on mainly anecdotal evidence – that sentencing of international crimes at the ICTR and at domestic courts has

---

[3] For a brief summary of the dynamics and history of genocide see, eg, S Strauss, *The Order of Genocide, Race Power and War in Rwanda* (Ithaca, NY, Cornell University Press, 2006) 1.

[4] As well as Rwandan courts, courts around Europe and in Canada also prosecuted a handful of perpetrators of Rwandan genocide. For a brief overview see B Holá and A Smeulers, 'Rwanda and the ICTR: Facts and Figures' in A de Brouwer and A Smeulers (eds), *The Elgar Companion to the International Criminal Tribunal for Rwanda (ICTR)* (Cheltenham, Edward Elgar Publishing, 2017) 71–73.

[5] There has been an extensive amount of commentary on the functioning and legal developments at the ICTR; innumerable articles have been published in legal academic journals or in edited volumes; and a number of books have also been dedicated solely to the ICTR (see, eg, T Cruvelier, *Court of Remorse, Inside the International Criminal Tribunal for Rwanda* (Madison, WI, University of Wisconsin Press, 2006); K Moghalu, *Rwanda's Genocide, The Politics of Global Justice* (New York, Palgrave Macmillan, 2005); or L van den Herik, 'The Contribution of the Rwanda Tribunal to the Development of International Law' (PhD Disertation, VU University, Amsterdam, 2005). Fewer studies have focused on sentencing at the ICTR (eg, MA Drumbl, *Atrocity, Punishment, and International Law* (New York, Cambridge University Press, 2007); J Meernik, 'Proving and Punishing Genocide at the International Criminal Tribunal for Rwanda' (2004) 4 *International Criminal Law Review* 65; or B Holá, C Bijleveld and A Smeulers, 'Punishment for Genocide – Exploratory Analysis of ICTR Sentencing' (2011) 11 *International Criminal Law Review* 745). When it comes to Rwanda and its justice mechanisms, the focus of academic commentaries has predominantly been on Gacaca practices (see among many others, eg, B Ingelaere, *Inside Rwanda's Gacaca Courts. Seeking Justice After Genocide* (Madison, WI, Wisconsin University Press, 2016); P Clark, *The Gacaca Courts, Post-Genocide Justice and Reconciliation in Rwanda, Justice without Lawyers* (New York, Cambridge University Press, 2010); A Chakravarty, *Investing in Authoritarian Rule, Punishment and Patronage in Rwanda's Gacaca Courts for Genocide Crimes* (New York, Cambridge University Press, 2016)). Few works compared all three levels of justice, the ICTR, domestic criminal courts and Gacacas (N Palmer, *Courts in Conflict, Interpreting the Layers of Justice in Post-Genocide Rwanda* (New York, Oxford University Press, 2015); G Gahima, *Transitional Justice in Rwanda, Accountability for Atrocity* (Abingdon, Routledge, 2013); N Jones, *The Courts of Genocide, The Politics and the Rule of Law in Rwanda and Arusha* (Abingdon, Routledge, 2010)). None of the literature however examines practices of Rwandan domestic courts in detail (except Palmer's book, which is, however, a socio-legal analysis examining legal and institutional culture) and none looks in particular on sentencing. A descriptive, comparative analysis of sentencing outcomes at the ICTR, Rwandan domestic courts and Gacaca has recently been published in B Holá and H Nyseth Brehm, 'Punishing Genocide: A Comparative Empirical Analysis of Sentencing Laws and Practices at the International Criminal Tribunal for Rwanda (ICTR), Rwandan Domestic Courts, and Gacaca Courts' (2016) 10(3) *Genocide Studies and Prevention* 59. This chapter relies on the same database regarding the ICTR and domestic courts verdicts collected by the first author.

[6] The ICTR had a jurisdiction over international crimes committed from 1 January until 31 December. The Rwandan laws regulated prosecutions of crimes committed since 1 October 1990 until 31 December 1994.

been widely divergent.[7] A notorious example is the public execution in Amahoro Stadium in Kigali in 1998 of 22 individuals who were convicted of genocide by Rwandan courts. In contrast, at the ICTR, the top-level perpetrators could be subjected 'only' to the maximum sentence of life imprisonment. Up to this day, however, only one study has attempted to systematically compare and contrast sentencing outcomes at the three levels of justice, ie, the ICTR, domestic courts and Gacaca.[8] Authors concluded that sentence severity indeed varied across the three court levels and sentences in Rwandan domestic courts seem to have been harsher compared with the ICTR as well as Gacaca. In addition, over time the punishing practices in Rwanda seem to have evolved and become less punitive.

This chapter attempts to further elucidate and contextualise these findings by providing an in-depth comparative analysis of punishment laws and practices at domestic courts in Rwanda and at the ICTR.[9] In addition, the chapter explains the developments of punishing practices in Rwanda by pointing to the 'transitional' socio-political context, which has fluctuated and changed over time. In domestic contexts, such as in Rwanda, post-atrocity criminal justice and punishment are fundamentally context dependent and form a part and parcel of broader societal transformation.[10] Punishment for mass atrocity crimes designed and implemented in domestic settings reflects immediate political and pragmatic needs of transitional authorities and societies. It morphs alongside the evolution of the transitioning state and society, and its broader (societal and political) motives and goals. It not only punishes perpetrators of atrocities for the sake of punishment alone or other traditional utilitarian punitive goals, such as deterrence or protection of society. It often reflects future broader societal goals, such as reconciliation of divided societies or truth-telling and is largely shaped by the political context of the transition. These broader interests and goals are largely contextual and dynamic. They depend on specific historical, political, social and transitional circumstances and fluctuate over time, in turn transitioning modalities and severity of punishment itself. It is simultaneously 'punishment of transition' and 'punishment in transition'.

This chapter, after providing an in-depth comparison of punishment in law and in practice at the ICTR and at domestic courts in Rwanda will attempt to contextualise the punishment practices following the 1994 genocide, thus shedding light

---

[7] cf MH Morris, The Trials of Concurrent Jurisdiction: The Case of Rwanda' (1996–97) 7 *Duke Journal of Comparative & International Law* 349, 363; Jones, above (n 5) 145.

[8] Holá and Nyseth-Brehm, above (n 5).

[9] The comparison presented in this chapter is limited to sentencing practices at the ICTR and Rwandan domestic courts and excludes Gacaca jurisdictions. The data collected for the purposes of this research were limited to the ICTR and Rwandan domestic court judgments as these are arguably, when it comes to procedural modality (criminal trial) and case characteristics (those considered the most responsible), the most comparable. After the establishment of Gacaca the domestic courts were meant to deal only with cases of those most responsible Category 1 defendants, who are arguably the most comparable to those tried at the ICTR. See section III below for more detailed discussion on categorisation of perpetrators in Rwanda.

[10] cf C Murphy, *The Conceptual Foundations of Transitional Justice* (Cambridge, Cambridge University Press, 2017).

on the sentencing 'discrepancies' identified in the literature.[11] It is divided into five sections. After this introduction, section II addresses methodological issues and presents a summary of collected data. Section III discusses the sentencing approach at the ICTR and in Rwanda relying on the comparative analysis of the positive laws and case law. Then, section IV briefly presents and compares descriptive statistics regarding sentence severity at the UN tribunal and Rwandan domestic courts paying particular attention to changes over time. The concluding remarks are presented in section V.

II. Methodology

In order to compare punishment across different legal systems, such as in Rwanda and at the ICTR, one needs to analyse two interrelated aspects: (i) sentencing approach (ie, punishment in law); and (ii) sentencing outcomes (ie, punishment in practice).[12] The comparative analysis of sentencing approaches should focus on the convergence or divergence of sentencing goals, sentencing general principles and factors justifying sentence severity according to positive laws and as developed in jurisprudence. In order to evaluate consistency in sentencing outcomes, it is necessary to ascertain the extent to which similar defendants convicted of comparable crimes are being subjected to similarly severe penalties (ie, predictability of sentences). As we wanted to compare sentence severity at different courts governed by different laws and situated within different contexts (the ICTR and Rwandan domestic courts), a multivariate multilevel statistical modelling – enabling us to assess predictability of sentences across the two systems – would have been the most suitable methodology. Due to limitations of data collected in Rwanda, however, only descriptive analysis of sentencing outcomes (comparing sentence ranges and averages for different categories of cases) was possible.

The data collected and used for this analysis consists of: (i) the ICTR Statute, its Rules of Procedure and Evidence (RPE) and all ICTR judgments until the Tribunal's closure in December 2015;[13] and (ii) Rwandan organic laws regulating genocide prosecutions, and judgments handed out by Rwandan domestic courts collected during field work in 2014 and 2015. The ICTR indicted 90 individuals for genocide-related crimes.[14] Seventy-three individuals were tried and

---

[11] Holá and Nyseth-Brehm, above (n 5).

[12] For a more detailed discussion and conceptualisation of consistency of sentencing of international crimes see B Holá, 'Pluralism in Sentencing' in E van Sliedregt and S Vasiliev (eds), *Pluralism in International Criminal Law* (Oxford, Oxford University Press, 2014).

[13] All these documents are readily available on the ICTR/MICT website. See: unictr.unmict. org/en/cases   or   jrad.unmict.org/webdrawer/webdrawer.dll/webdrawer/search/rec&sm_fulltext= judgment&sm_udf3=judgement&sort1=rs_datecreated&count&template=reclist.

[14] The MICT and the ICTR list on their websites that the ICTR 'indicted 93 individuals for genocide and other serious violations of international humanitarian law committed in 1994' (see: unictr.unmict. org/sites/unictr.org/files/publications/ictr-key-figures-en.pdf). However, this figure is misleading as it

received a verdict: 14 were acquitted and 59 convicted. In case of the remaining 17, their cases were either referred to Rwanda and France, their indictments were withdrawn, defendants died before the final judgment or are still at large.[15] Almost all ICTR convicts – 52 out of 59 (88 per cent) – were found guilty of genocide and all were convicted for participation in killings and offences against persons, including sexual violence.[16] There were only seven individuals, who were not convicted of genocide (four pleaded guilty to charges of crimes against humanity and three others were convicted of crimes against humanity combined with war crimes). All sentencing judgments (trial and appeal) published in English on the ICTR website were collected, coded and analysed for the purposes of this study.

In contrast to the ICTR, it remains uncertain how many cases were actually tried by domestic courts in Rwanda.[17] During our fieldwork, we collected and coded cases concerning 639 individuals tried by domestic courts between 1995 and 2014.[18] In addition, we coded all judgments published by the NGO Avocats

also includes the two individuals convicted for the contempt of the Tribunal and in addition, one individual, Georges Ruggiu, is listed twice (once under those transferred to serve a sentence and for the second time under those who have already served their sentence).

[15] For a more detailed discussion of the ICTR population, see Holá and Smeulers, above (n 4).

[16] Twelve individuals were convicted of rape as an underlying act of genocide and/or crime against humanity.

[17] According to Martin Ngoga – the Deputy Prosecutor General of Rwanda at the time – approximately 4,122 individuals were judged by the end of 2001 (M Ngoga, *Rwanda 10 Years After the Genocide: Creating Conditions for Justice and Reconciliation* (Prosecutor's Colloqium, 25–27 November 2004:, available at: ictr-archive09.library.cornell.edu/ENGLISH/colloquium04/rwanda.html). Jones reports that an additional 2,335 individuals were tried in 2002 and 2003 (Jones, above (n 5) 88) and the United Nations suggests that the Rwandan domestic courts had tried over 10,000 individuals by mid-2006 (UN Outreach Programme on the Rwanda Genocide and the United Nations, *Justice and Reconciliation in Rwanda.* Background Note (2012, available at: www.un.org/en/preventgenocide/rwanda/pdf/bgjustice.pdf). In 2005, the vast majority of genocide-related cases were transferred to the Gacaca courts, however, and the domestic courts retained jurisdiction only over the most serious Category 1 cases. In 2008, the vast majority of Category 1 cases were also transferred to Gacaca courts, and only those 'most serious' of Category 1 cases were to be tried in domestic courts. According to the official report of the National Service of Gacaca Courts, the Gacaca courts prosecuted 1,003,227 individuals in 1,958,634 cases during this time. The outcomes of Gacaca judgments are not included in this analysis.

[18] Access to judgments of domestic courts and their availability proved to be much more complicated than expected in Rwanda. There is no centralised digital database of genocide-related cases and cases are typically archived in physical copies at each competent court. We visited each of these courts and sought access to its archive. However, the number of cases we were able to access is rather limited. For example, according to the Rwandan Supreme Court's annual reports, the domestic courts decided cases involving 567 individuals in the period between 2005 and 2012 (The Republic of Rwanda: Supreme Court: RAPORO, Y'IBIKORWA BY'URWEGO RW'UBUCAMANZA, 2004–11, 2011–12, 2012–13, on file with authors). During the field study, however, we collected cases involving only 353 individuals tried between 2005 and 2014. The difference in the reported and collected cases can be ascribed either to over-reporting in the official statistics or to weak archiving practices. Clark (above (n 5) 175) discusses a similar phenomenon with respect to the national figures regarding the number of individuals tried by Gacaca, where he notes that government 'grossly overstates' the number of suspects prosecuted by Gacaca. One might also speculate to what extent 'the logic of the performance' in Rwanda can also account for the difference in numbers (reported by Reyntjens with respect to local governments (F Reyntjens, *Political Governance in Post-Genocide Rwanda* (New York, Cambridge University Press,

Sans Frontiéres (ASF) concerning the cases of 527 individuals decided between 1997 and 2005.[19] We have thus collected case files concerning 1,166 individuals tried at Rwandan domestic courts. Out of these, 715 individual verdicts were issued by first instance courts and 451 are appeals or review judgments.[20] From our sample, 731 persons were convicted, 220 acquitted and in the case of 215 individuals the case was dismissed or the defendant had died or was absent. All defendants were convicted of genocide (only very rarely (in four cases, in combination with crimes against humanity), of which the vast majority was condemned for 'participation in killing' (685 individuals: 93.7 per cent), either exclusively or in combination with sexual violence or property crimes. In the remaining 4 per cent of cases (29 individuals) the underlying crime of conviction was either causing injuries to a person, sexual violence, or property related offences, such as looting or stealing. In case of 17 individuals, the underlying crime of conviction is unclear. The vast majority of defendants were convicted of membership of killing groups. In these cases, judges established that perpetrators had been part of a group, which executed an attack and killed and/or injured and/or sexually assaulted a number of victims, and/or looted property, during the period of the genocide. The defendants in these cases were often found guilty of these offences irrespective of whether they had actually harmed victims themselves. Only approximately 10 per cent out of those convicted (73 individuals) were sentenced for the organisation, planning, encouragement or leading the attacks, acts comparable to ICTR crimes. Among the latter was, for example, former Minister of Justice Agnes Ntamabyariro, the

2013) 53, 182) and by M Witteveen with respect to the Prosecution service (M Witteveen, 'Assessment Genocide Fugitive Tracking Unit (GFTU), Building the System from the beginning of the Pipeline', 1 December 2014, report prepared for the National Public Prosecution Authority in Rwanda, paras 25, 26, on file with author). Very roughly, 'the logic of performance' entails that state authorities and officials are evaluated by achieving pre-set numerical targets per month and a performance of a unit or office is judged by evaluating whether the target has been achieved. Therefore, one might wonder to what extent the figures reported to the central authorities (in order to reach the quota) and summarised in the annual reports actually reflect reality on the ground. According to Human Rights Watch similar pressures to achieve (numerical) outcomes are imposed by judicial authorities on judges. (Human Rights Watch, 'Law and Reality. Progress of Judicial Reform in Rwanda' (2008) 28), available at: www. hrw.org/reports/2008/rwanda0708/index.htm. Additionally, the archives we visited were not very well organised, according to Western standards and in comparison to the ICTR. It is possible that files got lost or were simply nonexistent in the first place. Despite these obstacles, we have collected and coded all judgments that were made available to us.

[19] The ASF collected and published in French a selection of genocide-related cases decided by specialised chambers established at domestic courts to deal with suspected genocide perpetrators and military courts in Rwanda in the pre-Gacaca period. The cases were published online in French in seven volumes. ASF Belgium, *Recueil de Jurisprudence Contentieux du Genocide*, 1–7 (Brussels, 2002–06). The volumes can be found at the website of the ASF, together with other reports relating to the Rwandan genocide, here: www.asf.be/nl/blog/category/theme/rwandan-genocide/.

[20] As discussed in Holá and Nyseth Brehm, above (n 5) 65, case files we gained access to in Rwandan domestic courts hardly ever contained files on the complete trajectory of an individual via the justice system. We have collected and coded all judgments we gained access to. That however means that for some individuals only first instance judgments were available (and we do not know whether a verdict was later modified); for some we have only a final judgment issued on appeal or review.

only member of the so-called interim government, which was in power during the genocide between 12 April and 19 July 1994, included in our sample of cases from Rwanda. The Intermediate Court in Nyarugenge convicted her in 2009 to life imprisonment for, inter alia, planning and organising the genocide in Nyanza and Kibuye, sensitising people to participate in genocide and creating criminal groups.

Therefore, in contrast to the whole population of cases stemming from the ICTR, the sample of analysed cases from domestic courts is non-representative and incomplete. We have collected cases made available to us by the Rwandan authorities and complemented them with cases published in the ASF volumes. Given the limited number of cases included in our sample and potential for various biases in the data, it proved impossible to conduct any more advanced statistical analysis. In addition, the descriptive statistics presented in this chapter must also be read with caution, keeping in mind the limitations of the collected data. On the other hand, ours is the only academic study which attempted to collect and analyse original empirical data concerning prosecutions of the genocide-related crimes in Rwanda by domestic criminal courts. In this sense, irrespective of the challenges of the fieldwork and collected data, it is highly unique and unprecedented.

III. Punishment in Law at the ICTR and in Rwanda

In contrast to the ICTR, where judges were given ample space for tailoring the sentence in individual cases, in Rwanda the laws a priori stipulated systematisation of sentences and provided for mandatory sentences with hardly any leverage/ discretion left to judges. Despite the different ways in which sentencing was regulated in the positive laws at the ICTR and in Rwanda, it appears that punishing *génocidaires* has been based on a comparable 'logic' and similar principles underlying the approach to determine a severity of punishment. At both systems, punishment severity was to be differentiated predominantly based on the culpability of a defendant and his or her position in the overall state hierarchy, and his or her role and degree of involvement in the crimes.

The regulation of sentencing in the ICTR Statute[21] and its RPE[22] have been discussed extensively elsewhere.[23] It is enough to mention that at the ICTR positive sentencing law did not stipulate any particular sentencing goals, nor principles or sentencing factors. In Arusha, judges were provided with only very general

---

[21] Article 23 ICTR Statute, as appended to the UN Security Council Resolution 955 (1994), November 8, 1994, UN Doc. S/RES/ 955 (1994).

[22] ICTR Rules of Procedure and Evidence; adopted on June 29, 1995, as amended, available at: unictr.unmict.org/sites/unictr.org/files/legal-library/150513-rpe-en-fr.pdf.

[23] See literature referred to above (n 5). B Holá, 'International Sentencing – "Game of Russian Roulette" or Consistent Practice?' (PhD Dissertation, BOXPress, Oisterwijk, 2012) 209; S D'Ascoli, *Sentencing in International Criminal Law, The UN Ad Hoc Tribunals and Future Perspectives for the ICC* (Oxford, Hart Publishing, 2011).

guidelines for sentence determination in individual cases. They were mandated to take into account and consider: the gravity of the offence; the individual circumstances of the offender; the general practices regarding prison sentences in Rwanda; and any individual mitigating and aggravating circumstances they deemed relevant. A modality of ICTR punishment was limited to imprisonment, including life imprisonment, and no sentencing ranges for individual offences were stipulated in the law. Consequently, ICTR judges were vested with a large amount of sentencing discretion. Given the fact that there had been no international precedent for sentencing offenders of genocide and the fact that the ICTR in a way functioned as a self-referential system, the Tribunal's sentencing approach consolidated over time, building upon previous cases and jurisprudence. The following paragraphs briefly describe how sentences were justified and argued on a general level, while taking into account all the ICTR cases and patterns over a 20-year timespan.

The starting point of sentence determination according to ICTR judges was the gravity of the offence.[24] For the purposes of sentencing, gravity was primarily determined *in concreto* by looking at the particular circumstances of the case.[25] In most cases, the concept of gravity was interpreted as encompassing two aspects: (i) the magnitude of harm caused by the offender and represented by, for example, the scale of the crime, the number of victims and the extent of victims' suffering; and (ii) a form and degree of the accused's participation in the crime, or in other words, the offender's culpability.[26] The principles of proportionality, totality and gradation seemed to have governed judges in delimiting a severity of punishment and distinguishing among sentence severity in individual cases. According to the case law, a penalty ought to reflect the totality of the crimes committed by a person and be proportionate to the gravity of the crimes in general, while taking into account one's position in the overall conflict and role in the particular crimes. After evaluating the gravity of crimes, ICTR judges further individualised the sentence by assessing aggravating and mitigating circumstances in each case. Only those circumstances directly related to the charged offences and to the offenders themselves when they committed the offence were accepted in

---

[24] cf *Prosecutor v Akayesu* (Appeals Judgment) ICTR-96-4-A (23 November 2001) para 413; *Prosecutor v Rutaganda* (Appeals Judgment) ICTR-96-3 (26 May 2006) para 591.

[25] Over time, ICTR judges rejected a notion of abstract hierarchy between individual categories of international crimes. In an early jurisprudence, genocide was denoted as the crime of crimes and judges argued that for the purposes of sentencing, genocide as a category of international crimes is considered more serious compared with war crimes. (*cf Prosecutor v Serushago*, ICTR-98-39 (5 February 1999) para.13; *Prosecutor v Rutaganda*, ICTR-96-3 (6 December 1999) para. 451; *Prosecutor v Musema*, ICTR-96-13 (27 January 2000) para 981; *Prosecutor v Kambanda*, ICTR-97-23 (4 September 1998) para 14). Later on, however, judges have emphasised that there is no hierarchy among individual categories of international crimes and that *all* crimes under their jurisdiction represent very serious violations of international humanitarian law. *cf Prosecutor v Renzaho*, ICTR-97-31-T) (14 July 2009) para 817; *Prosecutor v Rukundo* (Appeals Judgment) ICTR-2001-70 (20 October 2010) para 260.

[26] For more elaborate discussion of the concept of gravity see Holá, 'International Sentencing', above (n 23) 47–56.

aggravation. Amongst the most common aggravating factors cited was 'abuse of a position of authority, leadership, influence or trust'. Conversely, mitigating factors did not have to relate directly to the offences for which the person had been convicted, and in the majority of cases, the personal circumstances of the offender relating to his character, family circumstances or behaviour prior to and during the genocide were discussed and accepted as mitigating in sentencing. The most frequent mitigating factor cited by ICTR judges was 'assistance to victims'.[27]

Consequently, ICTR judges have used their large discretion to develop a sentencing 'algorithm' that they seem to have applied across all cases. Arguably, since all the crimes coming before the ICTR were very grave and serious offences (in the majority of the cases defendants were convicted of genocide-related killings of tens, hundreds and often thousands of victims, which in many national jurisdictions would attract the severest sentences), ICTR judges seem to have differentiated between 'serious and horrendous' and 'even more serious and horrendous' criminal acts and involvement of defendants in these acts. This differentiation was primarily conducted by applying the principle of gradation, which focuses on evaluation of a defendant's culpability as reflected by a position in the state hierarchy and the role one played in particular crimes. Judges thus differentiated between 'crimes which are of the most heinous nature, and those which, although reprehensible and deserving severe penalty, should not receive the highest penalties'.[28] Consequently, life imprisonment as the severest sentence was according to ICTR judges reserved for the most serious offenders,[29] being those at the upper end of the sentencing scale, such as those who planned, led or ordered atrocities, or those who committed crimes with particular zeal or sadism. Hence, judges often reiterated that offenders receiving the most severe sentences tended to have been in senior positions of authority, such as ministers in the interim government.[30] Conversely, secondary or indirect forms of participation, such as complicity in genocide or facilitation of crime, would according to judges usually result in lower sentences.[31]

In one of the first ICTR cases – *Kayishema and Ruzindana* – for example, the judges enumerated the factors that distinguished the different levels of culpability of the two accused, both of whom were convicted of genocide. Kayishema, who was the prefect of Kibuye, was convicted for his leading role as well as active participation in several massacres and attacks on sacred places such as churches resulting in the deaths of thousands of victims. He was considered a leader in his prefecture who had instigated and ordered attacks. In contrast, Ruzindana, a commercial trader in Kigali, played a leadership role during only one attack,

---

[27] For a more detailed discussion regarding aggravating and mitigating factors and a complete list, see Holá, 'International Sentencing', above (n 23) 56–72, 77–82.

[28] *Prosecutor v Elizaphan & Gerard Ntakirutimana*, ICTR-96-10 & ICTR-96-17 (21 February 2003) para 773.

[29] *Prosecutor v Nahimana, Barayagwiza, Ngeze*, ICTR-99-52 (3 December 2003) para 1097.

[30] *Prosecutor v Setako*, ICTR-04-81 (25 February 2010) para 500.

[31] *Prosecutor v Karera*, ICTR-01-74 (7 December 2007) para 583.

in which he also personally participated in killings. In sentencing him, the judges emphasised the heinous means by which he committed murders, such as

> the vicious nature of the murder of a sixteen-year old girl named Beatrice. Ruzindana ripped off her clothes and slowly cut off one of her breasts with a machete. When he finished, he cut off her other breast while mockingly telling her to look at the first one as it lay on the ground, and finally he tore open her stomach.[32]

Despite the horrendous nature of Ruzindana's acts, the judges concluded that Kayishema deserved more punishment than Ruzindana. The principal reasons for this decision can be traced back to the principle of gradation: Kayishema occupied a position of authority, while Ruzindana did not. Kayishema's conviction also covered a more extensive crime base; he was educated, a medical doctor and, at the time of genocide, the prefect of Kibuye, who betrayed the ethical duties that he owed to his community. Moreover, on at least one occasion, Kayishema instructed and praised Ruzindana, thus indicating his more senior and leading role in the atrocities. Taken together, these considerations led the judges to sentence Kayishema to life imprisonment, while Ruzindana was given a sentence of 25 years.[33]

Consequently, ICTR judges seem to have developed a sentencing approach where particular attention was dedicated to the principle of gradation. The principle of gradation is mainly concerned with a defendant's culpability for systematic and organised criminality. In this respect, a particular emphasis is placed on factors such as the defendant's position within the state's hierarchy, his or her exercise of authority and influence over others and his or her particular role in the offences. These factors were utilised by judges to distinguish between different levels of culpability of defendants and consequently, to justify differences in sentence severity in individual cases.

In Rwanda the post-genocide government had issued a set of so-called Organic Laws (OLs), which specifically governed prosecution and punishment of those suspected of involvement in genocide and related offences. These perpetrators were initially tried at the specialised chambers set up in domestic courts, which were abolished in 2000. Since then genocide cases were tried by domestic courts where the Chambers were located, along with ordinary crimes. With the establishment of the Gacaca courts in the early 2000s (during the pilot phases of Gacaca in 2002 and subsequently nationwide since 2005) the OLs regulated prosecutions and punishments at both domestic and Gacaca courts.[34] In contrast to the loose legal regulation at the ICTR and the subsequent development of sentencing doctrine in its case law, the OLs constrained the sentencing options of Rwandan judges to a considerable extent. The laws contained fixed mandatory sentences and narrow

---

[32] *Prosecutor v Kayishema and Ruzindana* (Sentence) ICTR-95-1 (21 May 1999) para 18.
[33] ibid, para 26.
[34] For one of the most recent books based on an extensive empirical research and analysis of a range of Gacaca courts see Ingelaere, above (n 5).

sentencing tariffs with a very limited margin of appreciation given to judges to individualise a sentence and take into account the particularities of each case.

In 1996, the first law enacted in Rwanda to regulate genocide-related prosecutions, OL 08/96, introduced the categorisation of genocide suspects and gradation in sentence severity depending on the defendant's category.[35] Category 1 suspects included planners and organisers of genocide; those, who committed the crimes while being in a position to exercise state authority; notorious murderers, who killed with a particular zeal and cruelty; and perpetrators of sexual violence.[36] Category 1 defendants would receive a death penalty with no possibility of sentence reduction or mitigation.[37] Category 2 encompassed those who participated in killings and murders, and the mandatory sentence for this type of offender was life imprisonment. Then, Category 3 suspects (those, who participated in acts causing personal injuries short of death) were eligible to penalties stipulated for similar offences by the Rwanda Penal Code. Finally, Category 4 suspects, who committed offences against property, were not subjected to incarceration and their punishment was limited to reparations. OL 08/96 also stipulated a possibility for Category 2 and 3 defendants to confess and plead guilty, which, if accepted, would lead to a significant sentence reduction. For example, a Category 2 defendant, who pleaded guilty, could be given either between seven and 11 years (if the guilty plea took place prior to the prosecution)[38] or between 12 and 15 years (if he confessed during the trial).[39]

OL 08/96 set the scene for the subsequent development of regulation of sentencing structures for convicted *génocidaires*. The genocide prosecution laws were frequently revisited and amended, with the most important changes in the 2000s.[40] According to the 2000 OL, the majority of genocide cases (all cases concerning Category 2, 3 and 4 defendants) were to be transferred to the Gacaca community courts.[41] The OL on Gacaca was amended several times,[42] most substantially in 2004[43] and 2008.[44] Besides changes relating to the organisation

---

[35] Organic Law 08/96 on the organization of prosecutions for offences constituting the crime of genocide or crimes against humanity committed since October 1, 1990, adopted 30 August 1996.

[36] ibid, Article 2.

[37] ibid, Article 14.

[38] ibid, Article 15.

[39] ibid, Article 16.

[40] Organic Law 40/2000 setting up Gacaca jurisdictions and organizing prosecutions for offences constituting the crime of genocide or crimes against humanity committed between October 1, 1990 and December 31, 1994, adopted 26 January 2001.

[41] In 2008 the majority of Category 1 defendants were transferred to Gacaca jurisdictions, leaving courts to deal only with planners and organisers; and leaders who at the time of genocide occupied a position of authority at the national and regional/prefectural level.

[42] eg, in 2001 by OL 33/2001 modifying and completing OL 40/2000.

[43] OL 16/2004 of 19 June 2004 establishing the organization, competence and functioning of Gacaca Courts charged with prosecuting and trying perpetrators of the crime of genocide and other crimes against humanity, committed between October 1, 1990 and December 31, 1994, adopted on 19 June 2004.

[44] OL 13/2008 modifying and complementing OL 16/2004 of 19 June 2004 establishing the organization, competence and functioning of Gacaca Courts charged with prosecuting and trying

and structure of the Gacaca tribunals and to broadening their jurisdiction also with respect to the majority of Category 1 offenders, the modifications also pertained to offender categorisation[45] and sentence severity, which, as discussed further below, became increasingly more lenient. Irrespective of these developments, however, sentence severity in all the laws was clearly gradated depending on the categorisation of a defendant. In turn, the category was determined by the role of a defendant in crime (leaders, organisers, planners, with those who incited others being considered the most culpable); one's position of authority (those who occupied any position of authority at the national, prefecture, sub-prefecture or communal level were also deemed to be the most culpable); and finally perpetrators of sexual violence were ranked among the most culpable. Category 1 defendants were upon conviction eligible to the most severe sentences. The remaining Category 2 and 3 offenders (basically all 'hands-on perpetrators' and their accomplices) were divided depending on whether the crimes they committed or participated in targeted persons (Category 2) or property (Category 3) with a decrease in sentence severity depending on the type of crime committed (torture, killing, injury). Sentences within each category were also applicable to 'accomplices', defined as persons, who by any means provided assistance to individuals specified in each category.[46] The OL left the other individual terms further undefined and thus provided those implementing them with a relatively broad discretion on who to classify as 'an organiser' or who to consider 'a notorious murderer', for instance. As the categorisation of an offender obviously had serious consequences for sentence severity 'the legal straitjacket' imposed by Rwandan law when it comes to sentencing was actually not as tight. A large amount of discretion was only shifted to one of the steps preceding trial and the actual sentence delivery and that is the offender categorisation. According to OL 16/2004 the Gacaca courts were competent to categorise offenders.[47]

The severity of mandatory sentences stipulated in the OL was also largely dependent on two types of the so-called mitigating 'excuses',[48] which could lead to a considerable sentence reduction: (i) confession and guilty plea;[49] and (ii) minor age of a defendant at the time of genocide (offenders between 14 and 18).[50] Judges could also adjust a sentence within the predetermined ranges, in case mitigating

---

perpetrators of the crime of genocide and other crimes against humanity, committed between October 1, 1990 and December 31, 1994 as modified and complemented to date, adopted on 19 May 2008.

[45] As of 2004, eg, Categories 2 and 3 relating to offences against persons were merged into Category 2 and offences against property (previously Category 4) became Category 3.

[46] OL 16/2004, above (n 43) Article 53.

[47] ibid. The list of Category 1 suspects has been since OL 08/96, above (n 35), published by the chief prosecutor at the Supreme Court periodically. Initially the information on who to put on the list was forwarded by local administrative and judicial authorities (see Des Forges, above (n 2) 751), after the Gacaca the information was forwarded by the Gacaca courts.

[48] S Rugege and AM Karimunda, 'Domestic Prosecution of International Crimes: The Case of Rwanda' in G Werle et al (eds), *Africa and the International Criminal Court*, International Criminal Justice Series 1 (The Hague, TMC Asser Press, 2014) 90.

[49] OL 16/2004 as amended, above (nn 43 and 44) Articles 72, 73.

[50] ibid, Article 78.

or aggravating circumstances were present.[51] At the same time, the OL did not provide any list of relevant mitigating circumstances, and left it to the discretion of judges to accept any circumstances they deemed relevant to be mitigating.[52] In the cases collected for the purposes of this study, judges hardly ever discuss and accept any factors in mitigation of a sentence. In contrast, the OL explicitly stipulated as aggravating: (i) a position of authority at the level of a Cell or a Sector;[53] and (ii) conviction for a multiplicity of offences.[54] In such cases, judges were directed to hand out the most severe penalty envisaged within the defendant's category. In contrast to the ICTR, where incarceration was the only possible sentence, the OLs in Rwanda also stipulated an additional penalty to incarceration, which was the withdrawal of civic rights, the extent and duration of withdrawal depending on the category of offender.[55]

Arguably, the offender categorisation in the Rwandan OLs was based on comparable considerations underlying the approach developed by ICTR judges in their case law. Similar to the sentencing principles the ICTR judges had developed over time, it seems that in Rwanda one of the organising principles of this categorisation was a differentiation between offenders on the basis of their level of culpability. Assessment of culpability level in turn primarily depended on a position of authority, the particular role in the committed offences, and the way in which the crimes were executed. The type of underlying offence influenced the sentence severity only secondarily as those found responsible for the same offence, such as killing, were ultimately categorised depending on their position of authority or role in crime. These considerations primarily determined whether an offender was classified as the most culpable, Category 1, and thus subjected to the severest sentences. Similarly, as of 2007 Category 2 defendants were further divided into those who 'just' participated in killings and those labelled as notorious murderers, who committed the killing with particular zeal or cruelty. More severe sentences were reserved for the latter. Again, it is the individual role in a group crime as distinguishing criterion between these different levels of culpability resulting in more severe sentences. This is, however, not to say that the type of underlying offence was insignificant. Sexual violence, for instance, was considered the most serious (as all those who are found to have participated in sexual violence were Category 1), followed by other offences against persons (torture, killings and non-fatal injury) and the least serious were offences against property. It was, nevertheless, principally the position of authority and the organisational or planning role in the crime, or execution of a crime with particular zeal and cruelty, as the factors considered to increase a defendant's culpability within both systems, at the ICTR and in Rwanda.

---

[51] ibid, Article 81.
[52] Rugege and Karimunda, above (n 48) 90–91. The authors also provide examples where judges for example accepted remorse or cooperation with the court as mitigating circumstances.
[53] OL 16/2004 as amended, above (nn 43 and 44) Article 52.
[54] ibid, Article 77.
[55] ibid, Article 76.

Despite these similarities, two significant differences between the ICTR and Rwandan courts can be identified: (i) the approach to the culpability of accomplices; and (ii) the possibility to individualise sentences.

First, according to the OLs in Rwanda, an accomplice (ie, a person who has by any means provided assistance to commit offences) was subjected to the same sentences as individuals specified in each category, be it hands-on perpetrators, order-givers or instigators. Accomplices were thus put on a par with principals and subjected to the same sentences with no distinction as to their potentially different levels of culpability. In contrast, in the ICTR case law judges argued for a difference in culpability level between the principals and accomplices (aiders and abettors), with a lesser culpability level for the latter.[56] This difference in sentencing approach is even more significant if one takes into account that the vast majority of those in our sample collected in Rwanda are convicted as accomplices, based sometimes on a very broad interpretation of complicity, and subjected to relatively severe sentences nonetheless. The following two cases can further illustrate this relatively broad application of criminal responsibility for genocide in Rwanda, which essentially blurs the boundaries between bystanders and perpetrators. In one case, a woman was found to be an accomplice to killings committed by a group of *Interahamwe*, because, before and after the killings, the *Interahamwe* regularly gathered in her bar and drank beer. In her case, the judges argued that she provided them with support by offering them a meeting place and sentenced her to 25 years' imprisonment. On account of the fact that her husband worked for the government at the time, judges considered her actions to have more weight in the eyes of the local population and took it into account in ascribing her a criminal liability.[57] In another case, a defendant was convicted of killing a victim, whom he claimed he was hiding during the genocide. However, the victim disappeared without trace and nobody was able to locate the body. The court argued that by refusing to reveal the place where the body was hidden the defendant must have been responsible for the killing or for allowing others to kill the victim. The defendant claimed that he took the victim to a different hiding place and did not know what happened afterwards. He was sentenced to life imprisonment.[58]

Second, possibilities to individualise sentences were almost non-existent in Rwanda compared with the ICTR. At the ICTR, judges had ample space for individualisation and could also take into account the personal circumstances of an offender, such as his or her character, education or family circumstances. The OL offered judges in Rwanda a limited space for this type of individualisation by providing a narrow possibility to adjust a sentence and account for individual circumstances within predetermined sentencing ranges. However, judges in the

---

[56] However, it should also be noted that in practice the empirical multivariate studies of sentencing predictability have not so far discovered a detectable difference in sentence severity between the main perpetrators and accessories. *cf* Holá, 'International Sentencing', above (n 23) 218–19.

[57] *Prosecutor v Consolee Mukobwjana*, Intermediate Court Karongi (Trial Judgment) (30 July 2014).

[58] *Prosecutor v Silas Iyamubonye*, Intermediate Court in Muhanga (Trial Judgment) 17 October 2014.

collected cases do not seem to have taken this opportunity and do not refer to the individual circumstances of defendants for the purposes of sentence determination at all. This difference in approach might not in practice be very significant, however, as the ICTR judges primarily emphasised the gravity of crimes and often argued that given the seriousness of offences individual circumstances are only of a very limited relevance in sentence determinations. Therefore, despite being mentioned in all the ICTR cases as relevant factors in sentence determinations, it might be questioned to what extent the individual circumstances of the offender, such as his or her character or behaviour prior to the crimes, actually in practice had any tangible effect on sentence severity.[59] The sentencing practices at the ICTR and in Rwandan domestic courts are compared and contrasted in the following section.

IV. Sentencing Outcomes at the ICTR and in Rwandan Domestic Courts

Due to the quality of data collected in Rwanda, the analysis of sentencing outcomes is limited to presentation of descriptive statistics. As stated above, the collected data is not sufficient to make any definitive and valid conclusions with respect to consistency or inconsistency of sentencing outcomes at the ICTR and in Rwanda. There are essentially two reasons for this: (i) it is impossible to ascertain to what extent the data collected in Rwanda is representative; and (ii) the majority of collected cases did not concern Category 1 defendants (a group arguably most comparable to those tried at the ICTR) but Category 2 defendants convicted predominantly as accomplices, often based on a very loose link to the actual crimes.

Table 1 presents descriptive statistics relating to sentence severity divided per category of defendants, ie, ICTR and Category 1, 2 and 3 in Rwanda as classified by judges in the collected judgments. The first column shows a percentage of those sentenced to the maximum sentence (life imprisonment or death)[60] within each category, the second column shows the average determinate sentence, followed by a sentence range. In the final column, cases are divided according to the fact of whether a defendant pleaded guilty and the plea was accepted by judges.

---

[59] None of the empirical studies on the ICTR sentencing has examined a significance of individual circumstances for sentence severity. Compare also the most recent empirical study of the ICTY and ICTR sentencing, where the authors argue that the ICTY and ICTR sentences are exclusively predicted by factors relating to gravity and aggravating factors. JW Doherty and RH Steinberg, 'Punishment and Policy in International Criminal Sentencing: An Empirical Study' (2016) 10 *American Journal of International Law* 49.

[60] The death sentence was abolished in Rwanda only in 2007. Despite many convictions to death in the early trials, however, according to the public record only 22 individuals were actually executed in 1998.

Table 1 Life and determinate sentences at the ICTR and Rwandan domestic courts (collected cases)

	% Max sentence (life/ death)	Average determinate sentence	Sentence range	Accepted Guilty Plea			
				YES		NO	
				% Max sentence**	Average determinate sentence	% Max sentence**	Average determinate sentence
ICTR (59)	29% (17)	28.1 years (42)	6–47 years	11% (1)	10 years (8)	32% (16)	28.1 years (34)
Rwanda Category 1 (150)	76.7% (115)	16.7 years (35)	2–30 years	27.5% (11)	15.4 years (29)	94.5% (104)	23 years (6)
Rwanda Category 2 (567)	40.4% (229)	15.3 years (356)	1–30 years	8.1% (17)	12.9 years (192)	54.2% (194)	18.2 years (164)
Rwanda Category 3 (14)	0%	Reparations (11)	1–10 years (3)	0%	Reparations (9)	0%	4.7 years (3) Reparations (2)

*The numbers in brackets refer to the number of convicted individuals included within each category.
**Percentages here refer to each individual sub-category, ie a proportion of those: (i) who pleaded guilty; or (ii) did not plead guilty.

In Rwanda sentence severity is clearly gradated depending on the category of a defendant. This finding is not surprising at all given the rigid mandatory sentencing structures in the OLs. However, what might be striking is that judges do not seem to fully adhere to mandatory sentences and sentence ranges prescribed in law. For example, Category 1 defendants, who did not confess, should have been, according to all the OLs, sentenced to maximum imprisonment as a mandatory sentence, which was initially death and subsequently life imprisonment with special provisions. However, in the collected sample some of them actually received determinate sentences. As Rwandan judges hardly ever explain their sentencing choices it is difficult to discern reasons for these decisions. Similarly, it is almost impossible to understand (by reviewing the judgments) why certain defendants are given sentences in the lower end of the prescribed sentence range and why others are sentenced to the most severe sentences mandated for a particular category. Given the fact that sentencing argumentation in the judgments issued by the domestic courts in Rwanda is rudimentary, it is difficult to ascertain the reasons for particular sentencing outcomes from the judgments. Judges in Rwanda justify sentence severity in individual cases by reference to particular laws and discuss factual allegations underlying the case, but sentencing principles or aggravating or mitigating factors are hardly ever mentioned in the case law.

Figure 1 provides a comparison of proportions of defendants convicted to the maximum sentence at the ICTR and in Rwanda. It appears that Category 1 defendants in Rwanda have the highest proportion of maximum sentences (over 75 per cent of individuals in the collected cases were convicted to death or given life imprisonment), followed by Category 2 offenders in Rwanda (slightly over 40 per cent) and finally at the ICTR (almost 30 per cent were convicted to life imprisonment).

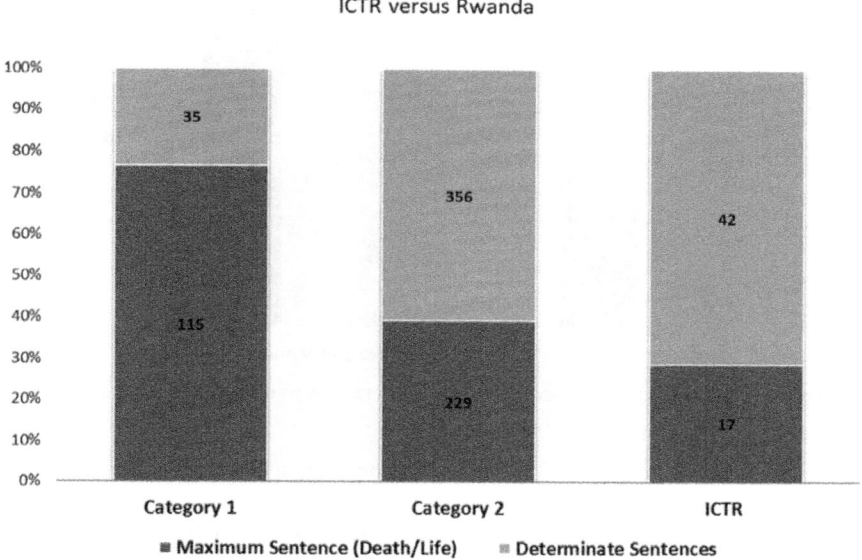

Figure 1 Proportion of maximum sentences for different groups of offenders

To make the picture more complete, Figure 2 further illustrates average determinate sentences of the same groups dividing them further on the basis of whether a defendant's guilty plea was accepted by judges or not. The average determinate sentence of those, who did not plead guilty at the ICTR, is the highest. In contrast, those who pleaded guilty at the ICTR, have received very lenient sentences, not only compared with their counterparts at the ICTR but also compared with all defendants in our sample in Rwanda who confessed. Besides the mitigating effect of the guilty plea, this relative 'leniency' might also be explained by the fact that, in the majority of cases, these ICTR defendants confessed only to a relatively limited crime base and a relatively limited participation in the crime. Often multiple charges (including charges of committing genocide and/or sexual violence) were dropped in exchange for the accused's cooperation. This resulted in comparatively less serious cases compared with other ICTR cases. The only exception is Jean Kambanda, the former prime minister, who pleaded guilty to the entire very broadly formulated indictment and was convicted to life imprisonment.

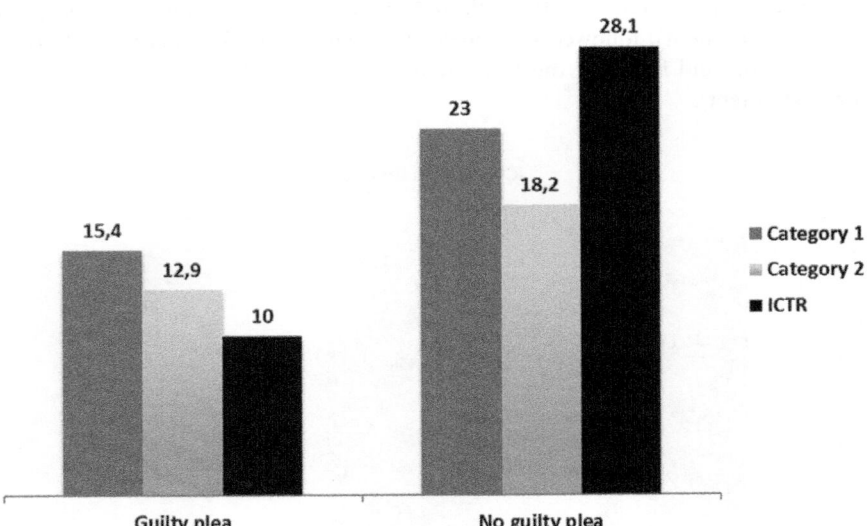

Figure 2 Average determinate sentences for different groups of offenders

Looking at Figures 1 and 2 combined, one can see a gradual decrease in sentence severity across the different groups. The most severe sentences in our sample have been handed out to Category 1 defendants in Rwanda, followed by Category 2 defendants (especially if one considers the proportion of those convicted to a maximum sentence) and finally those who did not admit to their guilt at the ICTR (whose determinate sentences, on the other hand, seem to have been the most severe). Those pleading guilty at the ICTR were subjected to the most lenient sentences. Without making any conclusive claims and provided that the presented data offers only a very limited picture of 'sentencing reality', perpetrators tried by the Rwandan courts in our sample indeed seem to have been subjected to more severe sentences compared with the individuals tried at the ICTR. One of the possible reasons for this might be that, despite the fact that the ICTR defendants would most probably have all been classified as the most culpable Category 1 in Rwanda and subjected to the most severe sentences, the ICTR has not treated them as a homogeneous category. At the ICTR, judges seem to have made an additional differentiation in their culpability level and severity of sentences. In general, empirical studies evaluating the ICTR sentencing found that there seems to be a decrease in sentence severity depending on the level of an official/state authority exercised by a defendant during the genocide. The majority of high-ranking state governmental, regional and military leaders tried at the ICTR were convicted to the maximum sentence, life imprisonment, or relatively high determinate sentences. In this sense sentences of this ICTR sub-group are the most comparable to Category 1 in Rwanda. In contrast, those who did not occupy higher positions or did not exercise any state derived authority received comparatively lower sentences, in particular if their participation in crime was not judged as zealous and cruel.[61] The position of the offender in the overall state hierarchy was certainly not the sole determining factor of sentence severity at the ICTR. Other factors, such as an extent/scope of crimes (which tend to be broader in case of higher-ranking individuals) or a role an individual played in crime, were arguably also influencing sentencing outcomes at the ICTR as well. For example, those who played an ancillary role and only provided assistance seem to have been sentenced less severely than hands-on perpetrators or those who planned, incited or ordered the atrocities.[62] These considerations are irrelevant according to the OL in Rwanda. Given the fact that legal and factual reasoning, when it comes to sentence determinations, is very rudimentary or non-existent in collected judgments it is impossible to ascertain whether similar considerations played a role at all when Rwandan judges exercised their limited discretion in individual cases.

The fact that sentences delivered by the Rwandan domestic courts seem to have been more severe than those handed out by the ICTR should, however, also be seen in light of developments of sentencing structures in Rwanda. As the majority of our data collected in Rwanda comes from the earlier period (57.6 per cent of cases in our sample were decided by 2001 (ie, under th OL 8/96), and in total 83.4 per cent of cases were concluded by 2007, when OL 10/2007 was introduced) the statistics presented above are skewed towards the earlier prosecutions. When one compares OL 8/96 with the subsequent laws regulating prosecution of genocide-related crimes, there is a discernible trend leading to progressive reduction in severity in the prescribed sentences over time. Not only were the prescribed sentences becoming more lenient but also in many cases imprisonment was being substituted by alternative sanctioning mechanisms such as community service ('Travail d'Intérêt Général' (TiG)) or suspended sentences, which are not reflected in the presented statistics.[63] According to the OLs (and as shown in Table 2 below) half of the pronounced sentences of Category 2 offenders, who pleaded guilty, were as of 2000 to be served in community service camps and not in prisons. In addition, as of 2000, for example, sentence reduction due to a confession and guilty plea was also made available to Category 1 offenders, initially only in cases if they pleaded guilty before the investigation and prosecution, and from 2007 also if they did so after the proceedings against them started. Furthermore, in 2007 Rwanda

---

[61] This finding is also in line with empirical studies conducted to assess consistency of sentencing at the ICTY and ICTR. *cf* D'Ascoli, above (n 23) or Holá, 'International Sentencing', above (n 23).

[62] Holá, Bijleveld and Smeulers, above (n 5) 769.

[63] *cf* Articles 73, 78 and 80 of OL 16/2004, as amended, above (nn 43 and 44). These Articles stipulate that sentence of imprisonment for Category 2 defendants (both adults and minors), who confess should be only partially served in prison and the rest suspended and commuted to community service.

abolished the death penalty and substituted it with a sentence of life imprisonment or life imprisonment with special provisions.[64]

Therefore, increasingly over time, sanctions envisaged for genocide-related crimes in Rwanda were becoming less and less punitive. This trend can be best illustrated by the example of Category 2 offenders, who participated in offences against a person with intent to kill and did not confess to their crimes. Were such individuals tried under OL 8/96 their convictions would have led to a manda-tory sentence of life imprisonment. In 2000, however, they would face a minimum sentence of 25 years and a maximum of life imprisonment. And were they tried as of 2004, they would be subjected to 'only' a sentence ranging from 15 years to 19 years. Consequently, as demonstrated in Table 2,[65] which illustrates the evolu-tion of sentencing ranges for Category 1 and 2 of genocide perpetrators (adults) as stipulated in the OLs over time, the mandatory sentences became progressively more and more lenient.

The reasons for this 'fade of retributivism' are arguably multiple and largely interconnected. They can be: (i) principled (such as the fact that over time in the governmental rhetoric prosecutions and punishment of genocide perpe-trators were increasingly more aimed at other goals than 'mere' retribution); (ii) pragmatic and practical (a pressing need to deal with the problem of over-crowded prisons and backlog of cases); (iii) socio-economic (including economic and social repercussions of having a majority of the adult Hutu male popula-tion detained); or (iv) political (a ruling regime trying to consolidate its power by offering significant concessions to those, who had done 'wrong' but nonethe-less cooperated with the system).[66] All these considerations are briefly addressed below.

---

[64] OL 31/2007 relating to the abolition of the death penalty. In the cases where the death penalty had been pronounced before the adoption of OL 31/2007 and in cases of all legal texts containing the death penalty as a punishment, death penalty was substituted for life imprisonment or life imprisonment with special provisions (Article 3, Article 6). Given that crimes against humanity and genocide are subject to life imprisonment with special provisions (Article 5, para 3) those sentenced to the death penalty in all likelihood had their sentences changed to life imprisonment with special provisions. As noted above, however, despite pronouncing the death penalty as maximum sentence before 2007, only a very limited number of individuals were actually executed.

[65] Offender categorisation presented in Table 2 is based on the later OLs' 3-ranked categorisation, which in essence meant that Category 1 offenders encompassed those in position of authority or specific organisational role in crime, and all those who participated in sexual violence, while Category 2 offenders encompassed all those involved in offences against persons (previously Category 2 and 3 offenders). It should also be noted that in 2007 (as shown in Table 1) some of the sub-categories initially considered Category 1 were moved to Category 2, with more lenient sentences stipulated compared with the remaining Category 1 offenders, as illustrated in Table 2. The OLs also envisaged substantially mitigated sentence ranges for minors, who were at the time of the genocide aged between 14 and 18 years old. For a more detailed discussion of prosecutions and punishment of minors in Rwanda see J Barrett, 'What a Difference a Day Makes: Young Perpetrators of Genocide in Rwanda' (2014) University of Cambridge, Faculty of Law, Legal Studies Research Paper Series, Paper No 24/2014.

[66] For a similar argument regarding the set-up and functioning of Gacaca courts, see Chakravarty, above (n 5).

Table 2 Development of sentence ranges for Category 1 and Category 2 offenders in OLs in Rwanda

CATEGORY 1		OL 8/96	OL 40/2000	OL 16/2004	OL 10/2007	OL 13/2008
leadership/organizers/ sexual violence	**No guilty plea**	DEATH PENALTY	DEATH or LIFE	DEATH or LIFE	DEATH or LIFE	LIFE with special provisions
	Guilty plea after prosecution	DEATH PENALTY	DEATH or LIFE	DEATH or LIFE	25–30 years	25–30 years
	Guilty plea before prosecution	DEATH PENALTY	25–LIFE	25–30 years	20–24 years	20–24 years

CATEGORY 2		OL 8/96	OL 40/2000	OL 16/2004	OL 10/2007	OL 13/2008
notorious murderer/ torture/dehumanizing corpses (until 2007 included in Category 1)	**No guilty plea**				30 years-LIFE	30 years-LIFE
	Guilty plea after prosecution				25–29 years (1/2 TIG)	25–29 years (1/2 TIG)
	Guilty plea before prosecution				20–24 years (1/2 TIG)	20–24 years (1/2 TIG)
intent to kill	**No guilty plea**	LIFE	25–LIFE	25–30 years	15–19 years	15–19 years
	Guilty plea after prosecution	12–15 years	12–15 years (1/2 TIG)	12–15 years (1/2 TIG)	12–14 years (1/2 TIG)	12–14 years (1/2 TIG)
	Guilty plea before prosecution	7–11 years	7–12 years (1/2 TIG)	7–12 years (1/2 TIG)	8–11 years (1/2 TIG)	8–11 years (1/2 TIG)
no intent to kill	**No guilty plea**	Penal code	5–7 years (1/2 TIG)	5–7 years (1/2 TIG)	5–7 years (1/2 TIG)	5–7 years (1/2 TIG)
	Guilty plea after prosecution	1/2 of applicable penalty	3–5 years (1/2 TIG)	3–5 years (1/2 TIG)	3–4 years (1/2 TIG)	3–4 years (1/2 TIG)
	Guilty plea before prosecution	1/3 of applicable penalty	1–3 years (1/2 TIG)	1–3 years (1/2 TIG)	1–2 years (1/2 TIG)	1–2 years (1/2 TIG)

Besides 'eradicating the culture of impunity' following the genocide, the Rwandan authorities were emphasising societal reconstruction, reconciliation[67] and reintegration of perpetrators, increasingly as additional goals of prosecutions and punishment. Compare this with the goals stipulated in the first OL 8/96, which was strictly conceived of as an instrument 'to organize criminal proceedings'[68] and break the cycle of impunity. With the introduction of the Gacaca courts, however, in OL 40/2000 the goals were formulated much more broadly and encompassed truth-finding, popular participation, achieving justice and reconciliation, reintegration of perpetrators, reparation of harms and even promoting repentance. The Preamble of OL 16/2004 clearly stipulated these varied, much broader transitional justice goals:

> Considering that [the genocide and crimes against humanity] were publicly committed before the very eyes of the population, which thus must recount the facts, disclose the truth and participate in prosecution and trying the alleged perpetrator
>
> …
>
> Considering the necessity to eradicate for ever the culture of impunity in order to achieve justice and reconciliation in Rwanda, and thus to adopt provisions enabling rapid prosecutions and trials of perpetrators and accomplices of genocide, not only with the aim of providing punishment, but also reconstituting the Rwandan society that had been destroyed by bad leaders who incited population into exterminating part of the Society
>
> Considering that it is important to provide for penalties allowing convicted prisoners to amend themselves and to favour their reintegration into the Rwandese society without hindrance to the people's normal life.

These goals would in turn be reflected in stipulated modalities of punishment (for example, in a possibility of alternative sentences, ie, TIG camps for those who confess and cooperate) and in severity of prescribed sanctions (a possibility of significant reductions in sentences to those who come forward and sincerely apologise).

In addition to these certainly principled reasons and lofty goals, however, pressing pragmatic considerations, such as extremely overcrowded prisons, a backlog of cases at the specialised chambers and economic and social repercussions of having a majority of the adult Hutu male population detained, might also explain these developments. The shifting of categories, progressively more lenient

---

[67] eg, in 1999, the National Unity and Reconciliation Commission (NURC) was established as the principal organ to coordinate and supervise programmes aimed at promoting 'unity and reconciliation' and 'sensitise' Rwandans towards these goals. *cf* Law No 03/99 of 1999 establishing the National Unity and Reconciliation Commission, 12 March 1999. On its website, the NURC lists, among other reconciliation 'tools', also Gacaca prosecutions and *ingando* (solidarity camps), which on a very basic level can be described as re-education 'boot-camps' promoting a unified official version of history and 'teaching' attendees the values of being Rwandan. All (provisionally) released prisoners and those in TIG camps have been subjected to these 're-education' programmes. See, eg, A Purdekova, *Making Ubumwe: Power, State and Camps in Rwanda's Unity-Building Process* (Oxford, Berghahn Books, 2015).

[68] OL 08/96, above (n 35) Article 1.

sentence ranges and the introduction of alternative sentences might also be, at least partially, explained by the unintended effects of instituting the Gacaca proceedings. In the first phases of the Gacaca system many persons, who were not suspected of involvement in genocide, ended up on lists of suspects that were compiled by communities in the Gacaca information-gathering phase. This meant that many individuals, who were not initially considered or who were already released by the criminal justice system, actually ended up being detained (or reconvicted), in turn again increasing the prison population. This led to an increase in detainees and a further burden being placed on already overcrowded prisons, contrary to the initial goals of the government. Arguably the laws and sentence ranges were being continually adjusted to respond to these practical developments and to make the system more effective and efficient in the eyes of the Rwandan government.[69]

Finally, in contrast to some other transitional contexts, the Rwandan government and the ruling party (Rwandan Patriotic Front), which took over power after a military victory and has since then ruled in an increasingly more authoritarian way,[70] had the ability to unilaterally shape and design (criminal law) responses to atrocities, including the design and application of punishment, without any major political opposition and constraints.[71] In general, transitional justice measures implemented in Rwanda had a largely punitive character. The massive, large-scale prosecutions implemented in Rwanda are indeed unprecedented compared with other transitioning societies. The enforcement of criminal accountability in Rwanda was largely one-sided and some argue meant to control the majority Hutu population.[72] The Rwandan government indeed put a big emphasis on broadly conceived criminal accountability and severe punishments in the aftermath of the genocide. Over time, however, these strictly punitive impulses seem to have been thwarted with the criminal justice system being overwhelmed, and with the increasing necessity to cater also for other needs of the transitioning society. In this respect, the developments of accountability and sentencing in Rwanda over time demonstrate how in domestic contexts, penal measures after atrocities are arguably shaped to a large extent by a variety of other societal, political and pragmatic needs and goals of transitioning societies. They represent 'punishment in transition', which morphs and reflects a multitude of other broader considerations, which are usually neither shaping nor reflected in conventional criminal punishment in ordinary, peaceful domestic contexts or at international courts.

---

[69] *cf* Ingelaere, above (n 5) 25, 29, 192.

[70] See, eg, Reyntjens, above (n 18); or T Longman, *Memory and Justice in Post-Genocide Rwanda* (Cambridge, Cambridge University Press, 2017).

[71] L Rueda Guzman and B. Hola, 'Punishment in Negotiated Transitions: A Case Study of the Colombian Peace Agreement with the FARC-EP' (2019) 19 *International Criminal Law Review* 127–159, which discusses the recent situation in Colombia where the transitional justice system, including criminal accountability and punishment modalities, was shaped and designed during peace negotiations, where former adversaries had to find a consensual solution and a compromise reflecting their different needs and goals.

[72] Longman, above (n 70) 103, 128, 134; Reyntjens, above (n 18).

V. Concluding Remarks

The aim of this chapter was to compare and contextualise the sentencing laws and practices of *génocidaires* at the ICTR and domestic courts in Rwanda. Due to difficulties in the data collection encountered in Rwanda and the limitations of the collected sample of cases, it proved impossible to make any conclusive claims regarding disparities in international sentencing. This research is, however, one of the firsts to attempt to systematically examine and compare punishment practices with respect to genocide-related crimes in Rwandan domestic courts and at the ICTR.

This chapter discussed empirically based indications that indeed those tried and sentenced by domestic courts in Rwanda seem to have been subjected to more severe sentences compared with those tried and sentenced at the ICTR. In order to make any sound comparisons, however, it is also necessary to consider the context in which the sentencing took place and reflect upon, for example, the quality of trials, detention conditions or standards applied by judges to convict someone of genocide. Analysis of sentencing laws and outcomes reveals only an extremely limited picture of reality. In Rwanda many Hutus suspected of participation in genocide were reportedly killed in revenge attacks immediately after the genocide and in the late 1990s,[73] while tens of thousands were detained without criminal charges, often for years in overcrowded prisons and improvised detention facilities in deplorable conditions with no access to basic hygiene, food, healthcare or legal aid whatsoever.[74] Even though the conditions in detention facilities improved over time due to successive waves of releases of the elderly and sick and provisional releases of those who confessed in expectation of Gacaca proceedings,[75] the conditions in most prisons are still incomparable to 'the prisoners of international community'. A shining example of these double standards is the Mpanga prison in Nyanza Province in Rwanda. Besides *génocidaires* convicted by Gacaca and domestic courts in Rwanda, it has also hosted eight individuals convicted by the Special Court for Sierra Leone.[76] As thousands of Rwandans are crowded in a common, soccer field sized courtyard of the 'domestic wing' sharing bathrooms and sleeping in dorm-like corridors or outside, due to a lack of available space inside, the international prisoners in the international wing enjoy single cells with private bathrooms.[77] Furthermore, when it comes to the quality of trials in Rwanda, especially in the early years after genocide, many commentators and NGOs pointed to the lack of fair trial guarantees, a lack of any defence available to

---

[73] Reyntjens, above (n 18) 1–25.

[74] C Tertsakian, *Le Chateau, The Lives of Prisoners in Rwanda* (London, Arves Books, 2008) 34.

[75] As reported by Barrett, above (n 65) 18.

[76] At the time of writing, two out of those eight have already been released.

[77] Observations of the first author during the field visit in Mpanga prison in 2014. For imprisonment conditions of international prisoners *cf* B Holá and J van Wijk, 'Life After Conviction at International Criminal Tribunals: Empirical Overview' (2014) 12 *Journal of International Criminal Justice* 109.

those suspected of genocide or the fact that prisoners were in reality presumed to be guilty, not innocent.[78] Arguably, the quality of trials and of the judicial system as such significantly improved over time;[79] however, the fact remains that in the collected sample of cases only 30.9 per cent were represented by a defence lawyer. And even if in a position to afford a defence lawyer, the possibility of actually being able to conduct an effective defence in genocide-related cases in Rwanda is still questioned to this day. Quite recently, in mid-2017 for example, a British court blocked and rejected the extradition of five genocide suspects to Rwanda on account of insufficient guarantees of effective defence.[80]

Keeping in mind these broader considerations, this chapter presented 'a magnifying glass picture' comparing sentencing laws, practices and outcomes at the ICTR and in Rwandan domestic courts. With respect to sentencing approach, the chapter argued that at the ICTR as well as in domestic courts in Rwanda, the culpability level of the offender was the main 'ordering device' in justifying differences in sentence severity within each system (be it a priori as in Rwandan laws or by the ICTR judges in the case law). The culpability level was determined predominantly by his or her position in the state hierarchy, exercise of authority and influence over others, and his or her role in the crime. One notable difference, however, relates to the treatment of accomplices, which were put on a par with principal perpetrators and subjected to the same sentences according to the Rwandan organic laws. In contrast, ICTR judges argued that for the purposes of sentencing accomplices should be in general considered less culpable, due to their secondary role in atrocities. This difference in sentencing approach is even more significant if one takes into account the fact that the vast majority of defendants in our sample of cases collected in Rwanda were convicted as accomplices (often based on a very broad interpretation of complicity) and subjected to relatively severe sentences. Regarding the sentencing outcomes, it was impossible to make any conclusive claims. Given the state of judicial archives in Rwanda, it will arguably never be possible to conduct a systematic and conclusive empirical review of all genocide-related cases decided by Rwandan domestic courts. Given that the official state statistics, often used and relied upon by researchers, might not be entirely representative and that the original case files are often not available,

---

[78] *cf* L Waldorf, 'Mass Justice for Mass Atrocity: Rethinking Local Justice as Transitional Justice' 2006 79(1) *Temple Law Review* 1, 45–46; or Amnesty International Report, *Rwanda. Unfair Trials. Justice Denied* (London, 1997) or Human Rights Watch, 'Law and Reality. Progress of Judicial Reform in Rwanda', above (n 18); or M Drumbl, 'Rule of Law amid Lawlessness: Counselling the Accused in Rwanda's Domestic Genocide Trials' (1998) 29 *Columbia Human Rights Law Review*, 545 550.

[79] See, eg, Palmer, above (n 5) at 89–113.

[80] *The Government of the Republic of Rwanda v Nteziryao and others* [2017] EWHC 1912 (Admin), High Court of Justice, 28 July 2017. But compare, eg, the case in the Netherlands of Jean Claude Iyamuremye and Jean Baptiste Mugimba, where the two accused after being initially not extradited to Rwanda due to concerns regarding fair trial rights, were in the end sent to Rwanda for trial: *The Government of the Republic of Rwanda v Jean-Baptiste Mugimba and Jean-Claude Iyamuremye*, Supreme Court in The Hague, 5 July 2016.

we might be left in the dark when it comes to sentencing practices of genocide-related cases by domestic courts in Rwanda.

Taking all this into consideration, the results, however, point in two directions: (i) the punishment of those considered 'the most responsible' and tried at the ICTR seems to have been less severe compared with the majority of defendants tried in Rwandan courts; and (ii) there has been a progressive evolution of punishment modalities and severity in Rwanda towards less punitive sanctions. This case study also demonstrated that in trying to understand and compare punishment after atrocities across different jurisdictions, the context matters greatly and must be reflected in the analysis. In this sense, of course each case is highly specific and cannot be generalised. In contrast to the relative vacuum of international courtrooms in isolation from the crime scenes and affected societies, criminal justice and punishment after atrocities at the domestic level is highly dynamic, conditional and instrumental. It is not simply the 'punishment for past wrongs' in the name of 'combating impunity'. It is part and parcel of a broader national transitional justice 'agenda' of regime change and social engineering within each state. It is context-dependent and ebbs and flows along the tidal waves of pragmatic, political and societal demands of transitioning societies. These in turn condition how punishment is designed, implemented and enforced. International prosecutions such as those at the ICTR are a principally distant, largely 'static' and symbolic form of justice, delivered in the name of an ambiguous 'international community'. However, when it comes to punishment and sentencing, the question remains what message the international community sends if, as in the case of Rwanda, those considered the most responsible tried at the ICTR seem to have been subjected to arguably preferential treatment and comparably more lenient punishments than the vast majority of their 'followers' prosecuted in domestic courts.

PART IV

Re-Entry of Victims and Perpetrators

8

Not in Our Name! Visions of Community in International Criminal Justice

MILENA TRIPKOVIC

I. Introduction

Having delivered its final judgment in November 2017, the International Criminal Tribunal for the former Yugoslavia (ICTY) ceased its work after nearly 25 years, which expectedly triggered attempts to give a closing verdict regarding its success in achieving various transitional goals. Although the main aim of the ICTY was to deliver justice by determining individual criminal responsibility, promoting peace in the former Yugoslavia also fared high on the list of objectives that the Court set out to accomplish. United Nations Resolution 827 by which the ICTY was founded in 1993, anticipated that the work of the *ad hoc* international criminal tribunal would, among other things, 'contribute to the restoration and maintenance of peace'.[1] Writing its first annual report, the former President of the ICTY Antonio Cassese suggested that the Court is 'a tool for promoting reconciliation and restoring true peace'.[2] Upon its closure, a quarter of a century later, the Court seems convinced that it has achieved even more than it had hoped for:

> Undoubtedly, the Tribunal's work has had a major impact on the states of the former Yugoslavia ... simply by removing some of the most senior and notorious criminals and holding them accountable the Tribunal has been able to lift the taint of violence, contribute to ending impunity and help pave the way for reconciliation.[3]

---

[1] United Nations Security Council, 'Resolution 827', available at: www.icty.org/x/file/Legal%20 Library/Statute/statute_827_1993_en.pdf.

[2] ICTY, 'Annual Report of the International Tribunal for the Prosecution of Persons Responsible for Serious Violations of International Humanitarian Law Committed in the Territory of the Former Yugoslavia Since 1991', available at: www.icty.org/x/file/About/Reports%20and%20Publications/ AnnualReports/annual_report_1994_en.pdf.

[3] ICTY, 'About the ICTY', available at: www.icty.org/en/about.

This self-assured view – that the Court's work on truth and justice paved the way towards reconciliation – is however shared by neither academic commentators nor many people who live in the former Yugoslavia. Most academics argue that the Court's proceedings have had little reconciliatory effects,[4] with some emphasising that, if anything, the ICTY has actually contributed to a heightened sense of mistrust and hostility,[5] although many have recognised that reconciliation was an unattainable goal for a court whose main purpose is to establish criminal responsibility.[6] These views are hardly surprising: since its foundation, the ICTY was, across the former Yugoslavia, persistently accused of prejudice and bias: for this reason, for example, 71 per cent of both Croatians and Serbs had a predominantly negative opinion of the Court, while 67 per cent of Croatians and 49 per cent of Serbs were against their countries' cooperation with the ICTY.[7] It is then understandable that 54 per cent of Croatians, 71 per cent of Serbs – and perhaps most significantly having in mind its multi-ethnic composition -- 50 per cent of people in Bosnia and Herzegovina think that the Court's work has had no influence on reconciliation in the region.[8] Even though perceptions differ across

[4] J Snyder and L Vinjamuri, 'Trials and Errors: Principle and Pragmatism in Strategies of International Justice' (2004) 28 *International Security* 5; J Meernik, 'Justice and Peace? How the International Criminal Tribunal Affects Societal Peace in Bosnia' (2005) 42 *Journal of Peace Research* 271; I Delpla, 'In the Midst of Injustice: The ICTY from the Perspective of Some Victim Associations' in X Bougarel, E Helms and G Duijzings (eds), *The New Bosnian Mosaic: Identities, Memories and Moral Claims in a Post-War Society* (Aldershot, Ashgate, 2007); J Mannegren Selimovic, 'Perpetrators and Victims: Local Responses to the International Criminal Tribunal for the Former Yugoslavia' (2010) 57 *Focaal* 50; JN Clark, *International Trials and Reconciliation: Assessing the Impact of the International Criminal Tribunal for the Former Yugoslavia* (Abingdon, Routledge, 2014); MI Khan, 'Historical Record and the Legacy of the International Criminal Tribunal for the Former Yugoslavia' in J Gow, R Keer and Z Pajic (eds), *Prosecuting War Crimes: Lessons and Legacies of the International Criminal Tribunal for the Former Yugoslavia* (London, Routledge, 2014).

[5] R Hayden, 'What's Reconciliation Got to Do with it? The International Criminal Tribunal for the Former Yugoslavia (ICTY) as antiwar profiteer' (2011) 5 Journal of Intervention and Statebuilding 313–330.

[6] JN Clark, 'From Negative to Positive Peace: The Case of Bosnia and Hercegovina' (2009) 8 *Journal of Human Rights* 360; JN Clark, 'The Limits of Retributive Justice: Findings of an Empirical Study in Bosnia and Hercegovina' (2009) 7 *Journal of International Criminal Justice* 463; JN Clark, 'Judging the ICTY: Has it Achieved its Objectives?' (2009) 9 *Southeast European and Black Sea Studies* 123; R Kerr, 'Peace through Justice? The International Criminal Tribunal for the Former Yugoslavia' (2007) 7 *Southeast European and Black Sea Studies* 373; J Subotic, 'Legitimacy, Scope, and Conflicting Claims on the ICTY: In the Aftermath of *Gotovina, Haradinaj* and *Perišić*' (2014) 13 *Journal of Human Rights* 170; Snyder and Vinjamuri, above (n 4); P Robinson, 'Creating a Legacy that Supports Sustainable Rule of Law in the Region' in R Steinberg (ed), *Assessing the Legacy of the ICTY* (Leiden, Martinus Nijhoff, 2011); D Orentlicher, 'From Viability to Impact: Evolving Metrics for Assessing the International Criminal Tribunal for the Former Yugoslavia' (2013) 7 *International Journal of Transitional Justice* 536.

[7] Organization for Co-operation and Security in Europe (OSCE), 'Public Opinion Poll: Attitudes towards War Crimes Issues, ICTY and the National Judiciary', available at: www.osce.org/serbia/90422; Beogradski centar za ljudska prava, 'Javno mnenje u Hrvatskoj i stavovi prema Međunarodnom krivičnom tribunalu za bivšu Jugoslaviju u Hagu', available at: www.bgcentar.org.rs/bgcentar/wp-content/uploads/2013/10/Javno-mnenje-u-Hrvatskoj-i-stavovi-prema-Medunarodnom-krivicnom-tribunalu-za-bivšu-Jugoslaviju-u-Hagu-ICTY-2011-detaljne-tabele.pdf.

[8] OSCE, ibid; Beogradski centar za ljudska prava, ibid; and Beogradski centar za ljudska prava, 'Javno mnenje u BIH i stavovi prema Međunarodnom krivičnom tribunal za bivšu Jugo-

ethnicities, 'exported'[9] or 'hijacked'[10] justice is seen unequivocally as a less than ideal solution.

This chapter is primarily motivated by a desire to explore some of the possible reasons why the ICTY failed to achieve the task of reconciliation among the peoples of the former Yugoslavia. To do so, the chapter consciously moves away from standard interpretations of relevant factors which cite geographical distance and insufficient attention to outreach, both of which refer to the point that the ICTY was a foreign court whose work was *unfamiliar* to the population of the former Yugoslavia. While at first this seems like a reasonable explanation, the chapter contends that a more comprehensive understanding of the relevant factors ought to be employed, which concerns the relationship between punishment and the community and emphasises the positive effects which the imposition of penal measures on wrongdoers can have for the wellbeing of the society. Stated simply, if prosecution and punishment by the ICTY did not have reconciliatory effects, then it must be the case that the positive effects which the punishment – as a theoretical possibility – may have on the community, were absent in this case. To understand what these are, we must seek to enlighten the deeper theoretical commitments which underlie this proposition.

The chapter develops in the following way. First, I expose the fundamental theoretical assumptions about the role of punishment in the community. This part of the chapter is not concerned with identifying the aims of punishment (its deontological or teleological foundations), but with the functions and role of punishment in the *community* to which the offender belongs. The second part of the chapter, drawing on the example of the ICTY's outreach programme in the former Yugoslavia, elucidates the key differences between the assumptions about the functions of punishment *within* one community and the role of punishment *at the international level*. This part emphasises the different ways in which communities are perceived on the domestic and international level by focusing on two key issues: the *authorship* and *ownership* of criminal punishment. Ultimately, it reaches a conclusion that international trials inherently suffer from the lack of appropriate moral bearing which is a precondition if punishment is to have a positive wide-scale effect on the society. Acknowledging the role that international criminal trials will increasingly assume in the future (particularly with regard to the International Criminal Court), the last part of the chapter concludes by seeking to reconcile the ever growing need for international prosecutions with the problems that international courts innately experience.

---

slaviju u Hagu', available at: www.bgcentar.org.rs/bgcentar/wp-content/uploads/2013/10/Javno-mnenje-u-BiH-i-stavovi-prema-Medunarodnom-krivicnom-tribunalu-za-bivšu-Jugoslaviju-u-Hagu-ICTY-2010-detaljne-tabele.pdf.

[9] D Saxon, 'Exporting Justice: Perceptions of the ICTY among the Serbian, Croatian and Muslim Communities in the Former Yugoslavia' (2005) 4 *Journal of Human Rights* 559.

[10] J Subotic, *Hijacked Justice: Dealing with the Past in the Balkans* (Ithaca, NY, Cornell University Press, 2009).

II. The Role of Punishment in the Community

When considering the role of punishment, one of the key issues that arises concerns the justification(s) of punitive measures that are imposed on criminal offenders. This refers to a long-standing debate regarding deontological (retribution) and consequentialist (deterrence, rehabilitation or incapacitation) reasons for which punishment may be imposed. The focus of this discussion is hence mostly on the offenders, while the assumptions about the effects of punishment for the community are mostly drawn indirectly from whatever is thought that punishment of criminals could achieve: a sense of righteousness derived from the knowledge that those guilty of crimes will not go unpunished (retribution); a sense of hope stemming from the belief that potential lawbreakers will be discouraged (deterrence) while current lawbreakers will be rehabilitated (rehabilitation); and a sense of security that draws on the knowledge that criminals have been prevented from reoffending, usually by way of incarceration (incapacitation). But all these assumptions are limited in that they do not go far enough in explaining whether punishment could achieve comprehensive, and not merely fragmentary, effects. To understand this, a sociological interpretation of the functions of punishment will be employed in this part of the chapter which examines the role of community in creating criminal laws (what I call the *authorship* dimension) and deriving the benefits from the application of punishment that is based on these norms (what I term the *ownership* dimension).

The sociological perspective on the role of punishment features perhaps most strongly in the work of Emile Durkheim, who developed a comprehensive account of the foundations and functions of punishment which (with some important caveats that will be mentioned below) figures strongly even today. In a well-rehearsed argument, Durkheim considered crime a 'normal' social fact which, even though it appears in diverse forms, is present across time and space.[11] For Durkheim, however, crime is not only 'normal' but is also not entirely negative:

> [T]o classify crime among the phenomena of normal sociology is not merely to declare that it is an inevitable though regrettable phenomenon arising from the incorrigible wickedness of men; it is to assert that it is a factor in public health, an integrative element in any healthy society.[12]

To understand this unconventional claim, we need to go back to Durkheim's examination of the foundations of criminal law. For him, crime is an action that 'offends certain collective feelings which are especially strong and clear-cut'.[13] These collective feelings – which Durkheim calls 'conscience collective' and which are spatially and temporally contingent – are moulded into laws, which thus purportedly become accurate representations of the common morality. Punishment can

---

[11] E Durkheim, *The Rules of Sociological Method* (London, The Free Press, 1964).
[12] ibid, 98.
[13] ibid, 99.

therefore be said to represent 'an index of society's invisible moral bonds'[14] and it is in this sense that I suggest that the community has *authorship* over criminal laws. A strong link between morality and crime is therefore established, but the link assumes an opposite direction from the one usually assumed – in Durkheim's words, we should not think that

> an action shocks the conscience collective because it is criminal, but rather that it is criminal because it shocks the conscience collective ... we do not condemn it because it is a crime, but it is a crime because we condemn it.[15]

However, the authorship role of the community in devising criminal laws is merely one dimension in Durkheim's analysis of the social functions of crime and punishment. The truly beneficial effects derived from punishment emanate from the *ownership* of the process through which punishment is imposed on criminal offenders and – even more importantly – the ownership of the *moral outcomes* of this process. Discussing this dimension of Durkheim's work, David Garland notes how punishment represents 'an occasion for the collective expression of shared moral passions, and this collective expression serves to strengthen these same passions through mutual reinforcement and reassurance'.[16] Therefore, a circular process is established whereby common morality provides the foundation for the definition of crimes whose punishment then works backwards to reaffirm that same morality and enhance social solidarity. Punishment then, rather than being merely expressive, has a functional effect as it 'is above all a moral process ... propelled by moral sentiments, its forms symbolize and express moral judgements, and its effects are primarily to reaffirm the moral order'.[17]

The most important conclusion emanating from the preceding discussion is that an intricate but robust link exists between *punishment* and *community* – the community not only creates criminal laws but more importantly, punishment does not exist and cannot be understood without reference to the community. Punishment is not an abstract, technical and instrumental response to crime that is separate from and bears no relevance to the social context within which it is imposed. While Durkheim's account has been criticised for assuming that 'conscience collective' is homogenous, but is more realistically a consequence of struggle thus becoming the 'ruling' or 'dominant' morality,[18] this critique does not significantly undermine the importance of punishment for the society and social solidarity, however these may come about.

Arguments which bear resemblance to Durkheim's position have been rehearsed more recently, within the debate on the best normative justification of punishment which emphasises the citizenship dimension and pays attention to the community within which such punishment is imposed. Starting from the

---

[14] D Garland, *Punishment and Modern Society* (Oxford, Clarendon, 1991) 2.
[15] E Durkheim, *The Division of Labor in Society* (New York, The Free Press, 1972) 123–24.
[16] Garland, above (n 14) 33.
[17] ibid, 47.
[18] ibid, 52.

premise that crimes are public rather than private wrongs, Antony Duff holds that 'common law' – the law of the community – is 'a form in which citizens speak to one another' because it 'embodies values shared by the community [and] flows from the traditions and practices of the community'.[19] The purpose of punishment is to communicate reprobation to the offender, make her understand the harm that she has caused and allow her to be reconciled with the community. This view, much like Durkheim's, also focuses on two dimensions: it examines both what the punishment 'does' to the offender (in Duff's words, it aims at 'inclusion' through communication), but also how such inclusive punishment benefits the community. Similarly, Nicola Lacey considers that criminal laws play a social function in upholding community values that are 'perceived as necessary to the maintenance, stability and peaceful development of the community'.[20]

Finally, the idea of the community's focal role in punishment has found its practical application within the restorative justice paradigm. Offenders, victims and the community are key actors in the restorative process as they are all considered to have a 'stake' in the given offence.[21] Conceptualising a crime as a conflict between the criminal and victim,[22] restorative justice nevertheless recognises the central role which the community plays in expressing moral reprobation and condemnation, but equally importantly in taking positive steps towards reintegration of the offender which invariably strengthens social cohesion.[23]

While common criticism, as already mentioned, holds that the empirical reality is often far removed from the notions developed in this section, the normative value of ideas that underlie them is not consequently undermined. If punishment is to have any beneficial effects on the community – and there is no reason to desire anything less than that – then reaffirming solidarity, and reasserting common values and common morality seem like valuable goals. Making the community an author of punishment therefore becomes a crucial condition for claiming ownership over the beneficial consequences which come about through its imposition.

III. The Community and International Criminal Punishment

The decision to put an international *ad hoc* tribunal, rather than any of the domestic courts which had actual jurisdiction over the matter, in charge of the

---

[19] AM Duff, *Punishment, Communication and Community* (Oxford, Oxford University Press, 2001) 59–60.

[20] N Lacey, *State Punishment* (London, Routledge, 1993) 176.

[21] T Marshall, 'Restorative Justice: An Overview' in G Johnstone (ed), *A Restorative Justice Reader: Texts, Sources, Context* (Willan, 2003)

[22] N Christie, 'Conflicts as Property' (1977) 17 *British Journal of Criminology* 1.

[23] H Strang and J Braithwaite, *Restorative Justice and Civil Society* (Cambridge, Cambridge University Press, 2001); H Zehr, *The Little Book of Restorative Justice* (New York, Good Books, 2014); F Fonseca Rosenblatt, *The Role of Community in Restorative Justice* (Abingdon, Routledge, 2015).

prosecution of crimes perpetrated during Yugoslavia's conflict, was essentially one of necessity. With the war still raging in 1993 when the ICTY was set up, there were no realistic prospects for prosecution other than to involve a geographically distant, and presumably impartial international court. According to Fausto Pocar, the ICTY's former President, the primacy of the ICTY was nevertheless intended to be only temporary, and the Court's 'completion strategy' which devised a plan for transferring the remaining cases to the countries in the region, was in reality a 'continuation strategy' aimed equally importantly at strengthening the rule of law and increasing judicial capacity in post-Yugoslav states.[24] Currently, a number of courts in the former Yugoslavia are facing the future prospect of conducting at least 3,000 trials for which the ICTY provided at least some evidence,[25] and while it remains to be seen how these processes will play out in reality, it is reasonable to suggest that the ICTY will remain the most important judicial body for the region, if for no other reason than because it succeeded in convicting a significant number of high-profile offenders for the most serious breaches of international humanitarian law.

Involving an international court in a domestic matter has, as is well known, led to numerous problems for the functioning of the Tribunal. Its fundamental deficiency was the lack of enforcement mechanisms to apprehend the suspects and secure evidence for prosecution, making the Court entirely dependent on the reluctant cooperation of the countries in the region.[26] The governments' unwillingness to cooperate was profoundly linked to (but also impacted) the negative way in which the people across the former Yugoslavia perceived the Tribunal's work.[27] The Tribunal was, from the start, seen to be not even an international, but essentially *a foreign court*, geographically removed from the region, alienated from the local population and the events that took place during the conflict. Even though the Tribunal at first enjoyed support within specific ethnic groups – such as Bosniaks and Kosovars – the ICTY's subsequent indictments against (a small number of) members of these groups irreparably damaged its reputation.

Aware of this damaging perception, seeking to reduce political obstruction,[28] and improve its reputation, the ICTY set up an outreach programme in 1999. The programme was essentially an information campaign, consisting of activities such

---

[24] F Pocar, 'Completion or Continuation Strategy?' (2008) 6 *Journal of International Criminal Justice* 655.

[25] Balkan Insight, 'Suspects Evade Justice as Prosecutors Ignore UN War Files', available at: www.balkaninsight.com/en/article/suspects-evade-justice-as-prosecutors-ignore-un-war-files-03-12-2018.

[26] C Jorda, 'The Major Hurdles and Accomplishments of the ICTY – What the ICC Can Learn from Them' (2004) 2 *Journal of International Criminal Justice* 572; V Peskin, *International Justice in Rwanda and the Balkans: Virtual Trials and the Struggle for State Cooperation* (Cambridge, Cambridge University Press, 2008); W Scharp, 'International Obligations to Search for and Arrest War Criminals: Government Failure in the Former Yugoslavia?' (1996) 7 *Duke Journal of Comparative and International Law* 411.

[27] OSCE, above (n 7); Beogradski centar za ljudska prava, above (n 7); Beogradski centar za ljudska prava, above (n 8).

[28] Kerr, above (n 6).

as organising workshops, preparing documentaries and prospects, and capacity-building of the judiciary.[29] Its ultimate goal was to 'work with the communities in the region to reflect on the Tribunal's achievements and carry that legacy forward'.[30] The Court thus felt that it was necessary to secure conditions in which its work would be seen as legitimate and to achieve this, it relied on spreading *information* about what it was doing: outreach was a manner of implementing international law into the (multi)national setting.

Reflecting back, however, the idea that obtaining additional information about criminal proceedings would influence various national and ethnic groups to view the Court's work more positively which would subsequently allow these groups to assume a more objective stance towards their own role in the conflict, now seems rather naive.[31] While the ICTY indisputably facilitated the uncovering of facts pertaining to the conflict which would have otherwise probably remained concealed,[32] the gap between knowledge and acknowledgement[33] was too wide and complex to be closed in such a simple way. Making the ICTY's work more visible in the region of the former Yugoslavia, therefore allowing the local popula-tion to 'participate' in its work, even if indirectly, was destined to achieve little in a contemporary world in which the public is in any case mostly excluded from and mostly disinterested in the punishment rituals.[34] As David Garland astutely observes,

> so long as the existing sanctions appear to convey a punitive effect in a manner which is broadly in keeping with current sensibilities, there tends to be limited moral interest in the details of how punishments are actually carried out.[35]

The key issue here is that the public is less interested in *how* punishment is imposed and more interested in *who* imposes it and on the basis of *what*. Anecdo-tal testimony which corroborates this position may be seen in the way in which the Serbian public perceived the trial of Slobodan Milošević. Each of his appearances before the ICTY was televised and the Serbian public had ample opportunities to understand the details of the crimes that he was charged with and comprehend the seriousness of the allegations that were put forward by the prosecution. But instead of changing the perception about Milošević through revealing the facts

---

[29] See for details, ICTY, 'Outreach Programme', available at: www.icty.org/en/outreach/outreach-programme> accessed on 23 June 2018; see also JN Clark, 'International War Crimes Tribunals and the Challenge of Outreach' (2009) 9 *International Criminal Law Review* 99.

[30] ICTY, 'Outreach Programme', above (n 29).

[31] Stanley Cohen similarly believes that a large gap exists between finding out the truth and coming to terms with atrocities perpetrated in one's name, see S Cohen, *States of Denial* (Cambridge, Polity Press, 2001).

[32] Jorda, above (n 26).

[33] Thomas Nagel, cited in L Weschler, 'Afterword' in L Weschler (ed), *State Crimes: Punishment or Pardon* (Washington DC, Aspen Institute, 1989).

[34] M Foucault, *Discipline and Punish: The Birth of Prison* (London, Penguin Books, 1991).

[35] Garland, above (n 14) 33.

about his alleged crimes, people across Serbia (even those openly critical of his regime) commended the skilled way in which he cross-examined the witnesses, revealing serious flaws in the prosecution's case and ridiculing the prosecutors who struggled to understand key actors and events, and even to pronounce words in the domestic language. Instead of coming to terms with the facts, the public seemingly became even more deeply enthralled into denial.

A response to this criticism was a suggestion that the way in which the ICTY's outreach programme was created had too many flaws – a pertinent one being that it was set up six years after the Court started its work. It was thus thought that while in theory outreach could achieve its goals, this task was undermined by the flaws in concrete measures which the Court had implemented: the programme was allegedly insufficiently thorough, understaffed and underfunded.[36] Resonating a general view that the ICTY is 'not our court', the Court's former spokesman Refik Hodžic held that it simply did too little:

> Eager to stay out of 'politics' and to 'let judgments speak for themselves', the Tribunal's decision-makers never saw the need to properly report to their true constituents on critical questions being raised in Sarajevo, Zagreb, Belgrade: Why were certain people indicted and others not? What was the philosophy of Tribunal's so-called sentencing policy? How was it possible to quash 1,300-page trial judgments with several pages of an appeal judgment? Why were defendants allowed to get rich by splitting Tribunal-provided fees with their lawyers? The list of such unanswered questions (often posed even by 'friends of the Tribunal' in the Balkans) is inexcusably long.[37]

In other words, as this argument seems to propose, had the ICTY's work in this domain been more serious, thorough and persistent, the Court would have been able to improve its image, convince the domestic population that it had legitimacy to conduct the criminal proceedings over foreign suspects, and perhaps reduce hostilities among the countries in the region, thus paving the way towards peace and reconciliation.

However, this position is essentially at odds with the theoretical notions regarding the role of punishment in the community that were developed in the previous section. While the Court's position seems to emphasise the beneficial effects which can be achieved if the domestic population *knows* what the ICTY is doing, the theoretical outlook holds that the beneficial effects can only take place if the community *feels* that the court 'belongs to them' and that the punishment

---

[36] R Zacklin, 'The Failings of Ad Hoc International Tribunals' (2004) 2 *Journal of International Criminal Justice* 541; A Fatić, *Reconciliation via the War Crimes Tribunal* (Aldershot, Ashgate, 2001); Clark, 'International War Crimes Tribunals and the Challenge of Outreach', above (n 29); Clark, 'Judging the ICTY', above (n 6); K Zoglin, 'The Future of War Crimes Prosecutions in the Former Yugoslavia: Accountability or Junk Justice?' (2005) 27 *Human Rights Quarterly* 41; L Dickinson 'The Promise of Hybrid Courts' (2003) 97 *American Journal of International Law* 295; J Ramji-Nogales, 'Designing Bespoke Transitional Justice: A Pluralist Process Approach' (2010) 32 *Michigan Journal of International Law* 32.

[37] R Hodžić, 'Accepting a Difficult Truth: ICTY is not Our Court, available at: www.balkaninsight.com/en/article/accepting-a-difficult-truth-icty-is-not-our-court.

imposed by such court is an authentic manifestation of communal sentiments.[38] These are two significantly different positions and the assumption that knowledge of how and why punishment is imposed will lead to a sense of ownership over this process[39] is rather tenuous, because it is debatable whether access to information can compensate for the lack of moral involvement.

It is at this point useful to go back to two concepts that were discussed in the previous section: the issues of authorship and ownership over criminal punishment, but the question now becomes how these concepts relate to the existence and functioning of international courts. While domestic communities are clearly the authors and owners (in other words beneficiaries) of punishment that is imposed by domestic courts, this is less obvious in the case in which punishment is imposed by a judicial body that is morally distant from the specific communal traits. Explaining Durkheim's position, Garland states:

> Punishment may be a legal institution, administered by state functionaries, but it is necessarily grounded in wider patterns of knowing, feeling and acting, and it depends upon these social roots and supports for its continuing legitimacy and operation.[40]

To achieve beneficial effects, then, the imposition of punishment as a legal process must not be disconnected from the community of people who are expected to experience the beneficial effects that arise therefrom: those whose 'conscience collective' ought to be reaffirmed through punishment. But in the case of international criminal tribunals – and the ICTY is a pertinent example of this – the imposition of punishment becomes a purely technical matter of proper administration of justice, which makes it profoundly disconnected from the moral sentiments of the domestic community and, as it was argued above regarding the outreach programme, makes the Court only superficially concerned with the impact of its judgments on the relevant community. While such punishment may be considered satisfactory from the standpoint of achieving the goal of justice,[41] punishment should not be expected to achieve other goals such as peace or reconciliation. The domestic population thus fails to see such punishment as morally relevant not because the Court is geographically removed and its work unfamiliar, but because it operates within an entirely alien moral framework. Suggestions on how best to 'internalise' justice achieved by international courts,[42] hence, seem to utterly miss the point: they seem to invoke an essentially top-down process in which domestic communities are mere recipients and passive participants in the process of punishment, but not enough concern is paid to whether they actually feel such justice their own.

---

[38] Durkheim, The Rules of Sociological Method, above (n 11).

[39] Saxon, above (n 9).

[40] Garland, above (n 14) 21.

[41] P Akhavan, 'Justice in the Hague, Peace in the Former Yugoslavia? A Commentary on the United Nations War Crimes Tribunal' (1998) 20 *Human Rights Quarterly* 737.

[42] S Ford, 'A Social Psychology Model of the Perceived Legitimacy of International Criminal Courts: Implications for the Success of Transitional Justice Mechanisms' (2012) 45 *Vanderbilt Journal of Transnational Law* 405.

At the same time, it would be wrong to assume that the ICTY functioned in a moral vacuum: it is merely that its target moral community is not the countries of the former Yugoslavia, but the *international community*. Judging from the way in which it was founded, as a last resort of the international community to stop the bloodshed in former Yugoslavia, and having in mind the nature of the values endangered by the crimes in ICTY's jurisdiction – universal values and the most severe attempts to undermine them – the authors and owners of such punishment are clearly located above and beyond the ex-Yugoslav community. Akhavan states this most succinctly when he observes how victims that appear before the international tribunals have the opportunity to 'hear and see their stories told ... in an officially sanctioned forum before the *international community*'.[43] Similarly, proposing that punishment imposed by international tribunals has an 'expressive function', Sloane points out that such punishment contributes to the 'world public order',[44] which means that it only indirectly concerns national communities and – in his opinion and as a normative matter – there is no reason why national communities should be the main addressees of international justice. Nevertheless, even though international trials were externally imposed on countries of the former Yugoslavia,[45] punishment by the ICTY should still benefit the region – after all, former Yugoslav countries are part of the international community and subscribe to the same universal values. It is, however, obvious that beneficial effects are undermined as the international community is the real author and owner of punishment imposed by international courts, whereas the domestic community is at best a passive recipient.

IV. Reconciliation Through International Courts: An Untenable Goal?

Judging from public opinion surveys that have been conducted in the former Yugoslavia, an appropriate response to violations of international humanitarian law which occurred during the 1990s conflicts, would have been criminal prosecutions conducted by the courts in the region, not the ICTY. While in Serbia 45 per cent of those surveyed believe that each country should put its own nationals on trial, 20 per cent would additionally support trials in the country in which the crimes were committed (and these would presumably be courts in foreign countries – Croatia or Bosnia and Herzegovina – since few crimes were perpetrated on Serbian soil), and only 11 per cent think that the ICTY should have been

---

[43] Akhavan, above (n 41) 766, emphasis added.

[44] R Sloane, 'The Expressive Capacity of International Punishment: The Limits of the National Law Analogy and the Potential of International Criminal Law' (2007) 43 *Stanford Journal of International Law* 39.

[45] Peskin, above (n 26).

solely responsible for the trials.[46] In Croatia, the percentages pertaining to regional prosecutions are reversed – 15 per cent support prosecution by the defendant's own state while 43 per cent support trials in the country in which the crimes were committed (this should come as no surprise because it would in reality mean Croatia's jurisdiction as most crimes that are of interest for Croatians were perpetrated within the country); however, an equally small number – 17 per cent – agree that the ICTY should have had sole jurisdiction.[47] This is an interesting finding – rather than the presumably impartial international court, those surveyed would have rather seen their co-nationals prosecuted by the courts of their former enemies. When asked why they would prefer such prosecutions over those conducted by an international court, the majority of respondents in Serbia (62 per cent) suggest that regional courts – regardless of whether domestic or foreign – would be more objective or fair.[48]

A notable level of distrust towards the objectivity and fairness of the ICTY can thus be observed in the surveys: regardless of differences between Croatia and Serbia, the Court clearly enjoyed less support than any of the courts in the region. This finding, along with the preceding discussion on the association between punishment and community, seems to paint a negative picture of the role that international criminal justice can play in the process of peacebuilding and reconciliation. Are international trials fundamentally ill-equipped to achieve anything more than (a necessarily partial) justice? Is the lack of moral authority to prosecute which is linked to the lack of authorship and ownership of domestic communities over international punishment an unsurmountable obstacle to the perceived legitimacy of international courts and their propensity to reaffirm the 'conscience collective' and restore solidarity at the domestic level? And, if so, what does all this mean for the future impact of the International Criminal Court on domestic communities that are 'unable' or 'unwilling' to prosecute?

To answer these questions, an additional layer of analysis needs to be introduced, which concerns the *capacities* of domestic communities to acquire a sense of authorship and ownership over international trials. While I have argued throughout the chapter that it is inherently difficult for domestic communities to experience beneficial effects from international punishment, this is made all the less likely whenever a domestic community does not have desired moral traits and is *effectively not a community*, which is undoubtedly the case with former Yugoslavia that has undergone a process of complete dissolution into ethnically homogenous states (Bosnia and Herzegovina, although multicultural, is nevertheless internally divided). It bears to emphasise at this point that Durkheim's view of the potential benefits that may come about from punishment is conceived from within the framework of fully functional communities, which have a desired level of solidarity. But, as Durkheim seems to suggest, 'punishment cannot by itself *create* moral

---

[46] OSCE, 'Public Opinion Poll', above (n 7).

[47] Beogradski centar za ljudska prava, above (n 7).

[48] OSCE, 'Public Opinion Poll', above (n 7); the question was not asked in the Croatian survey.

authority: on the contrary, punishment implies that authority is already in place and has been breached'.[49] In other words, for punishment to be able to reaffirm conscience collective it needs to refer to a morally robust community, a condition which is certainly not present in the case of divided post-conflict communities such as the former Yugoslavia. For reasons similar to those that Snyder and Vinjamuri put forward when they describe why pursuing accountability for crimes in ethnically or religiously divided communities is inherently difficult,[50] the probability of recognising and accepting the truth created by a foreign court will be additionally weakened – perhaps even made impossible – in circumstances in which bonds between citizens are not strong enough to create common moral sensitivities. The perceived legitimacy of an international court very much depends on *who* the Court prosecutes – 'indictments that conflict with the dominant internal narratives among the various groups will lead directly to lower perceptions of the court's legitimacy'.[51] The impact of the Court's work on the region is thus weakened not merely because the Court is perceived as irrelevant due to its weak moral links with the domestic community, but also because its judgments concern individuals that belong to multiple national or ethnic groups that are alienated from each other to the extent that they hardly make up a community. This furthermore causes many other problems which concern the outcomes of criminal punishment for the offenders and victims, and which do not usually appear in morally bounded communities. Divided communities are atypical to the extent that they tend to have sharply different perceptions regarding the causes and dynamics of conflict, and it is oftentimes the case that victims and offenders cannot easily be told apart as each 'can drift from one category to the other over the duration of the conflict'[52] and – perhaps more importantly – be due to a wider inability of social groups to acknowledge criminal responsibility of their co-nationals. While this is problematic enough, additional interference of an international court in such a setting and its inherent propensity to establish what is (or who was) right or wrong through its judgments, leads to problems in the appropriate social reactions towards offenders and victims, whose roles are conflated and viewed differently from the standpoint of various national and ethnic groups.

These realisations ultimately force us to reconsider the claims regarding the capabilities of international courts to achieve various transitional justice goals. On the one hand, having in mind the difficulties of making international courts morally relevant – especially when their judgments pertain to divided post-conflict communities – it would be sensible to reduce our expectations as to what they can achieve to merely determining criminal responsibility in individual (and an inevitably small number of) cases. This is surely a worthwhile goal and if we

---

[49] Garland, above (n 14) 42.
[50] Snyder and Vinjamuri, above (n 4) 37.
[51] Ford, above (n 42) 405.
[52] K Clamp, 'Restorative Justice as a Contested Response to Conflict and the Challenge of the Transitional Context' in K Clamp (ed), *Restorative Justice in Transitional Settings* (London, Routledge, 2016) 3.

additionally opt to pursue achievable aims of punishment – such as retribution or incapacitation – leaving those with dubious propensities to be achieved – such as deterrence or rehabilitation – aside, then punishment by international courts would serve its purpose of ending impunity for grave violations of international humanitarian law, regardless of the absence of the positive impact on the community.

However, aiming to achieve anything more than punishment of guilty offenders seems debatable from the theoretical point of view that was espoused in this chapter. Any attempt to do so could be doomed to failure simply because of the described moral irrelevance of international courts for the communities from which the offenders come. However, if any efforts are undertaken to bring international judgments closer to the community, these need to be cognisant of the domestic context and require skilful coordination of transitional justice mechanisms, which is something that international courts are themselves not equipped to do. Aiming to make international judgments relevant so that they can achieve desired beneficial outcomes would require that some positive steps are taken towards reforming and reestablishing the moral framework of a significantly disrupted community, so as to make it receptive to 'exported' justice. In other words, to even attempt reconciliation through punishment (however impossible this may seem based on the account developed in this chapter), some level of reconciliation at the domestic level must already exist which could be a paradox difficult to resolve (though not entirely impossible if we acknowledge that reconciliation is a term that can be understood in various ways).[53] Even if this kind of punishment cannot be a morally satisfactory substitute for punishment by domestic courts, acknowledging transitional realities in the domestic community would arguably at least reduce the danger of the court's judgments having a negative impact on the divided community.

V. Conclusion

The central argument of this chapter can be summed up succinctly through the words of a Srebrenica resident who, having been asked to comment on the impact of the ICTY on reconciliation, said: 'no reconciliation can come from a court than has so little relevance to our daily lives'.[54] The chapter has put forward an original claim which ascribes the inability of the ICTY to achieve reconciliation to its moral irrelevance to the ex-Yugoslav community, which is itself a consequence of the fact that the Court's proceedings are neither a sublimate of communal morality nor do its judgments have the capacity to reaffirm common morality in the

---

[53] For various ways in which reconciliation can be defined and understood, see D Crocker, 'Reckoning with Past Wrongs: A Normative Framework' (1999) 13 *Ethics & International Affairs* 43.
[54] Quoted in Clark, 'The Limits of Retributive Justice', above (n 6).

region of the former Yugoslavia. Rather than focusing on the perceived fallibilities of the outreach programme as an explanation for the lack of reconciliation through a failure to distribute *information* about the Court's work, I have instead focused on the lack of *shared perception and consciousness* that the ICTY acts in the name of and for the sake of the ex-Yugoslav community. The conclusion that I have subsequently proposed emphasises that international prosecutions can be a substitute for domestic processes only if the aim is to achieve (inevitably) partial justice, but they cannot be expected to reaffirm common morality and social solidarity, especially if they pertain to internally divided communities such as the former Yugoslavia.

9

Explaining (Away) Individual Agency: A Criminological Take on Direct Perpetrator Re-Presentations at the ICTY

ANETTE BRINGEDAL HOUGE

I. Introduction

'Today we know', Thomas Mathiesen wrote about the domestic criminal justice system in 1990, 'that [it] strikes at the "bottom" rather than at the 'top' of society'.[1] In contrast, international criminal justice is concentrated on those at the 'top': leaders, political elites and high-ranking commanders in armed organisations. As Schabas puts it, 'international criminal prosecution is not really concerned with thugs on the battlefield'.[2] Borrowing Christie's terminology, the 'ideal offenders' of international criminal justice are those who can be charged and convicted on the basis of their superior responsibility for collective crimes.[3] Such prosecutions, it is held, serve as a way to 'render justice to thousands of victims and their families'.[4]

However, as Smeulers and colleagues[5] show, more than half of the perpetrators international criminal justice institutions have ever convicted held only a low rank, or had no authority at all, at the time of their offences.[6] It was not until 2003

---

[1] T Mathiesen, *Prison on Trial: A Critical Assessment* (Winchester, Waterside Press, 2006) 76.

[2] WA Schabas, 'Criminology, Accountability, and International Justice' in M Bosworth and C Hoyle (eds), *What is Criminology?* (Oxford Scholarship Online, 2011) 357.

[3] N Christie, 'The Ideal Victim' in EA Fattah (ed), *From Crime Policy to Victim Policy. Reorienting the Justice System* (New York, St Martin's Press, 1986).

[4] 'About the ICTY', available at: www.icty.org/en/about.

[5] A Smeulers, B Holá and T van der Berg, 'Sixty-five Years of International Criminal Justice: The Facts and Figures' (2013) 13 *International Criminal Law Review* 7, 25–29.

[6] The Nuremberg and Tokyo tribunals prosecuted only high-ranking military leaders and individuals with high positions in the state apparatus – hence this development towards prosecuting individuals of lower ranks came with the establishment of tribunals and special courts in the 1990s and 2000s.

that the International Criminal Tribunal for the former Yugoslavia (ICTY),[7] with which this chapter is concerned, was mandated to concentrate exclusively 'on the prosecution and trial of the most senior leaders suspected of being most responsible for crimes within [its] jurisdiction'.[8] At the time, the ICTY was in its tenth year, and had already convicted and initiated proceedings against several individuals with lower ranks and little authority.[9] As a result, 60 per cent of the perpetrators convicted by the ICTY to date exercised little to no authority at the time of their offences. This percentage rises to almost 90 if middle-ranking perpetrators are also included. It follows that several of the defendants convicted by the ICTY were what Schabas refers to as 'thugs', interpreted here as direct perpetrators of the mass violence crimes that the Tribunal responds to. Their cases are the focal point of this chapter.

The chapter specifically focuses on the Tribunal's *narrative functioning* by way of examining the narratives that primary actors at the ICTY – defence, prosecution and the court – employ to explain (away) the individual agency of defendants in direct sexual violence and/or murder cases. I suggest that the arguments of the parties, which arguably epitomise the agency/structure debate, offer insights relevant beyond the constraints of the courtroom. The court and its actors are approached as storytellers that contribute and respond to the social construction of the phenomena, or crimes, that they address.[10]

I argue, using specific examples from ICTY proceedings, that defence, prosecution and judges each employ different narratives when drawing portraits of direct perpetrators of mass atrocities; and these distinct approaches provide important commentary to the ways we theoretically construct individual agency in relation to war-related mass violence. The defence counsel revert to narratives that range from complete denial to various degrees of acknowledgement of crimes, including out of character explanations, extraordinary circumstances, context specific pleas, as well as psychiatric assessments for mitigation purposes. To various extents these narratives explain *away* the agency of the defendant – as the *reasons* for their crimes are beyond that of their control. Prosecutors on their part tend to characterise the defendant as an opportunist who saw the war chaos, the political propaganda and the widespread impunity as a chance to '[revel] in what he could do, and what he

---

[7] The full name of the Tribunal is the International Tribunal for the Prosecution of Persons Responsible for Serious Violations of International Humanitarian Law Committed in the Territory of the Former Yugoslavia since 1991.

[8] UN SC Res. 1503/2003, in ICTY Updated Statute, 'Updated Statute of the International Criminal Tribunal for the former Yugoslavia' (UN Security Council, 2009) 57.

[9] Although it was always the aim of the prosecutors to target senior commanders and political leadership, the circumstances at the time of the establishment of the Tribunal – intervening in the midst of an ongoing war, and with strong opposition in former Yugoslav countries against the Tribunal's operations – apprehending and prosecuting leaders proved difficult, and the Office of the Prosecutor decided to start with lower-ranking suspected perpetrators until circumstances allowed for the prosecution of those always thought of as 'most responsible'. See Smeulers et al, above (n 5).

[10] M Burman, 'The Ability of Criminal Law to Produce Gender Equality: Judicial Discourses in the Swedish Criminal Legal System' (2010) 16 *Violence Against Women* 173, 177.

could do, he did'.[11] In the end, the court pays detailed attention to the overall war context and the wider policy landscape. Thus, the crimes are never presented as if committed in a political vacuum, independent of the war of which they form part. However, when it comes to the explanation of the individual defendant's participation in these crimes, the defendant is not portrayed as an ordinary man who fell apart under the extraordinary circumstances that war produced. Participation tends to be re-presented according to dispositional narratives that contain a sadistic agency on the part of the individual defendant – also in cases where the court accepts the remorse expressed by the defendant as genuine. The narratives that the prosecutors and court construct about the individual defendants often correspond poorly with the situational emphasis present in defence arguments and which is also dominant in scholarly debates about individual participation in mass violence.

The chapter first exposes a rationale for adopting a narrative approach to court proceedings. The second part offers narrative re-presentations of individual defendants adopted by the prosecution, defence and the judges at the ICTY in cases dealing with direct perpetrators. This part is based on two recent studies on sex crimes and murder cases before the ICTY,[12] and serves as a point of departure for the following discussion on the agency ascribed to individual, direct perpetrators of collective crimes during war.

II. The Narrative Functioning of the Court

The narrative focus on ICTY proceedings aligns well with an expressivist view on international criminal justice. Expressivism emphasises the court primarily as a normative, educational endeavour,[13] accentuating 'the social meanings communicated and interpreted in legal processes'.[14] However, there is no value judgement as to what is *the* primary or most important contribution of international criminal justice in this chapter's focus on the narrative functioning of the court. I simply

---

[11] Prosecutor in *Delić*, T 15535 (31 August 1998). In the following, transcript pages from oral proceedings are indicated by a capitalised T. Written submission such as sentencing or closing briefs and judgments ae specified as such. Defendants' names in italics refer to the case, whereas defendants' names in regular font refer to the defendants.

[12] AB Houge, 'Re-presentations of Defendant Perpetrators in Sexual War Violence Cases Before International and Military Criminal Courts' (2016) 56 *British Journal of Criminology* 419; AB Houge, '"He Seems to Come Out as a Personally Cruel Person". Perpetrator Re-presentations in Direct Murder Cases at the ICTY' in K Fitz-Gibbon and S Walklate (eds), *Homicide, Gender and Responsibility* (London, Routledge, 2016).

[13] MA Drumbl, *Atrocity, Punishment, and International Law* (Cambridge, Cambridge University Press, 2007) 17; MA Drumbl, 'Collective Responsibility and Postconflict Justice' in T Isaacs and R Vernon (eds), *Accountability for Collective Wrongdoing* (Cambridge, Cambridge University Press, 2011) 34–35.

[14] D Buss, 'Performing Legal Order: Some Feminist Thoughts on International Criminal Law' (2011) 11 *International Criminal Law Review* 409, 411.

hold that the narratives the court produce deserve attention. I agree with Osiel[15] who suggests that the mass atrocity tribunal and its proceedings can be seen as a 'theater of ideas'. Prior to the delivery of judgment and sentences, the court hears a myriad of stories or ideas pertaining to the individual defendant and his or her participation in mass violence crimes. It is the court and its primary actors as such storytellers that are my concern here. What stories does the court framework allow for, and how does the court negotiate the different conceptions of agency argued in the individual defendants' perpetration of collective crimes in its judgment?

The prosecution and judgment not only communicate an 'indignation [on behalf of] of humanity'[16] through their 'official condemnation of certain actions',[17] by which they arguably define war crimes as a breach of humanity's *conscience collective*.[18] The parties also offer and suggest *explanations* for these crimes.[19] As I have argued elsewhere, although trial narratives first and foremost serve the purpose of confirming the respective legal arguments of the parties, they 'are not constructed in a societal vacuum. They … also "reflect and construct social and cultural narratives" about the offenses charged and the perpetrators thereof'.[20]

A related aspect is the extent to which trial narratives can be seen as producing any kind of 'truth' or a credible historical record. In the scholarly community, Arendt's 'justice, not history'-approach to criminal justice has received wide acclaim.[21] Yet, the ICTY has made it one of its explicit aims to prevent historical revisionism through its documentation, archives and judgments. The Tribunal not only seeks to decide *which* crimes happened and *who* is responsible, but also attempts to answer the question of *how* it could happen, and *why*.

Thus, the analysis of the narrative functioning of the court is about the *meaning* of the narratives produced, and what stories prevail through judgment – not the level of truth or accuracy that they may entail. It is easy – and well advised – to be sceptical about the value of the narratives the primary court actors produce if these narratives are approached as established historical truths about the aetiology of the crimes. The court framework does not allow comprehensive life narratives, it exaggerates the meaning of some incidents and influences, and

---

[15] M Osiel, *Mass Atrocity, Collective Memory, and the Law* (New Brunswick, Transaction Publishers, 1997) 3.

[16] *Češić* (Sentencing Judgment) IT-95-10/1-S (11 March 2004) 7.

[17] JR Jason, 'Anarchy is What Criminal Lawyers and other Actors Make of it: International Criminal Justice as an Institution of International and World Society' in SC Roach (ed), *Governance, Order, and the International Criminal Court. Between Realpolitik and a Cosmopolitan Court* (Oxford, Oxford University Press, 2009) 137.

[18] For an elaborate critique of Durkheim and the global moral order claimed by international criminal justice, see K Lohne, *Advocates of Humanity. Human Rights NGOs in International Criminal Justice* (Oxford, Oxford University Press, forthcoming).

[19] See also N Christie's seminal text, 'Conflicts as Property' (1977) 17 *British Journal of Crimology* 1.

[20] Houge, 'Re-presentations', above (n 12) 425, citing S Harris, 'Fragmented Narratives and Multiple Tellers: Witness and Defendant Accounts in Trials' (2001) 3 *Discourse Studies* 72.

[21] R Wilson, 'Judging History: The Historical Record of the International Criminal Tribunal for the Former Yugoslavia' (2005) 27 *Human Rights Quarterly* 908, 911.

fails to pay attention to others, it enforces dichotomies, flattens personalities and necessarily reduces complexities. Individuals are re-presented as either good or bad, either with agency or without it, either as perpetrators or as victims.

Regardless of their historical or factual shortcomings or biases, however, the stories of the court actors, and in particular the stories emphasised in the judgments, are communicated to the extra-legal society. '[B]y selecting a guilty few and … exonerating the many [the court selects what will be remembered and in which way]', writes Karstedt.[22] This is part of what I call the narrative functioning of the court. It is not so much about the truth of the crimes, their causes and consequences, as it is about the *meanings* the court actors ascribe to them, and what understandings and explanations prevail and emerge from the court to a wider public.[23]

III. Re-Presentations of Direct Perpetrators at the ICTY

A number of stories about individual agency are told during court proceedings, and the judgment usually endorses only one of them. Up until judgment, what stories does the court framework allow for? And how does the court negotiate the different conceptions of agency argued by the opposing parties in its judgment? In two recent studies I have analysed the court transcripts, counsel briefs and judgments of the 22 cases before the ICTY in which the defendants have been finally convicted for their direct participation in murder[24] and/or sexual violence.[25] I found that the primary actors of the court portray the defendants, their offences and agencies according to five different narrative scripts. This section illustrates how the defendants and their agencies are re-presented in these narratives. This, in turn, contextualises the discussion on the degree and form of agency ascribed to individual direct perpetrators of collective crimes during war.

The court cases that constitute the basis for the analysis cover a wide repertoire of violent offences that is described in acute detail by witnesses, prosecutors

---

[22] S Karstedt, 'Introduction: The Legacy of Maurice Halbwachs' in S Karstedt (ed), *Legal Institutions and Collective Memories* (Portland, OR, Hart Publishing, 2009) 3.

[23] See also AB Houge on 'narrative expressivism' in '"Thugs" on Trial. Narrating Conflict-Related Sexual Violence in and for International Criminal Justice' (PhD dissertation, Oslo, University of Oslo, 2017) 33–35, 55–62.

[24] Houge, '"He Seems to Come Out"', above (n 12). The cases analysed are: *Bala* (IT-03-66), *Banović* (IT-02-65/1), *Bralo* (IT-95-17), *Češić* (IT-95-10/1), *Delić* (IT-96-21), *Landžo* (IT-96-21), *Erdemović* (IT-96-22), *Jelisić* (IT-95-10), *Lukić* (IT-98-32/1), *Mrđa* (IT-02-59), *Nikolić* (IT-94-2), *Sikirica* (IT-95-8), *Tadić* (IT-94-1), *Todorović* (IT-95-9/1) and *Zigić* (IT-98-30/1).

[25] Houge, 'Re-presentations'. The cases analysed are: *Bralo* (IT-95-17), *Furundžija* (IT-95-17/1), *Češić* (IT-95-10/1), *Delić* (IT-96-21), *Kunarac, Kovač & Vuković* (IT-96-23), *Zelenović* (IT-96-23/2), *Radić* (IT-98-30/1), *Simić* (IT-95-9/2), *Todorović* (IT-95-9/1), and *Landžo* (IT-96-21). Bralo, Češić, Delić, Todorović and Landžo were convicted both on murder charges and on sexual violence charges. The victims of the sexual violence charged were not the same as the murder victims.

and judges, and are available in the court records.[26] The crimes include mass rapes and public sexual violence committed against women, men and girls, and murders ranging from individual killings through beatings, shooting and stabbing, to executions in the form of mass shootings or by barricading hundreds of people into buildings and setting them on fire. The defendants represent all parties to the conflict in the former Yugoslavia. The youngest defendant was 19 at the time of his offences; the oldest was 40 years old. Eleven of the 22 defendants were convicted on the basis of their guilty pleas. Hence, there are a lot of factors that separate the individual defendants from each other. What links them – besides being an all-male group prosecuted and later convicted by the ICTY – is their direct, personal participation in the offences. They were not passive associates of the crimes, bystanders or responsible only through the chain of command. Some of them were order-givers too, commanding others to commit war crimes, but all of them, personally, sexually abused and/or murdered the victims of their offences. Also, they were all re-presented in the form of one or several narrative scripts before the court. These narratives can be grouped according to two primary categories that emphasise the defendant as either an ordinary man (position typical for defence) or a man with deviating personal characteristics (frequent prosecutorial stance).

IV. Defence Narratives About Ordinary Men

The first category of narratives comprises three different typical narratives that portray the defendant as an ordinary man. These narratives are primarily employed by defence counsel and range from complete denials, to partial denials, to narratives where the situational pressures are claimed to have reduced the defendant to a piece in a puzzle over which he had no control and within which he could not act otherwise.

Complete denials typically re-present the defendant as an innocent scapegoat, as in the case against Tadić, a local leader of the Serbian Democratic Party. Tadić, who was convicted for killing two Muslim policemen, was presented by his defence counsel as an intelligent, sociable man, not '[the stereotypical bloodthirsty Serb] who like a fanatic, is involved in all kinds of atrocities, one after the other' as he claimed the prosecution portrayed him. Rather, the defence depicted Tadić as a person with 'talent for art' and stated accordingly that 'artists are surely not prone to the commission of any grave offenses'.[27] The defence counsel of Furundžija on their part, suggested that the prosecutor should 'win an award for best fictional script'.[28]

---

[26] ICTY redacted case records are available at: icr.icty.org/default.aspx.
[27] Defence in *Tadić*, T 9244 (7 July 1997).
[28] Defence in *Furundžija*, T 672 (22 June 1998).

Partial denials consist of narrative re-presentations of the defendant and his acts in which the acts are accepted but their interpretation is denied. For instance, the counsel of Češić, who was convicted for forcing male detainees to perform fellatio on each other, emphasised that the offence was committed to 'cause great humiliation and degradation' and that he therefore could not be convicted for rape. His defence, thus, portrayed Češić as a rational man who acted as he did for a larger purpose, not because he was an opportunist sadist as the prosecution suggested. This narrative persisted also in relation to the murders with which Češić was charged. In the sentencing arguments his counsel stated that 'in almost (sic!) all murder cases for which [he was found] guilty, the victims did not suffer any additional suffering, pain, degradation or humiliation since they were shot from firearms and thus instantly killed'.[29] Again, Češić is tentatively portrayed as a rational man. Because he knew his victims were to be killed anyway, he did not, according to his defence, subject them to any harm beyond the act of killing.

Partial denials about sexual violence against women was, in contrast to sexual violence against men, argued to be committed for purely personal reasons, to satisfy sexual urges. These 'lust, not politics'-narratives serves the purpose of disconnecting the offence from the armed conflict, as an attempt to distort the prosecutors' case. The offence cannot be a war crime, if it is not related to the conflict.[30] The defendants' agency is also depicted as if it is somehow reduced by the defendants' claimed attraction to their victims, as if they are acting out of physiological and emotional needs.

Narratives of situational pressures portray the defendants as ordinary men under extraordinary circumstances. In these defence narratives, the war-specific circumstances, including orders and duress, are argued to have forced the defendant to commit crimes. The defendants were put in situations over which they had no control and within which they exercised no or limited agency. *Erdemović* offers the primary example of such a narrative. Erdemović admitted to having personally shot and killed about 70 people and held that he was following orders and acting under threats on his own life. The defence argued that Erdemović was 'neither the creator, the ideologist, the one giving the orders, a religious-nationalistic fanatic, nor a sadistic soldier, but above all a victim sowing victims, a mere "tool for killing" which has to kill in order not to be killed'.[31] Here, the defendant is portrayed as deprived of his capability to act otherwise lest he would be killed himself. Both the prosecutor and the court accepted this narrative and found duress to be a mitigating circumstance.

---

[29] Defence Sentencing Brief in *Češić* (12 November 2003) 11.

[30] See, eg, *Kovač* Defence Closing Brief (10 November 2000) 258. For a more detailed discussion about the differences pertaining to the type of sexual violence, and the gender of victims and perpetrators, as well as the nuances that emerge in comparison between murder and sexual violence cases, see the original publications.

[31] Appellants Brief in *Erdemović* (14 April 1997) 18.

Another version of situational pressure narratives presents the war context as such a strong rupture in the defendants' lives that they for a limited period of time acted completely out of character. An example of such a narrative is the defence counsel's re-presentation of the defendant and his offences in *Nikolić*. Nikolić pleaded guilty to beating nine detainees to death. According to his counsel, Nikolić 'can now not understand what it was that caused him to commit those horrid acts. Nobody can'.[32] In other parts of the re-presentation, his crimes are described as 'dreadful', and Nikolić as 'extraordinarily cruel' during the war. Similarly, the defence counsel of Bralo, who voluntarily surrendered and admitted to having killed five detainees and raped a woman several times as part of an interrogation, presented his wartime behaviour as 'wholly uncharacteristic'.[33] The defence further argued that Bralo was acting on orders and that 'some value system collapsed' in him under the pressures of war.[34] According to these narratives, defendants for a limited period of time acted in ways they could have never imagined themselves, and which they can later not comprehend, except by reference to the war specific pressures and chaos.

V. Prosecutor Narratives About Deviant Defendants

The second category of narratives emphasises dispositional re-presentations of the defendant and his motives for committing the violence in question. These narratives engage two distinctly different scripts according to which the prosecution and the defence explain away the individual agency of the defendant.

With the clear exception of Erdemović, prosecutors tend to portray the defendant as an opportunist, or a sadist, who derived pleasure from inflicting harm on his victims. In the case against Tadić, referenced above, the prosecutor argued that 'the true nature of … Tadić fully appeared' when he entered the Omarska camp in Prijedor. Here, his crimes 'defy logic and demonstrate an evil that is beyond any civilized society'.[35] The prosecution suggests that the violence was the result of his evil character, his desire to harm others. In contrast to the 'out-of-character' narratives presented by defence counsel in *Nikolić* and *Bralo*, the prosecutor in *Tadić* argues that the war context permitted Tadić to unleash what had always been a part of him.

In the case against Landžo, who was convicted for a murder and several sexual violence offences, the prosecution stated that 'many, if not most persons, who commit horrific crimes, such as those committed by Landžo, have personality difficulties'.[36] Yet, they also emphasised that a lot of people have 'personality

---

[32] Defence in *Nikolić*, T 485 (6 November 2003).
[33] Defence Sentencing Brief in *Bralo* (25 November 2005) 4.
[34] Defence in *Bralo*, T 127 (20 October 2005).
[35] Prosecutor's Sentencing Brief in *Tadić* (9 June 1997) 12.
[36] Prosecutor in *Landžo*, T 16284 (13 October 1998).

difficulties' without committing such crimes. Hence, the prosecution argued that Landžo exercised individual agency, and decided what he would and wouldn't do while he was serving as a guard in the Čelebići prison camp.

Similarly, the prosecutor in *Jelisić* portrayed the defendant as someone who 'killed as if for pleasure', 'in happy obedience', and who expressed a 'delusion of grandeur and narcissistic tendency'.[37] Jelisić, who was convicted following a guilty plea that included 13 murders, introduced himself to detainees as the 'Serb Adolf'. The prosecutor asked during proceedings:

> What is the relevant background of a man guilty of crime in time of war? Principally it is the man himself. He is his own background and he can draw little or no comfort from the wider background of war against which it must be remembered some suffer as victims, some behave innocently, some behave nobly.[38]

Whereas prosecutors argue that defendants possess controllable sadistic traits or characteristics that constitute aggravating factors, defence counsel present limited mental capabilities and inherent personality traits as mitigating arguments in several cases. In these cases, the defence accepts the crimes but deny or partially deny the defendants' responsibility for their participation in them. For instance, the defence counsel in *Banović* held that the defendant's less than average intelligence made him less able to reject unlawful orders. Todorović was, according to the defence's medical expert, possessing dependent personality traits, which made him conform to the wishes and perceived expectations of others. Landžo was at some point portrayed by his counsel as 'the true victim', because others took advantage of his immaturity and dependency. These narratives do not ignore the war context but argue that the war had that effect on their behaviour *because* of their personality traits, for which they could not be blamed.

VI. Agency Narratives in Judgments

To a considerable degree, judgments map out a historical conflict context, and narrate the individual crimes into a wider policy campaign. In that sense, 'the collective nature' of the crimes is accounted for. According to Wilson, the court has to 'situate individual acts within long-term, systematic policies' because the crime categories the Tribunal operates with 'emphasize the collective nature' of the crimes.[39] For individual defendants to be found guilty of crimes against humanity, such as genocide and persecution, Wilson points out, it is not enough to prove that the violent acts happened and that they were committed by the defendants. The court also needs to establish a credible link between the defendant's individual act,

---

[37] Prosecutor in *Jelisić*, T 3069, 3073 (25 November 1999).
[38] ibid, T 3083-4.
[39] Above (n 21).

and the wider policy of which it is argued to be part. This, Wilson holds, impels 'the Tribunal to place contextual and historical interpretation at the center of the trial and the subsequent written judgment'. Although individual war crimes can be committed for 'purely personal reasons', this does not suffice for crimes categorised under the umbrella of crimes against humanity.

This is a valid point, but when it comes to the individual perpetrator on trial and his agency, it is not the structural, collective or social explanations offered by defence counsel that are reflected in judgments. In terms of the individual defendant, it is his depraved mind that explains his participation in these collective crimes. For instance, in *Tadić*, the judgment comments how the defence portrayed him

> as an intelligent, responsible and mature adult raised by his parents in a spirit of ethnic and religious tolerance and capable of compassion and sensitivity for his fellows. However this, if anything, aggravates more than it mitigates for such a man to commit these crimes requires an even greater evil will on his part than that of a lesser man.[40]

This is also implied in the judgment in *Bralo*:

> The Trial Chamber is aware of the deteriorating political and military situation ... While it is notorious that [enormous] pressures existed, the Trial Chamber nonetheless finds that they cannot be considered in any way relevant to the sentence to be imposed upon Bralo for the crimes of which he has been convicted. Large sections of the population ... were subjected to the same or similar pressures, and yet did not respond in the same manner as Bralo.[41]

It could be argued that in terms of the narratives produced, there is a discrepancy between the court's understanding of the larger contextual and collective framework of the crimes on the one hand, and on the other, the reasons the court presents for the individual defendant's participation in the same crimes. Rather than as offences committed by the defendants as deliberate parts of a wider policy, the violence is presented in the judgments as premised by the defendants' depraved minds, for which the war context creates only an opportunity. In the judgment against Delić, for example, the judges comment how 'the manner in which [his] crimes were committed [is] indicative of a sadistic individual who, at times, displayed a total disregard for the sanctity of human life and dignity'.[42] On Lukić, who was convicted for killing more than 130 civilians, the judges state that he was 'an opportunist who took advantage of an environment in which he could commit crimes ... with impunity'.[43] In *Nikolić*, one of the judges intervened during the proceedings and said that the defendant 'seems to come out as a personally cruel person'.[44] It follows that the crimes are framed contextually, while the defendant is re-presented individually – that is, his person and personality is central to the

---

[40] *Tadić* Judgment (14 July 1997) 32.
[41] *Bralo* Judgment (7 December 2005) 18.
[42] *Delić* Judgment (16 November 1998) 433.
[43] *Lukić* Judgment (20 July 2009) 326.
[44] *Nikolić*, T 496 (6 November 2003).

court. The ordinary man under extraordinary circumstances has limited appeal for the purposes of explaining defendants' participation in mass violence under international criminal law.

VII. Individual Agency and Collective Crimes

Different primary court actors narrate the defendant perpetrators' individual agency differently. Defence counsel apply several scripts according to which they attempt to deny or mitigate the responsibility of the defendant. Oftentimes these narratives focus on the war context, and on structural and situational pressures associated with warfare. If the defence counsel accepts the crime, they still try to allocate responsibility elsewhere. Prosecutors primarily employ a narrative that pathologises the crime. They construct an aetiology that is based in large part on the sadistic, deviant traits of the defendant. In this, the court tends to agree; the direct perpetrator is constructed and understood as someone who is, or at least during the war was, inherently different. The sadistic component of agency emphasised by the prosecutors and judges, however, tends not to be acknowledged in research on individual perpetrators of collective violence.

As Arendt states, '[t]he sad truth … is that most evil is done by people who never made up their minds to be either bad or good'.[45] Arendt is a central point of reference in any publication on the aetiology of mass violence, and in particular pertaining to criminal justice responses in their wake. Following her observation of the trial against Adolf Eichmann in Jerusalem in 1961, Arendt coined 'the banality of evil' which she held was not a theory, but a factual statement that referred to 'the phenomenon of evil deeds, committed on a gigantic scale, which could not be traced to any particularity of wickedness, pathology, or ideological conviction in the doer … However monstrous the deeds were, the doer was neither monstrous nor demonic'.[46] The banality of evil-thesis is, however, based on the trial of a man who was convicted for his role in administrative massacres, not as a direct physical perpetrator.

On direct perpetrators, the situationist theories inspired by the experiments of Milgram and Zimbardo equally claim that evil acts are not premised by bad people. Rather, emphasis is put on the extraordinary circumstances that emerge during conflict, and the meaning of external influences, such as authority figures, peer pressures and dehumanising, xenophobic propaganda, as well as training or lack thereof. These factors induce common human behavioural traits such as obedience and conformity, as opposed to any specific or deviant character of the individual offender. The explanations attempted by many defence counsel

---

[45] H Arendt, 'Thinking and Moral Considerations: A Lecture' (1984 [1971]) 51 *Social Research* 7, 28.
[46] ibid, 7; see also H Arendt, *Eichmann in Jerusalem: A Report on the Banality of Evil* (New York, Penguin, 2006).

when they employed narratives of situational pressures align well with this school of thought.

According to military sociologist Grossman, people have a 'natural resistance to killing'.[47] This resistance – both a natural and learned decency – necessitates a deliberate process through which soldiers are trained and enabled to kill during war. This process includes various forms of constructed distances achieved by dehumanising the enemy combatants, but depends also and in particular on peer bonding and group absolution. Group absolution facilitates the act of killing by diffusing the responsibility of the individual among the members of the group of which he is part.[48] Moral philosopher Vetlesen, however, suggests that this emphasis on group absolution in situational explanations of excessive, collective violence is misleading. He argues that perpetrators' claims that they became depersonalised, that they no longer considered themselves as individual agents – what Grossman sums up as 'the individual is not a killer, but the group is'[49] – are understandable from the retrospective point of view of repentant perpetrators who have to find a way to live with what they have done.[50] According to Vetlesen it should, however, not be understood as a fact of the offence, as reality, when it is likely that the perpetrators knew all along that their excessive offences were wrong, but chose to act *as if* there was no other way, *as if* they were depersonalised, and *as if* their victims were less than human.[51]

At the time of the offence, this '*as if*' may function either as a rationalisation of the urge to conform to the group or as an excuse to take part in the violence that is happening. In relation to the court narratives addressed above, Vetlesen's argument finds a parallel in a statement of the prosecution in *Delić* as they respond to defence counsel claims that the Tribunal should only focus on the big fish:

> To suggest that the conduct of individual soldiers or guards, all of whom have the power of life and death over others, *may not be influenced* … is, in our view, fundamentally wrong and fundamentally against one of the reasons why this Tribunal was created.[52]

To argue that individual perpetrators have at least some degree of agency, but choose to act *as if* they have none, is not the equivalent of saying that there are no relevant, strong, external pressures, or that individuals are never forced to

---

[47] D Grossman, *On Killing: The Psychological Cost of Learning to Kill in War and Society* (New York, Back Bay Books/Little, Brown and Co, 2009) 212.

[48] For a more detailed presentation of the ordinary man under the extraordinary circumstances-paradigm see Harrendorf, ch 10. It is also elaborated in Houge, 'Re-presentations', above (n 12) where a defence case at a US court martial included the expert testimony of Philip Zimbardo.

[49] Grossman, above (n 47) 149.

[50] AJ Vetlesen, *Studier i ondskap [Studies in evil]* (Oslo, Universitetsforlaget, 2014) 136–37.

[51] AJ Vetlesen, *Evil and Human Agency. Understanding Collective Evildoing* (Cambridge, Cambridge University Press, 2005) 87–89.

[52] Prosecution in *Delić*, T 16300 (15 October 1998) (my emphasis). Similarly, a judge commented in the proceedings against Kunarac, Kovač & Vuković that 'Political leaders and war generals are powerless if the ordinary people refuse to carry out criminal activities in the course of war. Lawless opportunists should expect no mercy, no matter how low their position in the chain of command may be (Judge Mumba, *Kunarac*, T 65619 (22 February 2001).

commit mass violence. It does, however, offer an opportunity to ponder the potential importance the availability of narratives of individual agency has, not only for retrospect justification purposes, but also in the immediate context of the offences.

In the preceding discussion, what Grossman calls 'a natural resistance to killing' concerns legitimate killings on the battlefield. But do the same factors sufficiently explain illegitimate killings, excessive violence and sexual violence, or does this kind of violence require added nuances? Much like the court rejects defence counsel references to the pressures of war as a mitigating argument by pointing to all the people subjected to the same pressures who never became war criminals, Vetlesen argues that there is 'a gap between the generality of the proposed [situational] explanation, and what constitutes the particular act of evil'.[53] He further argues that situationist scholars fail to address the *excess* with which many war criminals kill, maim and sexually violate, which is gratuitous and unnecessary in terms of the purpose it is claimed to serve. He reacts to the ways in which purported explanations that follow detailed and graphical descriptions of excessive violent acts do not pay specific attention to this violent profusion. Because of this ignorance, the explanations offered for evil acts are in form and content the same explanations they would offer for mundane social practices. But these explanations cannot be interchangeable, Vetlesen argues, because the perpetrators are not just conforming, obedient individuals. They can also be *willing* executioners, act independently of any orders, and, importantly: their violence suggests that they also derive pleasure from the suffering of their victims. The particularity of such excessive violence, Vetlesen holds, could not have happened without sadism: 'For the victims, this element of sadism and perversion is obvious: it is not a claim, but an experience'.[54] Yet for situationist scholars, sadism is a shunned concept, also in the face of excessive mass violence: 'They acknowledge the murders of women and children in hundreds and thousands, but in a petty bourgeois priggish way take exception to anyone's use of the word sadism. Well, the acts speak for themselves'.[55] Hence, Vetlesen's critique of the situationist school resonates well with the prosecution and judgment narratives about the individual defendants' agency at the time of their offences. Češić was characterised by his 'extraordinary barbarity' and 'depravity' of mind by the judges, Delić as a 'sadistic individual', Lukić as an 'opportunist', Nikolić as a 'personally cruel person'. Kovač's acts were described as 'cruel', Landžo's as 'sadistic', Zelenović's as a 'horrible odyssey' of 'heinous crimes'. Radić was described as someone who 'relished' in 'barbaric' acts. The sadistic element which is bypassed in situationist understandings, is emphasised in these court narratives. It seems as if the court cannot and will not refrain from seeing the wicked acts as the result of wicked minds.[56]

---

[53] Vetlesen, *Studier*, above (n 50) 127–28 (my translation).

[54] ibid, 130–33.

[55] ibid, 134–35.

[56] Except in the case against Erdemović, where the judgment explicitly emphasised that the defendant 'took no perverse pleasure from what he did' (29 November 1996) 21.

Pointing out that some of these violent profusions require a degree of sadistic intent is not the equivalent of stating that perpetrators of mass violence cannot be 'ordinary men'. Vetlesen aptly quotes Levi in this regard: 'The motivations which led us to an act and the passions within us which accompanied the act itself [are] an extremely fluid matter. States of mind are by nature labile and even more labile is the memory of them'.[57] The deliberate and systematic production of social and political conditions that favour collective evil doing is also a premise for their perpetration. Therefore, sadism is not to be understood as a universal, solitary ground from which all acts of mass violence can be deduced and understood. Following his argument, though, what Vetlesen seems to suggest is that sadism, a tabooed concept, should be part of the conversation, because it obviously is part of the excessive violence.

The preceding discussion on the degree and form of agency ascribed to individual, direct perpetrators of collective crimes during war illustrates how the different primary court actors construct narratives that are supported by different aetiological schools in the scholarly community. Many defence counsel narratives about the defendants draw on situationist explanations for perpetrators' involvement in war crimes, which emphasise the meaning of fear, peer pressures, group absolution and orders. The political, collectively violent context is important in the prosecution and court narratives too, but only to situate the crimes under the Tribunal's jurisdiction.

These contextual factors seem to constitute only the backdrop for the court's understanding of the individual defendant's agency in the commissioning of his crimes. Here, the court emphasises the individual sadistic agency that this backdrop allows for. These narratives correspond to Vetlesen's critique of situationist scholars, in that they do not account for the manifestations of excess violence. In Vetlesen's view, it does not suffice to state *that* people were murdered, raped or tortured en masse; *how* these crimes manifested, which indicates that the perpetrators derived pleasure from the suffering of their victims, also needs to be accounted for. The inclusion of sadism in the explanation of excess violence does not suggest that these forms of violence are committed by people who are inherently mad or bad – it is not a dispositional argument. It does, however, allow for a layer of individual agency that most current publications on the causes of mass and excess violence do not account for. Importantly, however, any use of court narratives to inform theory construction about complex social phenomena that take place outside the court context needs to be carefully situated within the constraints of the legal framework of their construction. Moreover, direct perpetrators prosecuted at international criminal tribunals are not randomly selected, but carefully chosen defendants, selected inter alia on the basis of their notoriety as perpetrators. The understanding of their crimes and their participation are important with regard to a selected few, but likely not fit for generalisable theorisation.

---

[57] P Levi, *The Drowned and the Saved* (London, Abacus, 1988) 17; Vetlesen, *Studier*, above (n 50) 131.

VIII. Concluding Remarks

This chapter has demonstrated how the court framework offers a limited set of scripts according to which the individual agencies of the defendants in direct murder and/or sexual violence cases are explained (away), and what kind of narratives these are. A simplified summary of these narratives would point out that the prosecutors overemphasise individual agency, whereas defence counsel mitigate or deny it by drawing on the dominant scholarly narrative about participation in collective violence. Judgments reflect prosecution counsel narratives. Although the court acknowledges the circumstances of the war and the political conflict, it also emphasises in its judgments that everyone experiences severe pressures in times of conflict, yet far from all commit mass violence. From this observation and through detailed references to the manifestations of the violence the court accentuates the individual agency of the defendant and the sadistic manner in which he acted out on it. These court narratives, in turn, form the basis for a discussion about the degree and form of individual agency ascribed to perpetrators in scholarly works that seek to explain participation in excessive collective violence. However framed, the court narratives enable stories that are not so visible in theory, and which might add an important ingredient to the overall scholarly discussion about excessive wartime violence. At the very least, the court narratives force us to consider the relevance and presence of a sadistic component, and what that potentially means to theory construction. Insisting on individual agency as the court does, necessarily also means insisting on the existence of alternatives, of choice. Following Vetlesen, this is a choice perpetrators behave *as if* they do not have. When the court reiterates personal agency, whether it is defined in sadistic terms or not, it insists on an alternative narrative to the responsibility diffusing situationist narrative that explains away the agency of individual perpetrators of excessive violence.

Future implications of the ICTY's narratives pertaining to low-level perpetrators require further scholarly attention. If the narratives that the court produces contribute to the social construction and understanding of the crimes addressed and the actors involved, in the long term they may potentially influence the narrative pool from which actors extract information that support or guide their choices. As such, they may also influence agency.

PART V

Prevention

10

Social Identity and International Crimes: Legitimate and Problematic Aspects of the 'Ordinary People' Hypothesis

STEFAN HARRENDORF

'Us and them
And after all we're only ordinary men
Me and you
God only knows
It's not what we would choose to do'
(Us and Them, Pink Floyd, 1973).[1]

I. Introduction

In the criminological discourse, international crimes are often seen as a kind of exceptional category not only with respect to the scale of these crimes ('Makrokrim-inalität', as Jäger put it),[2] but also with respect to their inherent qualities. Hence, there is some agreement in scientific literature that such crimes cannot easily be explained when relying on theories of crime that were developed for 'normal', everyday crimes, but need a specific approach, which might, however, build on existing theories.[3] Moreover, the relationship between ordinary and international crimes is frequently described as a dichotomy between crimes of obedience or conformity on the one hand and crimes as acts of individual deviance from social

---

[1] The song 'Us and Them' appeared on Pink Floyd's album 'The Dark Side of the Moon' (1973).

[2] H Jäger, *Makrokriminalität: Studien zur Kriminologie kollektiver Gewalt* (Frankfurt aM, Suhrkamp, 1989).

[3] eg, Jäger, ibid, 187–213; D Rothe, *State Criminality: The Crime of All Crimes* (Plymouth, Lexington Books, 2009).

and legal norms on the other.[4] Save the masterminds behind genocidal operations, the other perpetrators of international crimes are often seen as 'ordinary people within extraordinary circumstances'.[5]

Such a notion is also included in the above quotation from Pink Floyd's song 'Us and Them', which was released in 1973 on the album 'The Dark Side of the Moon'. While the band seems to have never made a clear statement on the meaning of this song, it is usually understood as an anti-war song, probably influenced by the experience of the war in Vietnam,[6] but also by the fate of Roger Water's father in the Second World War.[7] Hence, it is not a song directly about genocide or mass atrocities, but it could as well be (especially if you take into account that war situations are typically prone to such crimes and that both the Second World War and the Vietnam war show various examples of this).

What is especially interesting with this quotation is that it seems to assume a social psychological interpretation of the individual's involvement in mass violence. It could summarise the basic assumptions of a Social Identity Approach[8] not only to war, but also to international crimes. In the song, such occurrences are understood as a product of group polarisation, of a strict, depersonalised differentiation between an in-group ('us') and an out-group ('them'), leading people to do things they would not do as individuals: 'Me and you … It's not what we would choose to do'.

In the following, I will try to unfold such a Social Identity Approach to international crimes. I will also show that it leads to the interpretation of international crimes as products of the *interaction* of individual and situational characteristics.[9] An interactionist theory of (international) crimes needs, however, also to identify the characteristics of individual perpetrators that make them prone to adopt a potentially genocidal or politically violent social identity. Based on the assumption that there are at least three different possible actions in a context of collective violence (participate, do nothing about it or resist/rebel) it is necessary to identify

---

[4] See, eg, HC Kelman and VL Hamilton, *Crimes of Obedience: Toward a Social Psychology of Authority and Responsibility* (New Haven, CT, Yale University Press, 1989); Jäger, above (n 2).

[5] A Smeulers, 'Perpetrators of International Crimes: Towards a Typology' in A Smeulers and R Haveman (eds), *Supranational Criminology: Towards a Criminology of International Crimes* (Antwerp, Intersentia, 2008); likewise JJ Savelsberg, *Crime and Human Rights: Criminology of Genocide and Atrocities* (London, Sage Publications, 2010) 52; CR Browning, *Ordinary Men: Reserve Police Battalion 101 and the Final Solution in Poland* (New York, Harper Collins, 1992).

[6] Newseum, 'Vietnam Music Monday: "Us and Them"' *Newseum.org* (2016), available at: www.newseum.org/2016/02/01/vietnam-music-monday-us-and-them/.

[7] O Klatt, 'Pink Floyds Jahrhundertalbum: Die dunkle Seite des Menschen' *Spiegel Online* (2013), available at: www.spiegel.de/einestages/pink-floyd-und-the-dark-side-of-the-moon-a-951078.html.

[8] For this theoretical position, see the seminal work by H Tajfel and JC Turner 'The Social Identity Theory of Intergroup Behavior' in S Worchel and WG Austin (eds), *The Psychology of Intergroup Relations*, 2nd edn (Chicago, IL, Nelson-Hall, 1986); JC Turner, MA Hogg, PJ Oakes, SD Reicher and MS Wetherell *Rediscovering the Social Group: A Self-Categorization Theory* (Oxford, Basil Blackwell, 1987).

[9] *cf* SD Reicher and SA Haslam, 'Rethinking the Psychology of Tyranny: The BBC Prison Study' (2006) 45 *British Journal of Social Psychology* 1.

the 'sleeper'[10] traits of potential perpetrators. As a result, a clarification of the meaning of 'ordinary' in the abovementioned 'ordinary people' hypothesis will be suggested.

The chapter also advocates a differentiated view on the position of international crimes in criminological theory. The spectrum of crimes is seen like a continuum with international crimes as an extreme form of criminal conduct, which, however, could be explained by the same, comprehensive theory as ordinary crimes. Group interaction is not only important for international crimes. All crimes in which groups are involved cannot only be understood as deviant acts (with regard to social norms of a larger society), but also as conformist acts (with respect to group norms). This is an assumption that also has historical roots in subculture theory,[11] but was not in the focus of most of the more recent developments in criminological theory. One aim of this chapter is therefore also to rediscover the social group[12] in criminology and try to integrate it into modern criminological action theories, most prominently the Situational Action Theory.[13]

II. A Social Identity Approach to International Crimes

The Social Identity Approach is probably the most influential[14] endeavour towards a social psychological understanding of group behaviour. It is based on two separate, but related theories, the Social Identity Theory[15] and the Self-Categorization Theory.[16] In these theories, social identity is defined as the part of the individual identity that derives from the individual's perceived belonging to a social group.

According to Social Identity Theory,[17] humans strive for a positive social identity. Now imagine the situation of a person who belongs to a group that does not provide him or her with a sufficiently positive social identity, since the group has a bad reputation and its members are seen as inferior or problematic by the members

---

[10] JM Steiner, 'The Role Margin as the Site for Moral and Social Intelligence: The Case of Germany and National Socialism' (2000) 34 *Crime, Law & Social Change* 61.

[11] AK Cohen, *Delinquent Boys: The Culture of the Gang* (Glencoe, IL, Free Press, 1955); JM Yinger, 'Contraculture and Subculture' (1960) 5 *American Sociological Review* 625.

[12] Turner et al, above (n 8).

[13] P-O Wikström 'Crime as Alternative: Towards a Cross-Level Situational Action Theory of Crime Causation' in J McCord (ed), *Beyond Empiricism: Institutions and Intentions in the Study of Crime* (New Brunswick, Transaction Publishers, 2004); P-O Wikström, 'Why Crime Happens: A Situational Action Theory' in G Manzo (ed), *Analytical Sociology* (Hoboken, Wiley, 2014); an application of this theory on international crimes can also be found in K Drenkhahn, 'Why Do People Engage in State Crime? Some Thoughts about Criminological Theory' in F Neubacher and N Bögelein (eds), *Krise – Kriminalität – Kriminologie* (Mönchengladbach, Forum Verlag Godesberg, 2016).

[14] *cf* SD Reicher, R Spears, and SA Haslam 'The Social Identity Approach in Social Psychology' in MA Wetherell and CT Mohanty (eds), *The SAGE Handbook of Identities* (London, SAGE, 2010).

[15] Tajfel and Turner, above (n 8).

[16] Turner et al, above (n 8).

[17] Tajfel and Turner, above (n) 8.

of other, relevant outgroups. Now there are different ways to try to achieve a positive identity, one individualistic and two group-related, social strategies: *individual mobility* would mean for the individual to try to leave his or her group and gain membership in a group with a higher social standing, which can then provide for a positive social identity. Yet, there is not always a possibility for such individual mobility. Take the example of a strongly racist or patriarchal society: Neither the racial nor the sexual classification of an individual can be easily changed by him or her.

Yet, there are other options to improve social identity for members of such groups that cannot easily be left. One option would be *social creativity*, which means a redefinition of the criteria of comparison, the value attached to it and the relevant outgroups against which to compare in order to come to a more positive result. The other option would be *social competition*, ie, a struggle with other groups in order to actually achieve an objectively better standing for the own group in the meaning of better access to scarce resources. Racial and sexual discrimination, for example, can be overcome by a mixture of social creativity (redefinition of the values associated with skin colour or sex) and social competition (a struggle to achieve a better, equal social position for females or black people).

Social Identity Theory is complemented by Self-Categorization Theory.[18] While Social Identity Theory focuses on group conflict, Self-Categorization Theory explains how humans categorise themselves, thus automatically or deliberately selecting a cognitive representation of the self that is adapted to the given situation. The theory differentiates between different levels of this self-concept. Hence, a person could categorise him- or herself as a human being, as just one member of the whole human species (human identity). More often, a person will categorise him- or herself as a member of a certain in-group in differentiation from a relevant out-group (social identity). Finally, it is also possible that in a certain situation the self-concept as a unique individual is activated (personal identity). The theory assumes that there is a functional antagonism between the different levels of self-categorisation. With increasing salience of an in-group/out-group categorisation the salience of personal identity decreases. This is called *depersonalisation* and means that a person begins to stereotype him- or herself, losing focus on his or her individuality, while concentrating on the assumed commonalities of the collective. Such depersonalisation must not be confused with deindividuation, a concept that was central to deindividuation theory.[19] While this older theory of group behaviour associated the deindividuated state of a person strictly with antinormative and disinhibited behaviour, a depersonalised person is simply more susceptible to

---

[18] Turner et al, above (n 8).

[19] L Festinger, A Pepitone, T and Newcomb, 'Some Consequences of De-Individuation in a Group' (1952) 47 *Journal of Abnormal and Social Psychology* 382; PG Zimbardo, 'The Human Choice: Individuation, Reason, and Order vs Deindividuation, Impulse, and Chaos' in WJ Arnold and D Levine (eds), *Nebraska Symposium on Motivation* (Lincoln, University of Nebraska Press, 1969) 237.

situational group and context norms. Adaptation to group norms occurs regardless of their accordance with general social norms.[20]

The validity of the assumptions of the Social Identity Approach has been proved by several experiments.[21] A thorough meta-analysis also showed that deindividuation effects found in different studies can better be explained with a social identity model based on the Social Identity Approach,[22] the 'Social Identity Model of Deindividuation Effects' (SIDE).

Human beings can be categorised by their belonging to very different groups. These groups can be small (like a group of friends) or large (like a group defined by nationality or religion). Obviously, not all of these possible group-related categorisations are important for a specific situational self-concept. According to Self-Categorization Theory, the relevant in-group/out-group dichotomy will be chosen based on the *salience* of the differentiation in a current situation. Salience is a function of *accessibility* and *fit*.[23] Accessibility of an in-group/out-group differentiation depends on how far a person is used to thinking in such categories. Fit, on the other hand, is an aspect of the situation: How strong are the situational cues that activate a certain in-group/out-group dichotomy?

The accessibility of a certain social identity can be enhanced by ideology: ideologies (ie, 'systems of shared beliefs, ideas, and symbols that help us make sense of the world around us', according to Alvarez)[24] are the backdrop of in-group/out-group categorisations. People tend to rely on ideologies allowing for positive group distinctiveness in problematic times.[25] Apart from manipulating accessibility, an ideology is also a tool of social creativity (in the meaning defined above) and redefines for the in-group the criteria of comparison, the value of these criteria and/or the relevant out-groups to compare with.

Alvarez[26] identifies several ideologies which are especially prone to political or genocidal violence.[27] These are nationalism, glorification or mythologisation of past victimisation, dehumanisation, scapegoating, an absolutist worldview and utopianism. I have explained the contents and relevance of each of these ideology

---

[20] T Postmes and R Spears, 'Deindividuation and Antinormative Behavior: A Meta-Analysis' 123 (1998) *Psychological Bulletin* 238, 254.

[21] Groundbreaking H Tajfel, MG Billig, RP Bundy and C Flament 'Social Categorization and Inter-Group Behaviour' (1971) 1 *European Journal of Social Psychology* 149; for further references, *cf* Reicher, Spears and Haslam, above (n 14).

[22] Postmes and Spears, above (n 20).

[23] Turner et al, above (n 8) 54–55.

[24] A Alvarez 'Destructive Beliefs: Genocide and the Role of Ideology' in A Smeulers and R Haveman (eds), *Supranational Criminology: Towards a Criminology of International Crimes* (Antwerp, Intersentia, 2008) 216.

[25] See E Staub, 'Individual and Group Identities in Genocide and Mass Killing' in RD Ashmore, L Jussim and D Wilder (eds), *Social Identity, Intergroup Conflict, and Conflict Reduction* (Oxford, Oxford University Press, 2001) 164–66.

[26] Alvarez, 'Destructive Beliefs', above (n 24).

[27] See also the partially differing approach by JL Maynard, 'Rethinking the Role of Ideology in Mass Atrocities' (2014) 26 *Terrorism and Political Violence* 821.

types elsewhere.[28] But it is necessary to take a closer look at dehumanisation from a social identity perspective. Dehumanisation helps persons overcome their natural inhibitions against murder and killing by defining others as sub-human or non-human. There are several examples for ideologies that dehumanise an out-group, like the anti-Semitic ideology of the Nazis that led to the Holocaust or the ideology of the Hutu in the Rwandan genocide of the Tutsi. In the light of the Social Identity Approach, the specific dangerousness of a dehumanising ideology becomes obvious: dehumanisation shifts the level of comparison. From the perspective of the Self-Categorization theory it allows people to understand these ideology-defined 'sub-humans' or 'non-humans' not simply as members of a certain out-group, but as enemies of humankind.

Now, how would ideology as a tool for social identity improvement play out in practice? Think of a group of lower-class, poor, insufficiently educated and socially disadvantaged persons, who, by the accident of birth, happen to be white males with a certain nationality. If they embraced a racist, sexist and nationalistic ideology, this would help to improve their social identity: they would continue to be uneducated, poor and socially disadvantaged, yet the groups they compare with and the categories of comparison would shift. According to their ideology, they could see themselves as automatically superior to others, who do not share the same criteria. Comparisons with such out-groups becomes both more relevant and more advantageous. Yet, they will perhaps feel that their being poor and disadvantaged is very unfair, given the reputed 'natural superiority' of their kind. Thus, such an ideology will also foster social competition and from the ideology-blurred perspective of the in-group justify violent acts against out-groups.

As mentioned before, ideology is also a powerful tool to manipulate accessibility: one subscribing to a racist, sexist and nationalistic ideology will get used to give priority to these criteria and will more often and more easily find situational cues triggering the specific in-group/out-group dichotomy. As ideology spreads and is learned and adopted by others, accessibility increases in a population and more situations fitting the ideology-based dichotomy will be identified.

Within groups sharing a social identity, the social influence of prototypical group members (for example, the group leaders) leads to an adaptation of individuals to group norms. Social influence is even important for the knowledge and information shared by the group. It could be shown that the social influence of the person sharing a piece of information is more important than the objective truth of it.[29] This is also the reason why fake news, superstitions or prejudice are gladly adopted and shared as long as they stem from influential in-group members. This leads to a distorted perspective on reality.[30]

---

[28] S Harrendorf, 'How Can Criminology Contribute to an Explanation of International Crimes?' (2014) 12 *Journal of International Criminal Justice* 234.

[29] Reicher, Spears and Haslam, above (n 14).

[30] See also with respect to such occurrences on the internet G Nordheim, 'Poppers Alptraum' (2016) *European Journalism Observatory*, available at: de.ejo-online.eu/digitales/poppers-alptraum; M Del Vicario, A Bessi, F Zollo, F Petroni, A Scala, G Caldarelli, HE Stanley and W Quattrociocchi

Social identity also underlies obedience effects. For example, Milgram's famous experiments[31] are open to a social identity interpretation,[32] which is more plausible than the classical way these experiments are understood. Before discussing this, it is necessary to recapitulate the experiments,[33] as we will have to go into some of the details of the experimental arrangements. Milgram's subjects seemingly had to administer increasingly strong electric shocks (from 15 up to 450 Volts in steps of 15 Volts) to a third person (the learner) by command of the experimenter each time the learner made a mistake in a simple memory test. The learner was just played by an actor and true electric shocks were not delivered, but this was unknown to the subjects. With increasing shock level, the learner reacted more strongly (up to outright screaming), showed growing protest and finally refused to give any further answers. If the naive subject wanted to stop, the experimenter used four different so-called 'prods':

Prod 1: Please continue, or, please go on.

Prod 2: The experiment requires that you continue.

Prod 3: It is absolutely essential that you continue.

Prod 4: You have no other choice, you must go on.[34]

If prod 1 was successful, the experimenter would not use the other prods. Otherwise, prod 2 would be chosen. If this was unsuccessful, prod 3 would be next and eventually the experimenter would come to prod 4.

Overall, many more persons conformed than anticipated, although with strong variation based on the proximity to the fake victim. In the so-called remote feedback condition, where the learner was placed in another room and was not heard by the subject, except for a loud banging on the wall at 300 Volts, followed by no response to any further questions of the naive teacher, 66 per cent of the subjects continued until the highest voltage level. In the touch-proximity condition, on the other hand, the subject was not only in the same room as the learner, but the learner also had to touch a metal plate in order to receive the (fake) shocks. From 150 Volts on, the learner refused to touch the plate voluntarily and the subject had to push his hand down onto the plate in order to execute the next shocks. In this condition, only 30 per cent of all subjects continued until the highest

---

'The Spreading of Misinformation Online' (2016) 113 *Proceedings of the National Academy of Sciences* 554.

[31] S Milgram 'Some Conditions of Obedience and Disobedience to Authority' (1965) 18 *Human Relations* 57; S Milgram, *Obedience to Authority: An Experimental View* (New York, Harper & Row, 1974); citations based on the 2017 e-book edition of the work.

[32] SD Reicher and SA Haslam 'After Shock? Towards a Social Identity Explanation of the Milgram "Obedience" Studies' (2011) 50 *British Journal of Social Psychology* 163.

[33] See also Harrendorf, above (n 28) 237–41.

[34] Milgram, *Obedience to Authority*, above (n 31) 48.

voltage level.[35] There were several replications of the experiments carried out by other researchers, which generally confirm Milgram's findings.[36]

Reicher and Haslam noticed that in all the transcripts of the experiments Milgram published, prod 4 is only used once, and with a negative effect.[37] Being confronted with prod 4, the subject states: 'If this were Russia maybe, but not in America' and refuses to continue. The experiment is terminated at the 150 Volts level.[38] If prod 4 was ever used successfully by Milgram cannot be found out. Yet, we can turn to the replication study by Burger for further information. As is shown in Burger, Girgis and Manning,[39] subjects confronted with prod 1 continued with the procedure in 64.3 per cent of all cases. After prod 2, 45.7 per cent of the subjects continued, 10.5 per cent continued after prod 3, and 0.0 per cent (!) continued after prod 4. This result casts some doubt on the common assumption that the continuation of subjects in Milgram's experiments was due to obedience to orders.

While it is true that many subjects conformed to the requirements of the experiments, seemingly this is not due to orders they received, as the only prod that is exactly phrased as an order was the one that was always unsuccessful. It is more plausible that the obedience Milgram found was due to group effects: the test subjects usually teamed up with the experimenter in the remote feedback condition and remained at his side, while the proximity conditions made it easier to change sides and support the victim. Milgram also saw this and clearly refers to this 'incipient group formation' in his 1965 publication.[40] Indeed, the experiments show that many test subjects were able to socially identify with the experimenter and join him in a seemingly important scientific endeavour. Accordingly, obedience rates drop as soon as the experimenter is not associated any more with the prestigious University of Yale, like in experiment 10, which is carried out in a rundown office building in Bridgeport.[41] Even lower obedience rates were found as soon as an ordinary man was chosen to give orders as a substitute for the experimenter, who seemingly had to leave the experiment earlier.[42]

But why did people conform less the more the prods were phrased as orders? The reason might be that the illusion of a shared social identity as partners in an important scientific endeavour is destroyed as soon as the experimenter tries to

---

[35] Milgram, 'Some Conditions of Obedience and Disobedience to Authority', above (n 31) 62.

[36] eg, JM Burger, 'Replicating Milgram: Would People Still Obey Today?' (2009) 64 *American Psychologist* 1; J-L Beauvois, D Courbet and D Oberlé, 'The Prescriptive Power of the Television Host: A Transposition of Milgram's Obedience Paradigm to the Context of TV Game Show' (2012) 62 *Revue Européenne de Psychologie Appliquée* 111. See also with further references A Smeulers and F Grünfeld, *International Crimes and other Gross Human Rights Violations* (Leiden, Martinus Nijhoff Publishers, 2011) 222–27.

[37] Reicher and Haslam, 'After Shock?', above (n 32) 167–68.

[38] Milgram, *Obedience to Authority*, above (n 31) 74–75.

[39] JM Burger, ZM Girgis and CC Manning 'In Their Own Words: Explaining Obedience to Authority Through an Examination of Participants' Comments' (2011) 2 *Social Psychological and Personality Science* 464.

[40] Milgram, 'Some Conditions of Obedience and Disobedience to Authority', above (n 31) 64.

[41] Milgram, *Obedience to Authority*, above (n 31) 93–97.

[42] Experiment 13, Milgram, *Obedience to Authority*, above (n 31) 119–24.

impose himself over the test subjects.[43] Therefore, while it can still be assumed that Milgram's experiments refer to legitimate authority, these are not experiments that show an isolated obedience effect with regard to orders or commands. It is plausible that – apart from situations where force or threat of force is present – authority depends on processes of social identification.

This is also somewhat confirmed by the seminal work of Tyler who showed that spontaneous conformity to legitimate authority can be separated from the effect of threat of force as a means of obedience enforcement, but also from conformity due to an internalised value system.[44]

There are further studies that show the relevance of a Social Identity Approach to international crimes. In an earlier publication,[45] I already showed how strongly processes of social identification influence the results of the (in)famous Stanford Prison Experiment.[46] In that experiment volunteer students were randomly assigned to become guards and prisoners of a mock prison and were briefed accordingly.

From a social identity perspective, it is especially important what Zimbardo, who was also playing the role of prison superintendent, told the students assigned to become guards in their initial briefing. As can be seen in original film footage of the experiment,[47] Zimbardo said that they can create in the prisoners

> feelings of boredom, … a sense of fear in them to some degree, you can create a notion of arbitrariness that their life is totally controlled by us, by the system, you, me, … and they have no privacy at all … We are going to take away their individuality in various ways. In general, what all this leads to is a sense of powerlessness. That is, we have total power in this situation and they have none.

Guards and prisoners also received costumes that were designed to reduce their individuality and increase a common group identity;[48] the prisoners' clothing additionally had a humiliating and degrading quality. They were only addressed by numbers instead of names.

The experiment had to be ended much earlier than planned, as mock guards had started to show increasingly abusive behaviour and some mock prisoners were in states of severe stress. Prison guards had set up an oppressive regime, with a faction of the guards group showing sadistic or very strong oppressive behaviour, another faction being tough but fair and a third faction reluctant to use their power.[49] Zimbardo himself preferred a purely situational interpretation, stressing

---

[43] Reicher and Haslam, 'After Shock?', above (n 32) 168.

[44] TR Tyler, *Why People Obey the Law* (New Haven, CT, Yale University Press, 1990).

[45] Harrendorf, above (n 28) 242–45.

[46] C Haney, C Banks and PG Zimbardo 'Interpersonal Dynamics in a Simulated Prison' (1973) 1 *International Journal of Criminology and Penology* 69; PG Zimbardo, *The Lucifer Effect: Understanding How Good People Turn Evil* (New York, Random House, 2007).

[47] K Musen and PG Zimbardo, *Quiet Rage: The Stanford Prison Experiment* (DVD, Stanford, Stanford University, 2004).

[48] Haney, Banks and Zimbardo, above (n 46) 75–76.

[49] ibid; Zimbardo, *The Lucifer Effect*, above (n 46) 196–97.

that he selected only persons for the experiment who did not show any psychological abnormalities and who were randomly assigned to play guards or prisoners.[50]

Yet, a more plausible explanation of the results of the experiment relies on the Social Identity Approach: apart from the symbols of power provided to the guards as social cues, the role expectations were clearly stated by Zimbardo in his initial briefing, which could be understood as an invitation to abuse of power.[51] In Reicher's and Haslam's own replication of the prison experiment, they left it up to the guards themselves to develop a joint social identity and did not provide them with role expectations. This newer experiment (the BBC prison study) ended very differently. The guards, who were never able to develop a strong group identity, did not install a regime of terror, but were overthrown by the prisoners.[52]

A Social Identity Approach also offers an excellent explanation for the well-known effect of group polarisation.[53] Groups whose opinions on a certain topic tend towards one extreme of the possible spectrum of opinions before a discussion of the topic develop an even more radical opinion on the topic after the discussion.[54] According to Self-Categorization Theory, this is due to adaptation processes towards the opinion of the prototypical group member. Prototypicality does not only require an opinion to represent the opinions of the other group members, but also to distinguish the in-group as well as possible from the out-group: the prototypical opinion needs an optimal meta contrast.[55] Indeed, studies have shown that polarisation mainly depends on the need to be distinct from a relevant out-group.[56]

Group stereotypes and group support[57] also help to reduce the amount of cognitive dissonance a person incurs who does not act in accordance with his or her moral standards. Social identity effects are therefore also important for the theory of neutralisation techniques, a theory that, although initially developed

---

[50] Zimbardo, ibid.

[51] Reicher and Haslam, 'Rethinking the Psychology of Tyranny', above (n 9).

[52] For a discussion of the BBC prison study, also see consenting JC Turner, 'Tyranny, Freedom and Social Structure: Escaping our Theoretical Prisons' (2006) 45 *British Journal of Social Psychology* 41; dissenting PG Zimbardo, 'On Rethinking the Psychology of Tyranny: The BBC Prison Study' (2006) 45 *British Journal of Social Psychology* 47; and summing up SA Haslam and S Reicher, 'Debating the Psychology of Tyranny: Fundamental Issues of Theory, Perspective and Science' (2006) 45 *British Journal of Social Psychology* 55.

[53] *cf* Turner et al, above (n 8) 142–70.

[54] See, eg, DG Myers, 'Group Polarization' in JM Levine and MA Hogg (eds), *Encyclopedia of Group Processes and Intergroup Relations* (Thousand Oaks, CA, SAGE, 2010) 361.

[55] Turner et al, above (n 8) 142–70; E-J Lee, 'Deindividuation Effects on Group Polarization in Computer-Mediated Communication: The Role of Group Identification, Public-Self-Awareness, and Perceived Argument Quality' (2007) 57 *Journal of Communication* 385.

[56] SP Nicholson, 'Polarising Cues' (2012) 56 *American Journal of Political Science* 52, 56; E Suhay, 'Explaining Group Influence: The Role of Identity and Emotion in Political Conformity and Polarization' (2015) 37 *Political Behavior* 221.

[57] Regarding the latter, see BM McKimmie, DJ Terry, MA Hogg, ASR Manstead, R Spears and B Doosje, 'I'm a Hypocrite, but so is Everyone Else: Group Support and the Reduction of Cognitive Dissonance' (2003) 7 *Group Dynamics* 214; also see L Festinger, H Riecken and S Schachter, *When Prophecy Fails* (Minneapolis, MN, University of Minnesota Press, 1956).

to explain juvenile delinquency,[58] has turned out to become perhaps the most preferred explanatory approach to international crimes.[59] Yet, the available variants of this theory, plausible as they seem as an at least partial explanation of international crimes,[60] do not sufficiently address group effects. These effects are somehow reflected in the technique called 'appeal to higher loyalties', but it needs to be considered that for group crimes (like international crimes) group effects interfere with the other techniques, too.

III. Individual Characteristics and Self-Selection of Perpetrators

Nowadays it is widely accepted that individual involvement in mass atrocities for the vast majority of perpetrators is not due to specific psychological abnormalities.[61] Only few of those who participate in such events can be diagnosed with a sadistic paraphilia or can be considered as 'psychopaths' in the meaning of a person scoring high on the PCL-R checklist.[62] When authors write that the perpetrators of international crimes are 'ordinary people', this is often done in relation to this fact. But what does this actually mean? From history[63] and from the famous social psychological experiments that are considered to shed light on the willingness of people to participate in international crimes, like the Stanford Prison Experiment[64] or Milgram's experiments,[65] we know that not everyone participates in international crimes. Even under the exceptional circumstances that allow for international crimes to occur, individuals retain the possibility to decide. And the decision to participate is only one option; the majority in a population usually acts as mere bystanders, not perpetrators. Finally, some try to resist or rebel against the murderous plans and actions of the perpetrators. The 'ordinary people' hypothesis somewhat obfuscates this finding, as it entails the notion that there is nothing special about the perpetrators. But perhaps there is?

---

[58] GM Sykes and D Matza 'Techniques of Neutralization: A Theory of Delinquency' (1957) 22 *American Sociological Review* 664.

[59] See A Bandura, *Agression: A Social Learning Analysis* (Englewood Cliffs, NJ, Prentice-Hall, 1973); Jäger, above (n 2); A Alvarez, 'Adjusting to Genocide: The Techniques of Neutralization and the Holocaust' (1997) 21 *Social Science History* 139; S Cohen, *States of Denial: Knowing about Atrocities and Suffering* (Cambridge, Polity Press, 2001).

[60] For a more detailed discussion, see Harrendorf, above (n 28) 249–51.

[61] Smeulers, above (n 5); T Blass, 'Psychological Perspectives on the Perpetrators of the Holocaust: The Role of Situational Pressures, Personal Dispositions, and their Interactions' (1993) 7 *Holocaust and Genocide Studies* 30.

[62] RD Hare, *Hare Psychopathy Checklist-Revised (PCL-R): Technical Manual*, 2nd edn (North Tonawanda, NY, Multi-Health Systems, 2007).

[63] See, eg, DR Mandel, 'The Obedience Alibi: Milgram's Account of the Holocaust Reconsidered' (1998) 20 *Analyse & Kritik* 74, 86–87.

[64] Haney, Banks and Zimbardo, above (n 46).

[65] Milgram, 'Some Conditions of Obedience and Disobedience to Authority' and Milgram, *Obedience to Authority*, both above (n 31).

Another problematic issue of this hypothesis is that being psychologically 'normal' is seen as something that is specific for perpetrators of international crimes. Yet, this is not true: criminological research shows that at least minor criminal offences are ubiquitous in every society around the world.[66] At least during adolescence, almost everyone commits at least some minor offences. Crime is a normal by-product of maturation processes.[67] And even 'career criminals' are usually not 'abnormal'. Of course, a relevant number of them can be diagnosed with an antisocial personality disorder,[68] but this is not surprising, as this disorder revolves around the core personality elements of habitual felons. Therefore, the notion of 'ordinariness' can mainly be explained with a view to the large discrepancy between the exceptional brutality and mercilessness of macro-criminal events and the unexceptional personality traits of the perpetrators. It is a means to express our astonishment and bewilderment about what humans are capable of, but it is of limited explanatory value.

All facts available on actual international crimes that have occurred in the history of humankind and all empirical results of social psychological experiments simulating atrocity-prone situations show that we must not only reject a purely individual, but also a purely situationist approach to explain international crimes. We have to assume that individual and situational factors interact.[69] The term 'ordinary people' refers to people, who would not have committed such acts under 'normal' circumstances, but it does not mean that there are no personality traits that foster participation. Therefore, it is necessary to identify such 'sleeper' traits.[70]

From a social identity perspective, we can systematise the interactionist approach as follows: although a Social Identity Approach to international crimes relies on group effects to explain individual behaviour, everything begins with self-selection. Which groups persons join or refrain from joining is not at all random but can be largely explained by processes of self-selection.[71] Joining the group then usually means self-categorisation of oneself as a group member in situations in which the social identity derived from this group becomes salient. In such situations, depersonalisation sets in, leading to an adaptation to group norms. Further polarisation of the whole group occurs after discussion of topics for which the group tends towards an extreme position. In addition, a common group knowledge emerges, not necessarily related to an 'objective' truth. Finally, criminal acts may occur, motivated by group ideology and in accordance with group norms.

[66] See, eg, E Durkheim, *Les règles de la méthode sociologique* (Paris, Félix Alcan, 1985).

[67] See M Rocque 'The Lost Concept: The (Re)emerging Link between Maturation and Desistance from Crime' (2015) 15 *Criminology & Criminal Justice* 340.

[68] SA De Brito and S Hodgins, 'Die Antisoziale Persönlichkeitsstörung des DSM-IV-TR: Befunde, Untergruppen und Unterschiede zu Psychopathy' (2009) 3 *Forensische Psychiatrie Psychologie Kriminologie* 116.

[69] SA Haslam and S Reicher 'Beyond the Banality of Evil: Three Dynamics of an Interactionist Social Psychology of Tyranny' (2007) 33 *Personality and Social Psychology Bulletin* 615.

[70] Steiner, above (n 10).

[71] Haslam and Reicher, 'Beyond the Banality of Evil', above (n 69).

The interactionist perspective, therefore, means that humans, as far as possible, decide which group to found or join. Each individual influences the topic, knowledge, norms and positions of the group. But the group also changes the persons who join it.

This interactionist perspective shows that it is crucial to identify the individual reasons leading people to join certain groups or feel like a group member, stay in the group and influence its position in a certain way. First, it is necessary to understand the ongoing self-selection processes. Take, as an example, the reserve police battalions in Nazi Germany. They might perhaps have consisted of ordinary reserve police officers, but not simply of 'ordinary men', as Browning insinuates.[72] Several had a policing career in Nazi Germany, were Nazi Party members etc.[73] Studies also show that police officers even in our times and in a democratic society often show a stronger tendency toward right-wing authoritarianism than average persons outside the police forces.[74]

For the Stanford Prison Experiment, Haney, Banks and Zimbardo report that they took out a newspaper advertisement, searching for male college students willing to take part in a psychological study on 'prison life'.[75] They carried out several psychological tests on the 75 volunteers found this way and only included in the study 'the 24 subjects who were judged to be most stable (physically and mentally), most mature, and least involved in anti-social behavior'.[76] Finally, the roles of guards and prisoners were also assigned randomly. Yet, self-selection might have been an important factor here, since the newspaper advertisement looked for volunteers for a study on 'prison life'. Carnahan and McFarland showed that such an advertisement attracts people with significantly higher scores of aggressiveness, authoritarianism, Machiavellianism, narcissism and social dominance, but lower scores on empathy and altruism than in a control group, where the words 'prison life' were omitted from the advertisement.[77] In addition, the test results of the participants in the Stanford Prison Experiment reported by Haney, Banks and Zimbardo for the authoritarianism (F-)Scale and the Machiavellianism scale seem to have been well above average,[78] although this cannot be fully confirmed due to a somewhat insufficient description of the exact versions of the scales used. In comparison, the participants in the BBC prison study, in which the guards did not show abusive behaviour, scored distinctly lower on the F-Scale.[79]

---

[72] Browning, above (n 5).

[73] M Mann, 'Were the Perpetrators of Genocide "Ordinary Men" or "Real Nazis"? Results from Fifteen Hundred Biographies' (2000) 14 *Holocaust and Genocide Studies* 331.

[74] J Gatto and M Dambrun, 'Authoritarianism, Social Dominance, and Prejudice among Junior Police Officers: The Role of the Normative Context' (2012) 43 *Social Psychology* 61; J Gatto, M Dambrun, C Kerbrat and P De Oliveira, 'Prejudice in the Police: On the Processes Underlying the Effects of Selection and Group Socialisation' (2010) 40 *European Journal of Social Psychology* 252.

[75] Haney, Banks and Zimbardo, above (n 46).

[76] ibid, 73.

[77] T Carnahan and S McFarland, 'Revisiting the Stanford Prison Experiment: Could Participant Self-Selection Have Led to the Cruelty?' (2007) 33 *Personality and Social Psychology Bulletin* 603.

[78] Haney, Banks and Zimbardo, above (n 46).

[79] Carnahan and McFarland, above (n 77).

Individual characteristics are also of explanative value for Milgram-type experiments. This becomes already visible in Milgram's original experiments. He wrote:

> This subject did not want to shock the victim, and he found it an extremely disagreeable task, but he was unable to invent a response that would free him from E's authority. Many subjects cannot find the specific verbal formula that would enable them to reject the role assigned to them by the experimenter. Perhaps our culture does not provide adequate models for disobedience.[80]

In a study by Begue et al,[81] which adapted the experimental condition of Milgram to a (fake) TV show context and found results very much in line with Milgram's original studies, the researchers showed that obedience is significantly and positively influenced by high scores of conscientiousness and agreeableness, two factors of the well-known five-factor personality model. Persons scoring high on conscientiousness tend towards self-discipline, sense of duty, aim for achievement and organisation and favour norms and conformity.[82] Agreeable persons also avoid norm violations and prefer not to upset people; they tend to conform with social expectations.[83] Hence, it is not so very surprising that these seemingly 'positive' character traits are connected with obedience in Milgram-type experiments. The above quotation by Milgram seems to be a good description of the inner conflicts a highly conscientious or agreeable person has to endure when confronted with such a task.[84] He also found significant influences of political orientation and political activism: persons who defined themselves as being on the Left of the political spectrum tended towards less obedience. The same was true for people who showed higher political activism, measured by whether they had ever signed a petition, attended a lawful demonstration, joined an unofficial strike, and/or occupied buildings or factories, or if they would at least consider doing so in the future. Yet, a more detailed analysis showed that this factor was only significant for female participants (without any explanation given).

The above-mentioned replication study by Burger did not find any significant correlations between the decision to stop and empathic concern or desire for control, i.e. the desire to have personal control over occurring events.[85] Yet, he found at least correlations between these scores and the individual first prod score, ie, the moment at which the first of the standardised prods (ie, 'Please continue' or 'Please go on') had to be used to motivate subjects to continue. Obviously neither empathic concern nor desire for control were able to predict defiance. It can be theorised that they will not help much if a person is highly agreeable and

---

[80] Milgram, 'Some Conditions of Obedience and Disobedience to Authority', above (n 31) 67.

[81] L Bègue, J-L Beauvois, D Courbet, D Oberlé, J Lepage and A Duke 'Personality Predicts Obedience in a Milgram Paradigm' (2015) 83 *Journal of Personality* 299.

[82] *cf* ibid, 301.

[83] ibid, 300.

[84] ibid.

[85] Burger, above (n 36).

conscientious. With respect to the replication study by Burger, the individual comments of the test subjects during and after the experiment were also systematically analysed. Here, it turned out that significantly more persons who expressed a feeling of personal responsibility for what happened to the learner during the experiment or in the de-briefing session stopped their participation in the experiment before reaching the 150 Volts level.[86]

These important findings already show some personality traits and personality aspects that might predict participation in international crimes for 'normal' persons. They show that, apart from the occasional sadist or dark triad personality,[87] much more common traits are relevant.[88]

This also allows for some relevant prevention strategies to be developed. Conscientiousness and agreeableness are not necessarily fully positive character traits. Although some degree of compliance and friendliness in social contacts is obviously necessary for society to exist, we should educate our children to become critical thinkers, not accepting rules just because they exist, but only because they are useful and necessary. The ideals of the Enlightenment and the Kantian categorical imperative should become primary moral goals of education. Children should also learn that being a 'good boy' or 'good girl' is not a virtue in itself, and that there might come situations in which they need to stand up against someone and reject his or her demands politely, but firmly. This is, obviously, not only helpful for the prevention of international crimes, but also helps to prevent more common events like sexual abuse. It can also be assumed that the preventive effect of a left-wing political orientation found by Begue et al[89] is actually due to the absence of authoritarianism in these test subjects. Therefore, this result fits well with the results from experiments of the Stanford Prison type. The educational ideals described above should actually also reduce the prevalence of authoritarian personality traits. Finally, a feeling of personal responsibility for outcomes of situations and a desire for control should be related to each other from a theoretical viewpoint. An education aiming at raising children to become freethinking, independent adults should foster such traits, too.

IV. Towards a Comprehensive Interactionist Theory

Which consequences has the social identity perspective on international crimes developed here for criminological theory? Ideally, we should have a comprehensive interactionist theory, integrating personality and situational aspects in a general

---

[86] Burger, Girgis and Manning, above (n 39).

[87] 'Dark triad' = Machiavellianism, psychopathy and narcissism. See DL Paulhus and KM Williams, 'The Dark Triad of Personality: Narcissism, Machiavellianism, and Psychopathy' (2002) 36 *Journal of Research in Personality* 556.

[88] For an offender typology, *cf* Smeulers, above (n 5).

[89] Bègue et al, above (n 81).

causal model. Such a model should not be eclectic,[90] but should be based on a thought through general concept. It should also not be too specific and limited in applicability, as is the case for the Collective Action Theory of Genocide by Hagan and Rymond-Richmond.[91] Pruitt suggested certain expansions and modifications of the theory,[92] but it would still remain a theory aiming only at the explanation of genocide. Ideally, the same theory should be applicable for international crimes as for other crimes.

Which modifications would a Social Identity Approach to international crimes bring for criminological theory? As already mentioned in the introduction, it should lead to the rediscovery of the social group in criminology.[93] What we can learn from the study of international crimes is that criminality cannot simply be understood as deviance from legal and social norms, but also as a result of an adaptation to and conformity with group norms. This is not only true for international crimes, but also applies to 'normal' criminality.

It is a well-known fact that delinquent peers are a relevant risk factor for offending.[94] Behind this correlation, we can expect some situational aspects, but also the effects of group formation and social identity processes. Early subculture theories[95] have seen this prescriptive effect of deviant group norms, yet they over-simplified by assuming inverse normative values, while reality is much more complex. However, it is interesting to see that Cohen in an early publication had already stressed the importance of social identity for the understanding of criminality.[96]

Until now, the theory of neutralisation techniques[97] has been the one used most frequently to explain international crimes.[98] While there is some truth in this theory,[99] it cannot be expanded to a full explanatory concept. Neutralisation theories only explain how perpetrators may overcome moral inhibitions against offending by redefining a situation in a way that its immoral aspects are neutralised, but they cannot explain why someone would want to commit the crime in the first place: motivation is necessarily absent from this theory and can also not easily be added to it. Another theory commonly understood to be of explanatory value for international crimes is Tittle's Control Balance Theory.[100] Yet, in this respect it

---

[90] Like the one developed by Rothe, above (n 3).

[91] J Hagan and W Rymond-Richmond, *Darfur and the Crime of Genocide* (Cambridge, Cambridge University Press, 2009).

[92] WR Pruitt, 'How Criminology Can Engage in the Theorizing on Genocide?' (2014) 9 *International Journal of Criminal Justice Sciences* 1.

[93] To borrow from the title of Turner et al, above (n 8).

[94] Just see Wikström, 'Why Crime Happens', above (n 13).

[95] AK Cohen, *Delinquent Boys* above (n 11); Yinger, above (n 11).

[96] AK Cohen, 'The Sociology of the Deviant Act: Anomie Theory and Beyond' (1965) 30 *American Sociological Review* 12.

[97] Sykes and Matza, above (n 58).

[98] eg, by Bandura, above (n 59); Jäger, above (n 2); Alvarez, 'Adjusting to Genocide', above (n 58); Cohen, above (n 59).

[99] *cf* Harrendorf, above (n 28) 248–51.

[100] CR Tittle, *Control Balance: Toward a General Theory of Deviance* (Boulder, CO, Westview Press, 1995); CR Tittle, 'Refining Control Balance Theory' (2004) 8 *Theoretical Criminology* 395.

is mainly a theory that helps explain the criminality of the masterminds behind macro-criminal events,[101] while it has nothing specific to offer with respect to the participation of 'ordinary' people. It is very plausible that many of them live their lives in a state of control balance and should therefore not offend at all.

There have been many other approaches to explain international crimes in the recent years, inter alia, an approach trying to explain international crimes from a life-course perspective.[102] Yet, the most promising theoretical development of the last few years has emerged in the field of action theories. While for many years, criminology mainly knew one fully-fledged action theory, the overly simple rational choice theory,[103] in recent years theory development in this area has made important progress. In the English literature and internationally, it is mainly Situational Action Theory that comes to mind here.[104] German sociologists also developed the Model of Frame-Selection as a general sociological action theory,[105] which can also be applied to criminal actions.[106]

Such action theories are excellent candidates for an explanation of international crimes,[107] as they are interactionist per se. They explain the decision of an actor in a situation based on the interaction of him or her with a certain situational setting: 'It's all about interactions'.[108] Situational Action Theory explains crimes as 'moral actions'.[109] According to the theory,[110] the first important issue is that we automatically apply a moral filter, when assessing the action alternatives that are available to us when we react on motivations (temptations or provocations). The theory assumes that not only persons have moral values, but that the setting also provides us with moral cues. In situations in which a criminal action alternative runs counter to our own morality and is also against the morality of the setting, this option will not pass the moral filter and we will habitually choose a legal action. If, on the other hand, a criminal action alternative does not violate our individual morality and is also in line with the moral cues of the setting, it is equally plausible that only this criminal action alternative is seen and, once again, habitually chosen (or choice is only made between different criminal actions). Finally, if individual

---

[101] See HE Müller, 'Staatsführungen als Tätergemeinschaften am Beispiel der Gefangenenmisshandlungen und Folter in Guantanamo und Abu Ghraib' in HE Müller, GM Sander and H Válková (eds), *Festschrift für Ulrich Eisenberg zum 70. Geburtstag* (München, Beck, 2009) 83.

[102] HN Brehm, C Uggen and J-D Ne Gsanabo, 'Age, Gender, and the Crime of Crimes: Toward a Life-Course Theory of Genocide Participation' (2016) 54 *Criminology* 713.

[103] GS Becker, 'Crime and Punishment: An Economic Approach' (1968) 76 *Journal of Political Economy* 169.

[104] Wikström, 'Crime as Alternative' and 'Why Crime Happens', above (n 13).

[105] See C Kroneberg, 'Die Definition der Situation und die variable Rationalität der Akteure: Ein allgemeines Modell des Handelns' (2005) 34 *Zeitschrift für Soziologie* 344.

[106] S Eifler, *Kriminalität im Alltag: Eine handlungstheoretische Analyse von Gelegenheiten* (Wiesbaden, Springer VS, 2009).

[107] Situational Action Theory is insofar also utilised by Drenkhahn, above (n 13).

[108] P-O Wikström, D Oberwittler, K Treiber and B Hardie, *Breaking Rules: The Social and Situational Dynamics of Young People's Urban Crime* (Oxford, Oxford University Press, 2012) 405.

[109] Wikström, 'Why Crime Happens', above (n 13).

[110] Wikström, 'Crime as Alternative' and 'Why Crime Happens', above (n 13); Wikström et al, above (n 108).

morality is not in line with the moral cues of the setting, usually both criminal and legal action alternatives will be identified. Then, an actual conscious decision process is necessary. Here, morality becomes important once again. If the criminal action alternative does not run counter to our own moral standards and allows us to fulfil our motivation, we will, in principle, choose it, if no external controls active in the setting (deterrents) hinder us. If, on the other hand, the criminal action alternative is not in line with our moral standards, but fits the moral cues of the setting, we will still choose the criminal action alternative if it fulfils our motivation and the internal controls active in the setting (self-control) do not sufficiently hinder us.

The Model of Frame-Selection[111] also provides a (somewhat more complex) action theory. This theory assumes that the process of deciding upon an action can actually be structured into three phases: frame selection, script selection and action selection. Prior to each of these phases, a subconscious process of mode selection takes place, in which the brain decides whether the following selection process can be carried out in an automatic-spontaneous (AS) mode or needs to be carried out in a reflective-calculative (RC) mode. The AS mode is selected if accessibility and fit (two concepts already explained above) allow for it, since we already have an accessible frame, script or action available that fits the current situation. If such a frame, script or action is not available, we will need to decide in RC mode, which Kroneberg bases on rational choice criteria.[112] Frame selection means the initial definition of a situation, ie, the interpretation of what Wikström in his theory would call the 'setting'. Based on this frame selection, one would then choose a script, ie, a possible chain of action that is adapted to the setting that was identified before. Finally, an individual action from this script is chosen and carried out. Mode selections for each stage (frame, script, action) are independent from each other, ie, it is possible that frame selection happens in AS mode, but the setting identified is so unusual or complex that we do not have an automated script available for it, but need to choose our course of action in RC mode, etc. Crimes can, in this model, be explained as a product of rational deliberation in RC mode, but also as habitual actions in AS mode. Morality is relevant for both modes. In RC mode, Kroneberg treats it as a factor in the rational choice process.[113] The AS mode of the Model of Frame Selection works somewhat similarly to the moral filter in Wikström's theory if the individual morality and the moral cues of the setting are in line with each other.

Now to the most important question: how can we 'import' the assumptions of the Social Identity Approach into these action theories? As for Situational Action Theory, social identity affects the moral filter. If a certain social identity becomes salient, an actor becomes depersonalised, focuses on and adapts to group norms. This means that the individual morality is adapted due to moral cues active in

---

[111] Kroneberg, above (n 105).
[112] ibid.
[113] ibid, 352.

the setting. In group situations the moral cues of the setting can therefore actually change individual morality. This can result in a criminal action alternative passing the moral filter that would otherwise not have passed it. The Social Identity Approach therefore shows that individual morality is something flexible and depends on the self-categorisation that is active in a given situation. Social identity will also affect moral deliberation.

Similar to this, depersonalisation and group identification in the context of Kroneberg's Model of Frame Selection will affect frame selection (settings are interpreted differently), but also script and action selection (scripts and actions will be selected in line with group norms and group knowledge). As self-categorisation depends on accessibility of the categorisation and the fit of the situation, factors also relevant for automatic selections in AS mode, social identity is not only relevant in RC mode, but also influences all the automated decisions we make. A combination of the Social Identity Approach with action theories therefore also helps explain how biased interpretations of situations and biased decisions on a course of action can come about.

V. Conclusions

Summing up, a Social Identity Approach to international crimes helps to find a common framework for many situational aspects that have been discussed somewhat separately so far. It can be part of an interactionist criminological theory, for example based on the Situational Action Theory or the Model of Frame-Selection. Such a theory understands international crimes as elements of a continuum of crimes. In that sense, perpetrators of 'international' crimes are 'ordinary' in the same way as many perpetrators of 'normal' crimes are 'ordinary' as well, while the notion that everyone would have reacted exactly this way in that situation needs to be rejected.

11

Regional Criminal Justice, Corporate Criminal Liability and the Need for Non-Doctrinal Research

ELIES VAN SLIEDREGT*

I. Introduction

In this chapter, I want to focus on the system of regional criminal justice proposed by the African Court of Justice and Human Rights (ACJHR). Discussing the proposal for an ACJHR has a threefold purpose. First, because it taps into a wider trend. Discussing the idea for an 'African International Criminal Court (ICC)' can be understood in a post-globalised context where domestic justice and arrangements closer to home are preferred over global law and governance. Secondly, it allows for discussing what is currently lacking in the tool box of international prosecutors: corporate criminal liability. The constituent document for the ACJHR, the Malabo Protocol, opens up the possibility to prosecute corporations for committing or being complicit in war crimes, genocide and crimes against humanity and transnational crimes. This has the potential to radically change the international criminal law 'ball game'. Thirdly, discussing both these topics – regionalism and corporate liability – illustrates very well how recent developments in international criminal justice cannot be fully understood and analysed by solely focusing on the law and doing doctrinal research. This chapter demonstrates the need for criminological and socio-legal approaches to international criminal justice. Only then can we fully understand the cycle of mass atrocities and come up with solutions for breaking that cycle.

In the following, I explore the question whether the Malabo Protocol, adopted in 2014 by the African Union (AU), vesting the to-be-established ACJHR with

* This chapter is based on thoughts developed since the symposium in Copenhagen and draws on talks given at the University of Pretoria, in August 2016, and at the Lauterpacht Centre for International Law, Cambridge University, in May 2017. Parts of it have been published with Larissa van den Herik in the Liber Amicorum for Baroness Judge Christine van den Wyngaert: S de Wulf (ed), *Huldeboek Christine van den Wyngaert* (Antwerpen, Maklu, 2017).

jurisdiction over international crimes, has added value alongside the ICC and whether it can be regarded as a model for the future. I will focus on one of the novelties of this African justice system: corporate criminal responsibility. First, I will make a few preliminary observations about its reception.

II. The Malabo Protocol: Differing Views

The scholarly reception of the Malabo Protocol is informed by different approaches. Clarke and Jalloh's work[1] as well as Werle's commentary[2] are largely doctrinal, article-by-article exercises that have some parallels with ICC commentaries, including those of Cassese, Schabas or Ambos and Triffterer.[3] Other works reflect on the strategy of regionalising criminal justice from more theoretical perspectives. Nicole De Silva's paper draws on institutional choice theory, making clear how African states, after initially pursuing strategies of using and changing the ICC, eventually shifted their focus to pursuing proposals for regional criminal courts within the AU.[4] Asad Kiyani posits the establishment of an African criminal court in the context of the Third World Approaches to International Criminal Law.[5] He sees it as a response to the failure of global justice to deal with crimes that have special resonance in the Third World (drug trafficking, illicit exploitation of natural resources) and the recognition of corporate criminal liability.[6]

The ACJHR can be regarded as either a rebel court or a role model.[7] As a rebel court, it is inspired by anti-ICC sentiments and is meant to operate as a shield against further ICC scrutiny into African crimes.[8] By way of justification for the move away from the ICC it is argued that justice is better provided at the regional

---

[1] K Clarke and C Jalloh (eds), *The African Court of Justice and Human and People's Rights* (Cambridge, Cambridge University Press, 2017).

[2] G Werle and M Vormbaum (eds), *The African Criminal Court. A Commentary on the Malabo Protocol* (The Hague, Asser Press, Springer Verlag, 2017).

[3] A Cassese, P Gaeta and JRWD Jones (eds), *The Rome Statute of the International Criminal Court: A Commentary* (Oxford, Oxford University Press, 2002); and O Triffterer and K Ambos (eds), *Rome Statute of the International Criminal Court: A Commentary* (Munich, CH Beck, 2016).

[4] N De Silva, 'Africa versus the International Criminal Court: The Strategy of Regionalizing International Criminal Justice': African opposition to the ICC and proposed regional criminal courts, prize winning paper of ISA 2017.

[5] As a branch of the more 'settled' scholarship around Third World Approaches to International Law (TWAIL). See AG Kiyani, 'Symposium on TWAIL Perspectives on ICL, IHL and Intervention. Third World Approaches to International Criminal Law' (2017) 109 *American Journal of International Law Unbound* 255, 258.

[6] ibid, 259.

[7] L van den Herik and E van Sliedregt, 'International Criminal Law and the Malabo Protocol – About Scholarly Reception, Rebellion and Role Models' in S de Wulf (ed), *Huldeboek Christine van den Wyngaert* (Antwerpen, Maklu, 2017).

[8] See M Ssenyonyo, 'The Rise of the African Union Opposition to the International Criminal Court's Investigations and Prosecutions of African Leaders' (2013) 13 *International Criminal Law Review* 385, 415–16; M du Plessis, 'Implications of the AU Decision to give the African Court Jurisdiction Over International Crimes' (2012) Institute for Security Studies Paper 235, 1.

level. As a role model, the Malabo Protocol can be seen as offering a new template for international criminal law (ICL) with additional (transnational) crimes and novel forms of international responsibility. It could serve as a corrective or even a role model, albeit for the time being only on paper. I will reflect on each of these perspectives.

A. Rebel Court

The immunity provision can be viewed as the most obvious sign that the Malabo Protocol is a rebel; designed, not as a complementary mechanism but as an alternative that opposes the ICC. Article 46(B) provides the general position in ICL: 'Subject to the provisions of Article 46Abis of this Statute, the official position of any accused person shall not relieve such person of criminal responsibility nor mitigate punishment'. Article 46Abis, however, stipulates that,

> [n]o charges shall be commenced or continued before the Court against any serving AU Head of State or Government, or anybody acting or entitled to act in such capacity, or other senior state officials based on their functions, during their tenure of office.

The clause was originally not part of the Malabo Protocol. In the 2012 Draft there had been no immunity provision. Article 46Abis is a response to the ICC's investigations into the Kenya and Darfur cases. It is part of a campaign to undermine efforts to bring to justice heads of state, presidents and deputy presidents. Its late insertion creates legal uncertainty within the Protocol, not just in conjunction with Article 46(B) but also with regard to one of the crimes over which the Court has jurisdiction. Corruption, in Article 28I, criminalises 'illicit enrichment' by public officials. This provision is drawn from the AU Convention on Corruption[9] which defines public officials as follows:

> 'Public official' means any official or employee of the State or its agencies including those who have been selected, appointed or elected to perform activities or functions in the name of the State or in the service of the State at any level of its hierarchy.

Another indication that the ACJHR and the Malabo Protocol can be regarded as an initiative that opposes the ICC, is the fact that there is no mention of the ICC; the Malabo Protocol ignores the ICC completely.[10] All it does is mention in paragraph 15 that the ACJHR,

> [w]ill complement national, regional and continental bodies and institutions in preventing serious and massive violations of human and peoples' rights in keeping with Article 58 of the Charter and ensuring accountability for them whenever they occur.[11]

---

[9] AU Convention on Preventing and Combating Corruption (adopted 1 July 2003, entered into force 5 August 2006).

[10] Du Plessis, above (n 8) 12.

[11] See Article 46H of the Protocol for a more detailed regulation. Again, there is no mention of the ICC.

The fact that there is no mention of the ICC in the Malabo Protocol may be seen as an indication that the ACJHR is not envisaged as working alongside the ICC.[12] This is exacerbated by the fact that the crime definitions in the Malabo Protocol, which draw on ICC provisions, have been rewritten. The crimes against humanity definition is broadened in Article 28C of the Malabo Protocol by lowering the threshold of application: an attack or 'an enterprise' against a civilian population that is widespread or systematic qualifies as a crime against humanity. The war crimes provision in Article 28D of the Malabo Protocol has 16 more acts than the ICC provision in Article 8 of the Rome Statute. This tweaking of internationally accepted definitions would make cooperation with the ICC very difficult. It would also make cooperation with other states difficult. The Malabo Protocol may result in obligation 'overload' and an inextricable patchwork of differing obligations for states.[13] The argument could be made that if there was a genuine desire to strengthen regional accountability efforts, initiatives other than creating a new court should be considered and that, in fact, the Malabo Protocol is a distraction therefrom. Such initiatives could include reinforcing domestic systems and particularly also cooperation and mutual legal assistance schemes underlying domestic prosecutions. The Malabo Protocol poses additional hurdles to creating the legal environment needed to prosecute crimes at the domestic level. This all feeds into the idea that the Malabo Protocol is not a genuine initiative to establish regional justice but is rather grandstanding against the ICC.

B. Role Model

The Malabo Protocol can also be viewed as a role model, offering a new template. In this context, we should mention first the inclusion of transnational crimes.[14] The Malabo Protocol grants the Court jurisdiction over 14 crimes, 4 international crimes[15] and 10 transnational crimes.[16] The definitions of transnational crimes are drawn from a number of international and regional conventions.[17] Like the

---

[12] For a proposal of how such cooperation could work, see HG van der Wilt, 'Complementary Jurisdiction' in G Werle and M Vormbaum (eds), *The African Criminal Court. A Commentary on the Malabo Protocol* (The Hague, Asser Press, Springer Verlag, 2017).

[13] See van den Herik and van Sliedregt, above (n 7) 516–18.

[14] Transnational crimes are crimes that have a cross-border effect and that traditionally are countered domestically through transnational interstate cooperation.

[15] Aggression (Article 28A(1)(14)); genocide (Article 28B); crimes against humanity (Article 28C); war crimes (Article 28D).

[16] Crime of unconstitutional change of government (Article 28E); piracy (Article 28F); terrorism (Article 28G); mercenarism (Article 28H); corruption (Article 28I); money laundering (Article 28Ibis); trafficking in persons (Article 28J); trafficking in drugs (Article 28K); trafficking in hazardous waste (Article28L); illicit exploitation of natural resources (Article 28M).

[17] Convention for the Elimination of Mercenarism in Africa (adopted 3 July 1977, entered into force April 2002); OAU/AU Convention on the Prevention and Combating of Terrorism (adopted 1 July 1899, entered into force December 2002); AU Convention on Preventing and Combating Corruption

international crimes definitions, they are slightly tweaked (and thus come with the same problem of state cooperation) adding clauses on modes of liability or applying them to specific situations.

Some of these conventions provide that the crimes can be committed by legal entities. For instance, Article1(16) of the Bamako Convention, which prohibits the import of hazardous waste, stipulates that 'person' is both natural and legal person. Another example is Article 1(3) of the Convention on Elimination of Mercenarism in Africa, which provides that: 'any person, natural or juridical who commits the crime of mercenarism … shall be punished as such'. The Malabo Protocol adopts the corporate liability approach of the treaties it draws on in the realm of transnational crimes and provides for corporate criminal responsibility itself in Article 46C (discussed further below). This broad approach to criminal liability can be followed by other courts dealing with international crimes and fills a gap that some felt has been left by the ICC Statute.[18]

The fact that the Malabo Protocol criminalises both international crimes and transnational crimes should be welcomed. It comports with the increased recognition that the two categories of crime should not be kept separate since they are often committed in *tandem*, especially in Africa. The intersection between international crimes and illicit exploitation of natural resources is well documented. It is no coincidence that three out of four convictions (Lubanga, Katanga, Bemba) at the ICC concern individuals commanding rebel groups in the mineral rich area of Ituri. As the UN special rapporteur on HR in the Democratic Republic of Congo (DRC) reported in 2003, 'despite the ethnic appearance of the conflict, its root causes are of an economic nature'.[19]

One offence conspicuously lacking from the list of offences subject to international criminal jurisdiction in Article 28(A) is forced labour/slavery. In Nuremberg, it featured as one of the offences the industrialists were charged with and it can be found in the war crimes and crimes against humanity sections of the Malabo Protocol. However, for a long time this offence has been recognised as a stand-alone crime and I wonder why the drafters decided to leave it out. Lots of the illegal trade comes with forced labour, for instance in the diamond mines in Congo.[20] In the Malabo Protocol, forced labour features on the list of war crimes

(adopted 1 July 2003, entered into force 5 August 2006); Bamako Convention on the Ban of the Import into Africa and the control of Transboundary Movement and Management of Hazardous Wastes within Africa (adopted 30 January 1991, entered into force 22 April 1998).

[18] See J Kyriakakis, 'Corporate Criminal Liability and the ICC Statute: The Comparative Law Challenge' (2009) 56 *Netherlands International Law Review* 333; D Stoitchkova, *Towards Corporate Liability in International Criminal Law* (Antwerp, Intersentia, 2010).

[19] Interim report of the Special Rapporteur on the situation of human rights in DR Congo (A/58/534).

[20] See for instance, Global Witness report: available at: www.globalwitness.org/sites/default/files/library/Congo%27s%20minerals%20trade%20in%20the%20balance%20low%20res.pdf. The crime can be added under the residual clause of Article 28(A)(2): The Assembly may extend upon the consensus of States Parties the jurisdiction of the Court to incorporate additional crimes to reflect developments in international law.

and it could be brought under the 'rest clause' in Article 28A(2) where it says that the Assembly of the African Union could decide to add additional crimes to the jurisdiction of the ACJHR.

III. The Case for African Justice

Two arguments in favour of regional or local justice are that (i) it better expresses regional or local values and, as a result, (ii) it brings justice closer to home. The assumptions underlying these arguments have to do with the legitimacy of the international justice system. When there is justice closer to the victim communities, there is ownership, enabling a process of reconciliation. Can the ACJHR deliver on that and as such have added value alongside the ICC? Answering this question is not straightforward but some preliminary observations can be made that at least challenge these assumptions.

The Malabo Protocol is premised on Western conceptions of criminal justice, not on African values. It is largely modelled on other international(ised) criminal courts, including the ICC and provides for retributive criminal justice, individual criminal responsibility, prison sentences, and formal criminal procedures. This is likely to encounter critique from those who advocate justice that expresses African values in that it fits better with the social fabric and community-based values of African society.

The Western take on criminal justice seems to fit with broader developments within the AU. Olufemi Amao argues that there is a gradual movement from intergovernmentalism to supranationalism in Africa as a result of the AU's gradual move to set up an EU-style justice system on the African continent.[21] He detects a development of supranationalism affecting crucial issues such as human rights, democratic reforms, territorial matters, tribal and religious disputes, and economic relations. So, while voices in transitional justice and Third World Approaches to International (Criminal) Law argue in favour of local, non-Western values, in reality the lawmakers of the AU embrace Western concepts that lie at the basis of the global justice system.

The ACJHR, in its aim to deliver justice closer to home, is not unique in doing so. We can mention here the Special Court for Sierra Leone, the Senegalese court that tried Habré, the Cote d'Ivoire court that dealt with Simone Gbagbo, the Central African Republic (CAR) court that is currently being established[22] and of course grassroots justice in Rwanda: the Gacaca trials. Gacaca especially, which is based on regional practices, does better than the ACJHR in expressing local values.

---

[21] O Amao, *African Union Law. The Emergence of a Sui generis Legal Order* (London, Routledge, 2017).

[22] See *Reuters*, 'War crimes court due to start probes in Central African Republic: UN', available at: www.reuters.com/article/us-centralafrica-violence-un/war-crimes-court-due-to-start-probes-in-central-african-republic-u-n-idUSKCN1IT1T0.

In evaluating the case for African justice and exploring whether it has added value alongside the ICC, we need to know whether, and if so, why regional justice is more likely to achieve reconciliation. What does 'regional/local justice' really mean? Is justice regional/local when it reflects regional/local values? Or is it sufficient that justice or any process of reconciliation, is geographically/physically close? And if there is a turn to 'regionalism' in international criminal law, is this supported by the victim communities and societies affected? These are all questions doctrinal research cannot answer. We need to know more about how justice works in practice and what the facts on the ground are. This requires non-doctrinal research, for example, criminological, anthropological and socio-legal research. Some of the studies already undertaken actually demystify local justice in Africa and are critical of the reconciliatory effect of, for instance, the Gacaca process.[23]

The ACJHR, not delivering on the regional/local values and not standing out as a unique regional/local initiative, strengthens the case for viewing the ACJHR as a rebel court. It questions the ACJHR's added value alongside other regional justice mechanisms and the ICC. There is however one obvious point where the Malabo Protocol *does* have added value and where it potentially is a model for the future: corporate criminal responsibility. This will be the focus of the second part of the chapter.

IV. Corporate Misconduct in Africa

Corporations in search of extractive resources and inexpensive labour operate in countries such as the DRC, Angola, Guinea, Cote d'Ivoire, Nigeria, the CAR, Liberia and Zimbabwe. They are involved in the oil industry, mining business, diamond and timber trade and dodgy land deals in the palm oil industry. Companies come from all over the world: the UK, the Netherlands, the United States, Lebanon and China. Corporate misconduct qualifies as corruption, money laundering, illicit exploitation of natural resources.

Corporate liability and corporate complicity are multifaceted phenomena, which have been studied by criminologists going back to 1940, starting with Sutherland who coined the term 'white-collar crime'.[24] Very rarely are corporations involved in international crimes as direct perpetrators, through their employees and managers. The only example that comes to mind in the realm of international

---

[23] See Penal Reform International, *Kibuye Case Study* and the *Final Monitoring and Research Report on the Gacaca Process*, 2004–05, available at: www.penalreform.org/resource/. See also M Rettig, 'Gacaca: Truth, Justice, and Reconciliation in Postconflict Rwanda?' (2008) 51 *African Studies Review* 25.

[24] He referred to it in a speech for the American Sociological Association in 1939 and after the Second World War published it as EH Sutherland, *White Collar Crime* (New York, Holt, Rinehart & Winston, 1949). For an overview, see JF Galliher and TJ Guess, 'Two Generations of Sutherland's White-Collar War Crime Data and Beyond' 51 (2009) *Crime, Law and Social Change* 163.

crimes, is the private military company Blackwater whose staff (allegedly) tortured prisoners in Iraq.[25] Most often, corporations are accomplices through their assistance in the commission of international crimes.[26] Direct liability lies more in the ambit of economic crimes: corruption, money laundering, illicit exploitation of natural resources.

Corporations can facilitate the commission of international crimes by providing logistical support and by passing on certain information. For instance, Talisman Energy Inc was charged with aiding and abetting human rights abuses and international crimes in Sudan for providing logistical support (airfields, roads) to local military implicated in committing crimes against civilians.[27] A more indirect form of involvement is to benefit from the commission of international crimes.[28] Examples are the violent repression of protests against the companies' activity by the police or security forces of a certain regime. An even more 'detached' form of involvement is that of silent approval. By continuing to do business with dictatorial regimes, business entities contribute to the political legitimisation and economic viability of such regimes while they do not directly benefit from or contribute to international crimes. The Truth and Reconciliation Commission in South Africa, for instance, concluded that the Apartheid regime could not have survived without the business support of certain companies, such as IBM and Ford.

Greed and profit seeking are often presented as the prime motives for both corporate crime and civil wars in resource rich countries.[29] Criminological research, however, offers a more varied picture. While commercial and financial interests seem to be the main motive, financial interests can take different forms. In most cases, rather than profit maximisation, loss minimisation seems to be the dominant motive.[30] In particular in the capital intensive extraction of natural resources, such as oil and gold, the risk of loss of investments that were already made appears to be the most important reason for corporations to stay in a country or area and as a result become involved in international crimes.[31]

---

[25] Victims of alleged abuse by Blackwater filed common law tort claims for wrongful death and fraud in US courts. *Nordan v Blackwater Security Consulting, LLC* 382 F Supp 2d 801 (EDNC, 2005). There has not been a prosecution of Blackwater as such.

[26] See W Huisman, *Business as Usual? The Involvement of Corporations with International Crimes* (The Hague, Boom Legal Publishers, 2010). E van Sliedregt and W Huisman, 'Rogue Traders. Dutch Businessmen, International Crimes and Corporate Complicity' (2010) 8 *Journal of International Criminal Justice* 816.

[27] The company was taken to court under the Aliens Tort Claims Act (ATCA). The Court ruled in favour of the company, *Presbyterian Church of Sudan v Talisman Energy Inc* (582 5F 3 244, 259).

[28] Referred to by Clapham and Jerbi as beneficial or indirect complicity: A Clapham and S Jerbi, 'Categories of Corporate Complicity in Human Rights Abuses' (2001) 24 *Hastings International and Comparative Law Review* 339.

[29] M Punch, *Dirty Business: Exploring Corporate Misconduct, Analysis and Cases* (London, Sage Publications, 1990).

[30] B Prosansky, 'Mining Gold in a Conflict Zone: The Context, Ramifications and Lessons of AngloGold Ashanti's Activities in the Democratic Republic of the Congo' (2007) 5 *Northwestern Journal of International Human Rights* 236.

[31] Huisman, above (n 26).

For example, Anglo-Ashanti Gold had bought concessions for the extraction of gold in an area of 8,000 square kilometres from the Congolese state mining corporation in 1998. Shortly thereafter, a civil war broke out. When the area was relatively quiet in 2004, the corporation could not wait to start the exploitation of the gold. This turned out to be too soon, because the FNI rebel movement appeared to be in charge of the area and the corporation was forced to pay them and to provide logistical support to the movement's operations.

V. Corporate Criminal Liability in International Criminal Law

The focus of international criminal law has for a long time been on the individual. While there were attempts in Nuremberg to hold organisations criminally responsible for international crimes, the International Military Tribunal was not ready to punish an organisation or a corporation as such.[32] The collective criminality theory at Nuremberg, aimed at declaring political and military organisations 'criminal' with the purpose of using this finding in subsequent trials to enable prosecutions of large numbers of its members without a showing of individual guilt, failed.[33] Courts were uncomfortable with the idea of strict liability and mass punishment. At the same time, the trials of the industrialists – Krupp, IG Farben, Zyklon B – were about punishing individuals for their wilful and knowing involvement in corporations carrying out criminal activities. While the *IG Farben* trial has been referred to as the case where the Tribunal recognised that the company itself had committed violations of international law, there was at the end of the day a strong commitment to individual responsibility. As the Court stated:

> Corporations act through individuals and, under the conception of personal individual guilt to which previous reference has been made, the prosecution, to discharge the burden imposed upon it in this case, must establish by competent proof beyond a reasonable doubt that an individual defendant was either a participant in the illegal act or that, being aware thereof, he authorized or approved it.[34]

The tide is turning towards holding corporations accountable for criminal offences. For some time now, domestic jurisdictions have accepted that legal entities can

---

[32] For an interesting overview see A van Baar, 'Corporate Involvement in the Holocaust and other Nazi Crimes' in J van Erp et al (eds), *The Routledge Handbook of White-Collar and Corporate Crime in Europe* (London, Routledge 2015).

[33] NHB Jorgensen, *The Responsibility of States for International Crimes* (Oxford, Oxford University Press, 2001); E van Sliedregt, *Individual Criminal Responsibility in International Law* (Oxford, Oxford University Press, 2012).

[34] Trial of Carl Krauch and Twenty-Two Others (IG Farben Trial), United States Military Tribunal, Nuremberg, 14 August 1947–29 July 1948, *Law Reports of Trials of War Criminals* (UNWCC), Volume X (His Majesty's Stationery Office, 1949) 52.

commit offences and be held liable, either under civil law or criminal law.[35] At the international level, we have a normative system in place that provides for monitoring and supervision of corporations to ensure they respect human rights. Corporations can be taken to court for violating international law, in particular human rights. The *Talisman Energy*[36] and *Kiobel*[37] cases are notable examples.[38] In 2014, the Special Tribunal for Lebanon (STL) held that legal persons can be the subject of contempt proceedings. Three TV stations were held in contempt because of revealing names of witnesses that should have been kept concealed.[39] Corporate liability was read into the Statute; the term 'person' was thought to extend to natural and legal persons. In justifying this reading the Tribunal referred to Lebanese law and '[a] general trend in most countries towards bringing corporate entities to book for their criminal acts or the criminal acts of their officers'.[40] In this context, we should also mention the work of the International Law Commission on a Convention on crimes against humanity[41] where the Drafting Committee has been requested to consider including a provision on the criminal responsibility of legal persons.[42]

The Malabo Protocol, by *explicitly* providing for jurisdiction over legal persons alongside natural persons, changes international criminal law in a revolutionary way. It is worth reiterating the relevant provision, Article 46C(1): 'For the purpose of this Statute, the Court shall have jurisdiction over legal persons, with the exception of States'. In one simple sentence, by extending the power to adjudicate over legal entities, the Protocol recognises corporate criminal liability. Bearing in mind the fact that those drafting the ICC Statute discussed including corporate criminal responsibility in the Statute but abandoned the idea because of a lack of agreement on criminal responsibility of legal entities,[43] the Malabo Protocol takes international criminal law to another level.

---

[35] C Wells, *Corporations and Criminal Responsibility*, 2nd edn (Oxford, Oxford University Press, 2001); Stoitchkova, above (n 18); J Kyriakakis, 'Corporations before International Criminal Courts: Implications for the International Criminal Justice Project' (2017) 30 *Leiden Journal of International Law* 221.

[36] *Presbyterian Church of Sudan v Talisman Energy Inc* (582 5F 3 244, 259), 2 October 2009. See also US Supreme Court, *Presbyterian Church of Sudan et al v Talisman Energy Inc* (No 09-1262); Amicus Curiae of international law scholars, 30 April 2010; available at: www.scotusblog.com/wp-content/uploads/2010/07/09-1262_Amicus-brief-of-International-Law-Scholars-William-Aceves-et-al.pdf.

[37] *Kiobel v Royal Dutch Petroleum* 133 S Ct 1659 (2013).

[38] The *Kiobel* case, however, limits extraterritorial jurisdiction of American courts under the Alien Tort Statute.

[39] *In the Case against New TVS AL Karma Mohamed Thasin Al Khayat*, STL-14-05, 31 January 2014.

[40] ibid, para. 26 citing a report by Clifford Chance 'Corporate Liability in Europe', January 2012, available at: www.cliffordchance.com/content/dam/cliffordchance/PDF/European Technical_ Bulletin. pdf, 1.

[41] A/CN.4/680 and Corr.1.

[42] Official Records of the General Assembly, Seventy-first Session, Supplement No 10 (A/71/10), paras 79–81.

[43] See below (n 52).

VI. How to Construe Corporate Criminal Liability

In general, there are three approaches to construing liability of a non-natural person: (i) through individual liability (ii) aggregation, or (iii) separate self-identity.[44] The first approach comes in two forms: vicarious liability and direct liability. Vicarious liability is based on the legal fiction that whatever a person does through an agent, he or she is deemed to have done himself or herself. In attributing liability to an entity, you perform a two-pronged test and determine: (i) whether the elements of the offence were met in the conduct of the agent; and (ii) whether the conduct can be ascribed to the entity on the basis of the relationship of agency (for example, employment). Direct liability provides for liability of the entity through identifying actions and thought patterns of particular individuals within the corporation. As long as corporate agents act within the scope of their authority and on behalf of the corporate body, their conduct is regarded as the conduct of the legal body itself. Again, a two-pronged test applies, where individual conduct needs to fulfil the elements of the crime and is ascribed to the corporation when the agent can be considered a corporate organ. A combination of these two forms was part of the French proposal for the ICC Statute. Liability would attach to juridical persons alongside natural persons who were *in a position of control within the juridical person, and who acted on behalf of and consent of the juridical person and in the course of its activities.*[45] The proposal never made it.

In the second approach, aggregation, knowledge and intent of different agents is assembled and attributed to the corporation. The behaviour of one agent can be joined to the knowledge of the other. The fiction underlying attribution is that the corporation controls the agents' conduct. Again, there is a two-pronged test where elements of liability are fulfilled through the conduct of agents, which is then ascribed to the entity.

The third approach is a corporate approach, where liability is ascribed to the corporation for its *own* conduct and knowledge. Conceptually, this is the most challenging approach. Thinking about criminal responsibility in terms of abstract legal entities without a body to kick and a soul to damn does not sit well with the agency concept that underlies our thinking about culpability. The real problem with corporate liability and corporate complicity is mens rea. Some domestic jurisdictions dispense with it all together. In Australia for instance the statutory provisions providing for organisational liability in relation to federal offences rely

---

[44] E Lederman, 'Models for Imposing Corporate Criminal Liability: From Adaptation and Imitation Toward Aggregation and the Search for Self-Identity' (2000–01) 4 *Buffalo Criminal Law Review* 641.

[45] Working Paper on Article 23, paras 5–6, A/ Conf.183/ C.1/ WGGP/ L.5/ Rev.2, 3 July 1998. See A Clapham, 'The Question of Jurisdiction under International Criminal Law over Legal Persons: Lessons from the Rome Conference on an International Criminal Court' in M Kamminga and S Zia-Zarifi (eds), *Liability of Multinational Corporations Under International Law* (The Hague, Kluwer Law International, 2000).

on the concept of 'corporate ethos' and 'corporate culture'.[46] If intention, knowledge or recklessness is the fault element of the underlying offence, it is attributed to the entity that expressly authorised or permitted the commission of the offence. Such authorisation or permission is then established by proving that a corporate culture existed within the organisation that directed, encouraged, tolerated or led to non-compliance of the law.[47] The enquiry into the organisational mens rea, however, will often still rely on aggregation and assembling attitudes from a number of agents, often at management level. Reasonableness plays a role in circumscribing liability. For instance, was the risk of crimes reasonably foreseeable? Corporate fault can be established when the company operates flawed formal procedures or informal practices that have been approved, encouraged or condoned at management level.

VII. Corporate Criminal Liability in the Malabo Protocol

A. Article 46C MP

The provision on corporate liability in the Malabo Protocol is a combination of at least two of the three approaches mentioned above: the aggregate and self-identity approaches. Here are the relevant paragraphs of Article 46C:

> 2. Corporate intention to commit an offence may be established by proof that it was the policy of the corporation to do the act which constituted the offence.
>
> 3. A policy may be attributed to a corporation where it provides the most reasonable explanation of the conduct of that corporation.
>
> 4. Corporate knowledge of the commission of an offence may be established by proof that the actual or constructive knowledge of the relevant information was possessed within the corporation.
>
> 5. Knowledge may be possessed within a corporation even though the relevant information is divided between corporate personnel.
>
> 6. The criminal responsibility of legal persons shall not exclude the criminal responsibility of natural persons who are perpetrators or accomplices in the same crimes.

Section 2, referring to corporate intention by proof of a policy, displays the holistic approach: the corporation as a separate identity. Section 3 expands on that by stipulating how this may be established. The element of reasonableness, which requires answering the question what is generally perceived as reasonable, may be viewed

---

[46] 'Corporate culture' is defined as 'an attitude, policy, rule, course of conduct or practice existing within the body corporate generally or in the part of the body corporate in which the relevant activities take place'. Criminal Code Act, 1995 § 12.3(6)

[47] Lederman, above (n 44) 699–700.

as circumscribing liability.[48] Section 4 equates corporate knowledge to knowledge of information of wrongdoing within the corporation, which suffices as proof of intent. Sections 4 and 5 further make clear that knowledge can be construed by deducing it from reports and/or monitoring procedures and by combining it from a collectivity of agents: the aggregate approach. Section 6 stipulates that corporate liability and liability of natural persons are independent of one another: one does not depend on the other. This differs from the French proposal for the draft ICC Statute.

The corporate criminal liability provision is a rather vague and open provision and it remains to be seen how the different approaches to corporate liability play out and comport to one another. To a certain extent, the provision looks like those provisions in conventions that criminalise transnational crimes and require further implementation at the domestic level. Rather than fully legislating/outlining a legal concept, it quite roughly outlines a legal concept and provides for different options that states can further develop and choose from when implementing domestically.

B. Extended Liability

Article 28N of the Malabo Protocol provides for modes of liability and criminal attempt. It applies to legal persons as well natural persons ('any person'). So this is the provision, combined with Article 46C, that one would rely on for *corporate complicity*.

An offence is committed by any person who, in relation to any of the crimes or offences provided for in this Statute:

  i. Incites, instigates, organizes, directs, facilitates, finances, counsels or participates as a principal, co-principal, agent or accomplice in any of the offences set forth in the present Statute;

  ii. Aids or abets the commission of any of the offences set forth in the present Statute;

  iii. Is an accessory before or after the fact or in any other manner participates in a collaboration or conspiracy to commit any of the offences set forth in the present Statute;

  iv. Attempts to commit any of the offences set forth in the present Statute.

The Malabo Protocol does not contain a general provision on mens rea like the ICC Statute does in Article 30. The provision on corporate criminal liability in Article 46C, however, provides for knowledge as the appropriate mental standard with regard to the underlying offence ('base crime'). At the level of individual criminal responsibility, there has been debate about the appropriate mens rea standard for aiding and abetting international crimes. The ICC Statute, in Article 25(3)(c) requires a purposive attitude towards the commission of crimes

---

[48] Stoitchkova, above (n 18) 119 (so-called 'Laufer test').

by the perpetrator; knowledge of the base crime is insufficient. On the other hand, the knowledge test has been consistently applied in Second World War cases and the *ad hoc* tribunals' case law.[49]

The issue of which test – purpose/intent or knowledge – was central to the case against the Talisman Energy company under the Alien Tort Claims Act in the United States. The judges, in finding in favour of the company, had relied on the ICC standard and held that, '[p]laintiffs have not established Talisman's purposeful complicity in human rights abuses'.[50] As *amici curiae*, in a brief addressed to the US Supreme Court, a group of international scholars argued convincingly that under customary international law, aiding and abetting liability requires that an accused *knowingly* provides substantial assistance to the perpetrator or tortfeasor. The US Supreme Court never ruled on the issue: it would not review the case.

The Malabo Protocol is clear: corporate knowledge is the mens rea for corporate liability. This is appropriate. It is closer to the corporate reality where companies rarely have criminal *intentions* that make them complicit in international crimes.

C. The Question of Penalties

There is no provision on penalties for legal persons in the Malabo Protocol. Since corporations cannot be subjected to classic criminal law punishment – a prison sentence – and the default penalty is thus a fine, this should have been addressed. The Malabo Protocol could have drawn on Article 10(4) of the UN Convention against Transnational Organized Crime on penalties for legal persons. This clause requires effective and proportionate sentences for legal persons, including monetary sanctions (thus for serious crimes committed by a wealthy company, this means imposing a very serious fine). The drafters of the Malabo Protocol could have also looked at some of the domestic sanctions following a finding of corporate liability. Think of the American example of requiring companies to implement a compliance monitoring system alongside a monetary sanction, or the French penalty of closing down a company – the so-called corporate death penalty. If you are *really* serious about corporate liability, this is what you spend time on when legislating on the topic. This brings me to my conclusion.

VIII. Concluding Observations

The Malabo Protocol can be viewed as either a rebel court or a role model court. As a rebel, it provides for immunity of sitting heads of state. Moreover, by redefining existing and well-established crime definitions the Protocol risks obstructing

---

[49] See M Jackson, *Complicity in International Law* (Oxford, Oxford University Press, 2016) 75–76.
[50] See above (n 36) 2.

implementation at the domestic level and state cooperation. As a role model, it extends jurisdiction to transnational crimes and corporate liability. In this way, the Protocol aligns with the reality of international criminality in Africa. The ICC Statute with its focus on the 'classic' core crimes, applicable only to individuals and requiring a high, purposive attitude for complicity, risks not capturing the true origins of conflict and mass atrocities in Africa (or elsewhere). Also, it obscures the role of the West in many of the conflicts on the African continent. Joanna Kyriakakis, pointing to the expressive goals of international criminal justice and concepts of sociological legitimacy, suggests that corporate prosecutions may have a redeeming effect upon the esteem in which some audiences hold international criminal law.[51] Moreover, corporate criminal liability may be a useful tool in *preventing* crimes. The threat of an investigation and prosecution may limit business activity that fuels conflict and leads to gross human rights violations and the commission of international crimes.

So far, the Malabo Protocol is only a role model on paper. Many questions remain with regard to its functioning and relationship with other justice models, global and local. Yet, its mere proposal is of interest to the international criminal justice project, not least for the prospect of corporate prosecutions. It should spur on efforts to understand and hopefully one day break the cycle of mass atrocities. Hence, it should spur on interdisciplinary, doctrinal and non-doctrinal research into international criminal justice.

---

[51] Kyriakakis, 'Corporations before International Criminal Courts', above (n 35) 221.

Epilogue

Epilogue

12

Breaking the Cycle of Collective Violence: International Criminal Law's Contribution

HARMEN VAN DER WILT

I. Introduction

While criminal law enforcement in a domestic context is a daunting enterprise, the problems multiply in cases of international criminal justice. Over the last 15 years we have learned to appreciate the full breadth of the complexities involved in bringing perpetrators of mass atrocities to justice. The days of euphoria, echoing the words of former Secretary General Kofi Annan who qualified the Rome Statute and the International Criminal Court (ICC) as a 'gift to humanity' have waned, eliciting the wry comment by David Luban that the honeymoon for the ICC is over.[1]

For analytical purposes, it makes sense to address the differences between criminal law enforcement in a domestic and in an international institutional context and for at least two reasons the chapters in this book make a valuable contribution to such a quest. First, they transcend the purely legal area by engaging in criminological and sociological research, thus pursuing a truly interdisciplinary approach. Secondly, the structure of the book epitomises the sequence of episodes in the cycle of collective violence and demonstrates the inter-action between the commission of international crimes and the criminal law response.

Although I by no means pretend to offer anything near a comprehensive survey, let alone an explanation of the differences between domestic and international criminal law enforcement, I would like to single out two salient features that enable me to structure my comments on some of the findings in the previous chapters. The first distinction refers to the question of scale. International crimes are, by definition, mass events, involving many perpetrators and a multitude

---

[1] D Luban, 'After the Honeymoon: Reflections on the Current State of International Criminal Justice' (2013) 11 *Journal of International Criminal Justice* 505.

of victims.[2] Moreover, they are usually committed along preconceived systematic patterns. This specific feature affects criminal law enforcement in a myriad of ways. It requires the drafting of specific definitions of these crimes that stand out for their 'contextual elements' and the introduction or adaption of modes of criminal liability. It puts heavy strains on the institutional capacity, in terms of human and financial resources. It raises questions in the realm of attribution of responsibility and guilt for the purpose of sentencing, etc.

Secondly, international criminal law enforcement predominantly takes place beyond the familiar institutional context of the nation state. Admittedly, this contention may appear rather bold in view of the famous complementarity principle that postulates primacy of jurisdiction over international crimes for the States Parties to the Rome Statute. However, despite all the claims of the successes of positive complementarity, the relationship with the ICC is essentially an antagonistic one. Many operational difficulties can be attributed to the ICC's functioning outside the state system.

Obviously, these observations are not new and may appear even commonplace to those who are only faintly acquainted with the ICC. However, whereas these aspects are often conflated, I intend to disentangle them, in order to demonstrate how they hamper international criminal law enforcement in different ways. My assumption is that mass criminality is a challenge to (international) criminal law because the morality and culture of criminal law is strongly predicated on individual agency and guilt. While one may counter that group criminality occurs in the domestic context as well, and that international judges and prosecutors may borrow from its experiences, I will argue in section II that international crimes *stricto sensu* are still a separate category that yields specific complexities. In section III, I will briefly touch upon the well-known paradox in the architecture of the Rome Statute that any confirmation of admissibility implies to a certain extent a depreciation of the criminal law system of a state which is difficult to reconcile with a subsequent request for cooperation. Of course, the contradiction is most acute when the state itself is involved in international crimes. However, the problem strikes deeper, because the ICC's claim impinges upon sovereign prerogatives that are most deeply cherished in the realm of criminal law. That observation takes me already to section IV in which I intend to address the conflux of the two aspects. I will explore the assumption that mass criminality and the state's insisting on its sovereign rights have something in common in that they challenge the dominant moral paradigm of international criminal law. In section V, I try to defend the ICC against its most virulent critics and – very tentatively – suggest some ways for improvement of the system, building on the previous chapters in this book. Whereas the focus in this chapter is indeed on the ICC, this should be understood as a shorthand for the entire phenomenon of international criminal justice.

---

[2] L May, *Crimes Against Humanity: A Normative Account* (Oxford, Oxford University Press, 2005) 83.

II. Mass Criminality and Collective Guilt as Challenges for International Criminal Law

The Rome Statute is imbued with the notion of mass criminality. The so-called contextual elements of the crimes within the jurisdiction of the ICC connote the commission of multiple crimes by large groups or organisations, involving many perpetrators. The gist of genocide is the special intent to destroy (in whole or in part) a group, displaying special features, and such a dreadful enterprise requires concerted action. The clarification of an 'attack directed against a civilian population' which is the defining element of a crime against humanity, explicitly mentions 'a course of conduct involving the *multiple commission of acts ... pursuant to or in furtherance of a State or organizational policy to commit such an attack*' (italics added).[3] Article 8 of the Rome Statute stipulates that the 'Court shall have jurisdiction in respect of war crimes *in particular when committed as part of a plan or policy or as part of a large-scale commission of such crimes*' (italics added). And aggression is the leadership crime par excellence which implies a person (or group of persons) wielding control over the resources of a state.[4] In a similar vein, the modes of criminal responsibility reflect the reality of several persons acting together in more or less coordinated ways for the purpose of committing mass atrocities. Apart from the well-known concepts of criminal participation like aiding and abetting and inducement/instigation/soliciting, the Statute includes provisions on the contribution of members of a group acting with a common criminal purpose (Article 25 (3), sub (d)) and the responsibility of subordinates for the crimes committed by their subordinates (Article 28 Statute).

These are all highly familiar topics that have been extensively discussed in scholarly debates and need not detain us here. The point that I wish to emphasise is that criminal law, being engrafted on individual agency and individual guilt, has great difficulties in dealing with collectives engaging in crime.[5] Surely this problem is not only a nagging problem for international criminal law enforcement. Domestic criminal law systems also struggle with mass criminality which is

---

[3] Article 7(2), sub a Rome Statute. See on the controversial issue what should count as an 'organisational policy', or, in other words, who can qualify as a perpetrator of a crime against humanity, the deliberations of the Pre-Trial Chamber in *the Situation in the Republic of Kenya*, Decision Pursuant to Article 15 of the Rome Statute on the Authorization of an Investigation into the Situation in the Republic of Kenya, ICC-01/09, 31 March 2010, §§ 115–28 and the Dissenting Opinion of Judge Hans-Peter Kaul, ICC-01/09, 31 March 2010.

[4] See Article 8bis Rome Statute.

[5] The topic has been profoundly and extensively addressed by G Fletcher, 'The Storrs Lectures: Liberals and Romantics at War: The Problem of Collective Guilt' (2002) 111 *Yale Law Journal* 1499. Contrasting the liberal, individualistic attitude with romantics idolising the community, including the Nation, Fletcher observes that 'a single methodology dominates the legal discourse of our time. Whether the talk is of law and economics, of constitutional law, of corrective justice or of human rights, the methodology remains the same. What counts is individuals, their rights, their preferences, their welfare' (ibid, 1503).

demonstrated by the endless discussions on the proper limits of conspiracy law in light of basic principles of criminal law.[6] However, the problem is aggravated in international criminal law, for the simple reason that this discipline is more frequently – and inherently – confronted with the phenomenon.

In line with its individualistic leanings (international) criminal law reveals a natural inclination to consider each contribution separately and attribute responsibility in accordance with the actus reus and/or mens rea. Accordingly, the actus reus may vary from an 'essential contribution', including the control over the crime, for co-perpetration,[7] a 'substantial contribution' for aiding and abetting,[8] or a 'significant contribution' for participation in a Joint Criminal Enterprise (JCE).[9] Classification is also differentiated on the basis of distinctive mens rea in respect of the crime itself and the cooperation with others. Whereas the aider and abettor need not share the intent of the principal and the member of a joint criminal enterprise does not even have to possess knowledge of a specific crime, as long as he is privy to and wishes to further the common criminal purpose and the crime is a foreseeable consequence of that general plan, the mens rea for co-perpetration is more demanding: not only must the co-perpetrators have intent and knowledge on the criminal act and its consequences, they must also be aware of their mutual cooperation in accomplishing the crime and of the essential nature of their contributions.[10]

While this individualistic perspective corresponds with the dominant liberal current in criminal law, it yields a distortion of reality and is therefore not fully satisfactory. Apart from the distinguishing parameters being rather vague – how does one draw the line between significant, substantial and essential contribution? – opinions on the proper limits of criminal responsibility of accomplices in particular have constantly wavered over the last 20 years. Examples abound. The mens rea for aiding and abetting in the Rome Statute is arguably more stringent than under general international criminal law, because it adds the requirement that the aiding occurred with the purpose of 'facilitating the commission of an international crime'.[11] The mens rea for a military commander as a prerequisite for incurring criminal responsibility for the crimes of his subordinates is different in the Rome Statute ('should have known') when compared with the Statutes of the International Criminal Tribunal for the former Yugoslavia (ICTY) and the

---

[6] See for a concise but enlightening discussion, A Ashworth, *Principles of Criminal Law*, 3rd edn (Oxford, Oxford University Press, 1999) 471–80.

[7] Situation in the Democratic Republic of the Congo, *Prosecutor v Thomas Lubanga Dyilo*, Judgment pursuant to Article 74 of the Statute, ICC-01/04-01/06-2843, 15 March 2012, § 999.

[8] *Prosecutor v Blaskić* (Judgment of the Appeals Chamber) IT-95-14-A (29 July 2004) § 48.

[9] *Prosecutor v Milutinović and others*, Decision on Dragoljub Ojdanić's Motion Challenging Jurisdiction – Joint Criminal Enterprise (Appeals Chamber) IT-99-37-AR72 (21 May 2003) §§ 23–26.

[10] *Prosecutor v Lubanga*, above (n 7) §§ 1012/1013.

[11] Article 25 (3), sub c. After a heated discussion that started with the *Perisić* case, the Appeals Chamber concluded that such a specific intent to further the crime was not a requirement under international criminal law. *Prosecutor v Mrkšić and Šlijivančanin* (Judgment of the Appeals Chamber) IT-95-13/1-A (5 May 2009) § 159.

International Criminal Tribunal for Rwanda (ICTR) ('knew or had reason to know'). The difference reflects earlier collisions between Trial Chambers of the ICTY on the topic.[12] And perhaps most spectacular: the ICC rejected JCE doctrine entirely and replaced it with the 'control over the crime' theory.

One may perhaps contend that such are the childhood diseases of a burgeoning discipline of law and that the dust will settle after a while, but in my view these meanderings reveal the deeper problem of a lack of unanimity on how international criminal law should come to terms with the concept of collective criminal responsibility. One of the basic tenets of liberal criminal lawyers, I argue, is that guilt in the sense of being at fault/being blameworthy, is essentially personal. One cannot be guilty, so the argument runs, for the acts of another person, in the sense that the guilt transfers completely from one person to another. According to Feinberg, 'there *can be no such thing as vicarious guilt*'.[13] It is questionable whether international criminal law fully adheres to that laudable principle. After all, according to Article 28 of the Rome Statute, the military commander is responsible *for* crimes committed by his subordinates and the member of a group acting with a criminal purpose is criminally liable *for* crimes committed by other members of the group. In other words, the criminal acts and the 'guilt' of some people are – partially – imputed to others as well. Two attempts have been made to circumvent the quandary of collective guilt. First, it has been argued that guilt and liability can and should be separated. One person may bear the consequences and make up for the fault of another person, without the former being blamed for the latter's behaviour. In parent–children and employer–employee relations this is a common practice.[14] However, while in tort law this is an adequate solution, it is inconceivable in criminal law, as criminal responsibility is predicated on guilt. A second proposition is that blame (expressed in sentencing) within a criminal enterprise can be apportioned in accordance with each separate member's culpable contribution. Whereas this approach is apparently not favoured by the ICC, it is alluring to the liberal mind and it has informed the plea for considering the nature of command responsibility as a dereliction of duty (failure to exercise the necessary control), rather than a form of complicity in the very crimes committed by the commander's subordinates.[15] However, while this position has much to commend

---

[12] The Trial Chambers in the *Celibici* and the *Blaskič* cases did not agree on the proper *mens rea* standard for military commanders, the latter suggesting that a commander might incur criminal responsibility for negligence. The issue was settled by the Appeals Chamber that confirmed the stricter 'had reason to know'-standard and rejected negligence as an appropriate basis for command responsibility. Compare *Prosecutor v Delalić et al* (*Celibici* case) (Judgment of the Appeals Chamber) IT-96-21-A (20 February 2001) § 241 and *Prosecutor v Bagilishema* (Judgment of the Appeals Chamber) ICTR-95-1A-A (3 July 2002) § 35.

[13] J Feinberg, *Doing and Deserving; Essays in the Theory of Responsibility* (Princeton, NJ, Princeton University Press, 1970) 231 (italics in original).

[14] Compare Feinberg, ibid: 'even when it is reasonable to separate liability from fault, it is only the liability that can be passed from one party to another'.

[15] See on this discussion, M Damaška, 'The Shadow Side of Command Responsibility' (2001) 49 *American Journal of Comparative Law* 455. For a sympathetic assessment see H van der Wilt,

it, it does not fully resolve the problem of collective guilt, as a very simple example can demonstrate. John and Mary plan to rob a bank and it is agreed that Mary will compel the counter clerk to open the safe at gunpoint, while John will remain outside on watch. The assurance that John will 'only' be held responsible for his facilitating role immediately begs the question: facilitation of *what*? Complicity does not exist in a void. It is a relational concept that connotes the idea that the accessory's responsibility is rooted in and dependent on the culpable conduct of the main offender. This subordinate relationship is properly expressed in the concept of 'derivative responsibility'. From this perspective it is futile to divorce entirely the acts and intentions of participants in a criminal enterprise from each other, because they are mutually influential. The 'guilt' of each participant in the criminal enterprise is to a certain extent tainted by the actions of the others and it is the core business of international criminal courts and tribunals that are confronted with mass criminality on a daily basis to assess the degree of responsibility of an accused against the backdrop of the notion that guilt is an interactive and volatile concept. Common purpose and military hierarchy are auxiliary tools that serve to explain and justify the partial transfer of guilt and responsibility.

Now the big problem in cases of mass criminality is that it is highly problematic to determine how guilt is distributed. So far, we have assumed that guilt in cases of mass atrocities is augmented, both in a quantitative and a qualitative sense. By definition, of course, the circle of perpetrators is expanded, but they also each incur a greater responsibility than would be commensurate with their (single) contribution. The rationale for this aggravation of blame is that concerted action represents a greater societal danger, because it reinforces the resolve of all to persevere, augments (therefore) the chance that the crime(s) will materialise and produces more damaging effects. However, the argument can perhaps be made that collective action *diminishes*, rather than increases, the guilt of individual participants. Fletcher points at the possibility of mitigation of individual guilt in cases of collective action by contending that the nation creates a climate in which the commission of atrocities is the norm and deprives the offender of part of his freedom to choose the morally right course. The basis for this mitigation, Fletcher continues, is not guilt in an *aggregative*, but in an *associative* sense. The nation is a separate and abstract entity whose actions do not directly cause the conduct of the individual, like in a conspiracy. The guilt of the nation, though predicated on the guilt of individual members, is detached from them, because if the nation's guilt was simply an aggregation of the guilt of individuals, it could not dilute their guilt for wrongdoing.[16]

It is an interesting suggestion that will be discussed in more detail in section IV. For the moment it suffices to observe that the possibility of mitigation of guilt compounds the problem for international criminal law enforcement, as

'Why International Criminal Lawyers Should Read Mirjan Damaška' in C Stahn and L van den Herik (eds), *Future Perspectives on International Criminal Justice* (The Hague, TMC Asser Press, 2010).

[16] Fletcher, above (n 5) 1540.

courts may be at a loss when to aggravate or to mitigate punishment in cases of collective wrongdoing. Moreover, it is quite probable that individual judges may disagree on the issue.

Ultimately, the assessment of the degree of guilt is expressed in the sentencing decision. The issuing of sentencing guidelines is a common practice in domestic criminal law systems, but the provisions on penalties in the ICC Statute are rather general and hardly contain any references to the collective nature of international crimes.[17] Of course, there is abundant case law from the ICC, the *ad hoc* tribunals, mixed tribunals and domestic criminal courts. Even a cursory review of this case law would exceed the scope of this chapter. Scholars have initially focused on the sentencing practices of the *ad hoc* tribunals and the ICC.[18] Gradually, the emphasis has shifted to a wider perspective, in which the sentencing policies of international and domestic courts are compared, exposing different approaches towards the distribution of guilt/responsibility within a collective.[19] There is no general consensus on the question whether the categorisation in distinct modes of criminal liability is essential for a rough attribution of guilt.[20] Would it not be preferable to leave the assessment of the responsibility of the accused, relative to his partners in crime, and depending on his position in the criminal enterprise, entirely in the hands of the sentencing judge? While the present author subscribes to the conventional position in criminal doctrine that a differentiated theory of criminal responsibility is the right normative model for international criminal law as well, the sentencing practice of international tribunals sometimes casts doubt on whether such an a priori categorisation makes much difference. The Trial Chamber in the Taylor Sentencing Judgment after having convicted Charles Taylor as an aider and abettor to a prison sentence of 50 years, declared that his sentence would have been much longer if he had been found a principal perpetrator.[21] The finding may seem somewhat erratic in view of man's mortality, but at least it demonstrates that the Chamber attaches importance to the distinction. The chapter in this volume by Holá and Chibashimba demonstrates that Rwandan courts tend

---

[17] Rule 145 of the Rules of Procedure and Evidence ICC mentions 'the degree of participation of the convicted person' as one of the factors that should be taken into consideration in the determination of the sentence. The commission of the crime causing 'multiple victims' counts as an aggravating factor.

[18] See, for instance, S Beresford, 'Unshackling the Paper Tiger – The Sentencing Practices of the ad hoc International Criminal Tribunals for the Former Yugoslavia and Rwanda' (2001) 1 *International Criminal Law Review* 33; AN Keller, ' Punishment for Violations of International Criminal Law: An Analysis of Sentencing at the ICTY and ICTR' (2001) 12 *Indiana International and Comparative Law Review* 53; R Henham, 'The Philosophical Foundations of International Sentencing' (2003) 1 *Journal of International Criminal Justice* 64.

[19] See for a thorough 'pioneering' study: M Drumbl *Atrocity, Punishment, and International Law* (Cambridge, Cambridge University Press, 2007) 68–123. An interesting study, entirely dedicated to the topic, is B Holá, 'International Sentencing – "Game of Russian Roulette" or Consistent Practice?' (PhD Dissertation, VU-Amsterdam, BOXPress, Oisterwijk, 2012).

[20] For a sceptical view, see JG Stewart, 'The End of "Modes of Liability" for International Crimes' (2012) 25 *Leiden Journal of International Law* 165.

[21] *Prosecution v Charles Taylor* (Sentencing Judgment, Trial Chamber II) SCSL-03-01-T (20 May 2012) §§ 94, 100.

to blur all boundaries between bystanders and perpetrators, ignoring entirely the distinction between principals and accomplices.[22] It reveals the complexity of the assessment of collective responsibility and the wide array of different opinions on the topic.

III. The International Criminal Court and States: An Antagonistic Relationship

The second topic that I intend to briefly discuss is the fact that the ICC has to operate within the configuration of an international society dominated by states. This puts the legitimacy of the Court's decisions under constant pressure. Criminal punishment is traditionally considered as the prerogative of the state and as one of the strongest expressions of its powers. Any claim in this area by an international entity is a particularly grave menace to the state's sovereignty.

Several arguments have of course been advanced in order to mitigate these qualms. The Rome Statute is an international treaty, so States Parties have consented to any limitations of their powers in the realm of criminal law. Besides, as is often observed, the complementarity principle implies that states still have priority and it is suggested that they have it in their own hands whether the ICC will intervene and overrule their decisions. Moreover, the ICC Prosecutor has frequently attempted to downplay the negative, antagonistic connotation of the principle, by presenting 'positive complementarity' as a common endeavour of the ICC and states to end impunity.[23]

All these statements are slightly beside the point and none of them fully allays the concerns of states. The critical moment is the finding of the ICC that a case is admissible, in view of complete passivity of a state, or its lack of capacity or genuine intent to bring the perpetrators to justice. After all, this verdict implies a denunciation of the state's criminal law system, at least of its ability or willingness to apply its system to the case at hand, in conformity with international standards. Such a decision potentially has great repercussions for the ensuing cooperation, demanded from the state, in the Court's investigation and prosecution of crimes.[24] A state that is disqualified as 'unable, due to a total or substantial collapse or unavailability of its national system', is not likely to have the powers to obtain the accused or the necessary evidence and testimony for the purpose of

---

[22] B Holá and A Chibashimba, 'Punishment in Transition: Empirical Comparison of Post-Genocide Sentencing Practices in Rwandan Domestic Courts and at the ICTR' (ch 7).

[23] For the first time explicitly: Office of the Prosecutor, *Report on Prosecutorial Strategy* (14 September 2006) 5: 'the positive approach to complementarity encourages genuine national proceedings where possible; relies on national and international cooperation; and participates in a system of international cooperation'. On positive complementarity, see, amongst others, W Burke-White, 'Implementing a Policy of Positive Complementarity in the Rome System of Justice' (2008) 19 *Criminal Law Forum* 54.

[24] See Article 86, Rome Statute.

assisting the Court.[25] Apart from patent incapacity, states can be expected to show reluctance – if not to display outright obstruction – after having been summoned by the Court to cooperate. The Kenya situation provides a case in point. The Pre-Trial Chamber found the case admissible because of a lack of national prosecutions for crimes against humanity, possibly implicating (amongst others) the president elect and his running mate, without having to decide whether such inaction was due to unwillingness or inability.[26] The Prosecutor lamented the Kenyan authorities' non-cooperation in the production of witnesses and evidence, preventing the Office of the Prosecutor delivering a case to answer and suggested that this obstruction was inspired by the head of state being one of the accused.[27] As is well known, neither the Trial Chamber nor the Appeals Chamber allowed the Prosecutor a further adjournment and the charges were dropped in 2015.

Difficulties in the cooperation between States Parties and the Court after the latter's finding a case admissible invite a somewhat closer scrutiny into the reasons of states for non-compliance. The first – and most obvious – is the possible involvement of state agents. It refers to the well-known assumption that most international crimes are effectively committed through the use of the state apparatus, either against the state's own nationals or against enemy civilians. An alternative explanation reflects the observations at the beginning of this chapter that the claim of jurisdiction by an international criminal court or tribunal is a blow against sovereign prerogatives and extinguishes each incentive to assist. The best way to explore which one of these rationales prevails or whether they are both (equally) relevant, is to address some recent experiences and situations which hypothetically exclude one of the explanations.

In the case of 'self-referrals' the state on whose territory the international crimes are allegedly committed takes the initiative in triggering the jurisdiction of the Court. Although the practice is a matter of controversy, investigations in five of the current 11 situations have started by this mechanism.[28] It is reasonable to assume that the referring state, being the initiator of the investigations by the ICC, does not object to the Court's exercise of jurisdiction. Thus, this situation precludes the second explanation. However, the first explanation still stands, because the government that refers a situation to the Court may well manipulate the selection of cases

---

[25] See the implicit paradox of Article 17(3) Rome Statute that mentions such lack of the means of criminal law enforcement as an indication of the inability of a state to conduct its *own* criminal proceedings.

[26] Situation in the Republic of Kenya, *Prosecutor v Muthura, Kenyatta and Hussein Ali*, Decision on the confirmation of charges, ICC-01/09- 02/11, 23 January 2012, § 39.

[27] Situation in the Republic of Kenya, *Decision on the Prosecutor's application for a further adjournment*, ICC-01/09-02/11, 3 December 2014, § 25.

[28] Namely, Democratic Republic of Congo, Uganda, Central African Republic (CAR) (I), Mali and CAR (II). For a critical assessment, see (amongst others) A Th Muller and Ignaz Stegmiller, 'Self-Referrals on Trial; From Panacea to Patient' (2010) 8 *Journal of International Criminal Justice* 1267. More positive: P Akhavan, 'Self-Referrals before the International Criminal Court: Are States the Villains or the Victims of Atrocities?' (2010) 21 *Criminal Law Forum* 103; and H van der Wilt, 'Self-referrals as an Indication of the Inability of States to Cope with Non-state Actors' in C Stahn (ed), *The Law and Practice of the International Criminal Court* (Oxford, Oxford University Press, 2010).

to its own advantage by using the tool of cooperation. These tactics were allegedly employed by Uganda's president, Mr Museveni, during the first auto-referral when he attempted to cajole the ICC Prosecutor to focus his attention on the prosecution of Museveni's foes, the Lord's Resistance Army (LRA), while simultaneously distracting him from the crimes committed by Ugandan armed forces. He cleverly used the Prosecutor's dependence on Ugandan cooperation for the purpose of the prosecution of LRA suspects as a bargaining chip.[29] The ICC Prosecutor at least formally thwarted Museveni's attempt to steer the prosecution exclusively in the direction of the LRA by pointing out that he would investigate crimes committed by both sides. He submitted that 'the scope of the referral encompasses *all* crimes committed in Northern Uganda in the context of the ongoing conflict involving the Lord's Resistance Army'.[30] In spite of these assurances, the Prosecutor has not investigated any of the Ugandan army's attacks on the civilian population, advancing the 'gravity' standard as a justification for this selectivity.[31]

The Ugandan example demonstrates how states can capitalise on the ICC being dependent on their cooperation by shielding their own people while putting their enemies in the limelight of the ICC's attention. It may easily result in skewed international criminal law enforcement to the detriment of rebels.

It is interesting to contrast both the Kenyan entanglements and the Ugandan self-referral with the situation in Libya. As is well known, the jurisdiction of the Court was triggered by a resolution of the Security Council. What the situations in Uganda and Libya had in common was that the Prosecutor targeted – at least initially – two adversaries of the government in power: Saif Al-Islam Gaddafi and Abdullah Al-Senussi. Rather than following the Ugandan authorities in their attempt to outsource the prosecution of enemies to the ICC, the Libyan government decided to challenge the admissibility of the cases, by pointing out that national prosecutions were underway, showing the ability and genuine commitment of the Libyan state to apply its criminal law system to the case.[32] It is remarkable that the Libyan government, apart from advancing purely legal arguments, also emphasised socio-political advantages of domestic criminal law enforcement over international criminal jurisdictions. Referring to a report of

---

[29] Compare S Nouwen and W Werner, 'Doing Justice to the Political: The International Criminal Court in Uganda and Sudan' (2011) 21 *European Journal of International Law* 950: 'a referral of the situation concerning the LRA would make the ICC's Prosecutor dependent on the cooperation of the Ugandan government; and he might hesitate to jeopardize such cooperation by charging his cooperative friends with crimes committed in neighbouring DRC'.

[30] Situation in Uganda (ICC-02/04-01/05), Decision to Convene a Status Conference on the Investigation in the Situation in Uganda in Relation to the Application of Article 53, 2 December 2005, § 4 (emphasis added).

[31] Nouwen and Werner, 'Doing Justice to the Political' above (n 29) 951: 'To date, he (id est: the ICC Prosecutor) has not opened an investigation into alleged crimes by state actors, officially on the basis of (a dubious application of) gravity as selection criterion'.

[32] Situation in Libya in the Case of *Prosecutor v Saif Al-Gaddafi and Abdullah Al-Senussi*; Application on behalf of the Government of Libya relating to Abduallah Al-Senussi pursuant to Article 19 of the ICC Statute, ICC-01/11-01/11, 2 April 2013.

the UN Secretary General on the UN Support Mission in Libya that apparently sustained the government's plea, the latter contended that:

> It is committed to applying international human rights standards both for the conduct of its investigations and any eventual trials. Achieving this outcome will contribute to judicial capacity-building *and will provide Libya's long-suffering people a unique opportunity to assume ownership over the past, to avoid impunity, and to build a better future based on respect for the rule of law and fundamental human rights.*[33]

It is a matter of some speculation why the Libyan government sought to challenge the jurisdiction of the ICC wholesale, instead of copying the strategy of its Ugandan colleagues. Most likely, the Resolution of the Security Council, which represents the grim face of international criminal justice, elicited a sharper response. Perhaps the government had a stake in vindicating its own jurisdiction, fearing that the ICC would be too 'soft' on its adversaries.

What matters is that the Libyan example reveals that reasons for obstructing the ICC's activities may be more complex than the protection of state officials and other allies from criminal responsibility.

IV. Challenges to the Dominant Moral Narrative of the International Community

In the previous sections I have argued that two features of international crimes and the context in which they are committed – the collective nature of these crimes and the ICC's dependence on states – are the prime challenges to the ICC's functioning. However, they affect the Court's operations in different ways and at different levels. While mass criminality requires the Court to reconsider the time-honoured concepts of substantive criminal law doctrine, the laborious interaction with states may hamper the proceedings and enforcement of its judgments.

In this section I seek to discuss the common denominator of these aspects that is seated in the dynamics between the individual and his social environment. Arguably, the most conspicuous element of the core crimes under the jurisdiction of the ICC is that they are considered 'normal', 'lawful', 'the right thing to do' in the social context in which the individual acts. Shortly after the Second World War, Edgar Faure made acute observations on the crucial differences between 'ordinary crimes' and 'official crimes':

> If the expression 'common-law crime' has a precise meaning, this meaning presumes a revolt by the delinquent against the forces representing the social order in which he is

---

[33] ibid, § 14 (emphasis added). The Appeals Chamber has confirmed the ruling of the Pre-Trial Chamber by holding the case against Al-Senussi indeed inadmissible; Situation in Libya, *Prosecutor v Gadaffi and Al-Senussi*, Judgment on the appeal of Mr Abduallah Al-Senussi against the decision of Pre-Trial Chamber I of 11 October 2013 entitled 'Decision on the admissibility of the case against Abdullah Al-Senussi', ICC1/11-01/11 OA6, 24 July 2014.

acting. Now, the crimes of the Nazi leaders present precisely this singularity, of having been committed in conformity with an order, in the very exercise of its forces.[34]

The evil conduct obtains an imprimatur of legitimacy, making it very difficult for the individual in this inverted moral universe to follow his own moral impulses. How official policy at the macro-level is translated to the micro-level of individual action through processes of authorisation, routinisation and dehumanisation, inducing 'ordinary people' to commit crimes of obedience has been extensively analysed by others and need not detain us here.[35] I just wish to emphasise that the call to conformity need not only emerge from the state and that obedience to superior orders is therefore not the only incentive for people to engage in mass criminality. In a wider sense, social interaction and group pressure mould individuals, in search of recognition and approval, into acceptance of the collective's moral code which may involve, in criminal sub-cultures, engagement in deviant behaviour. As indicated earlier, George Fletcher has discussed this phenomenon in the context of the problem of distribution of guilt.[36] What I wish to do, is to change the perspective by enquiring what this actually means for the claim of universal moral imperatives that sustains the establishment of the ICC. My hunch is that this claim is still and constantly contested, perhaps not at the level of the common endorsement of what constitutes an international crime in the abstract, but rather in respect of the question whether concrete behaviour amounts to an international crime and who should decide on that issue. To a large degree, the attitude of challenging the 'laws of humanity' can indeed be attributed to the perseverance of the state system. One should not forget, after all, that the solidification of interstate agreements on and principles of international humanitarian law into international criminal law and the concomitant introduction of individual criminal responsibility at the international level, are of fairly recent date. Alain Finkielkraut neatly captures the traditional view that no superior power should sit in judgement over the conduct of states and its officials in his reflections on the Armenian genocide. Despite all expressions of abhorrence and the exhortations of the victorious powers after the First World War to the Ottoman government to hold the agents who were implicated in these atrocities personally responsible for these crimes, 'no tribunal was set up to judge the Turkish Youth Brigade, nor were their activities condemned as illegal'. And he continues by explaining the central reason: '*Cuius region, eius religio*: to every state its own religion, its own system of justice, its

---

[34] E Faure, 'Introduction' to *La Persécution des Juifs en France et dans les autres pays de l'Ouest* (Paris, Center of Contemporary Jewish Documentation, 1947).

[35] See, for instance, HC Kelman, 'The Policy Context of International Crimes' in A Nollkaemper and H van der Wilt (eds), *System Criminality in International Law* (Cambridge, Cambridge University Press, 2009); C Browning, *Ordinary Men; Reserve Battalion 101 and the Final Solution in Poland* (New York, HarperCollins, 1992); A Smeulers, *In opdracht van de staat; gezagsgetrouwe criminelen en internationale misdrijven*, inaugural address, (Tilburg, Tilburg University Press, 2012).

[36] Fletcher, above (n 5) 1541: 'If the dominant systems of belief encourage actions like *Kristallnacht*, lynchings, gay bashings, or domestic violence, those who succumb to violence are certainly to blame, but one has to wonder whether they alone are to blame and whether they must bear the guilt alone'.

own police and its own morality'.[37] Other forms of collective criminality, though definitely different in scale and political impact, have at least this in common with 'state criminality' in that they challenge the moral and legal paradigm of the ICC.

The ICC is vulnerable to attacks that essentially strike at its legitimacy. Penal law is an exceptionally strong and powerful instrument, both in an expressive sense in that it reflects the deepest moral feelings of a community and in an operational sense, as it requires the application of coercive measures by a well-equipped police force.[38] In neither of these aspects does the ICC perform particularly well. Lacking its own police force and being dependent on the assistance of states, the Court's law enforcement capacities are obviously weak. Moreover, it claims to speak on behalf of a rather elusive 'international community', which is inherently pluralist and comprises the very state which is contesting the Court's powers of jurisdiction.[39] Deconstructed to its essential components, the international community consists of human beings. The concept of 'crimes against humanity' postulates an entity comprising all the world's population that can be endangered by a mortal adversary. The odium of 'an enemy of all humanity' (*hostis generis humani*) – initially preserved for pirates – has been famously criticised by Carl Schmitt who argued that it would be conducive of dehumanisation and itself invite the cruelest atrocities.[40] One need not reject entirely the idea of a 'common humanity' as the basic concept sustaining international criminal law. However, it is prudent to express caution against its casual employment, because it lacks a firm political content and is easily available for abuse.[41]

A fundamental assault on the ICC's legitimacy is the contention that the Court does not act according to its own principles and propounded aspirations. The Preamble to the Rome Statute extols cultural, political and human diversity ('Conscious that all peoples are united by common bonds, their cultures pieced together in a shared heritage'). It claims that international crimes are likely to destroy such pluralism ('concerned that this delicate mosaic may be shattered at any time'). At the same time, however, the Court propagates individual criminal accountability as the single cure for mass atrocities, thereby ignoring or even

---

[37] A Finkielkraut, *Remembering in Vain; The Klaus Barbie Trial and Crimes Against Humanity* (New York, Columbia University Press, 1992) 6.

[38] On the first 'Durkheimian notion', see the interesting contributions in this volume by Marina Aksenova (ch 4) and Milena Tripkovic (ch 8).

[39] See on the manifold faces and interpretations of the concept of international community the fascinating article by I Tallgren, 'The Voice of the International; Who is Speaking?' (2015) 13 *Journal of International Criminal Justice* 135.

[40] C Schmitt, *The Concept of the Political* (trans George Schwab) (Chicago, IL, University of Chicago Press, 1996) 54: 'To confiscate the word humanity, to invoke and monopolize such a term probably has certain incalculable effects, such as denying the enemy the quality of being human and declaring him to be an outlaw of humanity, and a war can thereby be driven to the most extreme humanity'.

[41] Compare R Nollez-Goldbach, 'Crimes against Humanity; The Concept of Humanity in International Law' in P Kastner (ed), *International Criminal Law in Context* (London, Routledge, 2018) 107. For a searching genealogy of the concept of 'enemy of humanity, see D Luban, *The Enemy of All Humanity* (draft), available at: www.verenigingrechtsfilosofie.nl/wp-content/uploads/2018/05/David-Luban-Enemy-paper-VWR.pdf.

dismissing alternative conceptions of justice. It does, in other words, not abide by its own standards.[42] More damaging to the reputation of the ICC are the critical legal approaches that seek to denounce its cosmopolitan liberal legalism as either naive blindness to the structural causes of injustice or even as a wilful attempt to conceal its permanent linkages with predominant Western powers.[43]

What all the criticism has in common is that it challenges the pretence of the ICC that it occupies the moral high ground. As such, it is grist to the mill of those who have a stake in blemishing its reputation.

V.   Some Final Reflections: Suggestions for Piecemeal Improvements of the System of International Criminal Justice

Criticising the discipline of international criminal law in general and the ICC in particular is fashionable and a favourite pastime of many scholars.[44] The reason for this is not hard to grasp: the gap between sky-high aspirations and poor performance invites scathing criticism. However, that observation may be too superficial. Some of the criticism is warranted and profound in questioning whether, contrary to the ICC's presumptions, law can ever be detached from politics.[45] This line of reasoning is reminiscent of Derrida's famous essay 'The Force of Law' in which he contends that law (*droit*), as a substitute for man's craving for unattainable justice, must be enforced, as its application implies a decision on opposing or irreconcilable interests.[46]

The issue is too complex to discuss in depth in this brief chapter. Suffice to say that the criticism is here to stay, because the ICC has appointed itself as the protector of the realm of political pluralism. Such an assignment inherently involves contradictions. While inevitably embroiled in politics, the ICC must transcend them as well, because it is expected – and pretends itself(!) – to mete out

---

[42] For an eloquent expression of this criticism, see S Nouwen and W Werner, 'Monopolizing Global Justice; International Criminal Law as Challenge to Human Diversity' (2015) 13 *Journal of International Criminal Justice* 157.

[43] For a typical example, see T Krever, 'International Criminal Law: An Ideology Critique' (2013) 26 *Leiden Journal of International Law* 701.

[44] For an insightful analysis, see S Vasiliev, 'The Crises and Critiques of International Criminal Justice' (unpublished manuscript, on file with the author).

[45] See Nouwen and Werner, 'Doing Justice to the Political', above (n 29); J Hoover, 'Moral Practices: Assigning Responsibility in the International Criminal Court' (2013) 76 *Law and Contemporary Problems* 263; D Robinson, 'Inescapable Dyads: Why the International Criminal Court Cannot Win' (2016) 28 *Leiden Journal of International Law* 323.

[46] J Derrida, 'The Force of Law: The Mystical Foundation of Authority' (1990) 11 *Cardozo Law Review* 920. Derrida quotes one of the pensées of Pascal: 'And Pascal continues "La justice sans la force est impuissante" ("Justice without force is impotent" – in other words, justice isn't justice, it is not achieved if it doesn't have the force to be "enforced" a powerless justice is not justice, in the sense of *droit*'. It is telling that Derrida cares to make that clarification ('justice in the sense of *droit*').

justice without fear or favour.[47] David Luban seems to consider this meta-political dimension as the raison d' etre of international criminal justice, where he qualifies the deadly risk of 'politics gone cancerous' as the essence of crimes against humanity.[48] Building on Kant's depiction of mankind as 'unsociable, sociable' and Arendt's presentation of pluralism as an indispensable part of the human condition, Luban argues that man is condemned to resort to political organisation, in order to navigate between the urge to cooperate with and fear of others. That already fragile equilibrium is shattered if the state turns violently on its own citizens and by doing so denies them the secure environment to further their interests. International criminal justice not only aspires to accomplish that such radical evil does not go unpunished, but also entails the promise of a world in which politics are not automatically associated with violence and oppression.[49] That quest may appear Herculean, if not utopian, but it is worth the effort, because it is an honourable alternative – though by no means the only one(!) – to remaining entirely passive.[50]

The acknowledgement of an inherent value of the cause of international criminal justice paves the way for the improvement of the system and it is my impression that the criminological contributions in this volume offer some useful insights and suggestions to that purpose. I have already taken the opportunity to briefly refer to some chapters in the previous sections and I will now finish my chapter by commenting on others.[51]

While many scholars have emphasised the importance of reviving and conserving memories of atrocities as a function of (international) criminal trials,[52] Christopher Harding, in a thoughtful contribution, draws our attention to its pitfalls ('Destructive potential') to wit, its capacity to rekindle old feuds. He points at the biological and psychological function of erasure of memory as a prelude to reconciliation and argues that such insights should be considered in the choice between modes of conflict resolution.[53]

---

[47] This 'predicament' is eloquently described by Vasiliev, above (n 44), where he observes that 'International criminal justice is justice pro *omnibus*, done in the name of everyone ("international community", "humanity", "civilization", "us" and similar subjects ICTs write into existence. On the flipside, this justice is erga *omnes* and dispensed vis-à-vis all, including the powers on which courts depend for functioning and survival'.

[48] D Luban, 'A Theory of Crimes Against Humanity' (2004) 29 *Yale Journal of International Law* 85.

[49] D Luban, 'Beyond Moral Minimalism' (2006) 20 *Ethics & International Affairs* 353, 355: 'ICL represents the utopian belief that politics need not be this way – that liberal politics, noncriminal politics, is possible'.

[50] Here I disagree with Gerry Simpson: G Simpson, 'The Conscience of Civilisation and its Discontents; A Counter History of International Criminal Law' in P Kastner, *International Criminal Law in Context* (London, Routledge, 2018) 27, who disqualifies the ICC's law enforcement as a 'system of injustice' and seems to prefer doing nothing above affiliating with that system (although I must admit, to his credit, he shows sensitivity towards those individuals who have pursued the course of international criminal justice).

[51] Regrettably, the chapters by Colleen Rohan and Elies van Sliedregt became available after completion of this final chapter.

[52] See, as one of the most prominent advocates, L Douglas, *The Memory of Judgment: Making Law and History in the Trials of the Holocaust* (New Haven, CT, Yale University Press, 2001).

[53] C Harding, 'The Biology and Psychology of Atrocity and the Erasure of Memory' (ch 2).

A number of contributions address the position of the individual perpetrator, his motives, interaction with the collective and his 'guilt', a topic that is obviously of major relevance for international criminal justice. It is interesting to note that not all authors are 'on the same page'. In her study on prison guards, Kerstin Carlson points out that, due to a mismatch between the general and special part of international criminal law, the guilt of individual perpetrators looms large and is surely exaggerated. They are facing criminal trials, instead of the real culprits, acting behind the scenes.[54] Remarkably, Anette Bringedal Houge censures the explaining away of the agency of individual perpetrators by situationist scholars and demonstrates that the ICTY has definitely paid attention to the motives – like sadism – of direct perpetrators.[55] In a similar vein, Stefan Harrendorf contends that there is room for individual choice and action, even in the dire circumstances of extreme violence, but he is especially interested in those who, different from their 'ordinary' peers, resist the temptation of committing atrocities. Harrendorf suggests that moral education that teaches children to become critical thinkers is a clue to this difference in reaction.[56]

Another interesting topic that has been touched upon in a number of contributions is the distinction in context between international and national criminal law enforcement and how this might affect the outcome of the trials. Matilde Gawronski argues that institutional features influenced the Ongwen trial at the ICC far more than the Kwoyelo trial in Uganda which was primarily steered by political and legal parameters.[57] And Barbora Holá and Amani Chibashimba point at the divergent sentencing practices of the ICTR and Rwandan domestic courts, wondering whether discrepancy between the lenient punishment of higher-ranking perpetrators at the ICTR and the more severe punishment of lower-level perpetrators by domestic courts can be justified.[58]

The analysis of the appropriateness of the application of Durkheimian social theory of criminal law ignites – again – rather opposite conclusions. In a theoretical appraisal, Marina Aksenova confirms that, analogous to the domestic context, the most egregious crimes shock the conscience of mankind and that (international) criminal law reinforces the social bonds within the international community.[59] As a criminologist, Milena Tripkovic is much more sceptical about the ICTY's

---

[54] K Carlson, 'Agents and Agency in International Criminal Law: Intent and the "Special Part" of International Criminal Law' (ch 6).

[55] AB Houge, 'Explaining (Away) Individual Agency: A Criminological Take on Direct Perpetrator Re-presentations at the ICTY' (ch 9).

[56] S Harrendorf, 'Social Identity and International Crimes: Legitimate and Problematic Aspects of the "Ordinary People" Hypothesis' (ch 10).

[57] M Gawronski, 'International Criminalisation as a Pragmatic Institutional Process: The Cases of Dominic Ongwen at the International Criminal Court and Thomas Kwoyelo at the International Crimes Division in the Situation in Uganda' (ch 3).

[58] Holá and Chibashimba, above (n 22).

[59] M Aksenova, 'Solidarity as a Moral and Legal Basis for Crimes Against Humanity: A Durkheimian Perspective' (ch 4).

capacity to stir the hearts and minds of the people of the former Yugoslavia, attributing this inability to both the abstract and distance nature of the Tribunal and the highly different perceptions of the several communities on the Balkan war.[60]

It is not a weak point of this volume that its chapters issue different, sometimes even opposing, messages. On the contrary, it reflects a highly complex and multifaceted reality with political, legal, social, psychological and even religious features. It will assist international criminal law enforcement in walking the fine line between being firm on the prime objective and being sensitive to the pluralist world in which it is operating.

[60] M Tripkovic, 'Not in Our Name! Visions of Community in International Criminal Justice' (ch 8).

INDEX